DICKENS, REYNOLDS, AND MAYHEW ON WELLINGTON STREET

A glance over the back pages of mid-nineteenth-century newspapers and periodicals published in London reveals that Wellington Street stands out among imprint addresses. Between 1843 and 1853, *Household Words*, *Reynolds's Weekly Newspaper*, the *Examiner*, *Punch*, the *Athenaeum*, the *Leader*, the *Morning Post*, and the serial edition of *London Labour and the London Poor*, to name a few, were all published from this short street off the Strand. Mary L. Shannon identifies, for the first time, the close proximity of the offices of Charles Dickens, G.W.M. Reynolds, and Henry Mayhew, examining the ramifications for the individual authors and for nineteenth-century publishing. What are the implications of Charles Dickens, his arch-competitor the radical publisher G.W.M. Reynolds, and Henry Mayhew being such close neighbours? Given that London was capital of more than Britain alone, what connections does Wellington Street reveal between London print networks and the print culture and networks of the wider empire? How might the editors' experiences make us rethink the ways in which they and others addressed their anonymous readers as 'friends', as if they were part of their immediate social network? As Shannon shows, readers in the London of the 1840s and '50s, despite advances in literacy, print technology, and communications, were not simply an 'imagined community' of individuals who read in silent privacy, but active members of an imagined network that punctured the anonymity of the teeming city and even the empire.

T0298920

The Nineteenth Century Series
General Editors' Preface

The aim of the series is to reflect, develop and extend the great burgeoning of interest in the nineteenth century that has been an inevitable feature of recent years, as that former epoch has come more sharply into focus as a locus for our understanding not only of the past but of the contours of our modernity. It centres primarily upon major authors and subjects within Romantic and Victorian literature. It also includes studies of other British writers and issues, where these are matters of current debate: for example, biography and autobiography, journalism, periodical literature, travel writing, book production, gender, non-canonical writing. We are dedicated principally to publishing original monographs and symposia; our policy is to embrace a broad scope in chronology, approach and range of concern, and both to recognize and cut innovatively across such parameters as those suggested by the designations 'Romantic' and 'Victorian'. We welcome new ideas and theories, while valuing traditional scholarship. It is hoped that the world which predates yet so forcibly predicts and engages our own will emerge in parts, in the wider sweep, and in the lively streams of disputation and change that are so manifest an aspect of its intellectual, artistic and social landscape.

Vincent Newey
Joanne Shattock
University of Leicester

Dickens, Reynolds, and Mayhew on Wellington Street
The Print Culture of a Victorian Street

MARY L. SHANNON
University of Roehampton, UK

Routledge
Taylor & Francis Group

LONDON AND NEW YORK

First published 2015 by Ashgate Publishing

2 Park Square, Milton Park, Abingdon, Oxfordshire OX14 4RN
52 Vanderbilt Avenue, New York, NY 10017

Routledge is an imprint of the Taylor & Francis Group, an informa business

First issued in paperback 2019

British Library Cataloguing in Publication Data
A catalogue record for this book is available from the British Library

The Library of Congress has cataloged the printed edition as follows:
Shannon, Mary L.
  Dickens, Reynolds, and Mayhew on Wellington street: the print culture of a Victorian street / by Mary L. Shannon.
    pages cm. – (The nineteenth century series)
  Includes bibliographical references and index.
  ISBN 978-1-4724-4204-8 (hardcover: alk. paper)
  1. Newspaper publishing – England – London – History
– 9th century. 2. English newspapers – England – London – History – 19th century. 3. Periodicals – Publishing – England – London – History – 19th century. 4. Journalism – England – London – History – 19th century. 5. Publishers and publishing – England – London – History – 19th century. 6. Dickens, Charles, 1812–1870 – Criticism and interpretation. 7. Reynolds, George W. M. (George William MacArthur), 1814–1879 – Criticism and interpretation. 8. Mayhew, Henry, 1812–1887 – Criticism and interpretation. I. Title.

PN5129.L62S53 2015
052–dc23
                                                                              2014039118
  ISBN 978-1-4724-4204-8 (hbk)
  ISBN 978-0-367-88030-9 (pbk)

For Miss Ingham, my English Teacher,
who showed me what was possible;
and for my parents, who gave me everything else.

Writers absorbed London in many ways – in reading rooms, theatre boxes, drawing rooms and at the dinner table. But most of all, they absorbed it in the streets.

—Jerry White, *London in the nineteenth century: 'A Human Awful Wonder of God'* (London: Jonathan Cape, 2007), 252

Contents

List of Figures

Note: All uncredited figures are from the author's collection.

Acknowledgements

This book was begun at King's College London; King's location on the Strand was what first drew my attention to the rich literary and cultural history of the area. It gave me the chance to explore an area of London that I did not know very well, despite having been born and brought up in the city. That location enabled me to walk the same streets as Dickens, Reynolds, and Mayhew; I had fun imagining what they would have seen and heard, in what ways it would have been different, and what might have stayed the same. Wellington Street is one of those streets. To all those friends and family members who have tolerated my exclaiming, 'you do realise that we are on Wellington Street now, don't you?' during trips to Covent Garden over the past five years: my apologies! I hope you approve of the end result of my curious obsession with Post Office Directories.

My grateful thanks go to Clare Pettitt, Ian Henderson, and Josephine McDonagh in the English Department at King's College London, who encouraged me to pursue this project and supported me as it took shape. I owe a huge debt of gratitude to the English and Creative Writing Department at the University of Roehampton, London, where this book was completed. In particular, Ian Haywood read the manuscript, and I am very grateful for his insightful questions and suggestions. Laura Peters supported this project every step of the way, and found departmental funds to pay for the wealth of images presented in this volume. This book would have been much poorer without that assistance. I would also like to thank my research assistant, Erica Gillingham, for her diligent work in securing copyright permissions (and for remaining cheerful in the face of many forms); Charlotte Stroud; and Simon Potter at Roehampton, who drew Figures 1.3 and 3.1.

I have benefited from the help of many people who have been generous with their time and experience. Particularly notable amongst these are Rohan McWilliam and Joanne Shattock. Special thanks are due to David Green from King's College London's Geography Department, Simon Sleight from the History Department, and Sheila Anderson from the Digital Humanities Department. I am extremely grateful to Louis James for all his advice and support; he has read my work, offered so many useful insights, and in short been a kind mentor to a young scholar. Many scholars around the world have discussed this project with me and patiently answered my questions; in particular I would like to thank Clare Brant, Dick Collins, Guy Dicks, Anne Humpherys, Miles Ogborn, and John Stokes. Adrian Autton and his staff at the City of Westminster Archives Centre have been helpful and informative; thank you also to the London Metropolitan Archives, City of London, and to the Menzies Centre for Australian Studies at King's College London. Miles Lewis provided images of Bielefeld's *papier mâché* buildings. Trevor Bates helped me to access the census records online. I thank the editors of *19: Interdisciplinary Studies in the Long Nineteenth Century* for permission to reprint material as part of Chapter 2. My commissioning editor at Ashgate, Ann Donahue, has been a model of efficiency, and wonderful to work with.

I would also like to take this opportunity to thank the early-career scholars whom I met at King's and elsewhere, past and present, who have provided friendship, advice, encouragement, critical comments, and plenty of tea. Mary Henes, Brian Murray, and Alison Wood shared their insights on research survival; Jess Hindes has been a fellow Reynolds fan; Ellie Bass, Hannah Crummé, Tullia Griersberg, Jennifer Lo, Megan Murray-Pepper, Philippe Roesle, Matthew Sangster, and Fariha Shaikh filled the 8th floor kitchen and The Edgar Wallace pub with intellectual debate and a huge dose of fun. Thank you for all the British Library lunch breaks, everyone. As for Sarah Crofton, Maria Damkjaer, Jordan Kistler, and Will Tattersdill, I could not have got to this point without them.

As this project took shape and grew, Leanne Atkinson, Claire Bates, Josephine Benton, Sarah Paine, and Bethan Walters listened to me when I wanted to talk about Wellington Street, and distracted me when I didn't. Thank you, also, to all my friends from Cambridge days. In no small measure is the existence of this book down to you all, and to your support during Cambridge and after. Newnham and Peterhouse forever. Thank you to Amanda Ingham, for all those English lessons in classroom B11. How did you put up with us all? They say you never forget a good teacher; in my experience, that's true.

Finally, I would like to thank my parents. I am lost for the words to express fully my admiration and gratitude; here are 86,000, which I dedicate to them.

Epigraph Credits

Extract from *London in the 19th Century: 'A Human Awful Wonder of God'* by Jerry White. © 2007 Jerry White. All rights reserved. Published by Jonathan Cape. Reproduced by permission of the Random House Group Ltd and by permission of the author, c/o The Hanbury Agency Ltd, 28 Moreton Street, London SW1V 2PE.

Extract from *The Practice of Everyday Life* by Michel de Certeau, translated by Steven Rendall. Published by the University of California Press, 1984. Reproduced by permission of the University of California Press.

Extracts from *London: The Biography* by Peter Ackroyd. © Peter Ackroyd 2000. Published by Vintage. Reprinted by permission of the Random House Group Ltd and Sheil Land Associates Ltd. © Peter Ackroyd 2001. Used by permission of Doubleday, an imprint of the Knopf Doubleday Publishing Group, a division of Random House LLC. All rights reserved. Any third party use of this material, outside of this publication, is prohibited. Interested parties must apply directly to Random House LLC for permission.

Extract from *Trafalgar Square: Emblem of Empire* by Rodney Mace. Published by Lawrence & Wishart, 2005; first published 1976. Reprinted by permission of Lawrence & Wishart.

List of Abbreviations

ADB   *Australian Dictionary of Biography* online edition, http://adb.anu.edu.au/

Australian Facts   Horne R.H. *Australian Facts and Prospects: to which is prefixed The Author's Australian Autobiography.* London: Smith, Elder & Co, 1859.

Colonial City   Clarke, Marcus. *A Colonial City: High and Low Life. Selected Journalism of Marcus Clarke.* Edited by L.T. Hergenhan. St. Lucia, Queensland: University of Queensland Press, 1972

DJWN   *Douglas Jerrold's Weekly Newspaper*

DN   *Daily News*

DNB   *Oxford Dictionary of National Biography* online edition, http://www.oxforddnb.com

DNCJ   *Dictionary of Nineteenth-Century Journalism in Great Britain and Ireland.* Edited by Laurel Brake and Marysa Demoor. Ghent; London: Academia Press and British Library, 2009

HW   *Household Words*

ILN   *Illustrated London News*

Kelly's POD (1843–53)   *Kelly's London Post Office Directory.* London: W. Kelly, 1843–53. WCA microfilm collection, London Directories/1843–53/vols 253–67.

Life   Forster, John. *The Life of Charles Dickens, with 500 portraits, facsimiles, and other illustrations, collected, arranged, and annotated by B.W. Matz.* 2 vols. London: Chapman & Hall, 1911; 1st publ. 1872–74

London Labour   Mayhew, Henry. *London Labour and the London Poor.* 3 vols. London: Office of London Labour and the London Poor, 1851–52

MP   *Melbourne Punch*

Mysteries Series I   Reynolds, G.W.M. *The Mysteries of London, Series I.* 2 vols. London: George Vickers, ? October 1844– 26 September 1846

Mysteries Series II   Reynolds, G.W.M. *The Mysteries of London, Series II.* 2 vols. London: George Vickers, 3rd October 1846– 16th September 1848

OBPO   *Old Bailey Proceedings Online,* http://www.oldbaileyonline.org

OED   *The Oxford English Dictionary* online edition, http://www.oed.com

Pilgrim   *The Pilgrim Edition of the Letters of Charles Dickens.* Edited by Madeline House, Graham Storey, and Kathleen Tillotson (general editors). 12 vols. Oxford: Clarendon Press, 1965–2002

RM   *Reynolds's Miscellany*

RPI   *Reynolds's Political Instructor*

Robson's Directory   *Robson's London Directory, Street Key, and Royal Court Guide, For 1843.* 24th edn. London: Bowtell, 1843. WCA microfilm collection, London Directories/1843/vol 201

RWN   *Reynolds's Weekly Newspaper*

Watkins's Directory   Watkins's Commercial and General Directory and Court Guide for 1852. London: Longman, Brown, Green, and Longmans, 1852. WCA microfilm collection, London Directories/1852/vol 57

Introduction

Their story begins on ground level.
—Michel de Certeau, *The Practice of Everyday Life*, trans. Steven
Rendall (Berkeley, CA: University of California Press, 1984), 97.

Arrival on Wellington Street

Just off the Strand, leading up to Covent Garden from Waterloo Bridge, is a relatively insignificant street called Wellington Street. In the 1847 edition of John Tallis's serial publication *London Street Views*, we see it as just a tributary of the Strand, leading off from the main drawing into a less-detailed distance.[1] Tallis's use of perspective affords us a tantalizing glimpse of the street, but does not allow us to look down it fully (Figure I.1).

The street began at Wellington Street on the south side of the Strand (sometimes called Wellington Street South, for example on the 1851 census returns), and continued through Wellington Street North and into Upper Wellington Street.[2]

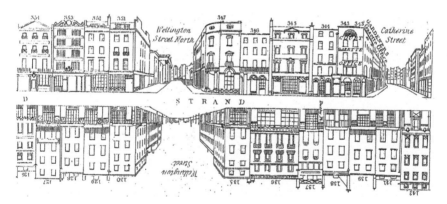

Figure I.1   Wellington Street North and Wellington Street (South) in 1847.
From *John Tallis's London Street Views* (1847 edition), 75.
Reproduced by permission of Guildhall Library, City of London,
and London Topographical Society.

---

[1]   *John Tallis's London Street Views: 1838–1840. Together with the revised and enlarged views of 1847*, ed. Peter Jackson (London: London Topographical Society and Nattali & Maurice, 1969), 75.

[2]   1851 census, National Records Office, HO107/151, ff. 190–91, accessed 15 July 2011 online via http://www.ancestry.co.uk/.

London guidebooks for the 1840s and 1850s pay little attention to Wellington Street; it is mentioned once, in passing, as an example of urban rebuilding in Cruchley's 1844 guide to London.[3]

On Wellington Street, however, you could find the offices of some of the most well known and influential newspapers, miscellanies, and serials of the mid-Victorian period. In 1850, Charles Dickens set up the office of his new periodical *Household Words* at 16 Wellington Street North. It is not surprising that Dickens chose this location; the three sections of Wellington Street – Wellington Street North, Upper Wellington Street, and Wellington Street (South) – were positioned at the heart of London's print networks, located as they were just off the Strand between Fleet Street and Covent Garden (Figure I.2). Vic Gatrell sets the creative heyday of this area firmly in the eighteenth century, but in fact its 'creative dynamism' continued, driven by its theatre and publishing industries.[4]

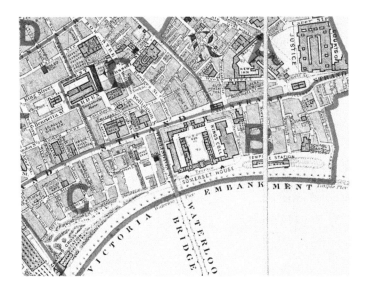

Figure I.2   Wellington Street, Wellington Street North, and Upper Wellington Street (1879). The streets are named separately and then crossed through, as all the streets had already been renamed as simply 'Wellington Street'. From *Map of the School Board District of Westminster* (London: Stanford, 1879). © The British Library Board, Maps.29.b.58.(9).

3   *Cruchley's Picture of London*, 9th edn (London: Cruchley, 1844), 253.
4   Vic Gatrell, *The First Bohemians: Life and Art in London's Golden Age* (London: Allen Lane, 2013), xxvii.

Between 1843 and 1853, Wellington Street played host to more than 20 newspapers or periodicals and 13 booksellers or publishers. The street was probably known to Dickens initially as a route through theatreland, as it was home to the Lyceum Theatre and lay just below Bow Street, home to Covent Garden Opera House. The Lyceum was managed by two sets of Dickens's friends: first the Keeleys, and then Charles Mathews and Madame Vestris (see Chapter 3). Wellington Street was also home to the office of *The Examiner*, edited by Dickens's close friend and biographer John Forster. From the bow window of the *Household Words* office in 1851, Dickens could see the Lyceum as well as the office of the radical publisher G.W.M. Reynolds (and Reynolds's business partner, John Dicks), from which was published *Reynolds's Miscellany* and *Reynolds's Weekly Newspaper* (see Chapter 2). A few doors up, Henry Mayhew had just opened the office of his new part-work, *London Labour and the London Poor* (hereafter *London Labour*). Mayhew's new office was next door to the building from which his father-in-law, Douglas Jerrold, had run *Douglas Jerrold's Weekly Newspaper*, two years previously, and in which the young G.A. Sala had rented a room the year before (see Chapter 1). This was a street where the print trade, entertainment culture, and reformist politics co-existed in a strange kind of melting pot. These interests and activities generated ideas and modes of thought and operation which spread out from Wellington Street itself; colonial emigration enabled the networks of Wellington Street to give life to the print networks on the other side of the globe. Writers, periodicals, and newspapers from Wellington Street found their way to colonial Melbourne, and print culture networks based on Wellington Street were reproduced by Melbourne immigrants like R.H. Horne and Marcus Clarke (see Chapter 4).

A study of the print culture of Wellington Street, then, is not one which confines itself to the Strand neighbourhood, to London, or even to the northern hemisphere. This book reveals, for the first time, that Dickens, Reynolds, and Mayhew all had offices on the same London street. It argues that the experience of Dickens and his contemporaries on Wellington Street was one of working in a remarkably interconnected community, made up of interlocking networks. I examine the print networks of Wellington Street between roughly 1843 and 1853 to show how print culture operated on the ground in the early to mid-nineteenth century, and how London's print culture intersected with the Empire. Given how important the closely packed nature of Wellington Street is to my reading of this print culture, the introduction of Melbourne into the picture may at first seem something of a stretch. However, the connections between Wellington Street in London and Collins Street in Melbourne show us that, because the print networks of Wellington Street were reinforced by strong ties of physical proximity, they had the background strength to sustain themselves when the networks became transnational, and could be replicated abroad. As Gillian Russell and Clara Tuite put it, in a period of British empire-building and exploration, 'sociable networks and communities had to be reconfigured and reimagined'.[5] Physical proximity in the city reinforced print networks, and this networked way of working and socializing created a virtual space which stretched across cities and connected writers, editors, and readers in a vast imagined network.

This book contributes to the interdisciplinary field of nineteenth-century print culture by using original archival research to inform new readings of well known and lesser known periodicals, newspapers, sketches, plays, and serial fiction. The similarities between work by Mayhew, Reynolds, and Dickens have been noted frequently.[6] Trefor Thomas, in his introduction to his abridged version of Reynolds's best-selling serial tale *The Mysteries of London* (hereafter *Mysteries*), writes of that text:

> Taken with Henry Mayhew's recording of the detail of street life [...] and with Dickens's apocalyptic vision of London in *Bleak House*, the text completes a literary triptych representing the culture of the metropolis from three distinctive perspectives at an epochal moment of social and political transition.[7]

This book asks where in London these writers were based and what their geographical location in the city can tell us about their work. I focus on urban journalism, sketches, and fiction by Dickens, Reynolds, Jerrold, Mayhew, and Sala, as well as sketches by Marcus Clarke in Melbourne. What emerges is a picture of print culture built upon the experience of face-to-face interactions.

Much critical attention has been given to the question of what kind of community, if any, is created by print culture. Perhaps most notably, Benedict Anderson argues that print culture helped to develop the modern conception of the nation state, because it created the condition whereby readers became accustomed to the idea of an 'imagined community'. For Anderson, 'all communities larger than primordial villages of face-to-face communities (and perhaps even these) are imagined'.[8] This is because 'the members of even the smallest nation will never know most of their fellow-members, meet them, or even hear of them, yet in the minds of each lives the image of their communion'.[9] Anderson argues convincingly

---

[5]   Gillian Russell and Clara Tuite, 'Introducing Romantic Sociability', in *Romantic Sociability: Social Networks and Literary Culture in Britain, 1770–1840*, ed. Gillian Russell and Clara Tuite (Cambridge: Cambridge University Press, 2002), 20.

[6]   See, for example, Anne Humpherys, *Travels into the Poor Man's Country: The Work of Henry Mayhew* (Athens, GA: The University of Georgia Press, 1977); Richard Maxwell, *The Mysteries of Paris and London* (Charlottesville, VA and London: University Press of Virginia, 1992); Robert Douglas-Fairhurst, Introduction to *London Labour and the London Poor: A Selected Edition*, ed. Robert Douglas-Fairhurst (Oxford: Oxford University Press, 2010), xiii–xliii.

[7]   Trefor Thomas, 'G.W.M. Reynolds's *The Mysteries of London*: An Introduction', in *The Mysteries of London*, by G.W.M. Reynolds, ed. Trefor Thomas (Keele: Keele University Press, 1996), vii–xxvii.

[8]   Benedict Anderson, *Imagined Communities: Reflections on the Origin and Spread of Nationalism*, 3rd edn (London: Verso, 2006), 6.

[9]   Ibid.

that from the eighteenth century onwards, the novel and the newspaper 'provided the technical means' for presenting this way of imagining community because they created 'that remarkable confidence of community in anonymity which is the hallmark of modern nations'.[10] Writers and editors assumed the existence of numerous readers; readers, in their turn, assumed the existence of fellow readers and enthusiasts whom they might never meet, but for whom the characters of their favourite fiction or the leaders of their favourite newspaper possessed a similar interest. At the same time, in a complicated double movement, the rise of a mass print culture made readers aware of exactly how large this 'imagined community' now was.

However, streets like the three sections of Wellington Street show that those involved in the actual production of this very print culture in mid-Victorian London themselves operated within very sociable face-to-face interactions, made up of interconnected (and also rival) networks. The son of Phiz recalled of the Strand area in the 1850s:

> London was a comparatively small town, and those who were engaged in the business of amusing the public, however they might hold themselves aloof, lived in a ring fence, and were continually in touch with one another. News spread mysteriously, as it is said to do amongst the Indians, but we must remember that there was a constant intercommunication between authors, artists, engravers, printers, and the like, and anything interesting was continually carried to and fro by a mob of subordinates.[11]

Notice the juxtaposition here between the sense of engagement in the technologically advanced arena of printing, and the resemblance of this London network to 'the Indians', with an implied suggestion of primitivism. The tribal metaphor is also one of kinship, which unites the idea of physical proximity with that of blood ties and mutual support. Benedict Anderson draws a distinction between 'primordial villages' and the imagined communities of print capitalism, but Phiz's son finds a certain wry humour in the fact that this is a distinction which he cannot draw. That this world of cliques and coteries could be suffocating as much as enabling is made clear by Antonia Harland-Lang, who suggests that some male writers in 1850s London felt caught in 'a fundamentally flawed system of networking which they nonetheless cannot do without'.[12]

I take the idea of face-to-face networks not just from Benedict Anderson but also from Raymond Williams, who, in his influential book *The Country and the City*, suggests that what he calls the 'knowable community' of 'face-to-face

---

[10] Anderson, 25; 36.

[11] Edgar Browne, *Phiz and Dickens as They Appeared to Edgar Browne* (London: J. Nisbet, 1913), 102.

[12] Antonia Harland-Lang, 'Thackeray and Bohemia' (PhD diss., University of Cambridge, 2010), 190.

contacts' is hard to find in a city novel, due to mass urbanization. He states that '[m]ost novels are in some sense knowable communities', but:

> the transition from country to city – from a predominantly rural to a predominantly urban society – is transforming and significant. […] In changes like these, any assumption of a knowable community – a whole community, wholly knowable – became harder and harder to sustain.[13]

According to Williams, a village is often idealized as a knowable community, 'an epitome of direct relationships', because 'people are more easily identified and connected' within them. In a knowable community, then, the connections between characters, or indeed between real people, are obvious. For Williams, this idea is, in fact, no more than a 'willing, lulling illusion of old country life' that masks less palatable social realities.[14] Williams does note that Dickens develops 'unknown and unacknowledged relationships, profound and decisive connections' between Londoners, and he rightly emphasizes the importance of these connections to Dickens's 'social and personal vision'.[15] Yet there is scope to think more about this idea in relation to both Dickens's writing and Dickens's networks.

This book argues that a networked way of working and socializing fed into the ways in which writers such as Dickens, Reynolds, and Mayhew represented their readers. Editors and writers on Wellington Street frequently addressed these anonymous readers as friends, as if they were part of their immediate social network. Helen Small has argued of Dickens's Public Readings in the 1860s that: '[n]ormally an invisible constituency, on these occasions the fiction reading public was to a significant degree made visible to itself as a collectivity'. For Small, Dickens presented a vision of reading as an activity that could be 'realised, through Dickens, as public and at the same time familial, intimate, personal'; he represented his audience as a group of friends linked by a shared experience of print, as well as an anonymous public.[16] The image of the anonymous yet sympathetic friend can be pushed further than this. Social networks enable the passing of information and social capital around the system; they involve active sharing and exchange.[17] Dickens, I argue, makes a claim that *Household Words* will unite his readers in a

---

[13] Raymond Williams, *The Country and The City*, 2nd edn (London: Hogarth Press, 1985; 1st publ. Chatto & Windus 1973), 165.

[14] Ibid., 180.

[15] Ibid., 155.

[16] Helen Small, 'A Pulse of 124: Charles Dickens and a Pathology of the Mid-Victorian Reading Public', in *The Practice and Representation of Reading in England*, ed. James Raven, Helen Small, and Naomi Tadmor (Cambridge: Cambridge University Press, 1996), 266; 277.

[17] See Charles Wetherell, 'Historical Social Network Analysis', *International Review of Social History* 43, supplement (1998): 125–44 (126); Gary B. Magee and Andrew S. Thompson, 'Networks and the British World', in *Empire and Globalisation: Networks of People, Goods and Capital in the British World, c. 1850–1914* (Cambridge: Cambridge University Press, 2010), 45–63 (49).

better understanding (Chapter 1); Reynolds hopes his readers will become radical protestors and vice versa (Chapter 2); Mayhew's readers write in to the office of *London Labour and the London Poor* with new information to contribute to the project, and debate with each other via the 'Answers to Correspondents' pages (Chapter 3). These writers and editors represented their readers as active participants in a network, who would react, respond, and feed information back to the 'hub' of the editor's office.

As is increasingly recognized, digitization has opened up a panoply of resources that must be assimilated and assessed in new ways, and the vast quantity and variety of works that comprised nineteenth-century print culture is becoming more and more evident. However, this book shows that, despite advances in literacy, print technology, and communications, London in the 1840s and '50s was not a place where face-to-face interactions within a knowable community (more commonly associated with the print trade in smaller early modern cities) disappeared. The proliferation of affordable print enabled communication with a greater number of anonymous readers, whom writers and editors would never meet. Yet this very disembodied form of communication was produced by participants in face-to-face print networks. Laura Rotunno has shown that a periodical could be a 'virtual' space for networking, for intellectual discussion and professional development on the part of those without access to an office space (this was true for women, as well as for scattered special interest groups).[18] But print networks themselves could create a virtual space where writers interacted face to face (in the office, at the theatre, in the street) and also via the printed page. This book unites the concepts of the 'face-to-face community' and the 'imagined community': an experience of the former by the editors and writers of Wellington Street was part of what led to an expectation of, and desire for, the latter – that is, a relationship between writer and imagined readers, conducted through print. This persistence of face-to-face networks is the significant backdrop to the fascination with connections and coincidences in work by Dickens, Jerrold, Mayhew, Reynolds, and Sala, as well as R.H. Horne and Marcus Clarke. The links between Wellington Street, Strand, and Collins Street, Melbourne, reveal a print network which stretched across the Empire, and so complicate Anderson's picture of print culture as a way of imagining the community of the imperial nation state.

This book is not interested in the geographies of reading or reception; rather, it is interested in how the writers of Wellington Street themselves conceived of their community of readers, and the ways in which the cultural geography of Wellington Street informed their representation of their imagined readers as part of the network. Readers, in this model, are not just an 'imagined community' of communicants who read in 'silent privacy' but active members of an imagined

---

[18] Laura Rotunno, 'Blackfriars: The Post Office Magazine: A Nineteenth-Century Network of "The Happy Ignorant"', in 'Victorian Networks and the Periodical Press', ed. Alexis Easley, special issue, *Victorian Periodicals Review* 44, no. 2 (Summer 2011): 141–64.

network, in ways which attempt to puncture the anonymity of the teeming city, and even the Empire.[19] However, as I show in Chapters 1 and 3, this is frequently an uncomfortable way of representing readers and representing the city, which undermines depictions of the city as a place of relief from social bonds created by anything other than simultaneity. Networks show that simultaneity – existing on the same street, or on the same page – reinforces links and connections in ways which can be both productive and unsettling. This is even more problematic when print networks are divided between London and Melbourne and by thousands of miles of ocean.

Situated within a square mile wherein much of the printed material of London, and indeed of the Empire, was produced, Wellington Street offers a particularly rich entry point into print culture networks in the mid-nineteenth century. Wellington Street contains a remarkable cluster of major figures in journalism, drama, and literature during the 1840s and '50s. The simultaneous presence of Dickens, Reynolds, and Mayhew on Wellington Street is one part of a rich, interconnected, cultural environment. Dickens had an office and living accommodation on Wellington Street right up to his death in 1870, and beyond the moment when the three sections of Wellington Street were united, renumbered, and renamed simply 'Wellington Street' in 1859, during the new Metropolitan Board of Works's drive to simplify and reorganize London's street names (see Chapter 1 for a detailed history of Wellington Street).[20] The period 1843–53, however, encompasses the last months of *Punch*'s residence on the street, as well as the radical protests of 1848 which spilled onto Wellington Street, the key year of 1851 (when Dickens, Reynolds, and Mayhew all had offices on the street), and the completion in 1853 of *Bleak House*, Dickens's novel about an interconnected world. It is before Reynolds's departure from London to Kent (1854); it is also before the start of the Crimean War (1854), the arrival of the Metropolitan Board of Works (1855), and the changed social and political landscape of the late 1850s. The period 1843–53 saw Wellington Street's three sections at their most dynamic, their most significant (in terms of print culture), and their most interlinked.

Even though Dickens, Reynolds, Mayhew, Jerrold, Forster, Lewes, and Sala had rooms or offices on Wellington Street during overlapping years, they were not necessarily influenced by each other's work in direct or straightforward ways. Inevitably, some of the connections that I draw in this book are speculative. We cannot know how many of the theatregoers at the Lyceum had read or went on to read texts written by the authors whose works they saw performed or adapted. The print networks of Wellington Street were not commented upon except by those who belonged to them. Despite their virtually adjacent offices, Dickens and Reynolds may not have met each other on the street every day, or even every week; we do not know if Dickens and Mayhew spoke after 1845. What this book argues, however, is that they were nonetheless aware of each other, because they

---

[19]   Anderson, 35.
[20]   Michael Slater, *Charles Dickens* (New Haven, CT: Yale University Press, 2009).

had offices on the same relatively short stretch of the city.[21] This meant that they had shared experiences of the print economy and its networks which operated on Wellington Street, filled as it was with booksellers, publishers, and editors. Close physical proximity to friends, rivals, and collaborators is a daily reminder of their existence, especially when connected by business and social ties. The proximity of the buildings – non-human agents – facilitated the creation and deepening of links and the development of rivalries among the social networks. Relationships between writers and editors were hostile as well as friendly; as Laurel Brake reminds us, 'networks accommodate rivalry as well as solidarity'.[22] Like a corridor in a university department, Wellington Street was a shared place of interactions and practice in the city. The remainder of this Introduction sets out the range of interactions at play in this book.

Urban Print Networks and the Everyday

Scholars of print networks are increasingly looking for ways to develop the study of networks beyond a focus on individual writers, titles, and groups, and towards an understanding of everyday practice and how networks function on the ground.[23] Laurel Brake has argued, in an article on networks in nineteenth-century journalism, that more work needs to be done on the intersections between networks of writers, editors, journalists, printers, illustrators, and publishers.[24] This book provides one answer to this problem: the study of a street rather than a house, or a group, allows us to examine all of these together. Brake's article is a call to arms for more research which moves away from life-writing studies of single authors or groups to consider 'the technics or structures of the industry' of print production, and she suggests that networking can be understood as 'part

---

[21] As Graham Law says of Reynolds and Dickens, given the proximity of their offices, 'it is likely that the two authors crossed paths occasionally'. Graham Law, 'Reynolds's "Memoirs" Series and "The Literature of the Kitchen"', in *G.W.M. Reynolds: Nineteenth-Century Fiction, Politics and the Press*, ed. Anne Humpherys and Louis James (Aldershot: Ashgate, 2008), 201–12.

[22] Laurel Brake, '"Time's Turbulence": Mapping Journalism's Networks', in 'Victorian Networks and the Periodical Press', ed. Easley, 119. See also David Knoke and James H. Kulinski, 'Network Analysis: Basic Concepts', in *Markets, Hierarchies and Networks: The Coordination of Social Life*, ed. Graham Thompson et al. (London: SAGE in association with Open University, 1991), 175.

[23] There has been useful work on print culture and technological networks, and print culture and transport networks: see, for example, Richard Menke, *Telegraphic Realism: Victorian Fiction and Other Information Systems* (Stanford: Stanford University Press, 2008), and Jonathan H. Grossman, *Dickens's Networks: Public Transport and the Novel* (Oxford: Oxford University Press, 2012). This book, however, is interested in the network as a social system.

[24] Brake, 'Time's Turbulence'.

of the *structure* of journalism'.[25] Recent work on networks within nineteenth-century print culture has focused on how male and female networks function, and how networks operate around one title or one publisher. Rosemary Ashton's *142 Strand: A Radical Address in Victorian London* (Chatto & Windus, 2006), which focused on John Chapman, and Patrick Leary's award-winning *The Punch Brotherhood: Table Talk and Print Culture in Mid-Victorian Britain* (The British Library, 2010), which focused on *Punch*, are examples of this kind of undeniably important scholarship.[26] *Dickens, Reynolds and Mayhew on Wellington Street* moves us beyond these investigations to show how networks of writers, editors, journalists, and publishers intersected between and across titles and social circles within the physical environment of a London street. It reveals how the material fact of buildings and streets affects the complexity, the contingency, and the dynamic flow of interactions, 'the unexpected range of connections' and the 'dynamic of interlocking structures, referenced [...] but otherwise invisible' that Brake says she began to visualize whilst compiling the *Dictionary of Nineteenth-Century Journalism*.[27] I map the crowded streets onto the crowded market of print culture itself to bring to life the full complexity of print culture networks in ways which a single-author study, as illuminating as that approach is in other ways, cannot do.

Uncovering the everyday practices of Wellington Street and its print culture enables us to recapture London's 24-hour print day, the round-the-clock interactions of editors and writers awake all day and into the night.[28] The 'everyday' is not easy to define; 'it is almost undefinable, being that realm of routine and humdrum which we take for granted'.[29] Following Lefebvre, however, the everyday might

---

[25]   Ibid., 117.

[26]   See also Linda H. Peterson, *Becoming a Woman of Letters: Myths of Authorship and Facts of the Victorian Market* (Princeton, NJ; Woodstock: Princeton University Press, 2009); Susan David Bernstein, *Roomscape: Women Writers in the British Museum from George Eliot to Virginia Woolf* (Edinburgh: Edinburgh University Press, 2013). Biographies of groups and individuals are also often implicit network studies, such as Michael Slater, *Douglas Jerrold: 1803–1857* (London: Duckworth, 2002) and P.D. Edwards, *Dickens's 'Young Men': George Augustus Sala, Edmund Yates, and the World of Victorian Journalism* (Aldershot: Ashgate, 1997).

[27]   Brake, 'Time's Turbulence', 115.

[28]   In a 2010 special issue of the *Journal of Victorian Culture*, Katharina Boehm and Josephine McDonagh identified what they believed was 'a significant shift in the direction of studies of the city'. This 'New Agenda', according to Boehm and McDonagh, focuses on material culture, on social networks, and on London as a place of mobility and exchange, 'as the minutiae of everyday life reveal stories of much larger significance'. This book contributes to this shift. See Katharina Boehm and Josephine McDonagh, Introduction to 'New Agenda: Urban Mobility: New Maps of Victorian Britain', ed. Katharina Boehm and Josephine McDonagh, special issue, *Journal of Victorian Culture* 15, no. 2 (August 2010): 196.

[29]   Lewis Holloway and Phil Hubbard, *People and Place: The Extraordinary Geographies of Everyday Life* (Harlow: Prentice Hall, 2001), 33.

simply involve work, leisure, and 'private life' and the places where these everyday activities occur.[30] The often coincidental and contingent interactions on Wellington Street between those who used the street for business and leisure on a regular basis fed into literary imitation, repetition, plagiarism, and competition across titles and texts. Wellington Street allows us to uncover new connections within the print culture of the 1840s and 1850s, as well as to synthesize existing knowledge about the networks that cluster around the key offices of *Household Words* and *Punch*. Wellington Street brings to our attention connections between men and women, newspapers and serial fiction, radical and 'respectable' culture, and metropolis and colony. It reveals the geographical connections lurking behind the texts, which have escaped notice until now, and the ways in which print networks were reinforced by physical proximity within a city in the mid-nineteenth century. Discussions of the city of Dickens, Reynolds, Sala, and Mayhew have often invoked the figure of the observing journalist or sketch-writer as if they are separate from the lived experience of the city streets.[31] However, the city can contain moments of spectacle without being held permanently in stasis; the mobile spectator is part of a mobile and busy city.[32] The shared exposure of writers and editors to the print culture visible each day on the streets around Wellington Street, I argue, reinforced the sense of participation in an active and recognizable community of print networks for Dickens and his contemporaries.

The study of networks of all kinds is a growing field in urban studies, sociology, historical geography, history of science, book history, and periodical studies. Book historians have increasingly adopted a geographical approach.[33] However, rather than limiting the study of print networks to the remit of biographers and book historians, how might geographical context and the everyday life of print networks

---

[30] Ibid., 35–6. See Henri Lefebvre, *The Production of Space*, trans. Donald Nicholson-Smith (Oxford: Blackwell, 1991).

[31] Jeremy Tambling's *Going Astray: Dickens and London* (Harlow: Pearson Longman, 2009), and Maxwell's *The Mysteries of Paris and London* focus on this observant figure.

[32] Peter K. Andersson is similarly critical of the figure of the late-Victorian flâneur: he points out that busy streets involve encounters and interactions – what he calls 'parochial behaviour' (using the term developed by the sociologist Lyn H. Lofland) – not simply an experience of anonymity or passive spectatorship. He concludes that 'late Victorian London had an extensive parochial realm, making the norms of behaviour dependent on notions of neighbourliness and commonality, but at the same time [...] parochial interaction was performative' and theatrical. See *Streetlife in Late Victorian London: The Constable and the Crowd* (Basingstoke: Palgrave Macmillan, 2013), 4–5; 130.

[33] For example, Adrian Johns and James Raven map locations of printers and booksellers to reveal the importance of the working practices of early modern and eighteenth-century bookselling to the development of the material form of the book itself. See Adrian Johns, *The Nature of the Book: Print and Knowledge in the Making* (Chicago: University of Chicago Press, 1998); James Raven, *The Business of Books: Booksellers and the English Book Trade, 1450–1850* (New Haven, CT: Yale University Press, 2007). See also Miles Ogborn's and Charles W.J. Withers's field-defining collection *Geographies of the Book* (Farnham: Ashgate, 2010).

inform textual criticism? This book combines archive work (both physical and digital) with literary criticism to show that the context of where texts were produced can make us look again at the language of the texts themselves. Such a geographical approach creates not a master-narrative for print culture, but a narrative of the everyday, which does not flatten out the landscape of interactions but shows how print culture was always fluid and in motion around the clock, and develops our understanding of the links between fiction, drama, and journalism. By focusing on the print culture of a specific street as a case study, we see how an understanding of everyday working and social practices for mid-nineteenth-century journalists and writers is crucial to any literary analysis of their written work. Wellington Street is a particularly rich location for study, given the simultaneous presence of the offices of Dickens, Reynolds, and Mayhew, writers fascinated by the minutiae of urban life. However, this approach could potentially yield results for other areas of London, other cities, or other periods.[34]

How do we map print culture without flattening the landscape of interactions, as Bruno Latour warns us against in *Reassembling the Social* (2005)? Networks are often viewed or displayed panoptically, with no sense of the flow of movement or information, like the London Underground map. In contrast, Latour advises us that:

> whenever anyone speaks of a 'system', a 'global feature', a 'structure', a 'society', an 'empire', a 'world economy', an 'organisation', the first ANT reflex should be to ask: 'In which building? In which bureau? Through which corridor is it accessible? Which colleagues has it been read to? How has it been compiled?'[35]

Following Latour's directive, this book searches for how networks operate on the ground. Place, the interactions that occur there, and the awareness of who shares the space with you are inseparable, for Latour, from questions of immaterial ideas like 'community', 'network', and 'culture'. As Latour puts it:

> Culture does not act surreptitiously behind the actor's back. This most sublime production is manufactured at specific places and institutions, be it the messy offices of the top floor of Marshal Sahlins's house on the Chicago University campus or the thick Area Files kept at the Pitts River *[sic]* museum in Oxford.[36]

If we are to investigate the everyday practice of urban print networks we must not lose the sense of the streets as complex formations, nor flatten them with a

---

[34] Angus Whitehead's work on Blake and Fountain Court, for example, investigates Blake's local networks to shed light on art history. See Angus Whitehead, 'The Will of Henry Banes, Landlord of Fountain Court, Strand, the Last Residence of William and Catherine Blake', *Blake: An Illustrated Quarterly* 39, no. 2 (Fall 2005).

[35] Bruno Latour, *Reassembling the Social: An Introduction to Actor-Network-Theory* (Oxford: Oxford University Press, 2005), 183.

[36] Ibid., 175.

panoptic gaze. Nineteenth-century print culture was itself always in motion, meaning that everyday narratives best reveal its far-from-static map. The very structure of Wellington Street itself was in a state of flux from 1834 onwards, with several rebuildings, renamings, and renumberings; Melbourne was only founded in 1835, but by the 1850s was an established centre for newspapers and periodicals.[37] Melbourne print culture pops up as a sudden new node on the interlinked networks, and turns physical proximity to London print networks into a metaphorical idea played out through the language and imagery of bodies and child-parent relations. The study of print networks on Wellington Street also sheds further light on the connections between literature, journalism, and drama in the mid-nineteenth century. The mutual influence of fiction and journalism, and fiction and drama, is now accepted; however, more understanding of the connections across all of these discourses is needed.[38] Wellington Street provides a concrete, physical location for the kinds of interactions between fiction, journalism, drama, and illustration explored by Martin Meisel in his 1983 book *Realizations*.[39] As well as the link between literature and journalism, the links between these and mid-Victorian drama must be considered if we are to have a complete picture of Victorian print culture. *Dickens, Reynolds, and Mayhew on Wellington Street* provides one methodological approach for achieving this.

---

[37]   Andrew Brown-May, *Melbourne Street Life: The Itinerary of Our Days* (Kew, Vic.: Australian Scholarly Publishing, 1998), 3. See also Elizabeth Morrison, 'Serial Fiction in Australian Colonial Newspapers', in *Literature in the Marketplace: Nineteenth-Century British Publishing and Reading Practices*, ed. John O. Jordan and Robert L. Patten (Cambridge: Cambridge University Press, 1995), 310.

[38]   Recent studies, such as Deborah Wynne's *The Sensation Novel and the Victorian Family Magazine* (Basingstoke: Palgrave, 2001), Matthew Rubery's *The Novelty of Newspapers: Victorian Fiction after the Invention of the News* (Oxford: Oxford University Press, 2009), and John M.L. Drew's *Dickens the Journalist* (Basingstoke: Palgrave Macmillan, 2003), have all contributed to the critical re-evaluation of the relationship between Victorian journalism and fiction. So has Anne Humpherys's and Louis James's edited collection *G.W.M. Reynolds: Nineteenth-Century Fiction, Politics and the Press* (Aldershot: Ashgate, 2008). At the same time there has been work on the links between melodrama and popular nineteenth-century fiction, informed by Peter Brooks's influential *The Melodramatic Imagination: Balzac, Henry James, Melodrama, and the Mode of Excess*, 2nd edn (New Haven, CT: Yale University Press, 1995). See Louis James, 'From Egan to Reynolds: The shaping of urban "Mysteries" in England and France, 1821–48', *European Journal of English Studies* 14, no. 2 (August 2010); Juliet John, *Dickens's Villains: Melodrama, Character, Popular Culture* (Oxford: Oxford University Press, 2001); Rohan McWilliam, 'The French Connection: G.W.M. Reynolds and the Outlaw Robert Macaire', in Humpherys and James, eds, *G.W.M. Reynolds*, 33–49.

[39]   Martin Meisel, Realizations: *Narrative, Pictorial and Theatrical Arts in Nineteenth-Century England* (Princeton, NJ: Princeton University Press, 1983).

Gender, Place, and Modernity

Wellington Street does place some limits upon the scope of our investigation of nineteenth-century print culture: the overwhelming majority of the writers who used Wellington Street regularly were male. There were, of course, many famous female contributors to *Household Words* and other publications. However, this book only discusses people who can be placed physically on the street, rather than contributors to a Wellington Street publication who have no geographical link to Wellington Street itself, who sent in work from another location, or who would not have been regular visitors to the street. For example, the two most important female contributors to *Household Words*, Elizabeth Gaskell and Harriet Martineau, were not based in London, were not regular office visitors, and mostly wrote in to the editor from afar.[40] This is exemplified by the story of Adelaide Proctor, a key member of Barbara Leigh Smith's Langham Place circle, who contributed several verses to *Household Words*. Dickens wrote in his preface to her *Legends and Lyrics*, published in 1866 after her death, that in 1854 he was

> going to dine that day with an old and dear friend [...] I took with me an early proof of that number [of *Household Words*], and remarked, as I laid it on the drawing room table, that it contained a very pretty poem written by a certain Miss Berwick. Next day brought me the disclosure that I had so spoken of the poem to the mother of its writer, in its writer's presence; that I had no such correspondent in existence as Miss Berwick; and that the name had been assumed by [B.W. Proctor's] eldest daughter, Miss Adelaide Anne Proctor.[41]

Because they communicated through correspondence alone, Dickens had been unaware for almost a year that one of his valued contributors was, in fact, well known to him personally. Contrast this with J.W.T. Ley's account of Dickens's friendship with a male contributor, G.A. Sala:

> Dickens took a deep interest in him. He was a frequent guest to dinners at Wellington Street, where the offices of *Household Words* were situated – 'to my great glee and contentment,' he says, 'I used to get an invitation to dine at *Household Words* office about once a month.' [...] he says, 'I learned once, quite accidentally, that the Conductor of *Household Words* had made strenuous, but fruitless, efforts to obtain for me a position on the staff of 'Punch', not as an artist, but as a writer.'[42]

---

40   J.W.T. Ley, *The Dickens Circle: A Narrative of the Novelist's Friendships* (London: Chapman & Hall, 1918), 322; 324.

41   Ley, 144. For more on the Langham Place circle, see *Barbara Leigh Smith Bodichon and the Langham Place Group. Women's Source Library*, ed. Candida Ann Lacey, 2nd edn (New York and London: Routledge, 2001).

42   Ley, 315.

That women writers did not have easy access to such professional positions is interesting in itself, as Joanne Shattock has shown. Shattock points out that 'women writers began to have a public visibility in the 1840s' and analyzes the different ways in which women maintained literary networks, but she emphasizes that women writers were constrained by their lack of access to university education and to the 'clubs and dinners enjoyed by their male colleagues'.[43]

There were some literary women on Wellington Street. Susannah Reynolds, wife of George, was an editor and writer who may well have worked side by side with her husband and who forms a connecting node between cheap print, radical print, Reynolds, and Dickens (see Chapter 1). Henry Mayhew's wife, Jane, daughter of Douglas Jerrold, was described by Mayhew as his '*right hand*, scribbling to my dictation night and day', so it is possible that she visited her husband's office on Wellington Street, although she could have assisted him at home.[44] George Eliot was at 142 Strand from January 1851 and had a tenuous connection to Wellington Street through G.H. Lewes, who, together with Thornton Leigh Hunt, set up the *Leader*, which moved to Wellington Street (South) in 1852.[45] She occasionally visited the theatre there, as did Elizabeth Gaskell, who went to the Lyceum Theatre with Forster and the Dickenses (see Chapter 3).[46] Tracy C. Davis's research on the 1840s diaries of the theatre critic Amelia Chesson suggests that there may have been an unknown myriad of female journalists about whom the official record is silent.[47] However, a picture emerges of a particular performance of masculinity, which self-consciously merges friendship with professional life. This was an environment in which 'ambitious individuals had to strike a tricky balance between social networking and shouldering their way through the crowd'.[48] Bohemia, I argue in chapters 3 and 4, becomes a sign which

---

[43] Joanne Shattock, 'Professional Networking, Masculine and Feminine', in 'Victorian Networks and the Periodical Press', ed. Easley, 128–9. See also Brake's discussion of gender in mid-century higher journalism in Laurel Brake, *Print in Transition, 1850–1910: Studies in Media and Book History* (Basingstoke: Palgrave, 2001). For a useful discussion of the effects of place and proximity on female literary networks later in the century, see Susan David Bernstein, *Roomscape: Women Writers in the British Museum from George Eliot to Virginia Woolf* (Edinburgh: Edinburgh University Press, 2013).

[44] Henry Mayhew, 'Dedication', in *German Life and Manners as seen in Saxony at the Present Day*, vol. 1 (London: Wm H. Allen & Co., 1864), iii–iv.

[45] Rosemary Ashton, *142 Strand: A Radical Address in Victorian London* (London: Chatto & Windus, 2006), 85; for the *Leader*, see Chapter 1.

[46] James A. Davies, *John Forster: A Literary Life* (Leicester: Leicester University Press, 1983), 92.

[47] Tracy C. Davis, 'Amelia Chesson Enters the Fourth Estate: "She must, therefore, be considered a pioneer in lady journalism"' (paper presented at the annual conference for the British Association for Victorian Studies, University of Birmingham, 1–3 September 2011).

[48] Robert Douglas-Fairhurst, *Becoming Dickens: The Invention of a Novelist* (Cambridge, MA and London: Belknap Press of Harvard University Press, 2011), 141.

unites men from many different backgrounds, in London and Melbourne, as locals of these particular streets and networks.[49]

The local and the global are not stable categories, of course; Wellington Street itself complicates these distinctions. Latour argues that no place can be described as truly local or truly global, as the two categories are porous. For Latour, any social interactions involve 'a bewildering array of participants' behind the scenes who have made these interactions possible and 'which are dislocating their neat boundaries in all sorts of ways'.[50] Therefore, 'no place dominates enough to be global and no place is self-contained enough to be local'.[51] This is certainly true for Wellington Street. However, Wellington Street was an important local 'neighbourhood', in Arjun Appadurai's terms, where a 'locality' is not a place in space but a structure of feeling, and the 'neighbourhood' is the form in which this structure of feeling is realized.[52] Therefore, a neighbourhood can be virtual as well as real (created by the media and communications and storytelling), and so can be transnational as well as local.[53] Appadurai redefines the idea of the local, although the implications of his idea mean that global networks (or 'virtual neighbourhoods') cannot exist without local ones (in the traditional definition of the word) to establish the principle of networks first. Or, to put it another way, to have a virtual neighbourhood that erases the differences of time and space, and can stretch between London and Australia, you need first to have the concept of an actual neighbourhood, with actual buildings and an actual face-to-face community.[54] Imitation of London print culture in Melbourne, and biographical ties to Wellington Street networks, meant that the neighbourhoods of Wellington Street and Collins Street were linked. Bohemia reinvented itself in Melbourne. As Magee and Thompson argue in *Empire and Globalisation,* networks can be both local and global:

> rather than signalling the end of old associations, emigration often provided the means by which those associations could expand and diversify trans-nationally [...]. In their new setting, new arrivals are often more reliant and intent on accessing and accumulating social capital, both of the old and new vintage, than they had hitherto been 'back home'.[55]

---

[49]   Andrew McCann makes a similar point, although without reference to links between London and Melbourne print networks, in *Marcus Clarke's Bohemia: Literature and Modernity in Colonial Melbourne* (Carlton, Vic.: Melbourne University Press, 2004), 160.

[50]   Latour, 202.

[51]   Ibid., 204.

[52]   Arjun Appadurai, 'The Production of Locality', in *Modernity at Large: Cultural Dimensions of Globalization* (Minneapolis: University of Minnesota Press, 1996), 178–9; 181.

[53]   Ibid., 195.

[54]   Ibid.

[55]   Magee and Thompson, 56.

A networked way of working, as Magee and Thompson stress, was not limited to the early modern world, but continued during the nineteenth century. Wellington Street's networks were replicated so quickly in Melbourne precisely because emigrants like Horne and Clarke considered themselves to be still 'local' to London print culture, even as they recognized and desired their distance from it.

Stretched across the Empire, the print networks of the three sections of Wellington Street reveal the uneven processes of modernity. Andrew McCann characterizes usefully the somewhat vexed term 'modernity' as the experience of dislocation and lack of social connections within urban space; for McCann, from the late eighteenth and early nineteenth centuries, 'visions of a people with an intimate, ancestral relationship to place seem to circulate at the very moment that "belonging", in this fundamental sense, has been disrupted or rendered problematic by the processes of urbanization, migration and alienation'.[56] The sense of dislocation is commonly associated with the crowded nineteenth-century city; Rick Allen argues that 'the streets are characterised by movement; they are emblems of the essentially kinetic quality of modern city life'.[57] McCann points out that urban modernity is not a phenomenon confined by national boundaries, but is global (although many English novels maintained a steadfastly national focus in their representations of urban modernity, as James Buzard has shown).[58] A sense of locatedness, of what McCann calls 'belonging' is, then, in McCann's terms, pre-modern. Yet the print networks of the three sections of Wellington Street, reinforced by physical proximity in London, are the very essence of locatedness. The tribal metaphors which (as we have seen) members sometimes used to describe their networks tap into this strong sense of 'belonging' and make use of 'the ethnographic topos of the native who inhabits a thoroughly naturalised cultural environment'.[59] The face-to-face networks of the writers and editors of Wellington Street were not a closed system, but connected with readers, audiences, and colonial counterparts in a vast imagined network of sometimes tense and uncomfortable 'belonging'.

Outline of Chapters

To further my end of reconstructing everyday practice, the following chapters are arranged thematically and according to times of the day.[60] This book, then, revisits mornings on Wellington Street as editors and print workers arrive for

---

[56] McCann, 2.

[57] Rick Allen, Introduction to *The Moving Pageant: A Literary Sourcebook on London Street-Life, 1700–1914* (London: Routledge, 1998), 2.

[58] James Buzard, *Disorienting Fiction: The Autoethnographic Work of Nineteenth-Century British Novels* (Princeton, NJ: Princeton University Press, 2005).

[59] Ibid., 24.

[60] This is a strategy borrowed from Sala and others; see Rick Allen, introduction to *The Moving Pageant*, 2.

work, afternoon on a specific day during a radical protest, evenings at the Lyceum Theatre, and nights on the streets. Chapters 1 to 3 establish the different kinds of print networks which operated in and around the three sections of Wellington Street. Chapter 4 then reveals connections and similarities between these networks and those based around Collins Street, Melbourne.

Chapter 1, 'Morning', explains the location, structure, and layout of Wellington Street. It reveals which editors and writers had premises on the three sections of the street, and where those premises were. It reconstructs the print networks of Wellington Street, and uses Dickens's routine to consider what editors such as Dickens would have seen when they arrived at their offices in the morning. The chapter argues that editors on Wellington Street shared the same experiences of the print economy on the same short street, and links this to Dickens's address to his imagined network of readers, 'The Preliminary Word', in the first number of *Household Words*.

Chapter 2, 'Afternoon', develops this by arguing that Reynolds went one step further than Dickens's 'Preliminary Word' and sought to address real and potential readers directly when he spoke before and after the Trafalgar Square riots in 1848 (in the Square and from his balcony in Wellington Street). The chapter starts by arguing that the accounts of his speeches that Reynolds inserted into *Mysteries* blurred the line between speechmaking and radical fiction and attempted to expand and personalize his relationship with his network of readers, and to agitate them to revolution. The chapter then reconstructs the social contrasts evident during afternoons around Wellington Street, and argues that Reynolds's actions were grounded in the radical tradition of his locality. The final section points to the contradictions of Reynolds's position, in that his writing career would be threatened if his readers did create a successful revolution. The chapter concludes by arguing that this is a tension which, in *Mysteries*, Reynolds has already failed to resolve.

Chapter 3, 'Evening', argues that interactions between the theatrical and the print communities on Wellington Street reveal the links between print culture and the culture of entertainment and spectacle. It contends that the buildings and their occupants on Wellington Street made it clear to the writers and editors that readers could also be audiences, and audiences could also be (or become) readers, and so their understanding of their wider network of readers was shaped partly by this local and specific urban space. This awareness of the potential connections between audiences and readers allowed members of the print networks to have a sense of a 'real' public: their tastes, their instant feedback on a writer's work or the work of colleagues, and even their faces looking back at the playwright from the pit and the gallery. The theatres in and around Wellington Street were places where the interdependence of print culture and entertainment culture became apparent, and where the members of a local face-to-face network confronted physically the wider readership which they addressed in print. The chapter argues that this tension between the 'local' and the 'alien', the familiar and the strange, is not always a benign one, and is addressed though fears of anonymity, exposure, and chance meetings at the theatre, in work by Mayhew and Reynolds, as well as Dickens and Jerrold.

Chapter 4, 'Night', argues that Wellington Street matters, not just because of its role in London print culture in the 1840s and 1850s, but because of its place in colonial Melbourne print culture, too. It asks what happens when emigration renders physical proximity no longer possible, by focusing on the Wellington Street emigrant R.H. Horne, *Melbourne Punch*, and Marcus Clarke. It uses the vexed relationships between Horne and Dickens, and Clarke and Dickens, to argue that despite the vast distances between London and Melbourne, cultural separation between the two cities did not occur straightaway. The chapter argues that replication of London's print networks enabled Melbourne's print culture to emerge fully functioning by the time of Clarke's arrival, less than three decades after the city was founded. The chapter ends with a comparison of Mayhew's *London Labour*, Sala's 'The Key of the Street', and Marcus Clarke's 'A Night at the Immigrants' Home' to argue that night-time in Melbourne comes to sound a lot like night-time on Wellington Street. It suggests that Clarke's sketches were more than just derivative, however, but were the product of an enabling cultural tension between the 'Old World' and the 'New'. The bodies of the readers, writers, and urban poor of both colony and metropole are drawn into a network of connections in Clarke's sketch, which talks back to the European metropolis.

The book concludes with a reading of *Bleak House* as a novel which emerged out of Dickens's experience of a world of coincidences, connections, and networks. Shared urban space reinforces and throws up connections, both in *Bleak House* and in the print networks of Wellington Street. I seek to show what the study of networks within print culture can do, not just for our understanding of the working conditions of mid-century urban writers, but for the close reading of their words on the page. Engels's view of urban life, that the 'isolation of the individual [...] is nowhere so shamelessly bare-faced, so self-conscious, as just here in the crowding of the great city', was a trope of London descriptions before and after he first published *The Condition of the Working Class in England* in 1845.[61] However, the truism that city life is experienced by countless individuals who exist next to each other in complete isolation is one which, as a Londoner myself, I wish to challenge. Social networks based on physical proximity can exist just as much in the city as in the country when significant numbers of actors in a network remain in the same area over an extended period of time. As Jerry White argues, in a city made up of several villages, nineteenth-century Londoners who spent long periods of their lives in the city certainly *did* know their neighbours.[62] The city is *not* a place where you can escape connections, partly because 'one's home town is really a sector, not the whole city'.[63] That this can be a threatening possibility for the urban writer, as well as an enabling one, is revealed in this book.

---

[61] Friederich Engels, *The Condition of the Working Class in England*, ed. Victor Kiernan (London: Penguin, 1987), 69.

[62] Jerry White, *London in the 19th Century: 'A Human Awful Wonder of God'* (London: Jonathan Cape, 2007), 124.

[63] Ronald Abler, John S. Adams, and Peter Gould, *Spatial Organization: The Geographer's View of the World* (Englewood Cliffs, NJ: Prentice-Hall, 1971), 382.

Chapter 1
Morning: 'The Smallness of the World'

Introducing the editors and writers of Wellington Street,
and suggesting that when writers walk to work,
they tend to look about them.

Certain groups and people are undoubtedly attracted to a certain locality,
the topography of which is strangely analogous to their situation.
—Peter Ackroyd, *London: The Biography*
(London: Vintage, 2001), 235. © Peter Ackroyd 2000

From 1850 onwards, Wellington Street was the frequent destination of Dickens's morning commute. Garret Dumas, at one time amanuensis to Dickens, described Dickens's morning routine:

> Dickens would arrive at his office No. 16 Wellington Street at about eight o'clock and begin dictating. He would walk up and down the floor several times after delivering himself of a sentence or a paragraph. He was generally tired out by eleven o'clock and would then go to his club. Dickens had a very odd habit of combing his hair. He would go through the performance a hundred times a day, and, in fact, seemed never to tire of it. It was invariably the first thing he did on arriving at the office.[1]

Dickens himself had a fascination with work routines: this description is reminiscent of Pip's interest in Mr Jaggers's habit of literally washing his hands of the working day.[2] This chapter reveals the locations of those who worked on Wellington Street, and reconstructs what editors like Dickens would have seen as they walked down the street in the morning. The 'business of amusing the public', as Phiz's son called it, was an occupation which thrived on networks, and neatly illustrates what Forster called Dickens's 'favourite theory as to the smallness of the world'.[3] Rosemary Ashton, Andrew King, Patrick Leary, Iain McCalman,

---

[1] Garret Dumas, quoted in Thomas Wright, *The Life of Charles Dickens* (London: Henry Jenkins, 1935), 207.

[2] Charles Dickens, *Great Expectations*, ed. Margaret Cardwell (Oxford: Clarendon Press, 1993), 210. Further references are to this edition and appear parenthetically in the text.

[3] John Forster, *The Life of Charles Dickens,* with 500 portraits, facsimiles, and other illustrations, collected, arranged, and annotated by B.W. Matz (London: Chapman & Hall, 1911; 1st publ.1872–74), 1: 46; Edgar Browne, *Phiz and Dickens as They Appeared to Edgar Browne* (London: J. Nisbet, 1913), 102.

and Joanne Shattock have all shown how print culture in this period was based upon collaboration and networks of acquaintances.[4] However, what has been less considered is exactly where in London these networks were situated. This chapter argues that close geographical proximity meant that the famous names of mid-Victorian print culture were more than just aware of each other in print, through their letters, and through social occasions at each other's homes. They would have seen each other in the street or seen each other's premises when they visited their own, and would have been aware that friends, rivals, and ex-colleagues were working, or had worked, on publications with addresses which were within a few hundred yards of their own editorial addresses. In all, there were more than 20 newspapers, miscellanies, and periodicals which had their offices on the three sections of Wellington Street between 1843 and 1853, and 13 publishers or booksellers. Wellington Street did not *create* all these networks; many friendships and collaborations existed or occurred before their members had connections with Wellington Street. However, what Wellington Street shows us is that members of these networks, which collaborated and competed closely in print, shared the same experiences of the print economy on the same short street.

Rosa Salzberg, writing about the geography of print culture in early modern Venice, argues that

> It is important to stress [the] clustering of purveyors of print for several reasons. From the customer's point of view, it suggests that the presence of print [...] was difficult to ignore, encountered whenever one passed through the central arteries of the city [...] For the printers and print-sellers, the rather intimate, parochial context in which many of them lived and worked mirrored the close-knit nature of the industry from its early days. Their lives were complexly interwoven, held together by ties of kinship and marriage, neighbourhood and shared provenance, friendship and partnership.[5]

A similar point could be made about Wellington Street (South), North, and Upper in early to mid-nineteenth-century London, as this chapter will show. The editors of Wellington Street were poised at a tipping point between the vestiges of early

---

[4]   Rosemary Ashton, *142 Strand: A Radical Address in Victorian London* (London: Chatto & Windus, 2006); Andrew King, '*Reynolds's Miscellany*, 1846–1849: Advertising Networks and Politics', in *G.W.M. Reynolds: Nineteenth-Century Fiction, Politics, and the Press*, ed. Anne Humpherys and Louis James (Aldershot: Ashgate, 2008), 53–74; Patrick Leary, *The Punch Brotherhood: Table Talk and Print Culture in Mid-Victorian Britain* (London: British Library, 2010); Iain McCalman, *Radical Underworld: Prophets, Revolutionaries, and Pornographers in London, 1795–1840*, 2nd edn (Oxford: Clarendon Press, 1993); Joanne Shattock, 'Professional Networking, Masculine and Feminine', in 'Victorian Networks and the Periodical Press', ed. Alexis Easley, special issue, *Victorian Periodicals Review* 44, no. 2 (Summer 2011): 128–40.

[5]   Rosa Salzberg, '"Per le Piaze & Sopra il Ponte": Reconstructing the Geography of Popular Print in Sixteenth-Century Venice', in *Geographies of the Book*, ed. Miles Ogborn and Charles W.J. Withers (Farnham: Ashgate, 2010), 120.

modern and eighteenth-century London and the modernized city. What Gatrell describes as the 'forgotten intimacy' of eighteenth-century Covent Garden – 'in which stellar talent and workaday street life and criminal life were closely compacted, where everyone knew each other and lived within minutes of each others' lodgings, tenements, workshops, studios, coffee-houses and taverns' – did not end as the century turned, or when Victoria came to the throne.[6] As Lynda Nead has shown, 'modernity' is not a stable category or a period in history that can be demarcated as 'uncompromised newness', but a working-through of 'uneven and unresolved processes of urbanization; it took the form of the improved street within a district of slums'.[7] The kinds of social networks which Salzberg describes as sustaining early modern print culture can be found on Wellington Street.

In human geography, 'agglomeration theory' is used to explain why groups of people engaged in similar activities cluster together. Abler, Adams, and Gould, in *Spatial Organization: The Geographer's View of the World*, argue that in what they call a 'traditional agricultural society', the dispersal of families over arable land was the best way of optimizing land use.[8] However, once people started to urbanize and then industrialize, this changed, as 'interaction potential increases with metropolitan size. [...] Specialized units occupy different places within the metropolis, and their specific complementarities provide the potential for spatial interaction within the metropolis'.[9] In other words, as the city gets bigger, trades tend to specialize in order to differentiate themselves, and then tend to cluster together according to their specializations. Because specialization occurs, one trade may need something very specific from another. This means they must interact. Therefore – before the widespread use of telephones and the Internet – the bigger the city, paradoxically, the more likely it was for citizens to communicate, interact, and interconnect. This points to the complexity of the processes of modernity; in fact, dislocation and dispersal (although on a different scale, and for different reasons) were just as much features of agricultural societies as they were of industrialization.[10] The population of London may have risen between 1841 and 1851, but print entrepreneurs on Wellington Street relied upon face-to-face interaction within their networks.[11] At the same time, modern print technology allowed them to reach far-flung readers. The final section of this chapter will argue that the everyday working conditions of

---

[6] Vic Gatrell, *The First Bohemians: Life and Art in London's Golden Age* (London: Allen Lane, 2013), xv.

[7] Lynda Nead, *Victorian Babylon: People, Streets and Images in Nineteenth-Century London* (New Haven, CT: Yale University Press, 2000), 10; 5.

[8] Ronald Abler, John S. Adams, and Peter Gould, *Spatial Organization: The Geographer's View of the World* (Englewood Cliffs, NJ: Prentice-Hall, 1971), 303.

[9] Abler, Adams and Gould, 209.

[10] Ibid., 303.

[11] 330,000 migrants arrived in the capital during this period; between 1800 and 1881 London's population rose from 1 million to 4.5 million. See Roy Porter, *London: A Social History*, 3rd edn (London: Penguin, 2000), 248–9.

editors on Wellington Street led Dickens to address these imagined readers in the language of face-to-face networks in *Household Words*.

Editors on Wellington Street

In the middle of the nineteenth century, as now, the three sections of Wellington Street were situated just off the Strand, the traditional artery between the Court and the City. The Strand sits between Holborn and Covent Garden to the north, Pall Mall, Whitehall, and St. James's to the west, Fleet Street and the City to the east, and the river Thames to the south. The editors and writers of the Strand area were surrounded by the theatres, the big newspaper offices, and the Inns of Court. They would have encountered playbills, law stationers, students from King's College London (founded on the Strand in 1829), and lawyers. There was a large cluster of printers on Fleet Street and the streets and courts just off it, such as Bouverie Street, where Bradbury and Evans started their printing business in 1830.[12] This made it easier to share tools and expertise. At the eastern end of Fleet Street, the traditional centre of the book trade still operated around St. Paul's Churchyard and Paternoster Row. Wellington Street was situated at the heart of London's print culture. In other words, printed matter was everywhere.

The story of Wellington Street itself – its gradual evolution between 1834 and 1859 – is further evidence for a conception of modernity as comprising unstable, uneven processes. What we now call Wellington Street has had a troubled birth and a chequered history. The stretch of Westminster from the bottom of Bow Street to the start of Waterloo Bridge is now called Wellington Street above the Strand, and Lancaster Place below it. This is the latest in a series of renamings, renumberings, and even rebuildings. Bow Street, home of the infamous 'Bow Street Runners' and later the police station and police court, has always finished at Russell Street. The section from Russell Street downwards was called Charles Street, after Charles II, and since the eighteenth century it had a very dubious reputation (see Figure 1.1). Charles Street was in the middle of one of the city's ancient Red Light districts, notorious for brothels and bathhouses.[13] *Harris's List of Covent Garden Ladies*, a list of local prostitutes printed from 1760 to 1793, listed upwards of 200 names of popular girls, some of whom had lodgings on Charles Street.[14] According to one memoir, '[Mother H's] night-house […], the great *rendezvous* for gay city birds, […] extended from Bridges Street to Charles Street, now called Wellington Street'.[15] Old Bailey records show that Charles

---

[12] Leary, 134.

[13] E.J. Burford, *Wits, Wenchers and Wantons: London's Low Life: Covent Garden in the Eighteenth Century* (London: Hale, 1986), 102.

[14] Ronald Webber, *Covent Garden: Mud-Salad Market* (London: J.M. Dent, 1969), 74.

[15] Renton Nicholson, *Autobiography of a Fast Man* (London: [n.pub.], 1863), 32–3. For more on Nicholson's own role in Strand nightlife, see Chapter 3.

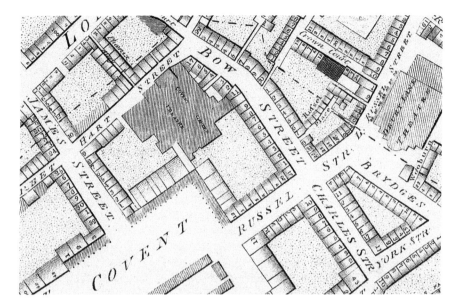

Figure 1.1   Charles Street in 1799. From Richard Horwood, *Plan of the Cities of London and Westminster, the Borough of Southwark, and Parts Adjoining. Showing Every House*, 1792–9. Reproduced by permission of Motco Enterprises Limited.

Street was also a hotbed of petty crime; a legal clerk called William Chaffey had his watch stolen from him there twice in less than a minute.[16] This is probably because Charles Street did not reach as far as the Strand, but finished at York Street. With no thoroughfare to the main road, it was a dark and disreputable cul-de-sac.

In 1834, Wellington Street North was built to connect Charles Street with the Strand, and south to Wellington Street (which rose north to the Strand from Waterloo Bridge). This was made possible because the English Opera House burnt down in 1830 (it was rebuilt and became the Lyceum Theatre).[17] Wellington Street and Wellington Street North became more respectable; businesses like Sotheby's auction house moved in. However, according to the *Survey of London*, Charles Street remained a problem. In 1835 locals complained to the parish vestry about the notorious brothels on the section near Russell Street, and in 1844 numbers 13 and 14, run by Mr and Mrs Stanley, were a brothel of 'the very lowest description'. According to the *Survey*, '[b]y that time the street had been opened to a greater

---

[16]   'October 1816, trial of FREDERICK BARKER MARY HARVEY (t18161030-86)', *Old Bailey Proceedings Online*, accessed 25 July 2012 via http://www.oldbaileyonline.org.

[17]   A.E. Wilson, *The Lyceum: Illustrated from the Raymond Mander and Joe Mitchenson Theatre Collection* (London: Dennis Yates, 1952), 51–5.

current of traffic by the making of Wellington Street. Charles Street was not widened or re-aligned, but because of "the bad repute" in which it stood, the old name was abolished in 1844'.[18] It was renamed Upper Wellington Street, which then brought it together with Wellington Street North and Wellington Street (South). This did not change matters straightaway; Mrs Stanley's brothel at 14 Upper Wellington Street was described gleefully in 1849 as 'of the filthiest kind to be found in London', and the Stanleys' 'coffee house' is still listed in the Post Office directory for 1853.[19]

In October 1859 the Metropolitan Board of Works decided to clarify matters by renaming the whole stretch Wellington Street and renumbering the houses (see Figure 1.2). However, between 1844 and 1859, the street that we now call Wellington Street was known as Upper Wellington Street and Wellington Street North, and it was a continuation of Wellington Street (South), now Lancaster Place (see Figure 1.3). Recovering the three sections of Wellington Street as they were between 1843 and 1853 may not be straightforward, but it is possible to piece together the street numbering before 1859 (see Figures 1.1–1.3).[20] The three sections of Wellington Street contained networks based upon business, friendship, and marriage. These networks formed, fragmented, and reformed over this 10-year span, and were connected to three key locations: the *Punch* office, which was at 13 Wellington Street (South) until January 1844, the office of *Reynolds's Miscellany* (*RM*) and later *Reynolds's Weekly Newspaper* (*RWN*) from 1847 at 7 Wellington Street North, and the office of *Household Words* (*HW*), established at 16 Wellington Street North in 1850[21] (Figure 1.4). Morning on the three sections of Wellington Street saw the arrival of the editors and press workers, as they hurried to their offices. According to Percy Fitzgerald, a young contributor to the periodical:

> The old original *Household Words* office was a graceful, highly-inviting, *dainty* little structure. It really seemed somewhat in keeping with the brilliant owner, and even with his genial, sympathetic character. It stood half-way up Wellington Street (north in those days), Strand, about half a dozen houses from York Street on the right-hand side as you looked from the Strand, and was number 16.[22]

---

[18]   'Bow Street and Russell Street Area: The former Charles Street', *Survey of London: volume 36: Covent Garden*, ed. F.H.W.Sheppard (1970), accessed 4 February 2011 online via http://www.british-history.ac.uk/source.aspx?pubid=362.

[19]   'Bawds and Brothels. No. III. Louisa Stanley', *Paul Pry: the Reformer of the Age*, 19 December 1849, 1; *Kelly's London Post Office Directory* (London: W. Kelly, 1843–53), WCA microfilm collection, London Directories/1843–45 (1853), 553.

[20]   Street numbering taken from the maps in Figures 1.1 and 1.2, together with Post Office Directories 1843–53 and census returns for 1841 and 1851.

[21]   Leary, 147; imprint, *RM*, 16 October 1847, 368, previously around the corner on Brydges Street, imprint, *RM*, 9 October 1847, 352; imprint, *HW*, 30 March 1850, 24.

[22]   Percy Fitzgerald, *Memories of Charles Dickens: with an Account of 'Household Words' and 'All the Year Round' and of the Contributors Thereto* (Bristol: J.W. Arrowsmith; London: Simpkin, Marshall, Hamilton, Kent & Co., 1913), 125.

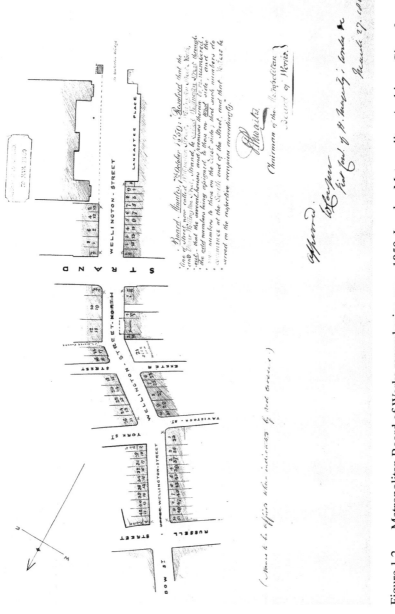

Figure 1.2 Metropolitan Board of Works renumbering map, 1859. London Metropolitan Archives, City of London. LCC/AR/BA/05/081.

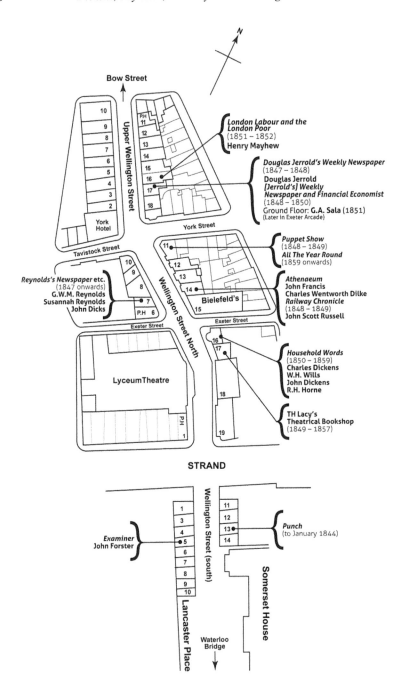

Figure 1.3   Approximate Plan of Wellington Street, *c.* 1843–53. Drawn by Simon Potter.

Figure 1.4   Wellington Street in 1893, showing the building which housed
             Household Words. City of Westminster Archives Centre Box
             G133 (6).

No. 16 Wellington Street North was a leftover of old London; it was demolished
sometime after the 1890s, during another of the continuous efforts to modernize
the area. A photograph from 1893 shows the building clinging to existence,
dwarfed by the buildings surrounding it (Figure 1.4).

    London in the 1840s and '50s was very much a walking city with no underground
railway, and the main streets were congested with traffic. Dickens, famous for his
perambulations around the city, walked the last stretch of his journey to the office,
as Fitzgerald recalled:

[Dickens] had a favourite private walk from the South Eastern Station to the office, always taking Chandos Street, perhaps a reminder of the childish 'blacking days', and through Maiden Lane into Wellington Street. Local tradesmen [...] / noted regularly his lithe figure briskly flitting past as the clock struck, his little bag in his hand.[23]

In the 1850s, 16 Wellington Street North played host to 'festive meetings [held] in the little rooms'; there was: 'but little room in the office for business purposes, but sufficient for Boz, and [...] was most convenient for his theatre going'.[24] These descriptions hold clues to the activities and sociability of the networks associated with Wellington Street. Dickens collected around him a network of like-minded friends, colleagues, and collaborators who took part in his festive meetings and his theatre trips, and who met him at the Garrick Club on nearby King Street. This network was largely based on and around Wellington Street, so on his morning walks Dickens could well have seen other famous faces of mid-century letters. If Dickens had occasion to walk down Wellington Street to his office, other editors must have done, too. Furthermore, just as the local tradesmen noticed Dickens, Dickens and his fellow editors must have noticed the bookshops, workshops, and other premises which they passed at the start of their day.

In *Sketches by Boz*, Dickens comments that the clerks who walk to work, heading for Chancery Lane just off the Strand, pay little attention to their surroundings:

> [They] plod steadily along, apparently with no object in view but the counting-house; knowing by sight almost every body *[sic]* they meet or overtake, for they have seen them every morning (Sundays excepted) during the last twenty years, but speaking to no-one. If they do happen to overtake a personal acquaintance, they just exchange a hurried salutation, and keep walking on, either by his side, or in front of him, as his rate of walking may chance to be [...].[25]

The buildup of clauses in this passage enlists the reader in the monotonous onward movement, and presents the Victorian commuter as one who sees nothing on his morning walk. However, it does suggest that these men are aware of those around them and of their participation in a shared ritual of travel on foot through the city streets. Furthermore, these are Dickens's own keen observations of the morning routine. Other pedestrians may keep their heads down, but writers and editors, on the lookout for their next material, were the very types of people who would be conscious of the landscape through which they moved: of its sounds, of its smells,

---

[23]   Percy Fitzgerald, 'Some Memories of Dickens and "Household Words"', in *The Dickens Souvenir of 1912*, ed. Dion Clayton Calthorp and Max Pemberton (London: Chapman & Hall, 1912), 22–3.

[24]   Ibid.

[25]   Charles Dickens, 'The Streets – Morning', in *Sketches by Boz and Other Early Papers 1833–39*, vol. 1 of *Dickens' Journalism*, ed. Michael Slater (London: J.M. Dent, 1994), 1: 53–4.

of the other people walking near them or past them, and of the shops and buildings which they passed along their way.

In 1843, before Dickens arrived, the offices of *Punch* magazine spent their last few months based at 13 Wellington Street (South) before the serial was sold to Bradbury and Evans and shifted to their Fleet Street premises.[26] The original *Punch* team included Mark Lemon and Henry Mayhew as co-editors, with Douglas Jerrold as a contributor and John Leech as illustrator. Other early members of the *Punch* team were W.H. Wills and Albert Smith, both of whom left or were ousted in the period of the Bradbury and Evans takeover in December 1842.[27] A few doors away, at 5 Wellington Street (South), was the office of the *Examiner*, founded by Leigh Hunt and his brother and edited at this point by Albany Fonblanque, whose literary editor was John Forster.[28] Forster was a friend of Douglas Jerrold and reviewed many of his plays, as well as being, of course, a friend to and associate of Dickens, whom he served in the capacity of literary advisor.[29] In 1846 Jerrold, Fonblanque, and Forster, along with Wills and the engineer John Scott Russell, formed a new network as they worked with Dickens on the *Daily News*, which had offices just off Fleet Street (10 minutes' walk from Wellington Street). Forster was briefly editor of the paper when Dickens stepped down.[30]

This network then fed back into the networks of Wellington Street. By 1853, W.H. Wills had moved to 16 Wellington Street North as assistant editor of *Household Words* under Dickens. There were further links back to *Punch* and the *Daily News*: *Household Words* was also published by Bradbury and Evans, with Douglas Jerrold's son Blanchard among the contributors to both Dickensian ventures.[31] Another famous contributor by 1853 was G.A. Sala, who is listed at 17 Upper Wellington Street in Kelly's 1851 *Post Office Directory*. Sala's morning walk at the turn of the decade was away from Wellington Street, rather than towards it. He describes how, in this period, he was training to be an engraver with a firm 'in Beaufort Buildings, Strand; and there I toiled and toiled during the day. At night I worked at artistic commissions in a studio on the ground floor of a house of which I was a tenant, in Wellington Street North, Strand'.[32] Between 1848 and 1849, at 14 Wellington Street North (next-door-but-one to the future office of *Household Words*), was the office of the

---

26 *Kelly's POD* (1843), 446; Leary, 147.

27 Leary, 19.

28 Laurel Brake, '*Examiner* [1808–1881]', in *Dictionary of Nineteenth-Century Journalism in Great Britain and Ireland*, ed. Laurel Brake and Marysa Demoor (Ghent and London: Academia Press and British Library, 2009), 211; *Kelly's POD* (1843), 446; imprint, *Examiner*, 2 January 1848, 16.

29 Michael Slater, *Douglas Jerrold: 1803–1857* (London: Duckworth, 2002), 94; 99.

30 Michael Slater, *Charles Dickens* (New Haven, CT: Yale University Press, 2009), 247.

31 Slater, *Dickens*, 242, and *Douglas Jerrold*, 197.

32 G.A. Sala, *The Life and Adventures of George Augustus Sala, Written by Himself*, 2nd edn, 2 vols (London: Cassell & Company, 1895), 1: 302. Even Sala is not immune here from the frequent confusion over which section of Wellington Street was which.

Railway Chronicle, edited by John Scott Russell.[33] This paper was published by John Francis, who also published the *Athenaeum* from the same building and who helped to prop up the *Daily News*.[34] The 1851 census shows that, unlike most of the other editors on the street, John Francis and his family lived as well as worked at number 14.[35] The editor of the *Athenaeum* until 1846 was Charles Wentworth Dilke, a family friend of Dickens who had worked with John Dickens at Somerset House.[36]

Mornings on Wellington Street must sometimes have been positively bustling with old friends and acquaintances. There were further connections to the networks of *Punch* and the *Daily News* between those working on newspapers and periodicals published from the three sections of Wellington Street. By 1853 Forster was overall editor of the *Examiner*, and so was a two-minute stroll away from Dickens. Jerrold's office for *Douglas Jerrold's Weekly Newspaper* had been at 17 Upper Wellington Street until 1848, before Sala arrived at that address, and Blanchard Jerrold had written articles for his father's paper.[37] After Jerrold left Upper Wellington Street his ex-*Punch* colleague, Henry Mayhew, set up an office at 16 Upper Wellington Street, next door to Sala, from which he published the serial version of *London Labour and the London Poor* between 1851 and 1852.[38] Mayhew's friend Henry Sutherland Edwards remarked that at the *Morning Chronicle* on the Strand, where the series originated, Mayhew 'had an army of assistant writers, stenographers, and hansom cab-men constantly at his call', but the suggestion is that Mayhew's mornings at his own office were much less bustling. Edwards comments laconically that 'Mayhew continued [his articles] in a publication of his own, but it was not the same thing. In the newspaper he had

---

[33]   Imprint, *Railway Chronicle*, 20 April 1844 and 24 and 29 December 1849, 896; *Kelly's POD* (1848), 596. The last number of the *Railway Chronicle* appeared in 1849; oddly, the office is still listed in *Kelly's POD* for 1853.

[34]   *Kelly's POD* (1843), 447 and (1853), 602; George S. Emmerson, *John Scott Russell: A Great Victorian Engineer and Naval Architect* (London: John Murray, 1977), 27; Peter Ackroyd, *Dickens* (London: Minerva, 1991; 1st publ. Sinclair-Stevenson, 1990), 505.

[35]   1851 census, HO107/1511, f. 148, accessed 15 July 2011 online via http://www.ancestry.co.uk/.

[36]   Slater, *Dickens*, 277.

[37]   *DJWN* moved from 169 Strand to 17 Upper Wellington Street in July 1847 (imprint, *DJWN*, 17 July 1847); *Kelly's POD* (1848), 553; Slater, *Douglas Jerrold*, 245. From July 1847 until December 1848, the paper continued at number 17 as *DJWN*. With the paper failing, Jerrold was forced to sell, and its name was changed in January 1849 to *Jerrold's Weekly News and Financial Economist*, and then again that year to *The Weekly News and Financial Economist*, when Frederick Guest Tomlins took over as proprietor (Michael Slater, 'Douglas Jerrold's Weekly Newspaper (1846–1851)', *DNCJ*, 117). Tomlins moved the paper to 1a Catherine Street, Strand (imprint, 22 June 1850, 600 and announcement, 29 June 1850, 601).

[38]   *Watkins's Directory* (1852), 1852; imprint, Henry Mayhew, *London Labour and the London Poor*, 3 vols (London: Office of London Labour and the London Poor, 1851–52). Further references to this edition appear parenthetically in the text.

his audience found for him. In his own publication he had to find it for himself'.[39] From 1848 to 1849, 10 years before Dickens used it for the offices of *All The Year Round*, 11 Wellington Street North was the office of *Puppet-Show*, a short-lived rival to *Punch* started by Henry Vizetelly in March 1848.[40] This miscellany was edited by John Bridgeman.[41]

These men headed each morning to small offices of the kind described by Sala himself in 1859:

> This is not, however, the monster journal that has all Printing House Square to roar and rattle in. No: our office is in the Strand. We are free of the charmed domains. We pass up a narrow court running by the side of the office, push aside a heavy door, ascend the creaking staircase, and discreetly tapping at a door, this time covered with green baize, find ourselves in the presence of Mr. Limberly, the sub-editor of the 'Daily Wagon.'
>
> Let us cast a glance round the room. What a litter it is in, to be sure! What piles of newspapers, home and country ones, mangled and disembowelled by the relentless scissors, cumber the floor! More newspapers on shelves – old files, these – more on the table; letters opened and unopened, wet proof-sheets, files of 'copy,' books for review, just sent by the publishers, or returned by the reviewers, after they have duly demolished the contents and the authors. And all about the room are great splashes and dried-up pools of ink, and the ceiling is darkened with the smoke of innumerable candles.[42]

This is the kind of scale of the smaller Wellington Street offices, although most of its newspapers and periodicals were weeklies, not dailies (Figure 1.5). Some of the more struggling writers and editors lived in the offices which they rented, so did not need to travel far in the morning. John Hollingshead described the Exeter Arcade, built around 1844 between Catherine Street and Wellington Street North, as:

> full of little shops which sold nothing to nobody, with the printed words 'To Let,' in every dusty window […] Here literary Bohemia of forty years ago and more 'squatted' – there is no other term – and succeeded in getting a few 'backers' – printers who thought they might 'strike' a catchpenny reef of periodical wealth […] The writers, when they were not frying sprats in the back-parlours, were 'publishing' these fly-sheets across the counters, and when the day's work was over they often slept under these counters […].[43]

---

[39]   Henry Sutherland Edwards, *Personal Recollections* (London: Cassell & Company, 1900), 60–61.

[40]   Henry Vizetelly, *Glances back through Seventy Years: Autobiographical and Other Reminiscences*, 2 vols (London: Kegan Paul, 1893), 1: 330.

[41]   *Kelly's POD* (1849), 570. Other well-known staff members included Henry Sutherland Edwards and John Hannay. See Vizetelly, 1: 330–31.

[42]   George Augustus Sala, *Twice Round the Clock; or The Hours of the Day and Night in London* (London: J. and R. Maxwell, 1859), 327.

[43]   John Hollingshead, *'Good old Gaiety': an Historiette and Remembrance* (London: Gaiety Theatre, 1903), 3.

Figure 1.5   *'Midnight: The Sub-Editor's Room'*. From Sala, *Twice Round the Clock*, 329. Reproduced with the permission of Senate House Library, University of London. MWC Sal.

One of these was Sala, who worked and slept in the office of the short-lived periodical *Punchinello* from about 1854, 'neatly constructing a couch and a pillow out of the back-stock of the publication' and despatching articles to the *Household Words* office almost next door.[44] Rosa Salzberg describes print culture in early modern Venice as 'an ever-changing constellation of collaborations and informal partnerships, some of which must have been concluded verbally', and argues that the geography of this print culture 'suggests that printers would have been aware of the work of their "rivals" via personal contact and observation in the neighbourhood'. She goes on to add that 'the shifting mass of press-workers moving from shop to shop created immediate links and promoted the flow of information between publishing operations'.[45] This account is remarkably like the one of 1850s London by the son of Phiz (see Introduction). The three sections of Wellington Street in the 1840s and 1850s contained similarly tight-knit networks. Despite the new construction and improvements in this area, it was still shaped by elements of its early modern and eighteenth-century past.

---

[44]   Sala, *Life and Adventures*, 1: 317–18.
[45]   Salzberg, in *Geographies of the Book*, ed. Ogborn and Withers, 120.

Such close working connections were helped by the close personal connections within these networks. The fact that these writers and editors worked on publications issued within a few doors of each other only made concrete and apparent the ties of friendship, marriage, and patronage already existing between them. Dickens knew Sala's mother; when Sala was 14, Dickens 'met them both at the Euston hotel and gave young George a letter of introduction to Mark Lemon [...] but Lemon did not employ him'. Later, Sala did a number of illustrations for publications by Albert Smith and Edward Lloyd.[46] Douglas Jerrold's daughter married Henry Mayhew, and letters in his biography record his exasperation and frustration with his rather hapless son-in-law, 'whom God make wiser!'[47] One letter reveals how Jerrold tried to promote Mayhew's series of articles in the *Morning Chronicle* (which became *London Labour*), hopeful that this venture might lead to Mayhew getting established:

> I send you the Chronicle of yesterday [...]. I am very proud to say that these papers of Labour and Poor were projected by Henry Mayhew, who married my girl. For comprehensiveness or purpose and minuteness of detail they have never been approached. He will cut his name deep. From these things I have still great hopes.[48]

Forster married the widow of Henry Colburn in 1856; Colburn was a major figure in the publishing world who owned a half-share of the *Athenaeum* and had started the *Court Journal* (which was at 17 Wellington Street North in 1850) and the *Literary Gazette* (based at 7 Wellington Street South, edited until 1850 by William Jerdan), among others. Both Dickens and Jerrold wrote to friends on Wellington Street asking for help in finding jobs for their more feckless relatives. Jerrold asked Forster for help in a letter dated 1850:

> MY DEAR FORSTER, – I believe you are acquainted with Mr. Hawes. If so, may I enlist your friendship to solicit of him any – however humble – appointment for my son Edmund – he is twenty-one – in any of the Colonies, though I should prefer that of New Zealand? He is, as you know, healthy, strong and active; and rather of the stuff for the bush than the clerk's desk.[49]

Dickens wrote a similar appeal to Scott Russell for help with his brother, 'a practical and persevering fellow', in the hope that 'I may possibly help him

---

[46]   P.D. Edwards, *Dickens's 'Young Men': George Augustus Sala, Edmund Yates, and the World of Victorian Journalism* (Aldershot: Ashgate, 1997), 8–9.
[47]   Douglas Jerrold, letter to Forster, 18 July 1850, in Walter Jerrold, *Douglas Jerrold: Dramatist and Wit*, 2 vols (London: Hodder & Stoughton, 1914), 2: 547.
[48]   Douglas Jerrold, letter to Mrs Cowden Clarke, 22 February 1850, in Walter Jerrold, *Douglas Jerrold*, 2: 530.
[49]   Douglas Jerrold, letter to Forster, 24 May 1850, in Walter Jerrold, *Douglas Jerrold*, 2: 538–9.

to some engineering employment'.⁵⁰ These people were guests in each other's houses, went on holiday together, and were godparents to each other's children. Edmund Yates, another famous contributor to *Household Words*, had Dickens as the godfather to one of his sons and Albert Smith as godfather to another.⁵¹ Such ties of kinship often pre-dated physical proximity on Wellington Street. However, the structure of the networks and the structure of the street were mutually reinforcing. It can hardly have been a coincidence that Mayhew established an office on Wellington Street so soon after his father-in-law, Jerrold, had also taken an office on the street.

Dickens liked to gather members of his network around him, demonstrated by Maclise's famous sketch of Dickens reading *The Chimes* to a group of friends including Forster, Jerrold, Laman Blanchard, and Clarkson Stanfield. Many of those working on Wellington Street were members of the Garrick Club, where Dickens usually headed at eleven o'clock; as well as literary acquaintances such as Wills, Gilbert Abbott à Beckett, and Thackeray, he could have expected to bump into a number of men connected with the Lyceum, including Charles Mathews, the playwright James Robinson Planché, who wrote extravaganzas for Mathews's Lyceum, and Stanfield the scene-painter, who designed sets for Dickens's amateur theatricals.⁵² I will discuss the importance of such clubs in more detail in Chapter 3. As Sala himself declared of a chance meeting at a club:

> This little incident once more reminds me that the world after all is not such a very big village.
>   Life is a chain of many links; but the spaces between are usually not very wide. 'The circles of our felicities,' writes Sir Thomas Browne, 'make short arches;' and the same, as a general rule, may be said of our sorrows.⁵³

Jerrold was also renowned for his sociability. Blanchard Jerrold declared that:

> He was a most social man: and in the neighbourhood of Covent Garden – the region sacred to social clubs – it was that, when a very young man, he met a number of friends who were clubbed together, in an humble tavern [...]. Other clubs succeeded [this]. The coterie of literary men and artists who were struggling together [had clubs which] were the merry meetings of wise men: and many wise heads still meet, to play like boys – and then go home to the studio again, the better for the laugh and the song.⁵⁴

---

⁵⁰   Charles Dickens, letter to John Scott Russell, 12 June 1854, in *The Pilgrim Edition of the Letters of Charles Dickens*, ed. Madeline House et al., 12 vols (Oxford: Clarendon Press, 1965–2002), 7: 351–2.

⁵¹   Henry Sutherland Edwards, 34; 35.

⁵²   Percy Fitzgerald, *The Garrick Club* (London: Elliot Stock, 1904).

⁵³   Sala, *Life and Adventures*, 1: 174.

⁵⁴   W. Blanchard Jerrold, 'Introductory Memoir', in *The Works of Douglas Jerrold*, ed. W. Blanchard Jerrold, 4 vols (London: Bradbury & Evans, 1863-4), 1: xxxiv–vi.

Jerrold's witticisms and in-jokes were famous amongst his literary network; Walter Jerrold records that when 'Forster was described by someone as playing the part of Boswell to Charles Dickens, Jerrold commented on hearing it, "He doesn't do the Boz well"'.[55]

One way in which members of this Wellington Street network represented themselves publicly as a united literary and artistic community was through amateur theatricals. In 1843, Dickens, Forster, Leech, Lemon, Mayhew, and Jerrold all took part in a benefit performance of *Every Man in His Humour* for Leigh Hunt.[56] The founder of the *Examiner*, Hunt was suffering from the twin evils of ill health and an irregular income.[57] A few years later, in 1851, Dickens put his amateur players into action again in *Not So Bad As We Seem*, in support of the 'Guild of Literature and Art' which Bulwer Lytton and Dickens were trying to set up to support struggling artists and writers.[58] The cast again included Dickens, Jerrold, Forster, and Lemon, with the addition of Charles Knight and Wilkie Collins. Such performances were one way of demonstrating unity across different generations of the network, such as between Dickens and Leigh Hunt. Such a connection to a renowned 'man of letters', who carried with him cultural capital from earlier decades, could only be beneficial to a younger professional like Dickens.

Rival Networks

These networks were not all harmonious on the three sections of Wellington Street, however. The morning walk to the office was done by friends and enemies alike, and the street was riven by rivalries, too, both personal and social. As I mentioned in the Introduction, G.H. Lewes and Leigh Hunt's son, Thornton Leigh Hunt, co-edited the *Leader* newspaper, founded in 1850, which moved to 10 and then 7 Wellington Street (South) in 1852–53.[59] Hunt had previously worked on the editorial team of Robert Rintoul's *Spectator*, with offices at 9 Wellington Street (South), where Rintoul lived.[60] Hunt's affair with Lewes's wife, and their subsequent children together, cleared the way for Lewes's relationship with George Eliot, whom he met in 1854 at the house of John Chapman, the bookseller and publisher, nearby at 142 Strand.[61] In business, the tension between emulation and competition caused friends and ex-colleagues with connections to Wellington

---

[55]   Walter Jerrold, *Douglas Jerrold*, 524.

[56]   See Chapter 3.

[57]   Nicholas Roe, 'Hunt, (James Henry) Leigh (1784–1859)', *DNB*, accessed 11 August 2012 online via http://www.oxforddnb.com/.

[58]   Slater, *Douglas Jerrold*, 247.

[59]   *Kelly's POD* (1852), 557 and (1853), 555; imprint, *Leader*, 1 January 1853, 24; Andrew King and Fionnuala Dillane, 'Hunt, Thornton Leigh (1810–1873)', *DNCJ*, 297.

[60]   *Kelly's POD* (1844), 156 and (1853), 555; 1851 census, HO107/1511, f. 190, accessed 15 July 2011 online via http://www.ancestry.co.uk/.

[61]   Ashton, 114.

Street to fall out. Again, Dickens was a focal point for much of the tension, as he had disputes with Jerrold, Thackeray, and Forster.[62] But there were other tensions within the networks, too. Albert Smith left *Punch* at the end of 1843, 'wounded' by his estrangement from Jerrold and Lemon, and went on to co-edit (with Angus B. Reach) the *Punch* rival *The Man in the Moon*. Jerrold employed Reach on his *Newspaper*, and continued to do so even after a parody of one of Jerrold's leaders appeared in *The Man in the Moon*; however, Michael Slater points out that Jerrold mentioned Reach to Dickens in the context of the ingratitude of one 'to whom I gave his first start in periodical literature, and in whose pocket I have put (for him) much money'.[63]

Feuds stoked by Wellington Street publications had ramifications in the wider neighbourhood of Fleet Street and the Strand, as Figure 1.6 shows. In this cartoon, *Punch* writers Jerrold, Thackeray, and Lemon discuss *Puppet-Show* in the street; print rivalry is linked specifically to the urban location of the *Punch* office. Furthermore, the rivalry between different networks is also expressed through the proximity of office windows. Mr Punch waves his stick from his office window at the window across the street, from which a figure who represents David Bogue glares back at him. David Bogue, one of many Scottish publishers and booksellers in London, had links with *Puppet-Show*, as his printer was Henry Vizetelly and he worked with Albert Smith. Bogue attempted a variety of publishing ventures, including collaborations with Cruikshank, with Sala, with Henry and Augustus Mayhew (with the publication of *1851: or, The Adventures of Mr and Mrs Sandboys*, a story designed to capitalize on the Great Exhibition), and with Thackeray.[64] However, Bogue's work with Smith led to Thackeray's break with Bogue; Albert Smith 'wrote the "phenomenally successful" first in a projected series of "social zoologies", on "gents", but when Bogue's printer Henry Vizetelly asked Thackeray to write as many of these little volumes as he pleased, he declined because he did not want to be associated with Smith'.[65] The *Puppet-Show* cartoon assumes that the reader has some knowledge of this spat, as the window of 'D. BOGUE' advertises 'GENTS', while the 'PUNCH OFFICE' has its own label: 'SNOBS' (Figure 1.6). Thackeray, notoriously proud of his status as a gentleman, has the tables well and truly turned on him in this cartoon.

One major rivalry on Wellington Street was that between G.W.M. Reynolds, the radical author and editor, and Dickens. It illustrates how the street was a place of fierce antagonism, just as much as it was of friendly competition. In a book published by the same William Tweedie (now at 337 Strand), John Dix (no friend to Reynolds) described Reynolds as he was in the 1840s when:

62   Slater, *Douglas Jerrold*, 180–81; Leary, 79–109.

63   Slater, *Douglas Jerrold*, 203.

64   When Bogue's business eventually failed, he sold some of his stock to William Tweedie, a bookseller of Wellington Street and fellow Scot.

65   Robert L. Patten, 'Bogue, David (1807/8–1856)', *DNB*, accessed 24 May 2012 online via http://www.oxforddnb.com/. See also Vizetelly, 1: 315–17.

FLY LEAVES, No. 3.

A TRIO OF PUNCHITES.

1st "Eminent Writer." I say, Douglas, what do you think of this Puppet-Show?

2nd "Eminent Writer." Why, I think we ought to put down all rival publications.

3rd "Eminent Writer." Otherwise we shall be sold at the butter shops free, gratis, and for nothing.

Figure 1.6   *A Trio of Punchites, Puppet-Show*, 25 March 1848, 16.
Reproduced with the permission of Senate House Library, University of London. PR [Z-Puppet].

he resided in apartments in King-square, Goswell-road, over a green-grocer's shop. I found him in a back room, wrapped in a dingy dressing-gown, and perched on a stool at a high desk, writing away like a steame-engine [*sic*]. [...] The whole expression of the face was that of a man who, when he looked in the glass, felt perfectly satisfied with himself on the score of personal appearance.[66]

No descriptions of Reynolds's Wellington Street premises survive, although he is careful to tell his readers that 'our Office is not a bookseller's shop: we only issue thence, or in plain terms "sell there", our own publications'.[67] However, the consensus among Reynolds scholars is that prior to 1851 (when Reynolds's address for letters to him as editor of his newspaper is given as Tollington Park), Reynolds would have been a frequent visitor to the office which he shared with his managing clerk and (from 1863) business partner, John Dicks (a different man, credited with

---

[66] John Dix, *Lions: Living and Dead; or, Personal Recollections of the 'Great and Gifted'*, 2nd edn (London: W. Tweedie, 1854), 282. I am grateful to Dick Collins for this reference.

[67] 'Notices to Correspondents', *RM*, 22 March 1856, 128.

saving Reynolds's business).[68] Dicks joined Reynolds's operation after Reynolds was declared bankrupt again in 1848, and Dicks is listed as the printer and publisher of *Reynolds's Political Instructor* and *Reynolds's Weekly Newspaper*.[69] In March 1850, Dickens delivered his opening appeal to the readers of *Household Words*. In it, Dickens made what is considered by critics an attack on Reynolds, as one of the 'Bastards of the Mountain, draggled fringe on the Red cap, Panders to the basest passions of the lowest natures – whose existence is a national reproach'.[70] In June that year, Reynolds returned the favour in his own new serial, *Reynolds's Weekly Newspaper*, by publishing a scornful denunciation of *Household Words*:

> [Dickens] sees the condition of [London's] population but dimly [...] and hopes
> to cure all the complaints and troubles of its inhabitants by a little small talk,
> 'familiar as household words', and about as much use as lip-sympathy to a
> starving man.[71]

This attack, similar to others in the Chartist press, aims to separate the politics, writings, and publications of 'true' radicals from those of Dickens. The implication is that if Dickens sees the true state of London 'but dimly', Reynolds not only observes it correctly, but transforms his observations into publications which are much better placed to help the poor. However, this denunciation of Dickens and of *Household Words* was published from the same street as the very serial which it attacked. Reynolds's office address was 7 Wellington Street North. He was only a few doors away from Dickens.

These two significant mid-century rivals, then, vented their diatribes in publications that were based just a few yards away from each other. When they visited their offices, it is conceivable that they could have passed each other on the street in the morning. The mutual antagonism between Dickens and Reynolds

---

[68]   I am grateful to Anne Humpherys, Louis James, and Guy Dicks for their help on this point. Reynolds later opened another office at 40 Parker Street, Drury Lane. See *Watkins's Directory* (1852), 407; Dick Collins, 'George William McArthur Reynolds: A Biographical Sketch', in *The Necromancer*, by G.W.M. Reynolds, ed. Dick Collins (Kansas City: Valancourt Books, 2007; 1st publ. *RM* 1851–52), xxxviii.
[69]   Other employees in 1851 included the compositor Mr Rudge and Mr Donaldson, overseer of the printing department in Parker Street. See Guy Dicks, *The John Dicks Press* (published by the author, 2005), 6; 20; 22. See page 19 in Dicks's book for Reynolds's account at his 1848 bankruptcy trial of being accosted 'at my own door' by a solicitor, while John Dicks was inside 'in the shop'.
[70]   [Charles Dickens], 'Preliminary Word', *HW*, 30 March 1850, 1.
[71]   GRACCHUS (probably Reynolds's younger brother Edward Reynolds), 'National Prosperity: Opinions of Ledru-Rollin and Charles Dickens', *RWN*, 16 June 1850, 3. For more on Edward Reynolds's work with his brother, see Michael H. Shirley, 'G.W.M. Reynolds, *Reynolds's Newspaper* and Popular Politics', in *G.W.M. Reynolds*, ed. Humpherys and James, 78–9, n. 13.

has been well documented.[72] Like many in the period, Dickens was probably made uneasy by Reynolds's vehement Republican beliefs and horrified by the semi-pornographic moments in his fiction.[73] However, Wellington Street is a physical and metaphorical example of just how complicated was their connection to each other, more complicated than has been previously argued. Reynolds had been in Wellington Street before Dickens arrived there. Dickens declared of Reynolds that 'I hold his to be a name with which no lady's and no gentleman's should be associated', yet he set up the offices for *Household Words* in the very street to which Reynolds was escorted back in triumph after he gave a rabble-rousing pro-Chartist speech in Trafalgar Square.[74] Wellington Street North was probably Reynolds's home address *c.* 1847–51, and was definitely the location for the offices of *Reynolds's Political Instructor* and *Reynolds's Miscellany*, before he ever began *Reynolds's Weekly Newspaper*.[75] Reynolds and Dickens operated within different networks of friends, and yet their world was still a small one, and they attacked many of the same social problems in both their fiction and their non-fiction (such as capital and corporal punishment, Chancery, the lack of education for all, and the so-called 'Taxes on Knowledge'). Reynolds contributed to *Bentley's Miscellany* while Dickens was editor, and Dickens's illustrator Phiz also illustrated Reynolds's novel *Robert Macaire*.[76] Dickens and Reynolds were both lampooned by co-editors Angus B. Reach and Albert Smith in the same volume of *The Man in the Moon*.[77] Yet in their addresses to their readers they worked to distinguish themselves from each other, to suit the politics, the demands, and the desires of different groups of readers. Those who worked to entertain and instruct the public through print may have been involved in the same business, on the same street, but this did not mean that their occupation was not a diverse, miscellaneous, and fragmented one.

However, as part of 'the business of amusing the public' (as Phiz's son put it), Reynolds and Dickens needed each other just as much as they tried to pull away

---

[72] See especially Michael Diamond, 'Charles Dickens as Villain and Hero in Reynolds's Newspaper', *Dickensian* 98, no. 457 (Summer 2002).

[73] Ibid., 127.

[74] In 1848, Reynolds gave an impromptu speech at the so-called Trafalgar Square Riot, which catapulted him into prominence in the Chartist movement. For more on this, see Chapter 2. Dickens's swipe at Reynolds comes from Dickens's letter to W.C. Macready, 30 August 1849, *Pilgrim*, 5: 603–4.

[75] Collins, xxviii; imprint, *RM*, 16 October 1847, 368.

[76] 'Biographical Sketches of Eminent Living Authors – Mr G.W.M. Reynolds', *London Journal*, 29 November 1845, 101. Reynolds's article 'Reflections in a Horse-Pond' was published under the pseudonym 'Max' (attributed by the Wellesley Index), in *Bentley's Miscellany*, January 1837, 470–73; Rohan McWilliam, 'The French Connection: G.W.M. Reynolds and the Outlaw Robert Macaire', in *G.W.M. Reynolds*', ed. Humpherys and James, 39.

[77] 'Advertisements Extraordinary' and 'Dips into the Diary of Barabas Bolt, Esq.', *Man in the Moon* 3 (1848), 1–58; 235–44.

from each other.[78] Evidently, Reynolds needed Dickens much more in the 1830s and '40s than the other way round, as his imitations of *Pickwick Papers* and *Master Humphrey's Clock* helped to launch his writing career in London on the back of Dickens's success, ensured a measure of crossover in their readerships, and must have been the main cause of Dickens's violent antipathy. Yet the many plagiarisms, imitations, appropriations, and re-writings of Dickens, of which Reynolds's were only a few, also helped to keep Dickens in the public eye. Philip V. Allingham points out that theatrical piracies of Dickens's characters and plots were extremely popular, as even after the 1842 Literary Copyright Act, adaptations of novels for the stage were not covered by copyright legislation. F. Dubrez Fawcett called the large number of Dickens adaptations on stage in the late 1830s and early 1840s 'The Boz Cascade' and 'The Dickens Deluge'.[79] Kathryn Chittick has shown how both serialization and the practice of inserting extracts from fiction in miscellanies and newspapers contributed to Dickens becoming 'a cultural phenomenon'.[80] The plagiarism of Dickens, including Reynolds's own, contributed to this widespread cultural notice and rapid rise to fame.[81] As Sally Ledger argues, they confirmed Dickens's position as a massive commercial success, and so as a writer worth emulating.[82] Furthermore, many critics have noted the influence of Reynolds's *Mysteries* on Dickens's *Bleak House*.[83]

The geography of London's print culture meant that the networks of rivals often touched at points, and Reynolds and Dickens were no exception. 332 Strand was the offices of the *Morning* and *Evening Chronicles*, where Dickens and Thackeray worked, which might have reminded Reynolds of his days in Paris when he gave the young Thackeray his first work as a writer on the *Paris Literary Gazette*.[84] Reynolds's younger brother worked for a time at Somerset House, as did Dickens's father. In 1850, Reynolds attended the first meeting of the National

---

[78]   Browne, 102. See Introduction.

[79]   F. Dubrez Fawcett, *Dickens the Dramatist: On Stage, Screen, and Radio* (London: W.H. Allen, 1952), 44; 72. For more on such adaptations, see Chapter 3.

[80]   Kathryn Chittick, *Dickens and the 1830s* (Cambridge: Cambridge University Press, 1990), 80.

[81]   Anne Humpherys calls works like Reynolds's *Pickwick Abroad* 'appropriations', not 'plagiarisms', because 'most of them make no effort to suggest that Dickens was the author'. See Anne Humpherys, 'Victorian Stage Adaptations and Appropriations', in *Charles Dickens in Context*, ed. Sally Ledger and Holly Furneaux (Cambridge: Cambridge University Press, 2011), 33.

[82]   Sally Ledger, *Dickens and the Popular Radical Imagination* (Cambridge: Cambridge University Press, 2007), 143.

[83]   See Cyril Pearl, 'Mr Dickens and Mr Reynolds', in *Victorian Patchwork* (London: Heinemann, 1972), 71; Anne Humpherys, 'Generic Strands and Urban Twists: The Victorian Mysteries Novel', *Victorian Studies* 34 (1991): 456; Richard Maxwell, *The Mysteries of Paris and London* (Charlottesville, VA and London: University Press of Virginia, 1992), 167.

[84]   See Jean Guivarc'h, 'Deux journalistes anglais de Paris en 1835 (G.W.M. Reynolds et W.M.T.)', *Etudes Anglaises* 28, no. 2 (avril/juin 1975).

Charter Association at the London Tavern, a large pub in 'Bishopsgate Within' (now 1–3 Bishopsgate) famous for its big meeting rooms.[85] Not only did Reynolds use it for meetings, but Dickens did, too. Dickens was there in 1841 for the meeting for the benefit of the Sanatorium for Sick Authors and Artists, and in 1851 for the annual dinner for the General Theatrical Fund.[86] Furthermore, the London Tavern is the location in *Nicholas Nickleby* for the public meeting 'in favour of the United Metropolitan Improved Hot Muffin and Crumpet Baking and Punctual Delivery Company'.[87] For a 'respectable' writer like Dickens, the danger of so much print being produced from a relatively tight geographic area in London, despite rivalries between different networks, is that the disreputable corollary of yourself may be working on a weekly serial publication just as you are, and be doing so from an office on the same street, only a few doors away.

George was not the only member of the Reynolds household with reason to feel antipathy towards Dickens's circle. 7 Wellington Street North was also the publishing address for George Reynolds's wife, Susannah Frances Reynolds. In a street full of male editors, Susannah Reynolds stands out as an important person in her own right, as well as an important part of Reynolds's network and of his public feud with Dickens. From the Post Office Directories for 1843–44, it is clear that number 7 Wellington Street North was used as living accommodation, as well as a publishing office, by the fabulously named Fortunatas Crisp before George and Susannah moved there with their children sometime between 1846 and 1847.[88] For the Reynoldses, then, there was no morning commute; until 1851 they simply had to walk downstairs. It was not unusual to have families living above the shop or the office on Wellington Street. A notice in the *Times* of 16 October 1846 announced that Mrs Black, wife of Alexander Black the bookseller, gave birth to her son at 8 Wellington Street North, next door to what would be the Reynoldses' premises.[89] Presumably this took place in their home above the bookshop. Mrs Francis, wife of the publisher of the *Athenaeum*, is listed at 14 Wellington Street with her three children on the night of the 1851 census, as is Mrs Bielefeld and her children, next door at Bielefeld's *papier mâché* works.[90] Susannah Reynolds is unusual, however, because of her literary activities; if she was not an equal partner in the business, she was certainly an important part of it. She wrote two novels serialized from Wellington Street in 1848: *Wealth and Poverty: A Domestic Tale* and *The Poacher's Daughter.* In 1847, she edited *The Household Book of Practical Receipts*, alongside

---

[85]   'Advertisements and Notices', *RPI*, 19 January 1850, 88.

[86]   Forster, *Life*, 2: 103.

[87]   Charles Dickens, *Nicholas Nickleby*, ed. Paul Schlicke (Oxford: Oxford University Press, 1990), 11.

[88]   *Kelly's POD* (1849), 570; Collins, xxviii; imprint, *RM*, 16 October 1847, 368.

[89]   'Births', *The Times*, 16 October 1846, 7.

[90]   1851 census, HO107/1511, f. 148, accessed 15 July 2011 online via http://www.ancestry.co.uk/.

W.E. Hall.[91] It is possible that she was the editor of the short-lived *Weekly Magazine*, an extremely rare halfpenny periodical which was eventually subsumed into *Reynolds's Miscellany*.[92] It is important to note the unusualness of a lady editor; George Eliot of the *Westminster Review* and Eliza Cook of *Eliza Cook's Journal* are well-known exceptions which prove the rule (see Introduction).[93] However, Susannah Reynolds's part in the Wellington Street community was a significant one, even though the majority of public comment on the rivalry between their network and the Dickens network came from her husband.

In November 1847, the *Daily News* (first edited by Dickens) published a negative review of Susannah Reynolds's 1847–48 serial novel *Gretna Green; or, All For Love* (which was published in volume form from the *Reynolds's Miscellany* Office in 1848).[94] The review was probably written by the son of Dickens's family friend, Charles Dilke junior, whose father (editor of the *Athenaeum* at 14 Wellington Street North) took on the role of manager of the *Daily News* when Forster was left as editor, after Dickens abandoned the paper in 1846. The column, 'Literature of the Lower Orders', mentions Susannah Reynolds's novel as part of a selection of 'insidious and deleterious' texts which 'act more directly and openly upon the worst passions, stimulating them to precocious and unnatural activity, and exercise an unsettling and disturbing power over the moral consciousness of the reader'.[95] In other words, Susannah's book was discussed as part of a group of texts said to promote sex and violence. Not only is this an overstatement of the excitement of the novel, it was a terrible threat to the moral standing – and therefore the livelihood – of Susannah and her husband. Susannah published as 'Mrs G.W.M. Reynolds' from the *Reynolds's Miscellany* office; any attack on her moral character as a writer was an attack on Reynolds's increasingly successful business.

This feud between rival networks on Wellington Street, begun in the public sphere of the printed page, continued to be played out there. The Reynoldses engaged their solicitors – Roche, Plowman, and Roche of 2 Upper Wellington Street – to demand an apology in print. The solicitors claimed to write under the instruction of Susannah herself, and the letter to the editor (Forster) offers a glimpse into how Susannah Reynolds wanted her life to be portrayed publicly:

---

[91] For a useful summary of what little is known about Susannah Reynolds and where the discrepancies lie in the public record of her life, see Collins, xxxix–xlvii.

[92] See King, '*Reynolds's Miscellany*', 63, and Louis James, 'A Bibliography of Works by G.W.M. Reynolds', in *G.W.M. Reynolds*, ed. Humpherys and James, 277. James's attribution of editorship to Susannah is only assumed.

[93] The *Westminster Review* was first published from 142 Strand, and *Eliza Cook's Journal* was published and printed by John Owen Clarke from 3 Raquet Court, Fleet Street, 1849–54. Both locations are within 10 minutes' walk of Wellington Street. *RM* frequently praised Eliza Cook.

[94] Michael Diamond refers to this incident in 'Charles Dickens as Villain and Hero' (129), as does Andrew King in '*Reynolds's Miscellany*' (63, n. 38).

[95] 'Literature of the Lower Orders', *DN*, 2 November 1847, 3.

[The review was] calculated to inflict a most undeserved, not to say wanton, injury upon the private property, and above all the reputation, of a lady who entertains a high respect for, and is anxious to preserve the favourable opinion of a numerous circle of valued friends. Having a large family of children to train up in the paths of virtue, she from this cause alone, is too deeply interested in carefully excluding from her writings all impurities, [...] and she feels that her true interests, as well as her disposition, lie in a different channel.[96]

A retraction followed swiftly the next week in the *Daily News*.[97] However, Reynolds continued to make public attacks on the *Daily News* across his different types of publications, no doubt out of concern for the Reynolds 'brand' as well as for his wife's reputation. The article in *Reynolds's Miscellany* about the affair declares of the *Daily News*: 'do you call this thing a newspaper?', while in *The Mysteries of London,* one character tells another that the *Daily News* is 'a paper which is contemptible in circulation and influence – scurrilous /or hypocritical, according to circumstances, in its literary articles – and wishy-washy in the extreme in its leaders'.[98] Reynolds directed his ire at all concerned:

the name of Charles Dickens was rather damnatory than useful to newspaper-speculation. Everyone must admit that *Boz* is a great novelist, [...] but he is totally incapable of writing for a newspaper. The proprietors of the *News* made a tremendous splash with his name; but they only created a quagmire for themselves to flounder in. (*Mysteries Series II*, 2: 74)

Dickens had to have been aware of these attacks, given his close relationship with Forster.

Interactions between people with distinct and otherwise separate 'trajectories' are, for the geographer Doreen Massey, important ways in which space is 'produced'. Space, for Massey, is not a given, but is 'always in the process of being made'. Following on from Lefebvre, Massey reads space as a human construct which emerges out of the interactions between people and is 'embedded in material practices' such as building and using streets.[99] This is one way of thinking about the rival editors and writers on the three sections of Wellington Street, with their competing trajectories. The clash between Dickens and Reynolds was a kind of territorial battle for a space within nineteenth-century print culture. However, for this clash to take place they both had to presuppose that there was such a territory over which to fight. Their war of words produced the very space over which they fought.

---

[96] "'Gretna Green," the "Daily News," and the "Express"', *RM*, 27 November 1847, 46.

[97] 'Literature of the Lower Orders', *DN*, 9 November 1847, 2.

[98] G.W.M. Reynolds, *The Mysteries of London Series II*, 2 vols (London: George Vickers, 3 October 1846–16 September 1848), 2: 74–5. Further references are to this edition and appear parenthetically in the text.

[99] Doreen Massey, *For Space* (London: SAGE, 2005), 9.

This rivalry, then, emerged precisely because Reynolds and Dickens were *not* on 'distinct trajectories', to use Massey's words.[100] Connections between Reynolds and Dickens were noticed during their own lifetimes. Mary Elizabeth Braddon openly acknowledged the influence of both writers on her sensation novels, and declared that she wanted to combine 'as far as my powers allowed, the human interest and genial humour of Dickens with the plot-weaving of G.W.R. Reynolds'.[101] Not only did writers link the two in their minds, but readers did, too. Readers of the *London Journal* and *Reynolds's Miscellany* also read Dickens; correspondents to Reynolds, the editor of these serials, assume names like 'Newman Noggs' (from *Nicholas Nickleby*) and 'Boz' alongside 'Tom Rain' (*Mysteries Series II*) and 'Richard Markham' (*Mysteries Series I* and *II*).[102] Indeed, one correspondent makes the connection explicit. We do not have the question, but Reynolds's answer is as follows:

> S.G. – Mr. Charles Dickens was born in 1812. Mr. G.W.M. Reynolds is several years his junior.[103]

S.G. obviously wanted to know whether Dickens and Reynolds were similar in age, but that such a question occurred to him (or her) is evidence that Reynolds and Dickens were paired in the imaginations of some readers.

Arguably, without the existence of rival publications on the same three sections of Wellington Street and on other streets in the Strand area, print culture would not have had such a physical presence in the city, as it would have been more dispersed. Spatial unity, even between publications marketed at different audiences like the *Athenaeum* and *Reynolds's Miscellany*, confers benefits. Salzberg remarks of early modern Venice that it is

> vital to note that there was no apparent spatial dislocation between the shops of the more prestigious publishers and printers and those who produced significant quantities of popular material [...]. Geographical proximity may have brought a stronger sense of identity and community to a trade that encompassed men spread over a broad spectrum of specializations and socio-economic levels, and that until later in the sixteenth century had no official guild to bring them together. The concentration of members of the print trade in these neighbourhoods also provided strong bases for new arrivals to access, [...] [especially when they were already] connected further by ties of marriage and business.[104]

In a period when copyright law for writers was a highly contested issue, and journalists and authors alike were struggling to be recognized as professionals

---

[100]   Ibid., 9.

[101]   M.E. Braddon, 'My First Novel', *Idler*, July 1893, 25.

[102]   'Notices To Correspondents', *RM*, 7 April 1849, 623; 'Notices To Correspondents', *RM*, 12 February 1853, 47.

[103]   "Notices To Correspondents", *RM*, 15 February 1851, 63.

[104]   Salzberg, in *Geographies of the Book*, ed. Ogborn and Withers, 120–21.

rather than 'scribblers', geographical proximity, even to one's rivals, had distinct advantages.[105]

Street Life

What, then, did Wellington Street look like to these editors and writers who headed to it (and away from it) in the morning? When mid-century Londoners and visitors walked up from Waterloo Bridge to Bow Street and Covent Garden in the morning, the shops, the offices, and the Lyceum, which they would have seen on their way, reinforced through urban space what they saw on the printed page: the close associations between different members of the print culture networks around the Strand and its side streets. For example, a page from the *Examiner* in 1847, with its address at 5 Wellington Street (South), advertised publications with offices also on the three sections of Wellington Street (Figure 1.7). This page contains advertisements for *Douglas Jerrold's Weekly Newspaper*, some new publications by Henry Colburn, a new work by Albert Smith, and the latest edition of *Punch*. It also advertises the fourth number of *Dombey and Son*, and fits Dickens alongside those already associated with Wellington Street three years before the first number of *Household Words*. The straight lines of the street are reorganized by the printed page, and the space of print culture is fitted onto its printed surface. This printed page makes a claim for print culture as a coherent space where a reader who enjoys the *Examiner* is encouraged to think that he or she may enjoy the other publications which it advertises, too. The urban space of the Strand area in general, and the three sections of Wellington Street in particular, made a similar claim. The street contained not just the newspaper and periodical offices, but also booksellers, a stationer, a lithographer, and a music copyist. It was the setting for many different types of engagement with print culture, and so our editors would have been made aware of their place in the print networks. At the same time, other trades less connected to the business of selling the printed word continued on the street. The street was a daily reminder to those who passed down it of print culture as a business, and of the business of print. Editors and writers on the street had a shared experience of its print culture all around them, and would have been very aware of their neighbours. This allowed them to understand and represent their occupations as a coherent field of work.

The *OED* defines 'coherent' as 'that which sticks or clings firmly together'; it can be used to refer to a mass or to parts, and has specific applications in physics. 'Coherent' also has a subsidiary sense of 'one who coheres or combines with others' and (now obsolete) of 'that which coheres or is connected'. In the eighteenth and nineteenth centuries, 'coherent' was also used to refer figuratively to things that were connected or unified in some way: the *OED* quotes H. Spencer

---

[105] For a useful discussion of battles over copyright law in the period, see Clare Pettitt, *Patent Inventions: Intellectual Property and the Victorian Novel* (Oxford: Oxford University Press, 2004).

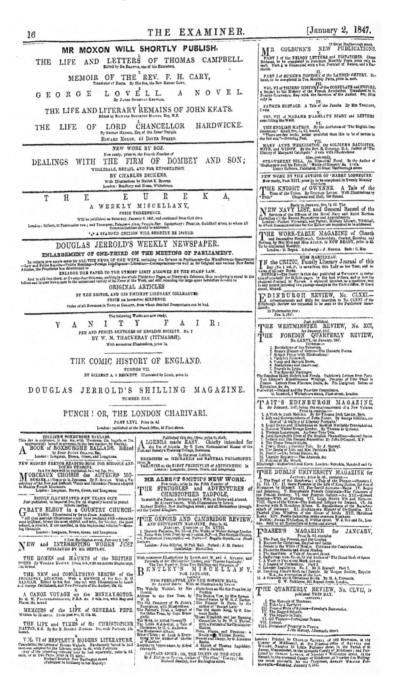

Figure 1.7   Advertisements and notices, *Examiner*, 16 January 1847, 16.
© The British Library Board. MFM.MLD63.

using it in 1870 to describe 'coherent combinations' of auditory feelings, and J.H. Newman in 1876 described the Ottoman Empire as 'more stable, more coherent than any Turkish rule before it'. To describe the networks of editors on Wellington Street as 'coherent', then, registers the connections between them. It emphasizes the ways in which they shared networks of acquaintances as well as geographical proximity and were (broadly speaking) doing the same work. It also describes the way in which they often chose to represent themselves.

Editorial addresses to the readers themselves often referred to print production as a 'field' of work. A correspondent in *Reynolds's Political Instructor* declares that '[a]s one who has for some years laboured in the field of political redemption, I experienced unmingled pleasure at the appearance of the *Political Instructor*', while Reynolds's new *Newspaper* is announced as 'the appearance of a new journalist in the field'.[106] Geographical, topographical, or spatial metaphors were frequently used in addresses to the reader in miscellanies and newspapers of the early to mid-Victorian period. Charles Knight declared in Volume 1 of his *Penny Magazine*:

> Ready and cheap communication breaks down the obstacles of time and space,
> – and thus, bringing all the ends of a great kingdom as it were together, greatly
> reduces the inequalities of fortune and situation, by equalising the price of
> commodities, and to that extent making them accessible to all.[107]

Geography, according to Knight, becomes irrelevant in the modern world, when canals can be dug and new, faster roads laid so that print can be distributed around the country cheaply and rapidly. By the 1840s, railways were beginning to cut a swathe across the countryside, allowing fast distribution of printed material, so that what was new in the metropolis could be known in Manchester the next day, and vice versa. The telegraph, developed into commercial potential by Charles Wheatstone (of King's College London, Strand) and his partner (the inventor William Fothergill), simultaneously transformed communication. Furthermore, Knight saw his miscellany as part of the way in which modern technology was, he believed, aiding the growth of understanding. In this way a printed serial publication, itself the product of technical innovation, could reduce physical distances between readers and editors, between readers and other readers, and between readers and sources of information. Cheap print could be 'as the small optic-glass called "the finder", which is placed by the side of a large telescope, to enable the observer to discover the star which is afterwards to be carefully examined by the more perfect instrument'.[108] For Douglas Jerrold, his *Shilling Magazine* can find its own space without displacing the work of anyone else; his original prospectus lays claim to its own 'hitherto unoccupied sphere of instruction, amusement, and utility'; this is

---

[106] JUNIUS, 'A Few Words on the Newspaper Press', *RPI*, 29 December 1849, 60.

[107] [Charles Knight], 'Preface', *Penny Magazine of the Society for the Diffusion of Useful Knowledge*, 1, 1832, iii.

[108] Charles Knight, 'Reading for All', *Penny Magazine*, 1 March 1832, 1.

a space in which the importance of 'community' is all.[109] For Edward Lloyd, his *Weekly Miscellany* fills a 'gap' in the country, but more specifically in the 'London Markets'.[110] In *Reynolds's Miscellany*, Reynolds also claims he is not competing for territory. His *Miscellany* is 'appearing in opposition to no existing cheap Publication, – started without the least idea of rivalry, – and issued in the full belief that there is room for its being without displacing any other'.[111] As we have seen, aggressive rivalry was actually something Reynolds did rather well. What these statements do show, however, are the ways in which editors tried to portray themselves as part of a recognizable set of networks, as part of a coherent field of work.

It is, of course, not surprising that all these writers and editors clustered around the Strand area in particular. Fleet Street had been synonymous with printing since Wynken de Worde set up his printing firm there in 1500, and the Strand had been home to periodicals and newspapers since the eighteenth century (Figure 1.8). St. Paul's Churchyard and Paternoster Row remained the key bookselling district, and Holywell Street was the place to go for cheap pornography, but printers and publishers clustered around Fleet Street and the Strand.[112] Between 1843 and 1853, the three sections of Wellington Street were at what could be called the mid-point of London, right near to where Temple Bar marked the dividing line between the City of London and the City of Westminster. They were also at the geographical heart of the early Victorian print trade. Jonathan Topham calls the

Figure 1.8   Area around Fleet Street and the Strand, showing Charing Cross, Trafalgar Square, and the National Gallery. From *Cruchley's New Plan of London, Improved to 1847* (London: G.F. Cruchley, 1847). © The British Library Board, Maps. Crace. VII.253.

---

[109]   [Douglas Jerrold], 'Preface', *Douglas Jerrold's Shilling Magazine*, 1, 1845, iii.

[110]   [Edward Lloyd], 'Preface', *Lloyd's Weekly Miscellany*, 1, 1850, iii.

[111]   'To Our Reader', *RM*, 7 November 1846, 16.

[112]   Peter Ackroyd, *London: The Biography* (London: Vintage, 2001), 401–2; see also Ashton; Nead; and James Raven, *The Business of Books: Booksellers and the English Book Trade, 1450–1850* (New Haven, CT): Yale University Press, 2007.

Figure 1.9   Houses once 16, 17, and 18 Upper Wellington Street. Number
16 was the office of *London Labour*; number 17 housed *Douglas
Jerrold's Weekly Newspaper*, and later Sala lodged there.

area around the Strand 'the heart of journalistic London', but it was also the heart
of print-producing London more generally.[113] As Andrew King puts it, this area
was 'a cultural field which is both geographically material and metaphysical'.[114]
Compared with the Strand itself, however, the three sections of Wellington Street
were shorter and more compact. Trafalgar Square to Temple Bar, the length of the
Strand, is a 15-minute walk; Waterloo Bridge to Bow Street takes barely 5 minutes
on foot. The eighteenth-century brick terraces still survive on what was Upper
Wellington Street and the top end of Wellington Street North, and their windows
are very close together. Each building within the terrace shared an internal wall,
and the terraces opened straight onto the street, with no gardens to separate them
from the bustle of the pavement. Therefore, even buildings on the opposite sides
of the street were relatively close, and occupants or visitors would have been very
aware of their neighbours (Figure 1.9).

---

[113]   Jonathan R. Topham, 'The Mirror of Literature, Amusement and Instruction and
cheap miscellanies in early nineteenth-century Britain', in *Science in the Nineteenth-Century
Periodical: Reading the Magazine of Nature*, ed. Geoffrey Cantor et al. (Cambridge:
Cambridge University Press, 2004), 53.
[114]   Andrew King, *The London Journal, 1845–83: Periodicals, Production and Gender*
(Aldershot: Ashgate, 2004), 76.

For example, from the offices of *Reynolds's Miscellany* at number 7 Wellington Street North, it would have been easy to see across to the windows of number 14, which housed the *Athenaeum* office and the office of the *Railway Chronicle*. Reynolds, when he visited the office, would have been faced with the concrete, physical existence of a periodical which served a very different market to his own largely working-class radical one, and a newspaper edited by someone who had worked with Dickens, a man Reynolds sought to both emulate and outdo.[115] In 1850, the existence of Dickens would have been even more inescapable once *Household Words* arrived at 16 Wellington Street North (Figure 1.10). The distinctive bow windows of number 16 are made much of in Percy Fitzgerald's account of the office, and would have been visible (albeit at an angle) from inside number 7:

> It was but a miniature sort of building, but sufficed. Exceedingly pretty was the bowed front, the bow reaching up for one story, and a ground floor window, each giving a flood of light, quite necessary for literary work [...]. As you looked from the other side of the street you could see well through the windows that the 'drawing-room floor', where the master sat, was handsomely furnished.[116]

From such big windows, an occupant would also be keenly aware of the street outside. Without double-glazing, street noise was intrusive, and the streets around the Strand were a noisy and busy marketplace from even the very early hours of the morning. The Strand itself (for centuries the main artery between Westminster and the City) was well known for 'the roar, and din, and bustle, and agitation of wheels, and horses, and men', as Reynolds himself described it.[117] One 1844 guidebook to London, reprinted for the Great Exhibition of 1851, warned the unwary visitor:

> The stranger, on his first visit to the metropolis, will be amazed at the immense number of all descriptions of vehicles, waggons, carts, &c. &c., to be seen in every direction, and how they all find sufficient employment must fill him with astonishment [...]. At times he will be much annoyed by the great noise which is always heard in the leading streets of the metropolis.[118]

The streets which gave access to Covent Garden were similarly congested. By half-past 5 in the morning, Boz tells us:

> Covent Garden market, and the avenues leading to it, are thronged with carts of all sorts, sizes and descriptions, from the heavy lumbering waggon, with its four stout horses, to the jingling costermonger's cart with its consumptive donkey.

---

[115]   See Diamond.

[116]   Fitzgerald, *Memories of Charles Dickens*, 125.

[117]   G.W.M. Reynolds, *The Necromancer*, ed. Dick Collins (Kansas City: Valancourt Books, 2007; 1st publ. in *RM*, Dec. 1851–July 1852), 122.

[118]   *Cruchley's Picture of London*, 9th edn (London: Cruchley, 1844), 243–4.

Figure 1.10   *Household Words* Office, *No. 16 Wellington Street, Strand.* From
Fitzgerald, *Memories of Charles Dickens.* © The British Library
Board, 010856.ff.7, facing page 125.

The pavement is already strewn with decayed cabbage-leaves, broken hay-bands, and all the indescribable litter of a vegetable market; men are shouting, carts backing, horses neighing, boys fighting, basket-women talking, piemen expatiating on the excellence of their pastry, and donkeys braying. These and a hundred other sounds form a compound discordant enough to a Londoner's ears, and remarkably disagreeable to those of country gentlemen who are sleeping at the Hummums for the first time.[119]

At five o'clock, the church bells of St. Mary-le-Strand, St. Clement Danes, and St. Paul's in Covent Garden rang out for morning services.[120] By seven o'clock the shops were completely opened, and the street sellers appeared to catch the early customers. Street selling of print went on in and around the Strand area, by those scratching a living on or below the poverty line. In *London Labour*, Mayhew described a multitude of street sellers who operated in the Strand area. He spoke to a groundsel and chickweed seller (1: 153), to ham sandwich-sellers who were '"working" the theatres' (1: 177), and to flower girls, some of whom also acted as prostitutes, 'mixing up a leer with their whine for custom or charity' (1: 134). He came across playbill-sellers who worked at the Lyceum Theatre (1: 288), street sellers of periodicals, books, newspapers, tracts, and back-numbers (1: 289), and a game-hawker (1: 124), as well as coffee stalls (1: 185). The fruit and fish stalls covered their tables in 'old newspapers or periodicals' (1: 99), as print became just so much waste paper in its final stages in the print economy. Horses and horse-drawn vehicles made a terrible din as they rattled and clattered along the roads. In streets inhabited by the wealthy, roadways were 'covered with gravel, and carefully watered […] to keep down the dust and deaden the rumblings of the carriages and the step of the horses', but in streets like Wellington Street there would have been no such protection.[121] Many side streets were still cobbled, and main roads like the Strand were surfaced with granite blocks or with layers of stones and gravel, which were easily displaced to block the street gullies. Some streets were laid with wooden blocks to deaden traffic noise, but in the summer you could smell and taste the dust.[122] Dickens's morning walk would not have been an altogether pleasant one.

Street life on Wellington Street North in the 1840s, once the day was underway, is shown in a newspaper image from 1843, reproduced on the cover of this book. It shows the entrance to the Lyceum and the offices of the *Morning Post* at no. 18. It also shows the building which will become (in 1850) the office

---

[119]   Dickens, 'The Streets – Morning', 51–2.

[120]   Emily Cockayne, *Hubbub: Filth, Noise and Stench in England 1600–1770* (New Haven, CT: Yale University Press, 2007), 110.

[121]   Max Schlesinger, *Saunterings In and About London* (London: Nathaniel Cooke, 1853), 13.

[122]   Liza Picard, *Victorian London: The Life of a City 1840–1870*, 2nd edn (London: Phoenix, 2006), 29–30.

of *Household Words* at no. 16.[123] As it is an advertisement for urban improvements, this view of Wellington Street's middle section gives the impression of a much wider, more stately thoroughfare than it was in reality. However, it provides a useful sense of the proximity of some key buildings. Once it arrived in 1850, *Household Words* was right by the office for the *Morning Post* newspaper, shown here, and clearly visible from the portico of the Lyceum. In this image, squashed between the building that will house *Household Words* and the *Morning Post* offices, is a slender building which, from 1849, was home to Thomas Hailes Lacy's theatrical bookshop. Lacy's business provided a point of intersection between print culture and theatrical culture (see Chapter 3), so it is entirely fitting that his premises came to stand between those of a miscellany and a newspaper and opposite a theatre. An account of a fire at number 15 Wellington Street North provides further evidence of how visible the offices and their occupants were to others at work producing printed material nearby. Number 15 was C.F. Bielefeld's famous *papier mâché* works (Figure 1.11).[124] The *Morning Post*'s report of the fire at Bielefeld's works in 1854 describes 'the densely-populated character of the neighbourhood' and states that at around ten o'clock at night, when the fire started, the usual 'crowded state of the Strand' meant that there were soon 'dense masses of spectators' gathered to watch. The Queen and Prince Albert themselves,

Figure 1.11   C.F. Bielefeld's *papier mâché* Works, 15 Wellington Street North. From an engraving on the frontispiece of Bielefeld's *On the Use of Improved Papier Mâché in Furniture, in the Interior Decoration of Buildings, and in Works of Art*, 2nd edn (London: C.F. Bielefeld, 1850). © The British Library Board, RB.31.c.409.

---

[123]   Wellington Street North in 1843. City of Westminster Archives Centre, Box 16, no. 35.

[124]   'Southampton Street and Tavistock Street Area: Wellington Street', *Survey of London: volume 36: Covent Garden* (1970), 226-229, accessed 22 June 2010 online via http://www.british-history.ac.uk/report.aspx?compid=46125.

we are told, had just left the Lyceum. The closeness of the buildings is very much a matter of comment when fires could spread so easily, so we hear about 'the cool and uninterrupted manner in which the printers of the Morning Post newspaper, almost next adjoining, pursued their ordinary avocation.' At the same time, 'Mr. Charles Dickens was doing good service at his office of "Household Words", by encouraging the firemen in their labours'.[125] Albert Smith, Charles Mathews, and the Lyceum ballet girls are also all out in the street. Dickens is so close to the Lyceum when at his window that the reporter from the *Morning Post* can see and hear him.

Such geographical proximity suggests that the morning commuters to the three sections of Wellington Street would have had a conception of themselves as part of a coherent print culture, a conception heightened by their relations within urban space. Dickens, when he stood at the window of his *Household Words* office at eight o'clock in the morning, would have looked out at the offices of people with whom he had collaborated, at his competitors, and at premises such as the Lyceum and Lacy's bookshop, which represented leisure industries that competed with printed matter for the leisure hours of the middle and the working classes. As well as the visibility of the buildings, the sense of operating within networks united by the production of print as much as by proximity would have been enforced by the presence and visibility of print on the streets. Despite the new innovations of gas lighting, advertising, and shop displays, many shops in this period still exhibited their wares on the street; Rosa Salzberg, writing about the print trade of early modern Venice, points out that selling print from shops and the sale of print in the streets were not distinct categories, as 'bookshops could be open to the street, and advertise their wares outside'.[126] That this was still the case with many old-fashioned booksellers in mid-Victorian London is, as Lynda Nead has discussed, made clear by contemporary images of Holywell Street, a hotspot for the radical and pornographic book trade only five minutes' walk from Wellington Street.[127]

In Figure 1.12, bookstalls outside the shop window are there to catch the attention of the passerby, and to entice them within to make a purchase. Wilkie Collins describes how books and pamphlets in cheap bookshops seemed to declare 'buy me, borrow me, stare at me, steal me – do anything, O inattentive stranger, except contemptuously pass me by!'[128] Those who did not make use of the street to advertise their wares made full use of their shop windows, as this image of the establishment of George Vickers, an early publisher of Reynolds's fiction, shows (Figure 1.13). The three sections of Wellington Street may not have been as renowned for bookselling as Paternoster Row or, less respectably, Holywell Street, but between 1843 and 1853 they were home to several booksellers with different specialisms, as well as Lacy. Alexander Black, seller of luxury foreign

---

125   'Destruction of Bielefeld's Papier Mache Works', *Morning Post*, 10 March 1854, 5.

126   Salzberg, in *Geographies of the Book*, ed. Ogborn and Withers, 121.

127   Nead, 161–89.

128   [Wilkie Collins], 'The Unknown Public', *HW*, 21 August 1858, 217.

Figure 1.12   C.J. Richardson, *House in Holywell Street, Strand*, June 1871.
City of Westminster Archives Centre B138 Holywell St. (687).

Figure 1.13   Anon., *Vickers – Publisher, Holywell St., Strand.* City of
Westminster Archives Centre B138 Holywell St. (13).

books, had premises at 8 Wellington Street North between 1843 and 1851, having
been there since the 1830s. In 1852, the business occupant of 11 Wellington
Street North was William Tweedie, the bookseller mentioned earlier, who was
a temperance publisher.[129] Martin Taylor sold books from 1 Wellington Street
(South) from 1843 to 1853. Nearby, at number 6, was Edmund Smith, listed in
the Post Office directory for 1843 as 'bookseller and publisher', who shared
the same building with another bookseller (and perhaps his business partner),
John Williams Rumsey, as well as a second Rumsey who is listed as a solicitor.
Finally, Sotheby's and Leigh, who started as book auctioneers, had premises at
3 Wellington Street (South) before they moved to their more famous New Bond
Street address. Other businesses which serviced the print economy were active
on the three sections of Wellington Street. For example, on Upper Wellington
Street between 1843 and 1853 we find a typefounder, a music copyist, and a
black-lead pencil maker. On Wellington Street North we find John Mabley's
stationery business at number 9, next door to Alexander Black's bookshop, and
on Wellington Street (South) is listed G.E. Madeley, lithographer and printer,
at number 3. The area was still one of mixed occupations, where a bootmaker
might work next to a printer, but it contained clusters of specialization in printed
material. The high-end, the speciality, and the more ordinary booksellers, then,
coexisted in the same street.

   Printed material, therefore, was hawked in the street by booksellers as well
as street sellers, and print was highly visible both for readers and for rival
editors. In fact, the visibility of print highlighted the fact that editors were
readers too, who might visit their offices and pass by a bookseller displaying

---

129   Brenda Ayres, 'Temperance Magazines', *DNCJ*, 618.

Figure 1.14   Anon., *Holywell Street, Strand, 1870*. City of Westminster
Archives Centre B138 Holywell Street (8–11).

the latest number of a rival publication in his window. The first number of *Puppet-Show* registers this rivalry in very concrete terms, exhorting its readers to 'purchase the *Puppet-Show*, and look at the illustrations of *Punch* through the shop-windows. You will thus obtain all the wit of both publications, and SAVE TWO-PENCE!'[130] In Figure 1.14, different types of advertising and display show how books are part of the commerce of a street. The gentleman in the bottom right corner scrutinizes a book from a display on the pavement; next to him a street seller carries her wares on a basket balanced on her head. Across the street, several women look at books through the large shop windows. On Wellington Street, these pedestrians and book-lovers would have included the editors and journalists, too.

Of course, many different types of people would have experienced the print culture of Wellington Street, as well as the editors and journalists; casual shoppers, visitors to the Lyceum, street sellers, pedestrians on their way to Covent Garden, cabmen, printers, and even the local firemen who fought the fire at Bielefeld's factory. The nature of a street as a thoroughfare meant that elements of Wellington Street's print networks were on display to the public. The composition of the street displayed the print economy as a coherent field of work to those outside of it, just as much as it played a role in the formation of that field, and this display invited outsiders to join in. Print was everywhere visible in this part of the city; one visitor to London commented that 'in the Strand, […] it is surprising to see how from bottom to top the various houses often display large signboards with painted letters'.[131] John Bolton Rogerson wrote in 1842 that he would 'feast' his eyes on a bookseller's window, as observation becomes a form of consumption. 'Reading' the metropolis is connected to reading metropolitan print, as Rogerson records that 'I have been told of people learning to read at a bookseller's window'.[132] This is dramatized by Dickens in *Little Dorrit*, when Arthur Clenham hears Maggy read the signs in the grocer's window:

> Nothing would serve Maggy but that they must stop at a grocer's window, short of their destination, for her to show her learning. She could read after a sort; and picked out the fat figures in the tickets of prices, for the most part correctly. She also stumbled, with a large balance of success against her failures, through the various philanthropic recommendations to Try our Mixture, Try our Family Black, Try our Orange-flavoured Pekoe, challenging competition at the head of Flowery teas; and various cautions to the public against spurious establishments and adulterated articles. When he saw how pleasure brought a rosy tint into Little Dorrit's face when Maggy made a hit,

---

130   'How to Save Two-Pence A-Week', *Puppet-Show*, 18 March 1848, 8.

131   C.P. Moritz, with an introduction by P.E. Matheson, *Travels of Carl Philipp Moritz in England in 1782: A reprint of the English Translation of 1795* (London: Humphrey Milford, 1924), 30.

132   John Bolton Rogerson, 'Walks In The Streets. – No. I.', *Bradshaw's Journal*, 19 March 1842, 314.

he felt that he could have stood there making a library of the grocer's window until the rain and the wind were tired.[133]

The official image of the office of John Tallis's *Illustrated News of the World* on the Strand makes a point of showing passers-by 'reading' the windows (Figure 1.15). The books and periodicals for sale in booksellers' windows, opposite the playbills posted outside the Lyceum, and next door to the sign which read 'Morning Post' on the front of that newspaper's building, all declared that although those amusing the public through print were competing for the attention and the business of passersby, they were not isolated scribblers, but professionals who were part of a coherent field of work. The same impulse lay behind Dickens's and Bulwer Lytton's scheme to create the 'Guild of Literature and Art'. A guild confers a sense of professionalism, permanence, and protection upon a trade, and on Wellington Street, that was just what the editors and writers needed.

It is important to recognize that although the majority of the businesses on the three sections of Wellington Street had some connection to the print trade, they were competing with the purveyors of other luxury goods or leisure facilities for the free time of their readers. This suggests that the print culture of Wellington Street was one influenced as much by an awareness of commerce, popular entertainment, and popular tastes as by any conception of 'high' art. Other premises were connected with leisure trades which both intersected with and competed with the business of amusing the public through print.[134] At 12 Upper Wellington Street were the premises of Abraham Haigh, listed in the *Post Office Directory* as a theatrical hosier. Haigh must have been a supplier to the many theatres nearby. As well as the leisure industry of the theatre and its service businesses, there were other competing leisure trades on the three sections of Wellington Street. This would have made visible and apparent to those working on the street, and walking down it, that the business of producing printed matter sat uneasily somewhere between a profession and a trade in this period. The coffee houses, the York Hotel, and the Coach and Horses on Upper Wellington Street were themselves in competition with the Old Bell and the Wellington Tavern lower down on Wellington Street North. Purveyors of luxury goods such as tobacco and wine were on Wellington Street (South), along with manufacturers of boots and ladies' shoes. Bielefeld's works provided luxury *papier mâché* goods. Other occupants included solicitors, surgeons, and a dentist, who would all have been educated professional men with money available to spend on the theatre and imported cigars. As I mentioned earlier, few of those engaged in the print business actually lived above their business premises; T.H. Lacy, for example,

---

[133] Charles Dickens, *Little Dorrit*, ed. Harvey Peter Sucksmith (Oxford: Clarendon Press, 1979; 1st publ. 1855–57), 99–100.

[134] For more on this, see Chapter 3.

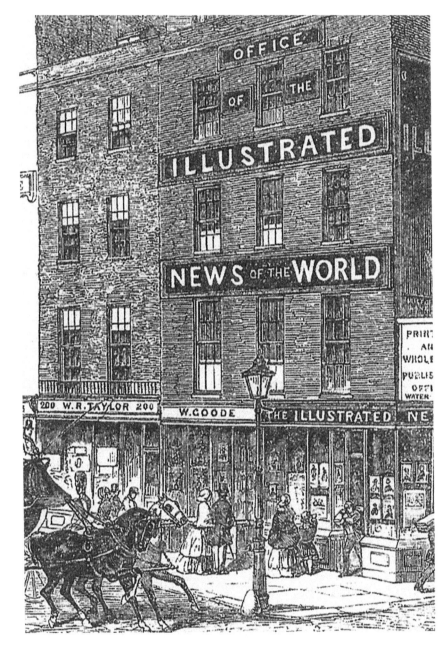

Figure 1.15   The windows of the *Illustrated News of the World* office, 199
Strand. Reproduced by permission of Guildhall Library, City of
London, and London Topographical Society.

commuted in across Waterloo Bridge from Newington.[135] As morning came, the makeup of the street shifted, as the commuters arrived and the householders left.[136]

Household occupancy itself was mixed; Old Bailey records of a prosecution for breaking and entering in 1845 reveal the multiple businesses carried out in 29 Southampton Street, Strand (a short walk from Wellington Street), where one of the tenants is a publisher:

> *Cross-examined by* MR. BALLANTINE. *Q.* Is the prosecutor a married man? *A.* Yes, and occupies the second floor, and one room on the third floor – the front room on the first floor is occupied by Mr. Newland, a solicitor, as an office – he has one clerk – his name is on a board in the hall – there are two back rooms on that floor, occupied by Mr. Barth, a publisher, who has now left – his name was on the board – his business is carried on in Brydges-street – the other room on the third floor is occupied by Mr. Hodson, a clerk in Somerset House – a Captain Moore lives in the attic – Mrs. Hart, the housekeeper, and her husband, lived in the kitchen below.[137]

One visitor to London commented that 'in the Strand [...] there is a constant succession of shop after shop; and [...], not infrequently, people of different trades inhabit the same house'.[138] The association with 'trade' clung to writers and journalists, and Reynolds uses this to take a swipe at *Household Words*:

> Mr Charles Dickens [...] has of late extended his business – from a manufacturer of Christmas stories (in which sentimental ticket-porters talk blank verse full of pathos as the language of everyday life, and in which an affected style of interrupted rhapsody, with occasional bursts of moralising, are the chief recommendations) to do a great business in the general line.[139]

Their surroundings would make the editors and publishers on Wellington Street well aware of their work as a business, rather than simply an art. In such an environment, networks, collaboration, emulation, and mutual endorsement become important business tools. The environment also led to cooperation between the other leisure industries and those involved in print production. London coffee houses stocked the latest newspapers and periodicals, and the Lyceum put on authorized adaptations of Dickens's fiction.[140]

---

[135]   1851 census, HO107/1568, f. 290, accessed 15 July 2011 online via http://www. ancestry.co.uk/.

[136]   Although printers and editors often worked late (see Chapter 3).

[137]   'March 1845, trial of RICHARD ELLIOTT, RICHARD VINCENT (t18450303-587)', *OBPO*, accessed 4 February 2010 via http://www.oldbaileyonline.org.

[138]   Moritz, 30.

[139]   GRACCHUS (probably Reynolds's younger brother Edward Reynolds), 'National Prosperity: Opinions of Ledru-Rollin and Charles Dickens', *RWN*, 16 June 1850, 3.

[140]   *Cruchley's Picture of London*, 16th edn (London: Cruchley, 1851), 250. For discussion of the Lyceum's adaptations of Dickens's fiction, see Chapter 3.

Peter Ackroyd sees Fleet Street as representative of what he calls London's 'topographical imperative', where not only is the same type of community, doing 'the same activity', drawn to the same place, but the very activities of that community (in this case print production) are coloured by the nature of that place. 'It can be said', Ackroyd continues, 'that the very earth and stones of London created their own particular inhabitants'.[141] This is a rather fanciful way of expressing what is nevertheless a useful insight: that mid-Victorian print networks were profoundly influenced by the area in which they were situated. As Lynda Nead suggests, paraphrasing Jane Jacobs, 'streets are much more than passageways, more or less congested; they are also environments and localities, with their own, distinctive economic, social and cultural forms'.[142] Streets are not simply places of practical purpose, devoid of cultural significance. Streets contain buildings and occupants, but they also contain the space between buildings. This space is a no man's land within the urban landscape, where all members of a network may move; a space of potential, where overlapping networks can meet and touch, and be influenced by shared experiences. At the same time, the existence of a street also situates members within their network in a very concrete way. In a reversal of Doreen Massey's reading of space, the form of a street gives form to its community.

'Tillers of the Field' and *Household Words*

If our editors, who knew that ex-colleagues and friends worked only a few doors away from them, had a sense of print production as made up of face-to-face networks and as a coherent field of work, then this has implications for how we might read the addresses to their imagined readers in their newspapers and periodicals. The composition of Wellington Street has an effect on the composition of the editorial addresses in two of the key publications with offices on Wellington Street North: *Reynolds's Weekly Newspaper* and *Household Words*.

The 'Preliminary Word' to the first issue of *Household Words* has a clear awareness of those publications which operate around it:

> Some tillers of the field into which we now come, have been before us, and some are here whose high usefulness we readily acknowledge, and whose company it is an honour to join. But, there are others here – Bastards of the Mountain, draggled fringe on the Red Cap, Panders to the basest passions of the lowest natures – whose existence is a national reproach. And these, we should consider it our highest service to displace.[143]

Publications (and, as the metaphor of 'tillers' implies, their editors and writers) that 'came before' are divided into two categories: those considered of 'high

---

[141]   Ackroyd, *London*, 401.

[142]   Nead, 173.

[143]   [Charles Dickens], 'Preliminary Word', *HW*, 30 March 1850, 1. Further references are given after quotations in the text.

usefulness [...] whose company it is an honour to join', and those 'whose existence is a national reproach'. Dickens's opinions on fellow inhabitants of Wellington Street North and Wellington Street (South) fit these two categories. We have already seen what Dickens thought of Reynolds, across the street at number 7. He felt very differently, however, about some of his other neighbours. Dickens followed the encouragement of William Jerdan, of the *Literary Gazette*, to make more of Sam Weller when that character appeared in *Pickwick Papers*. During the spring and summer of 1848, Dickens contributed articles to the *Examiner*, 'presumably either requested for the *Examiner* by Forster [...] or suggested to him by Dickens'. In November 1846, Dickens was thinking longingly of founding his own periodical, with the extremely successful *Athenaeum*, as well as Addison's *Spectator*, as models.[144] These publications, based on the three sections of Wellington Street, were ones whose existence Dickens certainly did not see as 'a national reproach'. The 'Preliminary Word' uses the word 'field' figuratively; those publications 'here', which *Household Words* hopes to 'join', are those already printed and published. 'Here' is the imagined space of the community of print culture. But it is also 'here', the geographical space of Wellington Street, where publications which Dickens admired and publications which he disliked sat almost side by side.[145] Space is both real and imagined in the 'Preliminary Word'.

Household Words made a claim to new ground in dramatic fashion in the 'Preliminary Word':

> Thus, we begin our career! The adventurer in the old fairy story, climbing towards the summit of a steep eminence on which the object of his search was stationed, was surrounded by a roar of voices, crying to him, from the stones in the way, to turn back. All the voices *we* hear, cry Go on! [...] With a fresh heart, a light step, and a hopeful courage, we begin the journey. The road is not so rough that it need daunt our feet: the way is not so steep that we need stop for breath, [...]. Go on! In a glow already, with the air from yonder height upon us, and the inspiriting voices joining in this acclamation, we echo back the cry, and go on cheerily! ('Preliminary Word', 2)

For Reynolds, on the other hand, any new ground is there to be claimed as his. In the *Instructor*, the advertisements for the *Newspaper* link London with the Continent, and the columns of *Reynolds's Weekly Newspaper* with those of the *Instructor*, in a network of associations. Readers are told that 'the writers who have hitherto sustained the spirit of the latter must now transfer their services to the columns of the former', and 'those who have admired the spirit in which [the Instructor] has been conducted and the varied democratic talents that were

---

144 Slater, *Dickens*, 74; 276; 277.
145 Reynolds's name may have been largely 'displaced' from accounts of nineteenth-century literature until relatively recently, but Dickens failed to 'displace' Reynolds; *Reynolds's Newspaper and the Sunday Citizen* was still published from the Strand neighbourhood in the twentieth century (Dicks, 107; 119).

united in the supply of its contents, will find the same recommendations in the columns of my WEEKLY NEWSPAPER'.[146] The columns of the *Instructor* will almost fit into the columns of the *Newspaper*; this is not altogether surprising when we consider that they were published (although not printed) from the same building. This elided printed space will become the space where London and the international radical scene are also elided:

> the services of able correspondents have been retained in Dublin, Paris, Madrid, Berlin, Vienna, Turin, Rome, Athens, Constantinople, New York, &c. The acquaintance of MR. REYNOLDS with the principal foreign patriots now dwelling [...] in the British metropolis, will likewise enable him to afford his readers the best and most accurate views of the progress of events on the Continent of Europe.[147]

This is a space of networks of writers and activists, and of readers, too. However, this space is presented to the reader as one controlled firmly by the overview of the editor-entrepreneur, who is the guiding presence behind 'my' newspaper.

The survey of print culture in the 'Preliminary Word' also looks out far beyond Wellington Street:

> We have considered what an ambition it is to be admitted into many homes with affection and confidence; [...] and to be associated with the harmless laughter and the gentle tears of many hearths. We know the great responsibility of such a privilege; its vast reward; the pictures that it conjures up, in hours of solitary labour, of a multitude moved by one sympathy [...]. The hand that writes these faltering lines, happily associated with *some* Household Words before to-day, has known enough of such experiences to enter an earnest spirit upon this new task, and with an awakened sense of all that it involves. ('Preliminary Word', 1)

This network also extends outwards across the nation and the Empire, as Dickens imagines how copies of *Household Words* will be carried with the reader on his travels, perhaps as a material link to home:

> to bring the greater and the lesser in degree, together, upon that wide field, and mutually dispose them to a better acquaintance and a kinder understanding – is one main object of our Household Words. [...] Our Household Words will not [...] treat of the hopes, the enterprises, triumphs, joys, and sorrows, of this country only, but, in some degree, of those of every nation upon earth. For nothing can be a source of real interest in one of them, without concerning all the rest. ('Preliminary Word', 1)

The whole nation here, and indeed the whole world, is a spectacle of connections, to be made evident to the sensitive reader and the sensitive observer. The small space of the editor's office is a space which creates networks in the outside world,

---

[146] 'To Our Readers', *RPI*, 11 May 1850, 1.
[147] Ibid.

and which enables knowledge of the 'Romance' in 'all familiar things' to be distributed to all the readers on that network. Wellington Street, in this model, becomes a hub for the print culture of the Empire, as *Household Words* aims

> to live in the Household affections, and to be numbered among the Household thoughts, of our readers. We hope to be the comrade and friend of many thousands of people, of both sexes, and of all ages and conditions, on whose faces we may never look. ('Preliminary Word', 1)

Dickens may never see his readers face to face, but he still knows how to address them as if they were part of his immediate network.

This chapter has argued that print was so effective at creating an imagined network out of people 'on whose faces we may never look' precisely because of the conditions of its production; that is, close, face-to-face networks. These conditions influence the way in which readers are conceived of and represented in Dickens's 'Preliminary Word'. The capital 'H' in *Household Words* finds its counterparts in the capitalized phrases 'Household affections' and 'Household thoughts'; the intellectual and emotional lives of 'our readers' are tied by typography to the very publication which they will read. The image of the editor as a solitary labourer is a disingenuous one, as the editor on Wellington Street was part of a community of networks, rivalries, and collaborations. Print in the 'Preliminary Word' envisages an imagined network of shared experience for both readers and writer precisely because, from the office in 16 Wellington Street North, Dickens could see participants in networks with shared experiences of print culture right outside his window. Dickens's rival Reynolds was, however, prepared to go one step further to engage with what he hoped were members of his own network of readers.

Chapter 2
Afternoon: 'Dissolute and Idle Persons'

Furthering our acquaintance with Reynolds, and proposing that radical writers like to step off the page and onto the streets.

> ... as in any drama, the stage and all that is on it form an integral and indissoluble historical link with the narrative.
>
> —Rodney Mace, *Trafalgar Square: Emblem of Empire*
> (London: Lawrence & Wishart, 2005; 1st publ. 1976), 21

G.W.M. Reynolds of 7 Wellington Street North was not content with merely addressing his readers in print. One afternoon in March 1848, he took a step out of the editor's office and onto the stage. In Reynolds's case, his stage was actually his balcony in Wellington Street, from which he addressed a crowd in the street below. His imagined network of readers had turned, he hoped, into real protestors there outside his building. His exact words were unrecorded, but they were most likely along the same themes – of republicanism and the 'People's Rights' – on which he had just delivered his first recorded public speech. Reynolds's 'finest hour', as Dick Collins has described it, began at around one o'clock in Trafalgar Square, the new public space in front of the National Gallery at the end of the Strand.[1] This new space, only begun in 1840, was about 15 minutes' walk from Reynolds's office in Wellington Street (see Figure 1.8).

Reynolds stood up in front of a protest meeting in Trafalgar Square about the introduction of income tax, and turned the issue of the day away from taxation and towards revolution. Afterwards, a significant number of the crowd followed him to Wellington Street. In that critical year of Europe-wide revolutions (and before the revolutions had lost their steam), Reynolds praised the recent French uprising which had deposed King Louis Philippe, and declared solidarity with the French people on behalf of 'the English nation'.[2] Five minutes' walk away in Whitehall, and just beyond in Westminster, the British government was already uneasy about the turmoil on the Continent and the presence of so many radical political refugees in London.[3] As Reynolds over-optimistically put it:

---

[1] Dick Collins, 'George William McArthur Reynolds: A Biographical Sketch', in *The Necromancer*, ed. Dick Collins (Kansas City: Valancourt Books, 2007; 1st publ. *RM*, 1851–52), xxxi.

[2] 'The Open-Air Meeting in Trafalgar-square', *The Times*, 7 March 1848, 8.

[3] Such as Louis Blanc, Giuseppe Mazzini, A. Ledru-Rollin, Louis Kossuth, and Karl Marx, all of whom came to London during this period. See E.J. Hobsbawm, *The Age of*

> Republicanism is the 'order of the day'; and there is not a throne in Europe that is worth twenty years' purchase, […]; – and from the banks of the Thames to the confines of Asia – from the cheerless regions of the North to the sunny shores of the tideless Mediterranean, the prevailing sentiment is adverse to the antiquated, useless, oppressive institutions of Monarchy.[4]

Reynolds's actions on that spring afternoon earned him immediate prominence in the Chartist movement, a place on the platform at the 'monster meeting' at Kennington Common on 10 April, the status of a radical celebrity, and a government file. The disorder after the meeting continued on and off over several days.

Reynolds inserted accounts of his afternoon into the pages of his best-selling serial narrative, *The Mysteries of London* (1844–48), published in penny weekly installments for two series, which was immensely successful in Reynolds's lifetime.[5] These insertions blurred the line between political speech-making, newspaper reporting, and radical fiction. This chapter argues that with these inserted accounts, *Mysteries* made use of Reynolds's move to Wellington Street in 1847, which put him at the heart of London's radical print networks and perfectly placed him to capitalize on the Trafalgar Square protest. His imagined network of readers became actualized as real protestors – some of whom Reynolds hoped had read his work, or might now go on to do so – gathered in the square and below his balcony to hear him bring his political comments in *Mysteries* to life. Reynolds's speeches also enabled him to overcome the barrier of illiteracy, to reach those he liked to call 'the industrious millions'. *Mysteries* reveals the links – for Reynolds – between fiction, the spoken word, radical politics, and urban space.

The networks of radical print culture had long interacted in the Strand neighbourhood; this tradition fed the riots and the disruption that March afternoon, as did the very visible poverty of the area in and around Wellington Street. That it occurred during the afternoon was crucial: this was the time when the city centre was at its busiest, and all classes were mingling in the streets. The second part of this chapter shows that Reynolds's own actions – and his accounts of them in *Mysteries* – were the latest dramatic manifestation of the radical tradition of his locality. The spatial theorist Michel de Certeau sees the rebellious reclamation of urban space on the part of the populace as praiseworthy 'social delinquency'.[6]

Capital: 1848–1875 (London: Sphere Books, 1985; 1st publ. Weidenfeld & Nicolson, 1975), 37.

  [4] G.W.M. Reynolds, *The Mysteries of London, Series II*, 2 vols (London: George Vickers, 3 Oct. 1846–16 Sept. 1848), 2: 199. Subsequent references will appear parenthetically in the text.

  [5] It was followed by *The Mysteries of the Court of London* (1848–56). For estimated circulation figures see 'G.W.M. Reynolds's *The Mysteries of London*: An Introduction', ed. Trefor Thomas (Keele: Keele University Press, 1996), xv; Anne Humpherys, 'An Introduction to G.W.M. Reynolds's "Encyclopedia of Tales"', in *G.W.M. Reynolds: Nineteenth-Century Fiction, Politics and the Press* (Aldershot: Ashgate, 2008), 126.

  [6] Michel de Certeau, *The Practice of Everyday Life*, trans. Steven Rendall (Berkeley, CA: University of California Press, 1984), 130.

The extreme radicals were associated popularly with other disreputable or offensive users of the streets: the obscene print trade, the pornographic press, the Strand's thriving prostitution trade, petty criminals, and dangerous republicans.[7] Reynolds objects to this very association with delinquency in the second series of *Mysteries*:

> The aristocracy and the men in power treat the people's assemblies with ridicule, and denominate the working-classes, when so assembled, as a 'mob'. They will not discriminate between honest politicians and the respectable working-classes on the one hand, and the ragamuffinery of society on the other. They confound us all together. (*Mysteries Series II*, 2: 233)

Reynolds the narrator uses the plural 'us' to link himself to his 'respectable' readers; Reynolds's links to the pornographic book trade of Holywell Street suggest that he was not as respectable as he would have liked to be considered, however. De Certeau declares that

> Social delinquency consists in taking the story literally, in making it a principle of physical existence where a society no longer offers to subjects or groups symbolic outlets and expectations of space.[8]

Reynolds tried to intertwine protest through radical storytelling with protest in urban space, in the hope that the combined work of both would push forward his radical agenda, as well as his own career. As Ian Haywood puts it, Reynolds 'intervened in history by utilising his literary skills both on the page and on the platform'.[9] By meeting in taverns, publishing pamphlets, speechmaking, and rioting in the streets, the radical members of the Strand's print networks made

---

[7] Reynolds was objected to by the more 'respectable' literary establishment on both political and literary grounds as too shocking and salacious, as well as too radical and too popular with the poor. Thomas Clark's stinging attack on Reynolds made much of his fiction, claiming that *The Mysteries of the Court of London* showed 'the diseased, corrupt, and sink-like mind from which it emanated', while Robert Louis Stevenson was 'revolted' by *The Mysteries of London* and by 'un-utterable Reynolds'; Thomas Clark, *A Letter Addressed to G.W.M. Reynolds, Reviewing his Conduct as a Professed Chartist, and also explaining Who He Is and What He Is, Together With Copious Extracts From His Most Indecent Writings. Also, A Few Words of Advice to his Brother Electors of Finsbury* (London: T. Clark, 1850), 21, British Library, Dex 251, MIC.B.613/58; Robert Louis Stevenson, 'Popular Authors', *Scribners' Magazine*, July 1888, 126; 124.

[8] De Certeau, 130. De Certeau sees a drive for social stability as inherent in city construction and urban planning. He argues that it is this very stability which threatens individuality and takes no account of the mobility of the individual and their developing experience as they walk around the city. Walking is a kind of narrative for de Certeau, and narrative itself is important because it is fundamentally not based upon any troubling sense of stability (no movement within a narrative – physical or metaphorical – means no story).

[9] Ian Haywood, *The Revolution in Popular Literature: Politics, Print and the People 1790–1860* (Cambridge: Cambridge University Press, 2004), 176.

delinquent use of urban space. These 'radicals' were not a united body and had many different aims and ideas. This chapter argues that despite this, Reynolds's speech (as reported in *Mysteries*) made use of his position in a hotspot for radical London. The streets around the Strand, including Wellington Street, gave geographic coherence to otherwise very disparate radical networks.

The final section of this chapter turns to *Mysteries* itself. Reynolds's speechmaking points to a contradiction already registered in *Mysteries*. The radical writers and pressmen in and around Wellington Street called for the clearing-out of poverty, bad housing, and exploitation, yet their narratives were often driven by the energy and excitement of this very world. *Mysteries* simultaneously registers the failure of revolution to take place in London, and recognizes that the narrative drive and excitement come from the very inequalities against which the text campaigns. Indeed, Reynolds exaggerates these inequalities by peopling his London with the very rich and the criminal poor. Richard Maxwell has argued that *Mysteries* is torn between the desire to weave mysteries and the desire to expose them, but there is a more political and spatial element to it than that.[10] The desperate conditions and the contrasts between rich and poor, seen every day around Wellington Street and the Strand, gave radical writers, editors, and pressmen a cause; but it also gave them a career. A successful revolution would only put an end to this narrative. If the 'real' or potential readers whom Reynolds saw protesting in the streets were successful, then the entire imagined network of Reynolds's readership would need different stories. It is a tension which, in *Mysteries*, Reynolds has already failed to resolve.

Delinquency on the Streets and on the Page: G.W.M Reynolds and the Trafalgar Square Demonstration

The *Times*, reporting on the Trafalgar Square meeting, focused its ire on the resulting disruption to Charing Cross, where Trafalgar Square meets the Strand:

> For several hours the peace of that busy thoroughfare was interrupted, business suspended, the shop-windows closed, and the passengers along the streets, whether on foot or in conveyances, put to considerable inconvenience, and even personal hazard.[11]

For the *Times*, the demonstrators were using space incorrectly, and so were 'out of place'; streets were to be used for business and shopping, not demonstrations. Note that even though the 'thoroughfare' is 'busy', it can still be at 'peace' if people and traffic can circulate freely, and the street can be used for its proper function. Reynolds himself claimed many years later that 'Trafalgar-square was

---

[10]   Richard Maxwell, *The Mysteries of Paris and London* (Charlottesville, VA and London: University Press of Virginia, 1992), 169.

[11]   'The Open-Air Meeting in Trafalgar-square', 8.

crowded on the occasion; all the thoroughfares were likewise densely thronged, and the working-classes had literally attended in their thousands'.[12] Whatever the true scale of the event, the demonstration was a precursor to the disorder which followed, when the crowd laid rowdy claim to a significant area of the city. Despite the large mass of people still gathered in Trafalgar Square, things seemed like they might end peaceably, with the resolution to hold a larger Chartist meeting at Kennington Common in a few days' time.[13] However, at about three o'clock the police attempted to break up the crowd.[14] When a small unit of police moved in on the crowd, they

> took stones from the building work around the base of Nelson's Column and pelted both the police and the column itself with them. When this supply of stones ran out, they tore down the palisades around Nelson's Column to replenish their arsenal and set fire to the contractors' sheds. At the height of the affray, a cry went up 'To the Palace! Bread and Revolution!', and a large section of the crowd moved off towards St. James' Park, smashing street lamps and the windows of the Reform Club on the way.[15]

According to the *Times*, the excited crowd broke shop windows, stole bread from bakeries, and demanded ale from publicans.[16] The *Times* report insists on the effectiveness of police action in controlling the protest. However, as Rodney Mace points out, the several days of disruption which commenced were enough to ensure that the authorities made extremely stringent preparations for the next, even bigger, Chartist demonstration at Kennington Common. Trafalgar Square itself continued to be occupied on and off for three days.[17] Some policemen and demonstrators needed hospital treatment, and several arrests were made. According to Mace, between 6 and 8 March the police arrested 103 people 'in or around Trafalgar Square', of which 73 were convicted.[18]

That Reynolds's big moment, reported in *Mysteries*, took place in the afternoon was significant, and the timing of the original meeting may well have been carefully judged. By one o'clock most of London was awake and on the move, from the poorest street seller to the wealthiest lady. The streets of London were open for business, and that business was shopping. As *Knight's Cyclopaedia of London* put it in 1851, '[a]lmost endless would be the task of enumerating the fine and elegant shops presented to view in the streets of London, and the dazzling

---

[12] 'The Festival of Messrs Reynolds's and Dicks's Establishment', *RN*, 11 July 1875, 1.

[13] The *Times* reported that there were 'nearly 15,000 persons' still in the square at this point; the *Freeman's Journal* reported 10–12,000 ('The Open-Air Meeting in Trafalgar-square'; 'Abolition of the Income Tax … (from the Sun of Monday)', *Freeman's Journal*, 11 March 1848, 3).

[14] 'Meeting in Trafalgar-square', *DN*, 7 March 1848, 4.

[15] Mace, 137.

[16] 'The Open-Air Meeting in Trafalgar-square', 8.

[17] Mace, 137–8.

[18] Ibid., 138.

array of commodities displayed in the windows'.[19] Afternoon was the time of day when all manner of Londoners mingled in busy streets like the Strand, and even on smaller streets like Wellington Street, positioned as it was on the easiest route from Covent Garden to Waterloo Bridge. In *Sketches by Boz*, Dickens describes how, as morning draws to a close,

> a new set of people fill the streets. The goods in the shop-windows are invitingly arranged; the shop-men in their white neckerchiefs and spruce coats, look as if they couldn't clean a window if their lives depended on it; the carts have disappeared from Covent Garden; the waggoners have returned, and the costermongers have repaired to their ordinary 'beats' in the suburbs; clerks are at their offices, and gigs, cabs, omnibuses, and saddle-horses, are conveying their masters to the same destination. The streets are thronged with a vast concourse of people, gay and shabby, rich and poor, idle and industrious; and we come to the heat, bustle, and activity of NOON.[20]

The multiple semicolons in this passage reinforce the sense of crowding, as clauses jostle up against each other like pedestrians on the pavement. Almost 20 years later, Max Schlesinger himself resorts to a cascade of commas and semicolons as the only way to describe daytime in Oxford Street. The passage works as a suitable description of the Strand, too:

> Its public is mixed; goods, waggons, and private carriages, omnibuses, and men and women on horseback, men of business, fashionable loungers, and curious strangers, are mixed up; shops of all sorts, from the most elegant drapers' shops down to the lowest oyster-stall, [...] legions of costermongers, and shoals of advertising vans.[21]

During an afternoon in the key thoroughfares of Westminster and the City, such as the Strand, 'the pavements are crowded with busy people, and the road is literally crowded with vehicles of every description'.[22] This activity would have spilled into the side streets too, especially along a main cut-through like Wellington Street, which is still one of the fastest ways to Covent Garden from the Strand. This crowding and mingling meant that the Strand and its surrounding streets were particularly susceptible to disruption that afternoon, as the *Times* registers indignantly. For Reynolds's purposes, however, it also meant that he was more likely to encounter real or potential members of his network of readers.

---

[19]   Charles Knight, *Knight's Cyclopaedia of London* (London: Charles Knight, 1851), 761.

[20]   Charles Dickens, 'The Streets – Morning', in *Sketches by Boz and Other Early Papers 1833–39*, vol. 1 of *Dickens' Journalism*, ed. Michael Slater (London: J.M. Dent, 1994), 54.

[21]   Max Schlesinger, *Saunterings In and About London* (London: Nathaniel Cooke, 1853), 103.

[22]   Schlesinger, 72.

Puppet-Show, with its office at 11 Wellington Street North, only just across the street from Reynolds at 7 Wellington Street North, reported on 'The Charing-Cross Revolution' in a gloriously mock-heroic style (Figure 2.1). It mocked participants in the event, but also newspaper reporting, for over-dramatizing what was, for *Puppet-Show*, a rebelliousness which needed to be deflated by humour.[23] Note how Reynolds is associated with his fiction and with his desire for readers:

> A dreadful rumour prevailed that MR. G.J.M.N.O.P.Q.W. REYNOLDS contemplated reading a chapter of his *Mysteries of London* to the populace! The military have been summoned to prevent this catastrophe.

And:

> Our worst fears have been confirmed. MR. G.J.M.N.O.P.Q.W. REYNOLDS spoke! [His speech was] a violent attack on the institutions of this country (including its grammar); and concluded with a pathetic reference to the fact that his journal, in which his speech would be reported verbatim, cost only a penny. His friends the rabble escorted him home.[24]

A reference to 'gentlemen distinguished for literary, scientific, and financial attainments' towards the middle of Figure 2.1 is another dig at Reynolds, who was declared bankrupt several times in the 1840s, including in 1848. Reynolds's commitment to radicalism is also called into question: is he not just another author and businessman advertising his wares, rather than a true believer? This charge has been levelled at Reynolds by many critics, both contemporary and modern.[25] But whether radicalism was a commercially or politically driven stance for Reynolds, he still needed a strategy to sell it. What *Puppet-Show* picks up on rather well is that the printed words of his fiction, and the spoken word within urban space, were connected for Reynolds. According to *Puppet-Show*, Reynolds wanted to read the printed text of *Mysteries* out loud to the crowd, and then proclaimed he would reprint his speech in his journal (*Reynolds's Miscellany*). In fact, he reprinted it in his fiction instead.

---

[23]   For more on satires of the Trafalgar Square protests and riots in the periodical press, particularly in *Punch* and *The Man in the Moon*, see Ian Haywood, 'George W.M. Reynolds and "The Trafalgar Square Revolution": radicalism, the carnivalesque and popular culture in mid-Victorian England', *Journal of Victorian Culture* 7, no. 1 (2002), 23–59.

[24]   'The Charing-Cross Revolution!', *Puppet-Show*, 18 March 1848, 8.

[25]   See, for example, Louis James, *Fiction for the Working Man 1830–1850: A Study of the Literature Produced for the Working Classes in Early Victorian Urban England* (London: Oxford University Press, 1963), 197. The debate continues in more recent scholarship: see Andrew King, 'Reynolds's Miscellany', 73–4; Michael H. Shirley, 'G.W.M. Reynolds, Reynolds's Newspaper and Popular Politics', 85; Stephen James Carver, 'The Wrongs and Crimes of the Poor: The Urban Underworld of The Mysteries of London in Context', 160–61; and Juliet John, 'Reynolds's Mysteries and Popular Culture', 169, all in *G.W.M. Reynolds: Nineteenth-Century Fiction, Politics, and the Press*, ed. Anne Humpherys and Louis James (Aldershot: Ashgate, 2008).

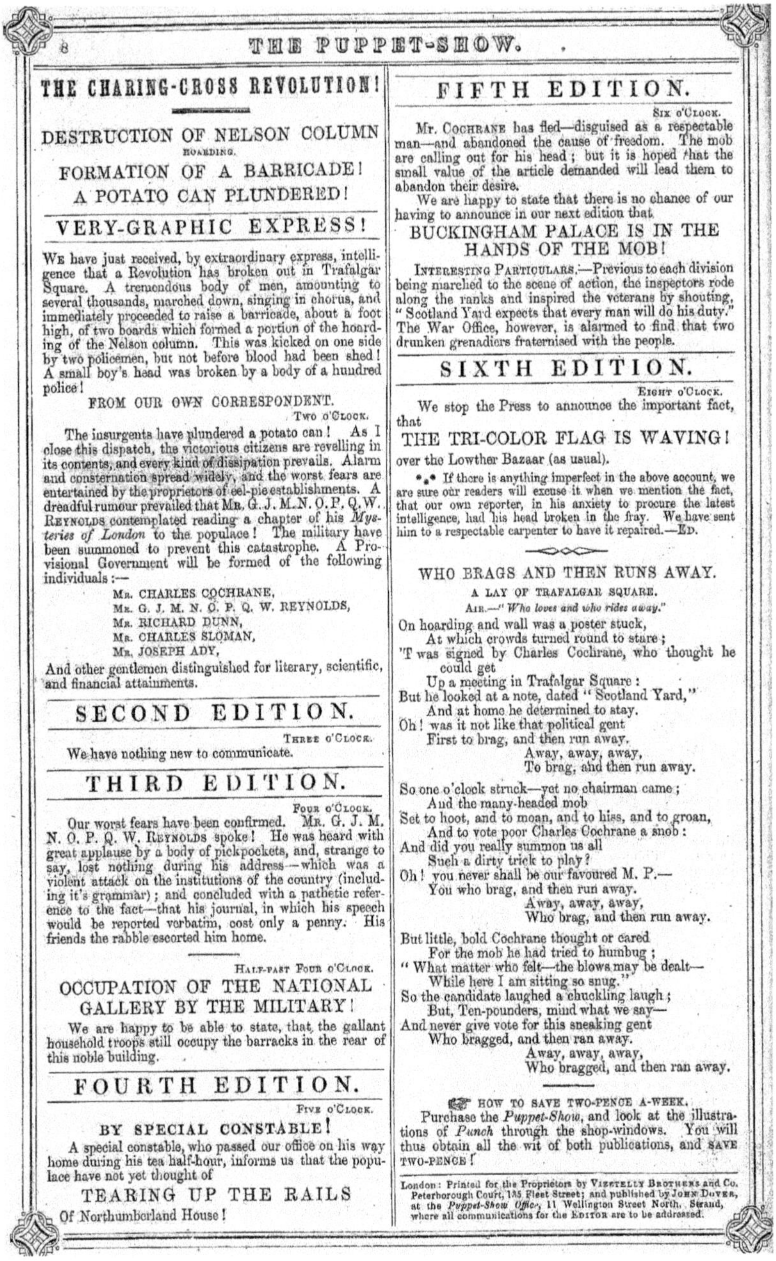

THE PUPPET-SHOW.

THE CHARING-CROSS REVOLUTION!

DESTRUCTION OF NELSON COLUMN
HOARDING.

FORMATION OF A BARRICADE!
A POTATO CAN PLUNDERED!

VERY-GRAPHIC EXPRESS!

WE have just received, by extraordinary express, intelligence that a Revolution has broken out in Trafalgar Square. A tremendous body of men, amounting to several thousands, marched down, singing in chorus, and immediately proceeded to raise a barricade, about a foot high, of two boards which formed a portion of the hoarding of the Nelson column. This was kicked on one side by two policemen, but not before blood had been shed! A small boy's head was broken by a body of a hundred police!

FROM OUR OWN CORRESPONDENT.
Two o'Clock.

The insurgents have plundered a potato can! As I close this dispatch, the victorious citizens are revelling in its contents; and every kind of dissipation prevails. Alarm and consternation spread widely, and the worst fears are entertained by the proprietors of eel-pie establishments. A dreadful rumour prevailed that MR. G. J. M. N. O. P. Q. W. REYNOLDS contemplated reading a chapter of his *Mysteries of London* to the populace! The military have been summoned to prevent this catastrophe. A Provisional Government will be formed of the following individuals :—

MR. CHARLES COCHRANE,
MR. G. J. M. N. O. P. Q. W. REYNOLDS,
MR. RICHARD DUNN,
MR. CHARLES SLOMAN,
MR. JOSEPH ADY,

And other gentlemen distinguished for literary, scientific, and financial attainments.

SECOND EDITION.
Three o'Clock.
We have nothing new to communicate.

THIRD EDITION.
Four o'Clock.
Our worst fears have been confirmed. MR. G. J. M. N. O. P. Q. W. REYNOLDS spoke! He was heard with great applause by a body of pickpockets, and, strange to say, lost nothing during his address—which was a violent attack on the institutions of the country (including it's grammar); and concluded with a pathetic reference to the fact—that his journal, in which his speech would be reported verbatim, cost only a penny! His friends the rabble escorted him home.

Half-past Four o'Clock.

OCCUPATION OF THE NATIONAL GALLERY BY THE MILITARY!

We are happy to be able to state, that the gallant household troops still occupy the barracks in the rear of this noble building.

FOURTH EDITION.
Five o'Clock.
BY SPECIAL CONSTABLE!
A special constable, who passed our office on his way home during his tea half-hour, informs us that the populace have not yet thought of

TEARING UP THE RAILS
Of Northumberland House!

FIFTH EDITION.
Six o'Clock.
Mr. COCHRANE has fled—disguised as a respectable man—and abandoned the cause of freedom. The mob are calling out for his head; but it is hoped that the small value of the article demanded will lead them to abandon their desire.

We are happy to state that there is no chance of our having to announce in our next edition that

BUCKINGHAM PALACE IS IN THE HANDS OF THE MOB!

INTERESTING PARTICULARS.—Previous to each division being marched to the scene of action, the inspectors rode along the ranks and inspired the veterans by shouting, " Scotland Yard expects that every man will do his duty." The War Office, however, is alarmed to find that two drunken grenadiers fraternised with the people.

SIXTH EDITION.
Eight o'Clock.
We stop the Press to announce the important fact, that

THE TRI-COLOR FLAG IS WAVING!
over the Lowther Bazaar (as usual).

•₊• If there is anything imperfect in the above account, we are sure our readers will excuse it when we mention the fact, that our own reporter, in his anxiety to procure the latest intelligence, had his head broken in the fray. We have sent him to a respectable carpenter to have it repaired.—ED.

WHO BRAGS AND THEN RUNS AWAY.
A LAY OF TRAFALGAR SQUARE.
AIR.—"*Who loves and who rides away.*"

On hoarding and wall was a poster stuck,
  At which crowds turned round to stare;
'T was signed by Charles Cochrane, who thought he could get
  Up a meeting in Trafalgar Square:
But he looked at a note, dated " Scotland Yard,"
  And at home he determined to stay.
Oh! was it not like that political gent
  First to brag, and then run away.
    Away, away, away,
    To brag, and then run away.

So one o'clock struck—yet no chairman came;
  And the many-headed mob
Set to hoot, and to moan, and to hiss, and to groan,
  And to vote poor Charles Cochrane a snob:
And did you really summon us all
  Such a dirty trick to play?
Oh! you never shall be our favoured M. P.—
  You who brag, and then run away.
    Away, away, away,
    Who brag, and then run away.

But little, bold Cochrane thought or cared
  For the mob he had tried to humbug;
" What matter who felt—the blows may be dealt—
  While here I am sitting so snug."
So the candidate laughed a chuckling laugh;
  But, Ten-pounders, mind what we say—
And never give vote for this sneaking gent
  Who bragged, and then ran away.
    Away, away, away,
    Who bragged, and then ran away.

☞ HOW TO SAVE TWO-PENCE A-WEEK.
Purchase the *Puppet-Show*, and look at the illustrations of *Punch* through the shop-windows. You will thus obtain all the wit of both publications, and SAVE TWO-PENCE!

London: Printed for the Proprietors by VIZETELLY BROTHERS and Co. Peterborough Court, 135 Fleet Street; and published by JOHN DUNCE, at the *Puppet-Show Office*, 11 Wellington Street North, Strand, where all communications for the EDITOR are to be addressed.

Figure 2.1   'The Charing-Cross Revolution!', *Puppet-Show*, 18 March 1848, 8. Reproduced with the permission of Senate House Library, University of London, PR [Z-Puppet].

The facts of how Reynolds came to speak at the meeting are as follows: the Trafalgar Square meeting was organized by Charles Cochrane, representative for Paisley at the Chartist convention, to protest about the new income tax.[26] However, Cochrane was informed by the commissioners of the police that he could not hold such a meeting so close to Westminster. This was due to the so-called 'Sidmouth's Gagging Act', passed in 1817 in response to increased rioting after the first French Revolution (1789–99), and more properly entitled 'An Act for more effectually preventing seditious meetings and assemblies'.[27] Hansard, the record of parliamentary debates, records that 'Mr. Cochrane accordingly abstained from attending the meeting himself, and put up placards informing the people that the meeting could not be held, and calling upon them to disperse'.[28] Disperse, of course, was exactly what those present did not do. Reynolds took charge of the meeting and delivered an impromptu speech which denounced the income tax and praised the newly reinstated French Republic. According to a reporter for the *Times*:

> At last 1 o'clock struck, and from the centre of the north terrace a gentleman, who announced himself as Mr. Reynolds, stated that in the absence of Mr. Cochrane he had constituted himself, or been constituted, chairman. He stated that he was an author, and that his works were, no doubt, known to many among his audience. He said much about the glorious French Republic, the tyrannical Louis Philippe, and the great Parisian people, whom he advised not to take the leading articles of aristocratic newspapers, nor the opinions of the west end oligarchy, as the expression of what the English nation thought of them.[29]

By moving from declaring himself to be an author to praising the French Republic, Reynolds connected fiction and politics. He made an implicit claim for fiction as being just as legitimate a medium for the discussion of radical politics as 'newspapers', because he was a fiction writer taking to the political platform. Furthermore, Reynolds's actions declared that printed matter was indelibly linked to the street theatre of political demonstrations; 'his works were, no doubt, known to many in his audience'.[30] His imagined network of readers, he hoped, had produced the real protestors there on the streets before him.

This is made clear by Reynolds on the pages of *Mysteries*. Reynolds's speeches in Trafalgar Square and Wellington Street were delivered when he was five months away from completing the second series. Using the editorial 'we', Reynolds writes his moment of triumph into the text of his story as a footnote, at a point where he has digressed to praise 'the grand work of moral agitation for the People's Rights':

---

[26] Collins, xxxi.

[27] Mace, 139.

[28] '7 March 1848, THE RIOT IN TRAFALGAR SQUARE. HC Deb 07 March 1848 vol 97 cc312-3', *Hansard Online* 97 (1848), accessed 20 May 2011 online via http://hansard.millbanksystems.com.

[29] 'The Open-Air Meeting in Trafalgar-square', 8.

[30] Ibid.

> At the 'monster meeting' in Trafalgar-square, on Monday, March 6th, we were called upon to preside in the absence of Mr. Cochrane. The *London Telegraph* contained the ensuing sketch or outline of the speech which we delivered on that occasion, and which we now transfer to the pages of 'THE MYSTERIES OF LONDON' simply for the purpose of convincing our readers that we are not afraid to proclaim in all possible ways the opinions which we have for years promulgated though the medium of our writings. (*Mysteries Series II*, 2: 202)

Reynolds used the public stage of urban space for a continuation and an articulation of political comment in his printed fiction, in order to come face to face with people he hoped were real members of his network of readers and to reach those who were illiterate. If the imagined network of readers became real protestors, then revolution might actually occur. Further on, Reynolds quotes from another *London Telegraph* report of the meeting held later that day at Clerkenwell Green. According to the report, 'Mr Reynolds, at some length, very ably and forcibly dwelt on the evils of class-legislation, and showed, from his writings, that he had ever been the friend of the working-men' (*Mysteries Series II*, 2: 202). In the footnote, Reynolds is keen to show that his opinions given on paper in his fiction and his opinions given orally are the same, and work towards the same goals. This is more than standard newspaper reporting of a political speech; it would be like one of Dickens's speeches to the working-men's institutes turning up in the text of *Bleak House*. Reynolds places this report in his fiction, not in *Reynolds's Miscellany* or in a recognized newspaper (his own newspapers, *Reynolds's Political Instructor* and *Reynolds's Weekly Newspaper*, did not exist until 1849 and 1850, respectively).[31] Indeed, the entire of the chapter in which these insertions appear (CLVII) is dedicated to elaborating on the subject of his Trafalgar Square speech about the superior political will of the 'glorious French'.[32] In these insertions, as in political reporting, the function of political speeches on the printed page of his fiction and the function of political speeches in urban space are elided.[33] But it is as a writer of fiction, not as a political journalist, that Reynolds stakes his claim to political and revolutionary credibility.

Just as Dickens's later reading tours turned fiction into theatre, so Reynolds's public speeches brought him into closer contact with his readership, many of whom may have been illiterate and so would only ever have heard his words read

---

[31]   The generic crossover between fiction and journalism in *Mysteries* has been noted by Humpherys, Maxwell, and in Helen M. Hauser's 'Miscellaneous Blood: GWM Reynolds, Dickens, and the Anatomical Moment' (PhD diss., University of California Santa Cruz, 2008). However, Reynolds was not paying much attention to his *Miscellany* in Spring of 1848; see King, '*Reynolds's Miscellany*', 65.

[32]   I am grateful to Louis James for this point.

[33]   Shirley makes a similar point about the cross-fertilization of Reynolds's journalism and Reynolds's fiction. But here I am interested specifically in Reynolds's oral speeches given in London, not his journalism. See Shirley, 'G.W.M. Reynolds, *Reynolds's Newspaper* and Popular Politics', 85–6.

aloud.[34] Communal reading and interpretation of Reynolds's *Mysteries* by the poor is described by Henry Mayhew in *London Labour and the London Poor*, which was of course first published as a periodical a few doors away from Reynolds's own office. As many scholars of Reynolds have noted, Mayhew records how 'the costermongers are very fond of hearing anyone read aloud to them, and listen very attentively. [...] Of all London, Reynolds is the most popular man among them. They stuck to him in Trafalgar-square and would again'.[35] The costermongers use their communal acts of interpretation to define themselves against the wealthy:

> 'Here all my audience', said the man to me, 'broke out with – "Aye, that's the way the harristocrats hooks it. There's nothing o' that sort among us; the rich has all the barrikin to themselves"'. "Yes, that's the b-way the taxes goes in", shouted a woman.' (*London Labour*, 1: 25)

His illiterate listeners interject their political opinions into the narrative, as listeners at a rally might shout 'hear, hear!' Politics, spectacle, and fiction, for the costermongers as well as for Reynolds, are intertwined. As Michael H. Shirley puts it, 'Reynolds's reliance on melodrama [...] proved to be in harmony with the assumptions of his readers'.[36] Reynolds's fiction reinforces what they feel they know about the organization of the city and of the country. Real readers (or listeners) can become real protestors, as Reynolds's neighbour Mayhew reports.

The same elision occurred during Reynolds's Trafalgar Square speech, where radical speechmaking appeared as a spectacle which brought the printed page to life, and continued the work done by radical storytelling. Reynolds's speech presented radical politics as a crowd-pleasing show, given as it was in a square near the heart of the West End theatre district. Someone from the crowd asked Reynolds if he would kill the French king, Louis Philippe, if he could. Reynolds replied 'that he certainly would not', but would 'put him in Woombles Menagerie and exhibit him at sixpence per head', as just another public spectacle on show in London.[37] However, this is a spectacle in which the audience, too, are the actors: Reynolds urged the crowd to 'shew the police and the Government-spies in plain clothes' that 'though met to demand their rights, they knew how to conduct

---

[34] See Helen Small on Dickens's Public Readings in the late 1850s and '60s: she likens them to Chartist rallies of earlier decades ('A Pulse of 124: Charles Dickens and a Pathology of the Mid-Victorian Reading Public', in *The Practice and Representation of Reading in England*, ed. James Raven, Helen Small, and Naomi Tadmor [Cambridge: Cambridge University Press, 1996], 284).

[35] Henry Mayhew, *London Labour and the London Poor*, 3 vols (London: Office of London Labour and the London Poor, 1851–52), 1: 25. Subsequent references to this work will be cited parenthetically in text. Also see, for instance, Carver, 151.

[36] Shirley, 'G.W.M. Reynolds, *Reynolds's Newspaper* and Popular Politics', 86. See also Anne Humpherys, 'Popular Narrative and Political Discourse in Reynolds's Weekly Newspaper', in *Investigating Victorian Journalism*, ed. Laurel Brake, Aled Jones, and Lionel Madden (London: Macmillan, 1990), 33–47.

[37] Mace, 137.

themselves' (*Mysteries Series II*, 2: 202). Reynolds became a celebrity for radicals across the country after 1848; notices in *Reynolds's Political Instructor* advertised his presence at meetings up and down the country.[38] The Chartist meetings at which Reynolds was frequently a star speaker turned radical politics into popular spectacle, and brought to vibrant life not only the leader articles which he wrote after 1848 for *Reynolds's Political Instructor* and *Reynolds's Weekly Newspaper*, but also his frequent outbursts within the text of *Mysteries*.[39]

Reynolds's second appearance, from his balcony in Wellington Street, also used urban space as a continuation of radical fiction. Once Reynolds had spoken in Trafalgar Square, he 'introduced several other speakers to the crowd, by whom resolutions condemnatory of the tax were successfully proposed'.[40] Three cheers were given to the French uprising, and somewhere between two and three o'clock in the afternoon, Reynolds headed back to Wellington Street. The cheap press described the scene jubilantly: if these reports are to be believed, it must have been as if his radical outburst in *Mysteries* had suddenly leapt off the page.[41] *Lloyd's Weekly London Newspaper*, a two-penny publication owned by Edward Lloyd and published from Salisbury Square, just off Fleet Street, reported that:

> Mr Reynolds then quitted his position on the terrace, and having had a vote of thanks tendered to him, retired, accompanied by several hundreds of persons, who followed, cheering him along the Strand.[42]

The Chartist *Northern Star*, edited by Reynolds's close associate Julian Harney, reported:

> The meeting gave thundering cheers for the brave Parisians, and the People's Charter, and the meeting was peaceably dissolved, on which Mr Reynolds was cheered up the Strand to his residence in Wellington-street, where he addressed the people from the balcony of his house.[43]

The *Lancaster Gazette* and the Dublin *Freeman's Journal* both copied a report from the *Sun*:

---

[38]   For one such notice, see 'Political Meetings in the Country', *RPI*, 23 March 1850, 160. For a discussion of the importance and popularity of such tours, see Haywood, 'George W.M. Reynolds and "The Trafalgar Square Revolution"', 43–5.

[39]   For a discussion of Reynolds's role in Chartism after 1848, see Rohan McWilliam, 'The Mysteries of GWM Reynolds: Radicalism and Melodrama in Victorian Britain', in *Living and Learning: Essays in Honour of JFC Harrison*, ed. Malcolm Chase and Ian Dyck (Aldershot: Scolar, 1996), 182–98.

[40]   'Disturbances in Trafalgar Square', *DN*, 8 March 1848, 3.

[41]   Collins remains somewhat sceptical of these accounts [Collins, xxxi].

[42]   'Serious Riots in the Metropolis', *Lloyd's Weekly London Newspaper*, 12 March 1848, 3.

[43]   'The Great Open-Air Meeting in Trafalgar-Square. – Brutality of the Police', *Northern Star*, 11 March 1848, 8.

Mr. Reynolds, who is the author of the 'Mysteries of London', and several other works, then proceeded down the Strand, followed by some two or three hundred persons, whom he exhorted to commit no act of violence, crying out 'Bravo, Reynolds!' They followed him to his residence, in Upper Wellington-street, from the balcony of which he addressed them for some time.[44]

It is Reynolds's status as the author of *Mysteries*, whose 'works were, no doubt, known to many among his audience', which he uses to invest himself with extra authority to speak to the crowds.[45] He recognizes that he is only known through his 'works', but this still allows him to connect the imagined network of his readers with the real crowds in front of him.

The relationship between real crowds in the streets listening to a speech and his imagined network of readers of his printed fiction also worked in the other direction for Reynolds: rather than speechmaking working simply as a continuation of ideas expressed in *Mysteries*, the pages of *Mysteries* were used to expand upon his speech. When he included the account of his afternoon in the spotlight as a footnote in the second series of *Mysteries*, he also repeated and expanded upon his speeches within the narrative itself. Reynolds declares:

> We cannot do otherwise, on reaching this point in our narrative, than avail ourselves of so fitting an opportunity to notice the grand and glorious struggle that has so lately taken place in the capital of France. (*Mysteries Series II*, 2: 199)

Through what becomes a lengthy digression in the narrative, the printed page is used to relive and to continue his successes within urban space. Reynolds's digression within the body of the narrative mirrors the report of his Trafalgar Square speech, as quoted by him in the footnote. Both digression and report emphasize the need for 'moral force', not violence; in the digression he decries the 'pitiable wages' of the workers, while in the report he is said to have called for 'fair wages'; in both there is criticism for the establishment newspapers, and for the sympathy shown towards Louis Philippe by Queen Victoria, as well as praise for the 'glorious' French (*Mysteries Series II*, 2: 200; 202).

'Control of position is everything in print', says Walter Ong; Reynolds explicitly paralleled the disruptive productions of the radical print community and its overlapping networks with the disruption of urban space by protestors on 6 March 1848.[46] Reynolds's Trafalgar Square speech, according to the *Times* report, staked a claim to space in London. According to Reynolds, the 'west end oligarchy' do not share the opinions of 'the English nation'. Politics is aligned with urban space: the 'west end' of London here evokes Parliament, Whitehall, and the gentlemen's clubs around Pall Mall. This is provocative, given that

---

[44]   'Abolition of the Income Tax [...] (from the Sun of Monday)', *Freeman's Journal*, 11 March 1848, 3. Notice the confusion over Reynolds's address.

[45]   'The Open-Air Meeting in Trafalgar-square', 8.

[46]   Walter J. Ong, *Orality and Literacy: The Technologizing of the Word* (London: Methuen, 1982), 121.

Trafalgar Square was positioned as a kind of gateway to all of these locations (see Figure 1.8).[47] Trafalgar Square was begun as recently as 1840, as part of urban improvement works, to provide a more dignified frontage to the new National Gallery as well as a memorial to England's naval victory and a reminder of the might of the burgeoning British Empire.[48] The *Illustrated London News* reported on the completion of Nelson's Column, and presented it as a patriotic reminder to all residents and visitors.[49] Trafalgar Square, therefore, was a particularly provocative stage for Reynolds's speech of praise for the French nation, given that he was standing under the shadow of a memorial to Britain's naval victory over the French at Trafalgar and was about to speak again from the balcony in a street named after Wellington, who defeated the French army at Waterloo.

The *Daily News* published a letter in its report which mockingly grumbled:

> Mr Reynolds, the new speaker of the occasion, had been escorted in triumph to his hotel, or his 'two pair back' in Wellington-Street, as the case may be. [...] There are always in London, as in Paris, enough of dissolute and idle persons [...] to be found to form such an assemblage.[50]

Dickens strikes a more sympathetic note in *Barnaby Rudge*, when he describes the rioting crowd as 'sprinkled doubtless here and there with honest zealots, but composed for the most part of the scum and refuse of London, whose growth was fostered by bad criminal laws, bad prison regulations, and the worst conceivable police'.[51] Reynolds the republican believed that political revolution could turn even the dishonest poor into happy and productive citizens (*Mysteries Series II*, 2: 375). The real protestors who gathered below Reynolds's balcony offered him the possibility that the crowd either contained members of his real network of readers, or that they would expand his readership by becoming so. If Reynolds's imagined network of readers could all become real protestors, then not only would Reynolds have a growing market for his fiction, but he would have succeeded in bringing radical fiction to life.

---

[47]   The 1848 demonstrations set a precedent for several protests throughout the nineteenth and twentieth centuries. When the student demonstrators of 2010 set off from outside King's College London, down the Strand to Trafalgar Square, they were following in this tradition.

[48]   Mace, 45. Work on clearing the site started as early as 1829. The square transformed the Charing Cross end of the Strand; several well-known buildings of Dickens's youth were knocked down. Nelson's column was finally erected in November 1843, although the bas-reliefs around the bottom of the column were only finished in 1854, and the famous lions were finally put in place in 1867. However, from the end of 1843, Trafalgar Square was in a form that would be recognizable to us now [Mace, 69; 90; 107–8. See also Michael Paterson, *Voices from Dickens's London*, 2nd edn (Cincinnati, OH: David & Charles, 2007), 28–9].

[49]   'The Nelson Column', *ILN*, 18 November 1843, 331.

[50]   'Disturbances in Trafalgar Square', *DN*, 8 March 1848, 3.

[51]   Charles Dickens, *Barnaby Rudge*, ed. John Bowen (London: Penguin, 2003; 1st publ. 1841), 407.

The Radical Press around Wellington Street

Reynolds's expectation of face-to-face contact with readers mirrors the face-to-face networks of radical writers and editors in the Strand neighbourhood. Reynolds's move to Wellington Street in 1847 put him at the heart of radical print production in London, and the association of the area with radicalism was something that underpinned his speeches in Trafalgar Square and in Wellington Street. The networks of radical print production were riven with rivalries and disagreements; they had different agendas, interests, and ideologies. Men like Dickens, Jerrold, and Mayhew, although they were Reynolds's neighbours on Wellington Street, would never have rallied to Reynolds's cry for revolution, despite their well-documented reformist beliefs. As Sally Ledger has shown, the term 'radical' was not a readily defined one in this period. She quotes Altick's explanation:

> There was no such thing as a uniform radicalism in the sense of all dissidents agreeing on an agenda of sweeping change. The radicalism of the 1840s was not coherently ideological or programmatic but was determined by the interests of the individual persons and groups. John Stuart Mill the apostate Benthamite, Feargus O'Connor the fiery Chartist leader, Joseph Hume the parliamentary reformer, Daniel O'Connell the Irish populist, Charles Dickens, and even Thomas Carlyle [...] were all 'radicals' in one way or another.[52]

However, Reynolds stood up to protest against the government and to praise the French Revolution in a part of London heavily associated with the publication of political and social protest. Those engaged with anti-establishment thought of all kinds clustered around the streets near Wellington Street, and by 1848 the neighbourhood had experienced a strong history of radicalism. Although Trafalgar Square was an extremely new urban space, it was fitting that London's first 1848 riot took place there and spread down the Strand. The form of the streets around the Strand, including Wellington Street, gave geographical coherence to the networks of print radicalism.

The protest on the streets paralleled the protests published in print, as print culture reaffirmed actual relationships between members of the radical network. The publications of the radical networks in and around the three sections of Wellington Street disrupted their readers' views of London with their exposure of the conditions endured by those 'of whom the public had less knowledge than of the most distant tribes of the earth', as Mayhew puts it (*London Labour*, 1: iii). Lynda Nead's study of the visual iconography of Holywell Street has shown how it 'stood as a symbol of old London', disrupting order and the march of modernity.[53] However, it was not just Holywell Street that was a potential threat to order; the

---

[52]   Richard D. Altick, quoted in Sally Ledger, *Dickens and the Popular Radical Imagination* (Cambridge: Cambridge University Press, 2007), 145.

[53]   Lynda Nead, *Victorian Babylon: People, Streets and Images in Nineteenth-Century London* (New Haven, CT: Yale University Press, 2000), 179.

street was one small part of the radical network of the Strand neighbourhood. Michel de Certeau argues that to tell stories about urban spaces is a fundamentally democratic activity which disrupts the 'imposed order' of the city. This is important because he sees cities as an 'operational concept' not designed with human freedom in mind.[54] For de Certeau, the 'rational organisation of the city' requires that it 'repress all the physical, mental, and political pollutions that would compromise it'. Despite 'the indeterminable and stubborn resistances offered by traditions', the city seeks to squash these in favour of control and stability. Stories about the city offer an escape from this order and stability, particularly if they are fractured, fragmented, and allude to other tests, like Reynolds's insertions of reports of his speech in *Mysteries*.[55] *Mysteries* is a good example of the kind of fragmented and disruptive narrative, celebrated by de Certeau, which seeks to challenge the political and social status quo. The threat of stability – of a lack of development on and off the page – is exactly what Reynolds fears in *Mysteries*, as the narrator exclaims 'we adjure ye not to remain at rest – […] not to stand still and gaze listlessly, while all the rest of the civilised world is in motion!' (*Mysteries Series II*, 2: 234).

Even though *Mysteries* was begun when Reynolds lived in King Square, Goswell Street, in Clerkenwell, it was completed after Susannah and George had moved to Brydges Street, Covent Garden, and then to Wellington Street.[56] The Strand neighbourhood had long been associated with such disruptive texts. The Trafalgar Square demonstration tapped into the lively and rebellious history of the area, which persisted despite the proximity of the Law Courts, Temple and Chancery, as well as the infamous Bow Street police court and New Bridewell prison. From the 1790s onwards, radicals clustered around the Strand, where what Iain McCalman calls the 'gutter' press busily attacked and satirized 'ruling-class vice and corruption' since the days of the Regency.[57] The radical London Corresponding Society (1792–99) met at the Bell Tavern at 6 Wellington Street North, and then at the Crown and Anchor tavern on Arundel Street, which hosted lectures by men like Coleridge and Daniel O'Connell.[58] A public meeting was

---

[54]   De Certeau, 107; 94.

[55]   De Certeau, 94; 107.

[56]   Collins, xxviii. Interestingly, in the District Surveyor's Returns for 23 December 1850, there is an application to make alterations to 7 Wellington Street North. Reynolds is listed in this as 'The Owner'; in all other planning applications for December, the 'Name of Party giving the Notice' is recorded as 'The Builder'. This suggests that the Reynoldses owned the building by this point, rather than leasing it, which could account for some of their greater financial stability from 1850 onwards. LMA MBO/DS/38A-H (1845–52) 38F (23 December 1850).

[57]   Iain McCalman, *Radical Underworld: Prophets, Revolutionaries, and Pornographers in London, 1795–1840*, 2nd edn (Oxford: Clarendon Press, 1993), 224; Nead, 161–89.

[58]   'The Strand (southern tributaries)', in *Walter Thornbury's Old and New London* 3 (1878), accessed 7 August 2012 online via http://www.british-history.ac.uk/source.aspx?pubid=341.

held there on 15 November 1847 'to explain the principles and objects of the People's International League', a radical organization founded by the exiled Italian revolutionary Giuseppe Mazzini and William James Linton with the aim of influencing Foreign Office policy.[59] The Crown and Anchor was later the site of Jerrold's Whittington Club.[60] The radical traditions of the Strand's eighteenth-century press stretched into the nineteenth century.

Near to Wellington Street is Fetter Lane, which leads north off Fleet Street; this was another enclave of anti-establishment thought. Thomas Evans, a Jacobin and a radical, operated out of Fetter Lane during the 1790s. As Peter Ackroyd puts it, Evans 'laced his revolutionary zeal with strong drink, and financed his activities by selling ballads and pornography'. The Falcon tavern in Fetter Lane was 'under surveillance as a centre for political activity'.[61] During the anti-Catholic Gordon Riots of 1780, fictionalized by Dickens in *Barnaby Rudge*, the distillery on the corner of Fetter Lane and Holborn was burned to the ground. Drawing on contemporary sources for his novel, Dickens described the scene: '[t]he gutters of the street [...] ran with scorching spirit [and many rioters] became themselves the dust and the ashes of the flames they had kindled, and strewed the public streets of London'; the rioters were dispersed in almost atom-like form over the surfaces of the streets along which they rioted.[62] Thomas Paine, author of the *The Rights of Man,* lived at 77 Fetter Lane, and William Cobbett produced his *Political Register* while he was at 183 Fetter Lane.[63]

There were strong continuities between this world and the radicalism and anti-clericism of the 1830s.[64] Indeed, Reynolds's first book, *The Errors of the Christian Religion Exposed, by a Comparison of the Gospels of Matthew and Luke*, was published in 1832 by a follower of Thomas Paine, Richard Carlile, who kept a radical bookshop off Fleet Street.[65] Vic Gatrell gives a lively account of how Carlile had to run his shop:

> In 1822, a Bow Street officer reported that Richard Carlile (or his wife: he was in prison) had invented a system in his little bookshop [...] that would thwart agents provocateurs by ensuring that the book-salesman's identity was concealed and that sales were wordless. The device consisted of 'two apertures in the back partition [of the shop] one for the receipt of money, the other for the transmission of the publication from behind, over which is a round dial with numbers on it, and a movable hand which may be turned so as to point to any number.

[59] Bishopsgate Library Howell Collection Pamphlet Box 46; George P. Landow, 'The People's International League in "Hudson's Statue" (Annotation to Carlyle's "Hudson's Statue")', *Victorian Web*, accessed 2 June 2012 online via http://www.victorianweb.org/authors/carlyle/hudson/people.html.
[60] 'The Strand (southern tributaries)', *Old and New London*.
[61] Peter Ackroyd, *London: The Biography* (London: Vintage, 2001), 235.
[62] Dickens, *Barnaby Rudge*, 571.
[63] Ackroyd, *London*, 235.
[64] McCalman, 219.
[65] Collins, xv–xvi.

These numbers correspond with others affixed to a list of books stuck up on one side of the shop, so any person by perusing this list may learn to what number to affix the head of/ the dial'.[66]

Dick Collins speculates whether Reynolds was ever 'one of those hidden, anonymous counter-assistants in Carlile's shop, or one like it?'; he uses the example of one Thomas Frost, who began by selling pornography in William Dugdale's bookshop and later became a Chartist and a writer.[67]

Richard Carlile did not operate in a vacuum; the group of Trafalgar Square protestors who followed Reynolds down the Strand passed through a hotbed of radical publishing. Early Victorian radical publishers developed a subversive 'underworld' which thrived around Drury Lane, Wych Street, the Strand, and especially Holywell Street, and became notorious for its association with pornography.[68] Reynolds tried to play down Holywell Street's dubious reputation in the first series of *Mysteries*, claiming that such things are now firmly in the eighteenth century and Regency past:

> The unprincipled venders of demoralizing books and pictures have, with few exceptions, migrated into Wych Street or Drury Lane; and even the two or three that pertinaciously cling to their old temples of infamy in Holywell Street, seem to be aware of the incursions of respectability into that once notorious thoroughfare, and cease to outrage decency by the display of vile obscenities in their windows.
>
> The reputation of Holywell Street has now ceased to be a by-word: it is respectable; and, as a mart for the sale of literary wares, threatens to rival Paternoster Row.[69]

A letter to the *Times*, however, in 1849 stridently decries 'Holywell-street and Wych-street, in which are shops the windows of which display books and pictures of the most disgusting and obscene character, and which are alike loathsome to the eye and offensive to the morals of any person of well-regulated mind'.[70]

Reynolds's own connections to the radical and pornographic publishing networks led him to gloss over the realities of Holywell Street, 'the home of the literature of radicalism and of a type of bawdy publishing dedicated to exposing the hypocrisy and immorality of the ruling classes'.[71] It was from Holywell Street and other premises nearby, for example, that by the mid-1830s the 'notorious'

---

[66]   Vic Gatrell, *City of Laughter: Sex and Satire in Eighteenth-Century London* (London: Atlantic Books, 2006), 503–4.

[67]   Collins, xv–xvi.

[68]   McCalman, 218.

[69]   G.W.M Reynolds, *The Mysteries of London, Series I*, 2 vols (London: George Vickers, ? October 1844 – 26 September 1846), 1: 319. Further references are to this edition and appear parenthetically in the text.

[70]   VERECUNDIA, 'To The Editor Of The Times', *Times*, 15 September 1849, 3.

[71]   Nead, 178.

William Dugdale became 'one of the most prolific publishers of pornography in the nineteenth century'.[72] Pornographers from the 1810s to the 1850s 'were part of the larger radical movement and saw themselves as political actors [...]. [They] create[d] a political platform that attacked old sexual and social standards and promoted new possibilities for society through sexuality'. Publishers and booksellers like William Dugdale 'adapted the language of the Enlightenment and the impulses of libertinism to argue for a new sexual order', as political and sexual satire went hand in hand.[73] Unlike McCalman, who argues that Dugdale and his fellows started off as radicals but then shifted to become pornographers, Lisa Sigel argues that 'it is quite possible, however, that the ultra-radicals saw pornography as a political medium. They published it alongside political tracts, and they continued to remain involved in key, working-class political issues'.[74] Dugdale's intended audience was the working class rather than, or as much as, the 'debauched aristocracy', hence the fear by many that the pornography of Holywell Street threatened more than just society's sexual mores, but its political stability as well.[75] Dugdale's next-door neighbour was none other than George Vickers, the first publisher of *Mysteries*.[76] R. Donaldson, 'Publisher and News Agent', sold the short-lived newspaper *Paul Pry: The Reformer of the Age* – which combined salacious illustrations with an anti-establishment slant – from 52 Holywell Street.[77] *The Progressionist*, a weekly penny paper 'devoted to the advocacy of the rights of the toiling Millions [...] and the fearless exposer of robbery, injustice, and wrong' was published by S.Y. Collins at 39 Holywell Street.[78] Yet from here, it was an easy walk to the far more respectable premises of Bradbury and Evans, Dickens's publisher from 1844 to 1859 and the owners of *Punch*, in Bouverie Street, just off Fleet Street.

The influence of this rebellious London print culture, resistant to regulation, continued throughout the 1840s. Physical proximity of offices and addresses in the streets reflected the connections within the printed page. Therefore, despite their rivalries and differences, Dickens, Jerrold, Reynolds, and Mayhew were, to some extent, part of this radical network. Sally Ledger argues that Dickens emerged out of radical Regency culture and operated as 'a cultural bridge' between 'radical' and 'popular' culture. She points out that the review of the *Chimes* in the Chartist newspaper the *Northern Star* shows that its editors assume their readers are familiar with Dickens.[79] Where Dickens chose to base the *Household Words* office,

---

[72]   Ibid.

[73]   Lisa Z. Sigel, *Governing Pleasures: Pornography and Social Change in England, 1815–1914* (New Brunswick, NJ: Rutgers University Press, 2001), 15–16. See also Gatrell, especially 501–4.

[74]   Sigel, 18.

[75]   Sigel, 23. See also Nead on women in Holywell Street, 184.

[76]   Nead, 176.

[77]   'Advertisements and Notices', *RWN*, 12 May 1850, 8.

[78]   'Advertisements and Notices', *RPI*, 23 March 1850, 152.

[79]   Ledger, 2; 150.

however, tells us just as much about his radical roots as anything else. Ledger has shown how Jerrold, like Dickens, was influenced by Regency radical culture and was 'determinedly anti-establishment', while Mayhew's articles for the *Morning Chronicle*, later to become *London Labour*, were extracted approvingly in Reynolds's *Newspaper*.[80] Lewes and Hunt's reformist paper the *Leader* had George Holyoake (an influential freethinker and journalist, whose friends included Lewes and Harriet Martineau and who wrote a biography of Richard Carlile) as a contributor.[81] F.D. Maurice, Professor of English Literature and Modern History from 1840 at King's College London on the Strand, founded the Christian Socialist movement – along with John Ludlow, Charles Kingsley, and Thomas Hughes. Maurice edited their weekly magazine *Politics for the People*, through which he became acquainted with some of the Chartist leaders.[82] Charles Kingsley had himself been a student at King's, entering in January 1837, and stood with Reynolds on the platform at the big Chartist meeting on Kennington Common in April 1848.[83]

Reynolds's own networks also clustered around the Strand. Reynolds's younger brother Edward lived at 14 Southampton Street in 1851, just two minutes west of Wellington Street between Maiden Lane and Tavistock Street, and in 1861 he was at Lancaster Place, just off the Strand below Wellington Street (South).[84] Edward Reynolds definitely wrote for *Reynolds's Weekly Newspaper* (when it became *Reynolds's Newspaper*) as 'Gracchus', and probably wrote the pro-Chartist Gracchus column from the inception of the paper in 1850.[85] In 1850 Reynolds was instrumental in setting up an office for the National Charter Association at 14 Southampton Street, where the secretary was 'in attendance daily from nine to two o'clock (Sundays excepted)'.[86] Regular Chartist meetings, attended by Reynolds, were held at Anderton's Hotel on Fleet Street between 1849 and 1850. Before this, the National Convention met in a hall off Fleet Street, described with Gothic relish by the writer and socialist Flora Tristan in her London diary:

---

[80]   Ibid., 107; see, for example, 'Street Musicians', *RWN*, 9 June 1850, 4.

[81]   Edward Royle, 'Holyoake, George Jacob (1817–1906)', DNB, accessed 11 August 2012 online via http://www.oxforddnb.com; George Jacob Holyoake, The life and character of Richard Carlile (London: James Watson, 1849).

[82]   Christine Kenyon-Jones, *King's College London: In the Service of Society* (London: King's College London, 2004), 48–9.

[83]   F.J.C. Hearnshaw, *The Centenary History of King's College London: 1828–1928* (London: George G. Harrap, 1929), 163.

[84]   1851 census, HO107/1511, f. 85; 1861 census, RG9/178, f. 149. I am grateful to Dick Collins for this information.

[85]   Collins, xxviii; For more on Edward Reynolds's work with his brother, see Shirley, 'G.W.M. Reynolds, *Reynolds's Newspaper* and Popular Politics', 78–9, n. 13.

[86]   'National Charter Association', *RPI*, 23 March 1850, 152; 'To the Public', *RPI*, 10 November 1849, 8; 'To the People of Great Britain and Northern Ireland', *RPI*, 6 April 1850, 176. By 1852, Arnott is the advertising agent for *RWN* (see 'Notice to Advertisers', *RWN*, 25 January 1852, 8).

In truth it was not very impressive: in one of the dirty, narrow little passages in Fleet Street there is a public house of mean appearance; inside the tavern a waiter will ask you if you would like a mug of beer; by the tenor of your reply he will know why you have come, and if you give him the password, he will take you through a back room, across a small courtyard and down a long corridor to the meeting hall.[87]

The *Northern Star*, owned by the Chartist leader Fergus O'Connor, moved to 340 Strand in 1844, and by 1845 it was edited by Julian Harney, an associate of Reynolds.[88]

All of these geographical connections mean that, despite Dickens's condemnation of Reynolds's actions at Trafalgar Square, there are moments when the networks of Dickens and Reynolds overlap.[89] Dickens met Mazzini, greatly admired by Reynolds, in 1846, after a fraudster sent a fake begging letter to Dickens in Mazzini's name. Dickens and Forster subsequently visited Mazzini's school for poor Italians at 5 Greville Street, Holborn (about 15 minutes' walk from Wellington Street), and became involved in championing it.[90] Douglas Jerrold worked with Dickens on the *Daily News* in 1846, but became editor of *Lloyd's Weekly Newspaper* in 1852 'and completed his journey from popular radical journalism to the mass-market newsprint of Edward Lloyd and G.W.M. Reynolds'.[91] The house of John Chapman on the Strand was a focal point for middle-class radicals and Unitarians, with a web of connections to people as diverse as George Eliot (then still Mary Ann Evans), Dickens, Holyoake, Marx, and Mazzini.[92] 'Popular radicalism' was such a loose category that Reynolds and Dickens expressed almost as many similar opinions as conflicting ones, and pursued 'radical' activities within interlinked networks.[93] However, Dickens seems

---

[87]   Flora Tristan, *Flora Tristan's London Journal, 1840: A Survey of London Life in the 1830s*, trans. Dennis Palmer and Giselle Pincett (London, Prior, 1980), 49.

[88]   'Welcome to the Metropolis', *Northern Star*, 23 November 1844, 1.

[89]   In his letter to Macready (see Chapter 1).

[90]   John Forster, *The Life of Charles Dickens*, with 500 portraits, facsimiles, and other illustrations, collected, arranged, and annotated by B.W. Matz, 2 vols (London: Chapman & Hall, 1911; 1st publ. 1872–24), 2: 93. Further references are to this edition and appear parenthetically in the text; Charles Dickens, letter to Mazzini, ? January 1846, in *The Pilgrim Edition of the Letters of Charles Dickens*, ed. Madeline House, Graham Storey, and Kathleen Tillotson (general editors), 12 vols (Oxford: Clarendon Press, 1965–2002), 4: 485 and footnote, 486; Charles Dickens, letter to Mrs Milner Gibson, 28 October 1845, *Pilgrim*, 4: 418–19 and footnote; Charles Dickens, letter to John Forster, ? 1846 – February 1848, *Pilgrim*, 5: 248.

[91]   Slater, *Dickens*, 242; Ledger, 149.

[92]   Rosemary Ashton, *142 Strand: A Radical Address in Victorian London* (London: Chatto & Windus, 2006).

[93]   Michael Diamond agrees that 'the two men could have agreed on many issues', in 'Charles Dickens as Villain and Hero in Reynolds's Newspaper', *Dickensian* 98, no. 457 (Summer 2002): 127.

to have dreaded any political association with his neighbour Reynolds.[94] Dickens became aware of the danger of being 'associated' with Reynolds in 1849, because the unthinkable happened: his name appeared on the list of subscribers to a fund that Dickens had organized to help an imprisoned Chartist. Horrified, Dickens separated the statement about the fund from the list of subscribers before he sent it to Burdett-Coutts, declaring that 'if anything could deprive this unfortunate young man [the Chartist] of his liberty ticket, I am pretty confident that it would be the knowledge on the part of the Government at home that he had such a champion'.[95] Physical proximity brought about overlaps that could threaten, as well as enable, a writer's career and reputation.

Even Reynolds's own Chartist network was to become a very unstable one, after the 1848 Chartist protests failed to secure the adoption of the People's Charter by Parliament. Margot Finn's question – how do you reinvigorate the Chartist cause after the perceived failures of 1848? – was a pertinent one for Reynolds the Chartist speechmaker.[96] His short-lived periodical *Reynolds's Political Instructor* expresses the frustrations of those involved in this very task; the ninth issue contains an open letter from 'The Council of the National Reform League to the People of Great Britain and Ireland', which pleads for those in favour of Chartism and social reform to unite.[97] For all that Reynolds declares that 'there is no division in the Chartist ranks', the pages of his *Instructor* and his *Newspaper*, with their proliferation of advertisements for multiple disparate radical organizations, reveal otherwise.[98] Ernest Jones successfully sued Reynolds for libel in 1859; Thomas Clark – who had been on the Provisional Committee of the National Charter Association with Reynolds, but then joined the rival National Reform Association as Chartism fell into disunity after the 'failure' of 1848 – made a very public attack on Reynolds's character, reputation, and politics in an open letter that he published himself. Reynolds denounced the National Reform Association as a 'Scandalous Attempt to Betray the Chartist Cause'; Clark hit back by describing Reynolds as 'a person of the most infamous practices […] and one whose enmity it is a compliment to have earned'.[99] By 1852, Reynolds was no longer on the Chartist executive, although his *Newspaper* continued as an important radical organ.[100]

What did unite the radical writers and editors based in the Strand neighbourhood, however, were the strong social contrasts evident in an area so close to the rookeries

---

94   See Chapter 1.

95   Charles Dickens, letter to W.C. Macready, 30 August 1849, *Pilgrim*, 5: 604.

96   Margot C. Finn, *After Chartism: Class and Nation in English Radical Politics, 1848–1874* (Cambridge: Cambridge University Press, 1993).

97   'The Council of the National Reform League to the People of Great Britain and Ireland', *RPI*, 5 January 1850, 68.

98   George W.M. Reynolds, 'To Sir Joshua Walmsley, MP.', *RWN*, 23 June 1850, 1.

99   G.W.M. Reynolds, 'The Council of the National Parliamentary and Financial Reform Association: Scandalous Attempt to Betray the Chartist Cause', *RPI*, 2 June 1850, 1; Clark, *Letter*, 3.

100   Collins, xxxviii.

of St. Giles, yet also accessible from St. James's.[101] These contrasts between rich and poor would have been visible to Reynolds and the protestors as they made their way to Wellington Street. The inescapable social contrasts of the area link to the trope in *Mysteries* of comparing the lives of rich and poor, and were also exploited by Dickens in *Bleak House* (which, as I noted in the Introduction, is a work often compared with the earlier *Mysteries*). In the opening of *Mysteries*, Reynolds sets up the image of London as 'the city of fearful contrasts':

> even the very pavement groans beneath the weight of grief which the poor are doomed to drag over the rough places of this city of sad contrasts.
>
> For in this city the daughter of the peer is nursed in enjoyments, and passes through an uninterrupted avenue of felicity from the cradle to the tomb; while the daughter of poverty opens her eyes at her birth upon destitution in all its most appalling shapes, and at length sells her virtue for a loaf of bread.
>
> There are but two words known in the moral alphabet of this great city; for all virtues are summed up in the one, and all vices in the other: and those words are
>
> WEALTH. | POVERTY.
>
> Crime is abundant in this city [...]. Crimes borrow their comparative shade of enormity from the people who perpetrate them: thus is it that the wealthy may commit all social offences with impunity; while the poor are cast into dungeons and coerced with chains, for only following at a humble distance in the pathway of their lordly precedents. ('Prologue', *Mysteries Series I*, 1: 2)

Anne Humpherys argues that there is no centre to Reynolds's London, and, although the Prologue suggests that the royal Palace, 'one delicious spot', provides a focal point to the city, this idea soon collapses.[102] Reynolds represents a city divided upon itself, and one where the fault lines are rich versus poor, feast versus famine, and virtue versus crime, in a version of Disraeli's 'Two Nations' image. In *Bleak House*, Dickens sets George's shooting gallery and Nemo's burial ground in the nearby vicinity of Wellington Street. Local conditions made it a particularly appropriate site for debating social change.

These local conditions were of great social divides. In May 1850, another piece of local news found its way onto the pages of the *Morning Post*:

> A portion of the valuable library of M. Guizot is to be submitted for sale, by Messrs. Leigh Sotheby, at the end of the ensuing week. The portion comprises some of the most sumptuous and expensive works ever issued from the French press.[103]

---

[101] This contrast is the driving force behind Jerrold's *The History of St. Giles and St. James*, where the names of these urban areas are turned into the names for the poor hero and the wealthy hero.

[102] Anne Humpherys, 'The Geometry of the Modern City: G.W.M. Reynolds and The Mysteries of London', *Browning Institute Studies* 11, no. 13 (1983): 76.

[103] 'Advertisements and Notices', *Morning Post*, 16 May 1850, 7.

Sotheby's book auctioneering business moved to 3 Wellington Street (South) in 1818, where they auctioned off the libraries of the wealthy: in 1849 they sold prints and books belonging to the Duke of Buckingham.[104] On the opposite side of the social scale, however, this was also an area full of people who scratched a living on the poverty line. This is shown by the fact that the neighbourhood inspired philanthropy. Number 11 Wellington Street (South) was briefly the home of John Simon, health and slum improvement campaigner, who was appointed demonstrator of anatomy at King's College London in 1838, was Medical Officer of Health for the City of London at just 32, and became 'the most famous medical man of the age'.[105] Exeter Hall on the Strand was the famous meeting place for several philanthropic societies, such as the Anti-Corn Law League and the London City Mission.[106] However, the Health Officer's report on the sanitary conditions of the Strand District decried the fact that in a district which was the seventh wealthiest in London, 'close-packing and overcrowding' created one of the highest child mortality rates in the entire metropolis:

> Nuisances arising from the various branches of industry, [...] the dust and refuse heaps of District Scavengers, the slaughtering of sheep and calves in the back-yards, [...] and the keeping of cows in the basements under private dwelling-houses – [...] notwithstanding the Nuisances' Removal Act and new Law for Licensing Slaughter-houses, continue to exist in the most crowded parts of this District.[107]

Several streets still had open cesspools instead of sewers.[108] In 1848, Douglas Jerrold's landlord put in a drainage application on behalf of Jerrold for 'leave, at the expense of the said Douglas Jerrold to flap the drain of No. 17 Wellington Street, Strand', presumably because the smell from the drain was offending Jerrold's nose.[109] In 1845, Mr Henry G. Bohm of 4 and 5 York Street complained of a cesspool on the adjoining premises; the District Surveyor found the pool was

---

[104]   G.D. Hobson, 'Appendix A: Some of the Principal Sales held at Sotheby's', in *Notes on the History of Sotheby's* (London: Sotheby, Wilkinson & Hodge, 1917), 23.

[105]   *Kelly's London Post Office Directory* (London: W. Kelly, 1843–53), WCA microfilm collection, London Directories/1843–45 (1844), 514; Christopher Hamlin, 'Simon, Sir John (1816–1904)', *DNB*, accessed 11 August 2012 online via http://www.oxforddnb.com; Jerry White, *London in the 19th Century: 'A Human Awful Wonder of God'* (London: Jonathan Cape, 2007), 459.

[106]   *Cruchley's Picture of London* (1851), 194–5; 'The thirteenth report of the London City Mission, as read at the annual meetings, held at Exeter Hall, Strand, and at Crosby Hall, Bishopsgate Street, on Thursday, May the 4th, 1848' (1848), Bishopsgate Library London Collection Pamphlet Box 27.

[107]   Conway Evans, *Reports Relating to the Sanitary Condition of the Strand District, London* (London: John Churchill, 1858), 19. British Library MIC.A.6906. (17.).

[108]   Ibid., 22.

[109]   LMA Metropolitan Commission of Sewers, Drainage Applications, MCS/305, vol. 1, 'Westminster 1847–1855' (21 January 1848), application no. 4.

'oozing through the Party wall and the smell offensive to the contiguous houses', but his superiors 'considered that they had no jurisdiction in the matter'.[110] Max Schlesinger comments upon how the poor men of Drury Lane try to escape 'the smell of the sewers that infect his dwelling' by spending Sunday afternoons in the gin palace.[111] Even as late as 1857, the date of the Health Officer's report, the Strand area was resistant to the march of modernity.

These were the conditions seen and smelt by the protestors as they followed Reynolds up the Strand. It was not just the sewage and livestock that made afternoons in the streets around Wellington Street a pungent experience. North of Wellington Street, Long Acre was well known for its coach manufactures and overlooked by the smoking chimneys of several breweries and foundaries. Schlesinger described how

> hundreds of high chimney-towers have belched forth their volumes of thick black smoke, and that smoke obscures the horizon with long streaks of black smut, [...] as the millions of chimneys on the house-tops contribute their quota, until a dusky atmosphere is formed, which intercepts the rays of the sun. Such is London by day.[112]

By 1853, number 13 Upper Wellington Street was the office for the Metropolitan and Stock Brewery Company, and the manager, William Stevens, kept samples of their beer ready for any who called in to the office.[113] Bielefeld's *papier mâché* works at 15 Wellington Street North (subsequently removed to a larger works at Staines) contributed to the noise and the smells of industry. The processes used to create Bielefeld's intricate designs were noisy and laborious:

> The paper and ingredients are placed in a mixer, and thoroughly well churned up, and afterwards rolled out into sheets, which are placed in metal dies and pressed [...]; the ornaments are then dried in a hot room, and afterwards trimmed [...]. The mixing, rolling, wood-cutting, and other machinery are driven by steam-power; the drawing and modelling requiring a high degree of skilled labour, are done on the premises.[114]

Bielefeld was not popular with his neighbours; locals complained that 'as well as tainting the neighbourhood with its smoke, the factory was an insufferable nuisance by reason of the "hordes of vagabond boys" employed there'.[115] As the protestors

---

[110]   LMA MBO/DS/38A-H (1845-52) 38A (9 January 1845).
[111]   Schlesinger, 268.
[112]   Ibid., 72.
[113]   *Kelly's POD* (1853), 553.
[114]   G. Lindsey, 'Papier Mâché', in *British Manufacturing Industries*, ed. G. Phillips Bevan (London: Edward Stanford, 1876), 179–80. This description is of the new works at Staines, but when done at Wellington Street the processes must have been similar.
[115]   'Southampton Street and Tavistock Street Area: Wellington Street', *Survey of London*, accessed 22 June 2010 online via http://www.british-history.ac.uk/report.aspx?compid=46125.

flooded the streets around Trafalgar Square, and the editors of Wellington Street laboured in their offices, manual and machine labour continued on the same street. No wonder Dickens described himself as 'putting on steam' when his work was going well (*Life*, 2: 37).

The other source of pungent smells that the protestors would have been aware of was the River Thames, as it flowed beneath Waterloo Bridge at the bottom of Wellington Street (South), parallel to the Strand. Even before the 'Great Stink' of 1858, when the noxious smell of the raw sewage dumped in the river was at its height, the Thames in the mid-nineteenth century was notorious as a polluted space. The waste from human sewage and from the many industries clustered along the riverbank turned a major source of drinking water into a death-trap. As early as 1849, the physician John Snow argued that cholera spread through London's slums from contaminated drinking water.[116] As Angus B. Reach laconically observed in his 1848 book about the Thames, the problem with 'the sewers of modern days' was that 'their influence upon the fish is decidedly of a prejudicial character'.[117] The polluted river became associated with social and moral pollution; Michelle Allen uses the example of Martha in *David Copperfield* to point out that often in Victorian iconography, 'when a sexually suspect woman makes her figurative fall, she comes to a halt quite literally on the banks of the river'.[118] However, the lively and industrial character of the Thames was also celebrated as a kind of urban picturesque.[119] Angus B. Reach asks his readers to imagine

> mud banks, dead cats, dead dogs, slimy hurdles, coal barges, grimy wharfs, common sewers, police-galleys, [...] waterside public-houses, penny steam-boats, mudlarks, [...] foreigners in funny hats, [...] tiers of shipping, lines of old tumble-down houses, rigging, chimneys, wharfs, bridges, boats, and everywhere muddy waters and restless currents – all moving – all commingling – and over all a canopy of ever-rolling smoke.[120]

The Thames here is the very antithesis of the stultifying stability feared by de Certeau; Reach turns a familiar London sight into an exotic world. The smell, however, from all this mud and smoke and slime, would have wafted off the river as Reynolds and his followers strode down the Strand (Figure 2.2).

Despite the relative prosperity of the Strand area, then, many of its inhabitants lived in unpleasant conditions and in desperate poverty. A report of a fire in 1846

---

[116]   Stephen Halliday, *The Great Stink of London: Sir Joseph Bazalgette and the Cleansing of the Victorian Capital* (Stroud: Sutton Publishing, 1999), 61.

[117]   Angus B. Reach, *London on the Thames: Or, Life Above and Below Bridge* (London: Vizetelly Brothers, 1848), 7.

[118]   Michelle Allen, *Cleansing the City: Sanitary Geographies in Victorian London* (Athens, OH: Ohio University Press, 2008), 63.

[119]   Ibid., 72–3.

[120]   Reach, 13–14.

Figure 2.2   Wellington Street from the Thames. From *Grand Panorama of London From the Thames*, Charles Evans (London: 6 Wellington Street [south] for the Vizetelly Brothers, 1849; first published in black and white, 1845). Reproduced by permission of Motco Enterprises Limited.

at the Castle public house, near the Adelphi Theatre on the Strand, records that 'the scene witnessed on this occasion defies all description from the number of poor families driven from their homes, who lost every portion of their humble property'.[121] Many poor families, such as Mayhew's costermongers, lived in close-packed houses in the courts behind the streets, like the one shown in Figure 2.3. Mayhew records how the 'the costermongers usually reside in the courts and alleys in the neighbourhood of the different street-markets' and includes Drury Lane, two streets east of Wellington Street, as one such 'coster district' (*London Labour*, 1: 47). Even the family he describes as 'a fair type of the thriving costermonger' lives in one room. One day he visits a 'struggling' costermonger, who

> lived with his family in a front kitchen and as there were [...] five persons and only one bed, I was somewhat puzzled to know where they could *all* sleep. The barrow standing on the railings over the window, half shut out the light, and when anyone passed there was a momentary shadow thrown over the room, and a loud rattling of the iron gratings above that completely prevented all conversation. When I entered, the mother-in-law was reading aloud one of the threepenny-papers to her son. (*London Labour*, 1: 47)

This scene is reminiscent of the costermongers listening to Reynolds's tales read aloud. Even worse off than the struggling costermongers were the vagrants who colonized the Strand and Charing Cross in large numbers and would have been

---

121   'Fire in the Strand – Narrow Escape of the Adelphi Theatre', *Morning Post*, 12 January 1846, 7.

Figure 2.3   *Golden Buildings, Strand, 1831.* City of Westminster Archives
Centre Box G133 Strand 10–16 (15).

seen by, or even joined, the protestors that afternoon. A saw-seller tells Mayhew that when he used to sleep 'in the dark arches by the Strand' he 'sometimes had twenty or thirty companions there' (*London Labour*, 1: 363).

This area was therefore one dogged by petty crime. St. Giles and Long Acre was notorious for 'cadging houses' (lodging houses that were home to petty criminals and prostitutes).[122] The Bell tavern in Wellington Street North is mentioned twice in the Old Bailey records for 1843, which report the theft of property belonging to the landlord, Robert Pyne.[123] In an area known for printing and publishing, paper theft was a common problem. Paper and even printed matter were valuable commodities. They could be sold on to other printers, or to stationers who served the nearby law courts, or to dealers in waste paper. Waste paper then served as easy packaging for other goods; in this way, print circulated between many different people. Mayhew writes:

> The sweet-stuff maker (I have never heard them called confectioners) bought his 'paper' of the stationers, or at the old book-shops. Sometimes, he said, he got works in this way in sheets which had never been cut (some he feared were stolen), and which he retained to read at his short intervals of leisure, and then used to wrap his goods in. In this way he had read through two Histories of England! (*London Labour*, 1: 204)[124]

Old Bailey records reveal the theft of printed paper in 1850 from George Stiff, publisher of the *London Journal* (which was edited by Reynolds until 1846) at 334 Strand, and the theft of actual numbers of the *London Journal* the year before. Numbers of *Lloyds's Penny Atlas* were stolen from Lloyd's premises in 1843, while in 1850 paper worth 26 shillings was stolen from the *Standard of Freedom* office at 319 Strand.[125] Fortunatas Crisp, proprietor of the *New Farmers's Journal*, who (as noted in Chapter 1) lived and worked at 7 Wellington Street North before Reynolds moved in, had goods stolen from his premises in 1844, including a ruler and three printer's composing sticks.[126]

---

[122] Anonymous, *Sinks of London Laid Open: A Pocket Companion for the Uninitiated. To which is added a Modern Flash Dictionary. Embellished with Humorous Illustrations by George Cruikshank* (London: J. Duncombe, 1848).

[123] 'January 1843, trial of WILLIAM SCOTT (t18430102-529)', *OBPO*, accessed 4 February 2011 online via http://www.oldbaileyonline.org; 'August 1843, trial of BENJAMIN HENMAN (t18430821-2446)', *OBPO*, accessed 4 February 2011 online via http://www.oldbaileyonline.org.

[124] For more on the sale of waste paper, see *London Labour*, 1: 190.

[125] 'June 1850, trial of WILLIAM GROVES (t18500610-1080)', *OBPO*, accessed 4 February 2011; 'October 1849, trial of FREDERICK ELLIOTT (t18491029-1975)', *OBPO*, accessed 4 February 2011; 'August 1843, trial of JOHN LEWIS (t18430821-2475)', *OBPO*, accessed 4 February 2011; 'December 1850, trial of CHARLES WALTERS, JONATHAN TANT (t18501216-272)', *OBPO*, accessed 4 February 2011 online via http://www.oldbaileyonline.org.

[126] *Kelly's POD* (1844), 514; 'January 1844, trial of JOHN WILLIAMS (t18440101-449)', *OBPO*, accessed 4 February 2011 online via http://www.oldbaileyonline.org.

Urban planners fought back, however. Local government aimed to clear out the dark courts and dingy streets where radical pressmen gathered; Parliament sought to destroy Holywell Street along with its radical and pornographic booksellers; legislation prohibited meetings within a certain radius of Westminster. The dirt, crime, and poverty of the area meant that the streets around the Strand were included in the urban 'improvements' instigated by Parliament and carried out by new civic bodies such as the Metropolitan Commission for Sewers, the District Board of Works, and, from 1855, the Metropolitan Board of Works.[127] Mayhew's interviewees map out a changing picture of the area. One of Mayhew's contributors speaks to a prostitute for the 1861–62 edition of *London Labour*, and she reminisces:

> Years ago Fleet Street and the Strand, and Catherine Street, and all round here was famous for women and houses. Ah! Those were the times. Wish they might come again, but wishing's no use, it ain't.[128]

Even by the 1850s, the crossing sweepers tell Mayhew that 'after the Opera we go to the Haymarket, where all the women are who walk the streets all night', as the prostitutes seem to have been pushed further west.[129] The drive to improve the area resulted in the demolition of Wych Street and Holywell Street to make way for Aldwych, Kingsway, and the widening of the Strand. By mid-century these ancient streets 'stood as a symbol of old London, against the modernising, improving thrust of the new city. [They were] disordered, crumbling, labyrinthine, [and] would have to come down before the march of modern improvements'.[130] The idea of widening the Strand was first proposed to a Select Committee in 1836, and again in 1838, 1847, and 1855, but it was not until the new century that the work was actually carried out.[131]

The drive for an ordered and modern city was already underway by the 1830s in the Strand neighbourhood, earlier than Nead argued.[132] However, the attempt to open up a disreputable area through the construction of Wellington Street North was not entirely successful. In 1840, James Pennethorne, later architect of the Public Records building on Chancery Lane (now part of King's College London), gave evidence before a House of Commons Select Committee. He argued that the policy of only purchasing the ground for the roadway of the northern part of Wellington Street, rather than ground on either side of it as well, had been

---

[127]   For the impact of such improvement works on Wellington Street's buildings and structure, including the removal of Charles Street brothels, see Chapter 1.

[128]   Bracebridge Hemyng, 'Prostitution in London', in *London Labour and the London Poor* (London: Griffin, Bohn, and Company, 1861–62), 4: 240.

[129]   Ibid., 2: 496.

[130]   Nead, 179.

[131]   Ibid., 165; 202. See also Percy J. Edwards, *History of London Street Improvements 1855–1897* (London: London County Council, 1898).

[132]   Nead, 5.

'a complete failure'.[133] According to the *Survey of London*, in December 1834 the Committee of Management for the parish of St. Paul's Covent Garden was dissatisfied with the length of time it took to get the street open. Since 1830, they complained, 'the neighbourhood has been in a most deplorable state, and many of its Inhabitants have been severe sufferers [...]. Instances have but too recently occurred where housekeepers have been driven to the Workhouse and the Gaol. This picture is not overdrawn'. Other projects begun more recently had already been finished 'whilst the short opening from Exeter Street to Charles Street – scarcely 200 yards in length – remains month after month and year after year without much visible progress towards completion'.[134] *The Companion to the Almanac* for 1835 apparently agreed that 'upon the whole, this improvement has not been carried forward with the spirit which has marked other things of the same kind'.[135] Modern 'improvements' did not change things drastically; Bracebridge Hemyng reveals that 'several showily-dressed, if not actually well-attired women, who are to be found walking about the Haymarket, live at St. Giles's and about Drury Lane'.[136] The prostitute interviewed by Hemyng explains that 'I live in Charles Street, Drury Lane, now'; she still uses the old street name, as the cultural memory of the area survives.

Street life, then, continued to resist the desire by urban planners to bring London under some kind of modernized control. The continuing fascination for readers of this aspect of the metropolis no doubt contributed to the popularity of *Mysteries*. There was a strong interest in the perceived vibrancy and exoticism of London street culture.[137] Books, pamphlets, and articles on street-cries, street-slang, thieves' dens, and 'fallen women' abounded, as the popularity of Pierce Egan's *Life in London* (1821) spawned many imitations.[138] *Mysteries* registers the potential for the failure of demonstrations like the one in Trafalgar Square, and ultimately of revolution in London, even before the revolutions of 1848 petered out. Reynolds's real protestors

---

[133]   'Southampton Street and Tavistock Street Area: Wellington Street', *Survey of London*, accessed 22 June 2010 online via http://www.british-history.ac.uk/report.aspx?compid=46125.

[134]   Ibid.

[135]   Ibid.

[136]   Hemyng, *London Labour* (1861–62), 2: 496.

[137]   See Seth Koven, *Slumming: Sexual and Social Politics in Victorian London.* Princeton NJ and Woodstock: Princeton University Press, 2004).

[138]   See, for example, Anon., *Sinks of London Laid Open* (1848) and Luke Limner (pseudonym of John Leighton), *London Cries and Public Edifices: Sketches on the Spot* (London: Grant & Griffith, 1847). For more on Pierce Egan see Louis James, 'From Egan to Reynolds: The shaping of urban "Mysteries" in England and France, 1821–48', *European Journal of English Studies* 14, no. 2 (August 2010): 95–106, and Gregory Dart, '"Flash Style": Pierce Egan and Literary London, 1820–8', *History Workshop Journal* 51 (Spring 2001): 181–205. See also Stephen James Carver, 'The Wrongs and Crimes of the Poor: The Urban Underworld of *The Mysteries of London* in Context', in *G.W.M. Reynolds: Nineteenth-Century Fiction, Politics and the Press*, 147–60.

were an example of what might happen if radical readers joined in with protests by radical networks. However, the clearing out of London's dangerous and filthy slums and dark places would threaten to put an end to melodramatic narratives of its 'mysteries'. If Reynolds's imagined network of readers really did all transform into real protestors, then it would not just be the streets of London that would be disrupted, but Reynolds's livelihood as a radical storyteller would be undermined as well.

'Spoilt by Improvement': *The Mysteries of London*

In *Mysteries*, Reynolds is caught between two conflicting and competing positions. On the one hand, he longs for a sense of unity in his depiction of London, so that he can establish some kind of coherent position from which to move his readers to radical political action. The mysteries of London can be solved, it is suggested, if one only overhears the right conversation, intercepts the right letter, and guesses someone's true identity or crimes. The narrative tries to contain multiplicity, and promises the reader a comprehensive view of the city. Yet at the same time, Reynolds wants the freedom of a lack of a centre, and a multiplicity of plot, to allow for the proliferation of mystery, and therefore the proliferation of narrative. Individual mysteries, like the whereabouts of a lost brother, may be solved, but Reynolds's real subject is London, and out of London's vast population a whole new set of mysteries can quickly emerge – more and more enticing instances of the exotic poverty and dramatic aristocratic vice which Reynolds evokes and which made his tales sell so well.

The text is divided between a desire to eliminate the social inequalities and open up the dark places of London, and a recognition that it is exactly its fanciful depiction of urban realities which provides the narrative with excitement and a sense of movement. Reynolds's London is a city that is resistant to easy resolutions. Its lack of a centre limits London's potential as a revolutionary city in *Mysteries*, a problem for a radical writer, but Reynolds needs London to remain a fragmented city, full of endless narrative possibilities, as this provides the energy for his tale. Fragmentation of the city in this text is both a barrier to the goal of revolution (like the fragmented state of the radical print networks) and a source of essential narrative dynamics. Reynolds the revolutionary cannot be reconciled with Reynolds the storyteller; ultimately, even Reynolds himself may unconsciously not want all of the mysteries of London to be solved.

Briefly, the first series of *Mysteries* focuses on two brothers: Richard and Eugene Markham. Eugene leaves home after a quarrel with his father, and he arranges to meet Richard in 12 years' time to compare their respective fortunes. Eugene vanishes into the city and reinvents himself as George Montague, then George Montague Greenwood, a crooked financier and politician. Richard is wrongfully imprisoned in Newgate, where he falls into the clutches of the villainous criminal the Resurrection Man, who pursues him through the many subplots of the series.

Ultimately, however, virtue wins the day; Richard saves a fictionalized Italian state from a despotic ruler, marries the Princess Isabella, and inherits a fortune. Eugene, however (or Greenwood, as he is referred to long after the reader has worked out his real name), loses his seat in Parliament along with all his ill-gotten gains, and dies repentant on the day he had appointed to reveal himself to Richard. Richard, of course, forgives Eugene wholeheartedly, like the impossibly virtuous hero he is. The second series introduces a new set of characters and an aristocratic mystery centred around a rape and an illegitimate birth, but it also returns to Richard Markham, now the much-loved Grand Duke of Castelcicala. Richard preaches democracy to the impulsive young hero of *Series II*, and goes on to lay down his crown for the benefit of his people. He is finally installed as First Magistrate of the new republic, under only his military title of General Markham. Along the way we have met all manner of Londoners: bankers, policemen, lawyers, soldiers, burglars, artists, undertakers, aristocrats, highwaymen, swindlers, and even Queen Victoria.

Reynolds's *Mysteries*, despite their radical tone and imagined working-class reader, were also read by the middle classes and survive in aristocratic bound volumes.[139] This suggests a cross-class readership for Reynolds, a potentially unified imagined community. Reynolds claims to aim for a unifying vision of London: he described his complete series of *Mysteries* fiction, which included the four series of *The Mysteries of the Court of London* (1848–56), as an 'Encyclopedia of Tales', and the world he describes as an 'omnibus' where 'the old and the young – the virtuous and the wicked – the rich and the poor – are invariably thrown and mixed up together'.[140] On one level, then, Reynolds's sensational plotting promises to create a sense of unity and coherence in London, what Anne Humpherys has called 'its effort at totalisation through multiple tales'.[141] The narrator asks the reader to follow him around the city, in a Mayhew-like role, to solve the mysteries of London. The Prologue to *Series I* of *Mysteries* promises readers that they will learn concrete answers to specific questions:

> Where is that city of fearful contrasts?
> Who are those youths that have thus entered upon paths so opposite the one to the other?
> And to what destinies do those separate roads conduct them? ('Prologue', *Mysteries Series I*, 1: 1)

---

[139] Trefor Thomas, 'Rereading G.W. Reynolds's *The Mysteries of London*', in *Rereading Victorian Fiction*, ed. Alice Jenkins and Juliet John (Basingstoke: Macmillan, 2000), 59.

[140] Anne Humpherys, 'An Introduction to G.W.M. Reynolds's "Encyclopedia of Tales"', in *G.W.M. Reynolds: Nineteenth-Century Fiction, Politics and the Press*, 123; *Mysteries Series I*, 1: 102. Compare Mayhew's preface to *London Labour*, which declares that '[t]he present volume is the first of an intended series, which it is hoped will form, when complete, a cyclopedia of the industry, the want, and the vice of the great Metropolis' (1: iii).

[141] Humpherys, 'An Introduction to G.W.M. Reynolds's "Encyclopedia of Tales"', 126.

These mysteries involving two characters are tied to much broader issues. London's mysteries, it seems, include not just why one female character is dressed as a boy, but extend to the 'true' oppression of the poor by the rich and the divisions, contradictions, and contrasts of the city:

> For we have constituted ourselves the scourge of the oppressor and the champion of the oppressed; we have taken virtue by the hand to raise it, and we have seized upon vice to expose it; we have no fear of those who sit in high places; but we dwell as emphatically upon the failings of the educated and rich, as on the immorality of the ignorant and poor. ('Epilogue', *Mysteries Series I*, 1: 416)

Unified knowledge of the city is fully possible if you trust in the narrator as your guide and follow him into the dens of criminals and the drawing rooms of the nobility. Armed with the narrator's encyclopaedic knowledge and detailed vision, London is to be revealed to us as a unified network where mysteries have a solution. Of course, the contradictions in Reynolds's position are already being revealed: is the reader being asked to have faith in Reynolds the writer, Reynolds the journalist-entrepreneur, or Reynolds the political activist? Reynolds's use of the editorial 'we' seems deliberately to obscure this question.

However, storytelling as a way of unifying the city and controlling its multiplicity is not the straightforward goal of *Mysteries*. By the end of Volume I of the first series, the narrative focus has enlarged beyond the Prologue. Although the main narrative strands are resolved eventually – we know what happens to Eugene – the sense of London as an 'inexhaustible' subject is emphasized:

> we have yet more to write, and [the readers] have more to learn, of the MYSTERIES OF LONDON [...] we have yet events more strange, and episodes more seemingly wild and fanciful, to narrate [...]. [...] For the word 'LONDON' constitutes a theme whose details, whether of good or evil, are inexhaustible: nor knew we, when we took up our pen to enter upon the subject, how vast – how mighty – how comprehensive it might be! ('Epilogue', *Mysteries Series I*, 1: 416)

The series ends, but the narrative continues; Richard reappears in *Series II*, and the depiction of London vice and virtue rolls on. There are too many fragments to the narrative for there ever to be a final resolution. This is, of course, a common conceit in serial fiction, but one which Reynolds exploits particularly well.[142] A reviewer in the *Critic* admitted grudgingly that Reynolds is

> skilled in the art of horrifying; he knows how to tread upon the verge of the prurient, without actually trespassing beyond the boundary defined by the law; [...] and he can frame a plot which will keep the reader in suspense through whole volumes without once losing the thread of his story, and yet continually branching off in pursuit of new personages and new incidents.[143]

---

[142]   See Laurel Brake, *Print in Transition, 1850–1910: Studies in Media and Book History* (Basingstoke: Palgrave, 2001), 31.

[143]   'Fiction', *Critic*, 20 November 1847, 326.

Readers may expect to solve the mysteries of London, but in fact they are continually presented with 'new personages and new incidents' which divert them from their path, send them in disconnected directions, and present them with further mysteries and further narrative.

Reynolds's *Mysteries*, then, needs the city to contain endless melodramatic narratives of the contrasts between the lives of the rich and the lives of the poor to maintain his serial tale. In this London, as I showed earlier in this chapter, economics takes precedence over morals, as the rich are punished less harshly for the same crimes as the poor, and the poor are driven to crime by hunger. In these contrasts lies the main drama of the narrative, which is represented graphically by the diagram:

WEALTH. | POVERTY.

and symbolically by the two brothers, Richard and Eugene, 'two youths' who travel down 'two roads' which lead in two different metaphorical directions ('Prologue', *Mysteries Series I*, 1: 2). These divisions correspond to the geographic division of London along its east-west axis, as the 'WEALTH' of the West End is contrasted with the 'POVERTY' of the East End, and Eugene (or 'Greenwood') heads first to the east side of the city while Richard begins his adventures in the west. The East End, represented by Bethnal Green, Tower Hamlets, and Globe Town, is described time and time again as a 'labyrinth' in which the unwary stranger from the west can be lost, but it is easily traversed by the Resurrection Man, who knows it well. In this diagram, the two halves of the city are very separate.

The contrasts drive the narrative because they link the very rich and the very poor together, as much as they pit them against each other. As Stephen Carver puts it, '[o]nly in the manner of their crimes and punishments do the social classes differ. [...] The contrast between wealth and poverty in this context is not contrast at all'.[144] For Reynolds, London is clearly divided into districts, but each district is, of course, porous. Crime is *not* safely contained in the east; one may find thieves in Grosvenor Square as well as in Tower Hamlets, and swindlers strolling through Mayfair. Eugene/Greenwood is just as dangerous as the Resurrection Man, for all that he uses different methods, wears different clothes, and lives on the other side of town. Thus, London may be fragmented into competing groups and individuals, but Reynolds suggests that this fragmentation might allow for a network of connections, too. London may contain resistance to resolution, but a focused attention on parts may build towards some kind of understanding of the whole. The juxtaposition of different components of the city allows for an awareness of links and connections, particularly between the rich and the poor. The disruption within the text is carefully choreographed. Yet these connections emerge more often through mutual abuse and criminal behaviour, not mutual benevolence or reformist fellow-feeling. The narrative enjoyment of the struggle

---

[144]   Carver, 'The Wrongs and Crimes of the Poor', 154.

Figure 2.4   A Party at Mrs Arlington's. *Mysteries Series I*, 1:9.

for survival in London sits very uneasily against Reynolds's insertions of radical political thought (like his speeches) into the text.

As well as the scenes alternating between rich and poor characters pointed out by Carver, the illustrations in *Mysteries* reveal the tensions in the text.[145] For example, a comparison of the illustrations to Chapters IV and LXIV show interesting similarities between the poses of the figures (Figures 2.4 and 2.5). The first woodcut is of a soirée at the residence of Mrs Arlington, a high-society mistress in Bond Street, to which our hero, Richard, is taken by the corrupt baronet Harborough and Mr Chichester. These men are tricksters and criminals who attempt

---

[145]   Carver, 154. For a useful discussion of the relationship between text and images in Reynolds's fiction, see Brian Maidment, 'The Mysteries of Reading: Text and Illustration in the Fiction of G.W.M. Reynolds', in *G.W.M. Reynolds: Nineteenth-Century Fiction, Politics, and the Press*, 225–46.

Figure 2.5   The Parlour of the 'Dark House'. *Mysteries Series I*, 1: 201.

to fleece the naïve Richard. The second woodcut shows a scene from the inside the 'Dark House', a tavern in Tower Hamlets frequented by the Resurrection Man and his friends. These scenes are, at one level, worlds apart, and separated in the text by many intervening chapters; these are not the neat, side-by-side juxtapositions of images found in Pugin's book *Contrasts*, as London is far too complex for that.[146] However, the woodcuts (which do not appear in the chapters they depict) suggest that the West End and the East End are not so very far apart after all. Both show groups of men seated around a central, standing female figure; the posture of the poor woman in the second illustration echoes Mrs Arlington's pose in the first, and the woman seated on the left of the second woodcut looks remarkably like the society mistress. Leighton and Surridge argue that scholars of serial fiction should '[consider] illustrations and layout as key constituents of plot rather than mere

[146]   A. Pugin, *Contrasts: or, A Parallel Between the Noble Edifices of the Middle Ages, and Corresponding Buildings of the Present Day; shewing The Present Decay of Taste. Accompanied by Appropriate Text*, 2nd edn (London: Charles Dolman, 1841).

bibliographical paratext',[147] and this is certainly as true for *Mysteries* as for the 1860s fiction that they choose as examples. The illustrations for *Mysteries* reinforce the message of the text: that rich and poor are entangled. However, these links arise more though vice and criminality than through understanding and benevolence.

Criminal activity drives the narrative. The porous nature of London's districts means that characters frequently cross the east/west boundary: Richard goes to meet the Resurrection Man at the 'Dark House'; Eugene buys a house in Park Lane, where he receives visits from East End criminals; and the poverty-stricken area of Seven Dials is found right in the West End. The Resurrection Man pops up everywhere, usually when least wanted; even Princess Isabella's pastoral retreat in Richmond, in the southwest, is not safe from him. Reynolds presents London as coherent in an *unexpected* way, or at least as a place that allows for a coming together, a mixing up, and new, uncontrolled combinations. There may be no 'centre' to Reynolds's London, in Anne Humphery's terms, but there are repeated and varying focal points where characters meet and touch, such as Newgate, which reveal how everyone is connected to everyone else. The very fragmented nature of Reynolds's London, paradoxically, reveals how inter-connected Londoners truly are. Perhaps analyzing fragments of information may, after all, provide some kind of resolution to the mystery that is London?

The correct way of 'reading' London, then, has political and moral overtones: Richard Markham triumphs in the end because he observes correctly, and then uses his observations to understand the plight of the suffering, and so enact reforms in his own state. Reynolds, too, is fascinated by local detail: by what clothes people wear, by what food they eat, and by how much money they earn. He uses such details, however, to make the move from the particular to the general, in a kind of social synecdoche. For example, Reynolds obsessively catalogues the earnings of Richard's eventual sister-in-law, Ellen Monroe, when she is a poor 'sempstress', complete with an accumulation of exclamation marks:

> Eighty blossoms for sixpence!
> Sixteen hours' work for sixpence!!
> A farthing and a half per hour!!! (*Mysteries Series I*, 1: 167)

Such details lead Reynolds outwards to other examples of poverty, rather than inwards into Ellen's inner character:

> She tried to avert her thoughts from the contemplation of her own misery [...]; and so she busied herself with thinking of the condition of the other lodgers in the same tenement which she and her father inhabited. She then perceived that there were others in the world as wretched and as badly off as herself. (*Mysteries Series I*, 1: 170)

---

[147] Mary Elizabeth Leighton and Lisa Surridge, 'The Plot Thickens: Toward a Narratological Analysis of Illustrated Serial Fiction in the 1860s', *Victorian Studies* 51, no. 1 (Autumn 2008): 68.

Details of Ellen's situation enable Reynolds to report further 'scenes of [...] destitution and suffering – of powerful struggle and unavailing toil – whose details are so very sad' (*Mysteries Series I*, 1: 167). Similarly, Reynolds includes interpolated first-person narratives from the criminal poor, which focus on their individual sufferings. These melodramatic 'tales of sorrow' set off his more generalized use of social reporting, statistics, and parliamentary reports, and argue that the poor turn to crime to survive, not because they are born wicked. Reynolds's melodrama provides cheap entertainment and sensational thrills, and works to gain the approval of his poorer readers, but also aims to educate the more middle-class reader in a humanitarian way of looking at the city. However, once again Reynolds is caught in his own contradictions. The sensational style of his prose uses poverty for entertainment. Thus, any reader is both thrilled by and distanced from Reynolds's dramatic descriptions of poverty, when what Reynolds declares is really needed is an urgent desire for political action.[148]

Therefore, despite the connections which Reynolds draws between his myriad Londoners, the contradictions of his depiction of London suggest that the divided, sprawling nature of the city is essential for fiction. The cry for unity between rich and poor through humanitarian vision, not criminal plots, comes under pressure if it is only the vitriolic narrator, or the saintly Richard Markham, who sees and champions the desire for change of the 'industrious millions'. Richard is not realistic enough, or the narrative around him is not fairy-tale enough, for him to be a viable saviour for London. If the poor have only Richard Markham to rely on, then they are doomed; he simply could not exist. In this context, revolution is not really an option. Reynolds warns that 'the meanest thing that crawls upon the earth may some day be in a position to avenge'; however, London fails somehow as a revolutionary city (*Mysteries Series I*, 2: 237). Violence does erupt, viciously, into the narrative, but it remains isolated and does not spread. There are crowds in *Mysteries*, but no mobs. News travels like wildfire throughout the city, fanned by the numerous newspapers which characters read and which are shown frequently in the illustrations (see Figures 2.6–2.8), but unified action does not spread so easily. Generally speaking, Reynolds's Londoners fail to look up from their own concerns.

This is partly because of the very divisions, fragmentations, and proliferations which Reynolds brings into his narrative. He controls his massive narrative with a sure hand, but can only do so with frequent use of the idea of 'meanwhile'. There is always something else going on at the same time as the chapter one has just read, just as in the city there is always something else to do, or to go to, instead of a demonstration. This includes, of course, reading *Mysteries*. It is all very well for Reynolds to juxtapose a chapter about a West End banker oppressing the poor with one about what an East End criminal is doing that same night, to draw out

---

[148]   See John Mullan, 'Sympathy and the Production of Society', in *Sentiment and Sociability: The Language of Feeling in the Eighteenth Century* (Oxford: Clarendon Press, 1988), 44.

Figure 2.6   The Advertising Agent. *Mysteries Series II*, 2: 73.

their connections and links. Yet this means that characters are forever separated by that chapter division, like separate encyclopaedia entries. Different events often have to occur at exactly the same time to maintain the complex plot, but while this allows the reader to spot how interconnected Reynolds's Londoners are, it limits revolutionary action. London is too complex a city for all the people to pour onto the streets together: they are far too busy plotting. Perhaps the time and space of London are somehow too chaotic for revolution.

Reynolds's own experience of revolt in London, with the Chartist demonstrations, was largely one of failure. In the second series of *Mysteries*, Richard Markham is first Prince, and then Arch-Duke, Ricardo, head of the Italian state which he liberated from a tyrant prince. The young Mazzini had himself wondered whether

Figure 2.7   Mrs Arlington at breakfast. *Mysteries Series I*, 1: 153.

a united Italy had to be a republic, or if some warrior-prince could lead a free Italy instead? Mazzini even wrote an appeal to Charles Albert of Piedmont to drive out the occupying Austrian forces; Charles Albert's son eventually united the Kingdom of Northern Italy in 1859.[149] Ricardo, however, chooses to step down from his throne in a highly idealized and bloodless revolution towards the end of the series. His noble actions are ecstatically received by the entire court:

---

[149]   David Masson, *Memories of London in the Forties*, arranged for publication and annotated by his daughter Flora Masson (London: Blackwood, 1908), 166–8; 189. Reynolds's Castelcicala is a fictionalized European state, like a prototype of Anthony Hope's Ruritania of the early 1900s – a fantasy land where able young Englishmen turn into warrior-heroes and win the love of princesses.

Figure 2.8   Queen Victoria and Prince Albert at breakfast. *Mysteries Series I*,
              2: 193.

> [T]he whole assembly rose and greeted him with the most joyous shouts – the
> most fervent applause that ever expressed the unfeigned admiration of a generous
> patriotism. The ladies in the galleries absolutely wept in the excitement of their
> feelings: for never – never was seen so sublime a spectacle as this of a mighty
> Prince casting his crown, his sceptre, and his titles at the feet of the Goddess of
> Liberty! (*Mysteries Series II*, 2: 377)

This is what Reynolds must have hoped Chartism would achieve in England;
Richard's capital of Montoni, however, only evokes London by being very different
to it. Like London, Montoni is 'a glorious spectacle' where 'the streets were thronged
with multitudes'. Unlike London, however, inequality is a thing of the past:

Not a mendicant was to be seen; the loathsome rags and hideous emblems of poverty which meet the eye in every thoroughfare and in every corner of London, had ceased to exist in Montoni. The industrious classes were all cheerful in looks and neat in attire; and instead of the emaciated women, and the pale, sickly children observable in such appalling numbers in the British metropolis, the wives of the working-men were all comely and contented, and their offspring ruddy with the hues of vigorous health. Oh! It was a blessed, blessed thing to behold those gay and happy multitudes – rendered thus gay and thus happy by means of good institutions, honest Ministers, and a Parliament chosen by the entire male adult population! Though the streets were thus thronged to excess, and the houses of entertainment were crowded, the utmost order, sobriety, and tranquility prevailed. There were no police visible: because none were required. (*Mysteries Series II*, 2: 375)

The disorder and poverty of London's streets creep in to Reynolds's description of Montoni, filling out his sentences, as if even Montoni cannot exist without its darker 'other'. Life on the streets of Montoni is an orderly experience in a way that daytime on the streets of Reynolds's London is not.

This is a source of frustration for Reynolds – why cannot London be more like Paris or Montoni? But maybe, strangely, it is also a source of relief. One character in *Mysteries* does fight back by posing as a maid in a lady's household to exact revenge, but the sympathies of the narrator move away from her and rest with her tormented employers (*Mysteries Series I*, 2, Chapter CCXIII). The clearing-out of London's darkness and distress, which must necessarily occur if Londoners empty onto the streets and tear down all that oppresses them, may be wonderful for a revolutionary, but disastrous for a writer. As one character puts it, in a foreshadowing of Bracebridge Hemyng's nostalgic prostitute:

Ah! London is a fine place – a very fine place; and I hope I shall never live to see the day when it will be spoilt by improvement! (*Mysteries Series I*, 1: 191)

It is the murk, the dark places, and the mysteries, the poverty, and the inequalities, that are the material for Reynolds's work and which provide it with its energy. Drama, for Reynolds, lies in strong contrasts; the lower middle classes are largely absent from his overview of London. As the Resurrection Man remarks, where would we be without 'St. Giles, Clerkenwell, Bethnal Green, and the Mint?' (*Mysteries Series I*, 1: 191). We certainly would not be reading the tale. Fragmentation and proliferation enable Reynolds to avoid solving all the mysteries of London.

In *Mysteries*, then, for all its rebellious tone, revolution is something that must be displaced onto the 'fairy-land' of a fictionalized Italian state (*Mysteries Series I*, 1: 149). Reynolds seems to be trying to have his cake and eat it: to argue for an end to monarchy while at the same time wanting to keep his glamorous fantasy world to appeal to the romantic among his readers. Reynolds must rely upon the printed page and the imagined network of readers, not urban protestors, to achieve his political aims, as he went on to do with his long-lasting *Newspaper*. The power of readers, however, is limited. At the end of the first series of *Mysteries*, the Epilogue declares that '[i]f, then, the preceding pages be calculated to engender one useful thought – awaken one beneficial sentiment, – the work is not without its value' ('Epilogue', *Mysteries Series I*, 1: 424). Reynolds aims to move the reader emotionally in a way which manifests itself physically, so that 'the tear of sympathy will be drawn from the eye', but this assumes that the eye of every reader works the same way and sees the same thing. Reynolds's use of affect is there to create proliferation: he asks the reader to tell others to '[p]eruse, ere you condemn!', and so widen Reynolds's audience. He uses his perceived power to move the reader to justify the proliferation of his narrative into a second series:

> And if, in addition to considerations of this nature, we may presume that as long as we are enabled to afford entertainment, our labours will be rewarded by the approval of the immense audience to whom we address ourselves, – we may with confidence invite attention to a SECOND SERIES of 'THE MYSTERIES OF LONDON'. (*Mysteries Series I*, 1: 424)

However, for all Reynolds's strong political beliefs, reading registers its failures here: he does not suggest that he will move his audience to political action, only to sympathy, sentiment, and the sensation of having been entertained.

Unity through reading, as a kind of political action, is not a story that can be taken seriously in London, where connections between urban dwellers are so complex and knowledge is so fragmented. In this chapter we have seen that if Reynolds had declared all the mysteries of London to be solved, then his series of tales could not have proliferated, but he may also have been aware that he might never resolve such a tangled knot of contradictions. Reynolds stood up in Trafalgar Square in an attempt to claim a space for 'the people' through unified protest across Europe, and across classes, as if he hoped that the sensational plotting of *Mysteries* could break out of its fictional context and into the real city itself.[150] However, if the imagined network of readers had *all* turned into real, successful protestors on that March afternoon in Trafalgar Square and Wellington Street, then where would the future of the radical pressman as inciter for revolution lie? Perhaps such public appearances as Reynolds made, where the writer became a showman trying to whip up the crowd, punctured the anonymity of the urban mass in potentially uncomfortable ways.

---

[150] The notion of 'the people' is itself problematic, of course, as there was much argument in the period over whether it referred to the whole of society or now meant the working classes.

Chapter 3
Evening: 'The Showman Introduces Himself'

*Examining the links between print culture and the culture of
entertainment and spectacle, and suggesting that the theatre can
be a place where writers and readers meet, with varied results.*

> ... we see in the fervent and fevered context of London that street life feels no
> compunction in taking on the lineaments of dramatic art.
> —Peter Ackroyd, *London: The Biography* (London:
> Vintage, 2001), 279. © Peter Ackroyd 2000.

Close encounters with your public could be a dangerous experience. When Henry
Mayhew's office arrived on Wellington Street in 1851, the Lyceum Theatre, then
as now, stood proudly towards the bottom end of the street near the corner with
the Strand.[1] Famous now for the management of Henry Irvine (1878–99) and for
the presence of his co-star Ellen Terry, less attention has been paid to the period
between 1843 and 1853, when the Lyceum was a key focal point for members of
London print networks.[2]

The office of *The London Labour and the London Poor*, at 16 Upper Wellington
Street, was practically equidistant between the Lyceum and Covent Garden
theatres (on Wellington Street North and Bow Street, respectively), and was in the
middle of a cluster of theatres which included Drury Lane, the Olympic (Wych
Street), and the Adelphi (Strand). Mayhew, his brothers, his colleagues, and his
competitors were ideally situated to make use of this theatrical district (Figure 3.1).
The proximity of Wellington Street to these theatres, as well as ties of business and

---

[1] *Watkins's Commercial and General Directory and Court Guide for 1852* (London:
Longman, Brown, Green and Longmans, 1852), WCA microfilm collection, London
Directories/1852/vol 57; *Kelly's London Post Office Directory* (London: W. Kelly, 1843–53),
WCA microfilm collection, London Directories/1843–45 (1852), 557. The office of the
serial version of *London Labour* (1850–52) started at 69 Fleet Street, but moved to
16 Upper Wellington Street by the eighteenth number, dated 21 April 1851. See imprints in
the British Library copy, item 8276.E.55.

[2] Michael R. Booth, *Theatre in the Victorian Age* (Cambridge: Cambridge University
Press, 1991), 54–5. For a biography of Irving, see Jeffrey Richards, *Sir Henry Irving:
A Victorian Actor and His World* (London: Hambledon & London, 2005). The only complete
book on the theatre is A.E. Wilson's *The Lyceum: Illustrated from the Raymond Mander
and Joe Mitchenson Theatre Collection* (London: Dennis Yates, 1952).

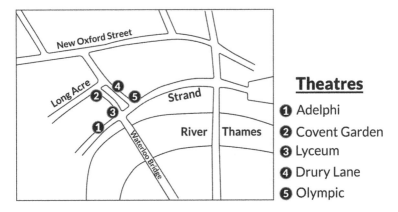

Figure 3.1   Map of theatres in the Strand area. Drawn by Simon Potter.

friendship between editors, writers, theatre managers, and actors in and around the street, shows how print culture and the culture of entertainment and spectacle were linked. The Lyceum on Wellington Street allowed members of the print networks to have a sense of a 'real' public: their tastes, their instant feedback on a writer's work or the work of colleagues, and even their faces looking back at the stage from the pit and the gallery (as in the watercolour below) if a playwright was called for a curtain call (Figure 3.2). Not all audience members were literate readers, but readers could become audiences, and audiences could contain those who might be (or become) readers. Audiences at the Lyceum would have covered the spectrum between literacy and illiteracy. This chapter suggests that the writers and editors who used the three sections of Wellington Street had their understanding of their wider audience shaped to a significant degree by this local and specific urban space.

Furthermore, as avid playgoers themselves, the writers and editors of Wellington Street (both male and female) frequently spent evenings sitting in the theatre as audience members, surrounded by many of the very people whom they perhaps hoped might read their work. *Puppet-Show*'s regular column 'Editor's Box' used the conceit of the Showman himself as a regular theatregoer to provide sharp-tongued reviews of local theatres.[3] Members of the print networks of Wellington Street mingled with theatre audiences on the same street, even though many of these audiences came from far and wide. Evenings just before and just after a performance at the Lyceum were busy times on Wellington Street. Figure 3.3 shows Wellington Street at the end of the century, when Irving and Terry drew the crowds, but it still gives a sense of the hubbub. Things had changed little since the start of the century, when Mary Lamb wrote to Dorothy Wordsworth:

---

[3]   See, for example, *Puppet-Show*, 24 June 1848, 115.

Figure 3.2   *[Interior of the Lyceum Theatre. Actors on Stage Mr and Mrs Keeley. Watercolour by Salmon?]*, 1846. City of Westminster Archives Centre Gardner Collection, Box 17, No. 18B.

here we are, living at a Brazier's shop, No. 20, in Russell Street, Covent Garden [which bisected Upper Wellington Street and Bow Street], a place all alive with noise and bustle, Drury Lane Theatre in sight from our front and Covent Garden from our back windows. The hubbub of the carriages returning from the play [...] is quite tremendous. I quite enjoy looking out of the window and listening to the calling up of the carriages and the squabble of the coachmen and link-boys. It is the oddest scene to look down upon.[4]

The theatres in and around Wellington Street were places where the interdependence of print culture and entertainment culture became apparent, and where the members of local face-to-face networks physically confronted members or potential members of the wider readership whom they addressed in print. However, this threatened a dangerous lack of anonymity, as public and private networks collided. By 'public', I mean both the literate debates in person and in print which Habermas

---

[4]   Mary Lamb, letter to Dorothy Wordsworth, 21 November 1817, Letter 226, in *The Works of Charles and Mary Lamb*, ed. E.V. Lucas, 7 vols (London: Methuen, 1905), 6: 506.

Figure 3.3   *1890. A First Night at the Lyceum, Strand Magazine*, 1891, 12.

calls the 'bourgeois public sphere' and the less homogenous, shared spaces of
the streets and the theatres where readers and non-readers, rich and poor, met
and mingled.[5] The public spaces of the city existed in an uneasy relationship with

---

[5]   Jurgen Habermas, *The Structural Transformation of the Public Sphere: An Inquiry
into a Category of Bourgeois Society*, trans. Thomas Berger with the assistance of Frederick
Lawrence (Cambridge: Polity Press, 1989; 1st publ. in German, 1962). Peter K. Andersson

the known networks of locality and coterie as the local and the strange, the familiar and the unfamiliar rubbed up against one another in the streets and at the theatre. This sense of public attention creates unease about theatricality, anonymity, and urban encounters in work by Mayhew, Reynolds, Jerrold, and Dickens.[6]

The Local and the Outsider

In 1850, Dickens wrote an article for *Household Words* about 'an evening [...] with a certain Inspector for a social conference between ourselves and the Detectives [of Scotland Yard, praised by Dickens over 'the Old Bow-Street Police'], at our Office [*sic.*] in Wellington Street, Strand, London'.[7] The article reveals how aware Dickens was of the activities of the Lyceum Theatre opposite, as the arrival of visitors to his office and the arrival of audience members to the theatre coincides:

> The reader will have the goodness to imagine the Sanctum Sanctorum of Household Words. Anything that best suits the reader's fancy, will best represent that magnificent chamber. We merely stipulate for a round table in the middle, with some glasses and cigars arranged upon it; and the editorial sofa elegantly hemmed in between that stately piece of furniture and the wall.
> It is a sultry evening at dusk. The stones of Wellington Street are hot and gritty, and the waterman and hackney-coachmen at the Theatre opposite, are much flushed and aggravated. Carriages are constantly setting down the people who have come to Fairy-Land; and there is a mighty shouting and bellowing every now and then, deafening us for the moment, through the open windows.

The scene in the office is described like a stage set, with the present tense adding to this effect. The Lyceum is not a building that is portrayed as separate from the *Household Words* office. Not only is it just across the street, but both workplaces are bustling at the same time, and the 'mighty shouting and bellowing' intrudes into Dickens's world 'through the open windows'. If Dickens can see across the street, then the 'people who have come to Fairy-Land' can probably see him, too, or at least see his candlelit bay window in the dusk. The presence of the theatre and the presence of journalists were equally inescapable during evenings on Wellington Street.

---

uses sociologist Lyn Lofland's work to suggest that the London streets which people use daily, and share with their neighbours, offer an example of a space between the public and the private spheres, Lofland's 'parochial realm', a space that is itself theatrical. See Andersson on the theatricality of late-nineteenth-century London streets in *Streetlife in Late Victorian London: The Constable and the Crowd* (Basingstoke: Palgrave Macmillan, 2013), 8–9.

6   Interestingly, according to Dick Collins, Rue Neuve-Saint-Augustine in 1830s Paris was where Thackeray lived during the time that Reynolds worked in the English-language bookshop (Collins, xix; xxii). If this street is the same as modern-day Rue Saint-Augustine, as I suspect it must be, then this was also in a 'Bohemian' theatre district, right by l'Opera and not far from Reynolds's French agents Galignani at 18 Rue Vivienne.

7   [Charles Dickens], 'A Detective Police Party', *HW*, 27 July 1850, 409.

Wellington Street and the Lyceum were tied from birth, as Figures 3.4 and 3.5 show. A fire in 1830 destroyed the original theatre, leaving the way clear for it to be rebuilt with the construction of Wellington Street North; the new Lyceum opened in 1834, and the much-delayed Wellington Street North was completed in 1835.⁸ The design for what was then called the 'Theatre Royal Lyceum and English Opera House' was much celebrated.⁹ The building was praised as 'a structure of great beauty' in 1834, and is recognized now as a key part of London's theatrical and architectural heritage.¹⁰ However, two successive managers failed to make a success of the theatre, and in 1844 it was taken over by Mr and Mrs Keeley under the new name of the 'Theatre Royal, Lyceum'.¹¹ Under the Keeleys, and afterwards under the management of Madame Vestris and her husband, Charles J. Mathews, Jr. (1847–55), the theatre (renamed again by Vestris as the 'Royal Lyceum Theatre', and soon simply referred to in newspapers as the Lyceum) finally came into its own. Despite bankrupting both husband-and-wife management teams, the Lyceum became well known for its popular burlesques, melodramas, pantomimes, and (under the Keeleys) for adaptations of novels by Dickens.¹² Reviews and comments on the Lyceum continued to fill the papers throughout the 1840s and '50s; Dickens would not have been the only Wellington Street editor well aware of events at the theatre.

The area that we now call the West End was not really so designated until much later in the century.¹³ However, as Jacky Bratton puts it, 'it is now generally agreed that the years from 1840 to 1870 [...] saw the emergence of the West End; but the period remains almost [...] unmapped'.¹⁴ The 1843 Theatre Regulation Act, which abolished restrictions on which theatres could put on so-called 'legitimate' drama, was a response to the growing number of minor theatres and 'the demand

---

⁸ Wilson, 51–2; 55. For the construction of Wellington Street North see 'Southampton Street and Tavistock Street Area: Wellington Street', in *Survey of London, volume 36: Covent Garden*, ed. F.H.W. Sheppard (1970), accessed 22 June 2010 online via http://www.british-history.ac.uk/source.aspx?pubid=362; and Chapter 1 of this book.

⁹ 'The New English Opera-House, Strand', *The Mirror of Literature, Amusement, and Instruction*, 2 August 1834, 1.

¹⁰ See, for example, *The Theatres Trust Guide to British Theatres 1750–1950*, ed. John Earl and Michael Sel, foreword Sir Donald Sinden (London: A. & C. Black, 2000), 123–4.

¹¹ Samuel James Arnold, previously manager of Drury Lane Theatre, was manager 1834–41; Michael William Balfe was manager 1841–44. See Wilson, 28; 62.

¹² Wilson. See also the Lyceum Collection in the Theatre Museum Archive, held by the Victoria and Albert Museum, Blythe House.

¹³ See Rohan McWilliam, *Talk of the Town: A History of the West End of London, 1800 to the Present* (forthcoming).

¹⁴ Jacky Bratton, *The Making of the West End Stage: Marriage, Management and the Mapping of Gender in London, 1830–1870* (Cambridge: Cambridge University Press, 2011), 1. See also Jim Davis and Victor Emeljanow, *Reflecting the Audience: London Theatregoing, 1840–1880* (Hatfield: University of Hertfordshire Press; Iowa City: University of Iowa Press, 2001), 167.

Figure 3.4   *Building the Lyceum and Wellington Street, 1830.* City of
Westminster Archives Centre Gardner Collection, Box 17, No. 12B.

Figure 3.5   *Lyceum Theatre (Wellington Street North under construction)
[1830?].* City of Westminster Archives Centre Gardner Collection,
Box 17, No. 12A.

for spectacle and sensation'.[15] The area around the Strand had more theatres than just the original patent theatres of Drury Lane and Covent Garden, and it had many more visual entertainments than just theatres. Furthermore, the area was full of small businesses which supplied the theatre industry by day, and supper rooms, taverns, and hotels which catered to the theatregoers by night. These were used by both what Davis and Emeljanow term the 'local' population (those with shops, offices, or residences nearby) and by visiting tourists and suburban commuters. The late 1840s and early 1850s were a time of crossover, when there were both a local playgoing audience of journalists and writers who recognized each other and a tourist audience of outsiders who were not part of those face-to-face networks.[16] Eighteenth-century practices persisted, even in the face of rapid urbanization and new transport links; the days of heading to the theatre from your rooms at the last minute, as Pip does in *Great Expectations*, were numbered, but Dickens slept at Wellington Street when he wanted to be in town (see Chapter 1). Therefore, 1843–53 on Wellington Street is a key moment for thinking about the connections between the anonymous imagined network of readers and audiences and the face-to-face community of London's print and entertainment networks.

The entertainment district growing up around Wellington Street drew many tourists into London, as has been well documented.[17] Wellington Street itself featured in a proposed walking tour of London which took in 'Charles Street [...] and the new street from Waterloo Bridge'.[18] Davis and Emeljanow note that the local population became of less and less interest to theatre managers with 'the huge increase in a travelling public using the new modes of transportation'.[19] The first railway to be built in London was the London and Greenwich Railway, from London Bridge to Greenwich, which opened in 1836. This was soon followed by the opening of great rail termini which linked London to every corner of Britain. By the time Mayhew, Reynolds, and Dickens all had offices on Wellington Street, these included Euston station (1837), Paddington station (1838), Fenchurch Street station (1841), Waterloo station (1848), and King's Cross station (1850).[20] Even before preparations for the expected influx of visitors to the 1851 Great Exhibition, London guidebooks detailed the hotels, railway connections, and omnibus routes available to the provincial tourist or the suburban commuter with money to spend.

---

[15]   George Rowell, *The Victorian Theatre: A Survey* (London: Oxford University Press, 1956), 11. For more on the 1843 Act see Booth, *Theatre in the Victorian Age*, 6; 145–46, and Tony Williams, *The Representation of London in Regency and Victorian Drama (1821–1881)* (Lewiston, NY and Lampeter: Edwin Mellen Press, 2000), 94.

[16]   Davis and Emeljanow, 179; See Rowell, 1–2, on the changes in nineteenth-century theatres and theatre practice.

[17]   Jeffrey A. Auerbach, *The Great Exhibition of 1851: A Nation on Display* (New Haven, CT: Yale University Press, 1999).

[18]   *Cruchley's Picture of London* (1844), 253.

[19]   Davis and Emeljanow, 182.

[20]   Jerry White, *London in the 19th Century: 'A Human Awful Wonder of God'* (London: Jonathan Cape, 2007), 37–44.

Cruchley's Picture of London for 1844 recommends that 'generally, the neighbourhood of Covent Garden and the Strand is preferred [as a place to stay], as forming a centre to the greater variety of places and objects of curiosity than any other spot in the Metropolis'.[21] The 1851 edition recommends Morley's Hotel in Trafalgar Square, The Golden Cross, Charing Cross, and the Bolt-in-Tun, Fleet Street, among others.[22] The York Hotel stood on the corner of Upper Wellington Street and Tavistock Street until it was taken over by a wine merchant.[23]

It was not simply the theatres which drew tourists from around the country on their visits to London. From 1851 in particular, with the impact of the Great Exhibition, the area around the Strand 'saw the rapid development of an entertainment district geared towards visitors with money in their pocket to spend either on shopping or the enjoyment derived from visiting theatres, exhibitions of technical achievements, and art galleries'.[24] From the early nineteenth century, however, and even stretching back to the eighteenth century, the entire Strand area became associated with spectacle, where to see and to view was suggested as a method of knowing things.[25] Just off the Strand stood Exeter Royal Exchange, now Exeter Hall, famous for its menagerie, which to great excitement exhibited an elephant in the 1820s.[26] Barker's Panorama on the Strand only closed down in 1831, and, according to Richard Altick, 'the panorama [was] an expression in popular art of the spirit which permeated much of literate London life in those decades'. Hornor's panorama of London, shown at the Regent's Park Coliseum, was sketched from the top of St. Paul's and looked directly down Fleet Street and the Strand, as if the city itself could be one vast entertainment or exhibition.[27]

Barker's Panorama became the Strand Theatre, next-door-but-one to the *Bell's Life in London* office. In May 1839, *Nicholas Nickleby and Poor Smike or, the Victim of the Yorkshire School* opened there, written before Dickens's serial was even finished. As Michael Slater describes it, this prompted a fierce attack by Dickens, in the June number of *Nickleby*, on those who spend their time 'cutting, hacking and carving' at the writing of others. The same theatre was to bring out a pirate dramatization of *Little Dorrit* in 1856, which Slater argues influenced

[21]   *Cruchley's Picture of London* (1844), 10–11.

[22]   Ibid. (1851), 248.

[23]   *Kelly's London Post Office Directory* (London: W. Kelly, 1843–53), WCA microfilm collection, London Directories/1843–53. (1850–51), 553 and (1852) 552.

[24]   Davis and Emeljanow, 179.

[25]   Richard D. Altick, *The Shows of London* (Cambridge, MA: Belknap Press of Harvard University Press, 1978).

[26]   Jonathan R. Topham, 'The Mirror of Literature, Amusement and Instruction and cheap miscellanies in early nineteenth-century Britain', in *Science in the Nineteenth-Century Periodical: Reading the Magazine of Nature*, edited by Geoffrey Cantor, et al., 37–66 (Cambridge: Cambridge University Press, 2004), 58–60.

[27]   Altick, 145, Figure 37.

Dickens's own plot workings before the novel was completed.[28] It is in nearby Covent Garden that David Copperfield goes to the theatre on first arriving in London as an adult and connects his own 'earlier life' with the spectacle he observes.[29] The theatre and print networks were engaged in a conversation which influenced the work of both sides. Davis and Emeljanow point to the existence in the West End of 'a resident community of hard-working men and women, pursuing a craft-based living in various small businesses, and a middle-class professional group attached to government bodies and commercial institutions together with artists, musicians, and actors'.[30] This 'resident community' also included, of course, many of the editors and writers who lived as well as worked in the area, and Davis and Emeljanow argue that this local population may have made up more of the West End theatre audiences than has previously been considered. The entertainments on offer in and around Wellington Street were where locals collided with outsiders, and so where writers and editors encountered their 'real' public.

People travelled in to Wellington Street, like Dickens, for work and for entertainment. As noted already, the number of editors, booksellers, and publishers who actually lived as well as worked on Wellington Street was small: the 1851 census lists the families of George Lapham, publisher of the *Examiner* (5 Wellington Street South); Stephen Rintoul of the *Spectator* (9 Wellington Street South); Charles Evans, publisher (6 Wellington Street South); Thomas Barton, managing clerk of the *Morning Post* (Wellington Street North); John Francis of the *Athenaeum* (14 Wellington Street North); James Matthews of the *Gardener's Chronicle* (5 Upper Wellington Street); and bookseller William Tweedie (18 Upper Wellington Street). Even those who lived on Wellington Street, either above their own businesses or above someone else's, were often not native Londoners. Out of 41 heads of households listed on the three sections of Wellington Street on the night of the 1851 census, 24 are recorded as born outside of London.[31] Few of the editors were born in London; Dickens was born in Portsea, Hampshire, and Reynolds was born in Sandwich, Kent. However, the *OED* defines a 'local' as not just 'an inhabitant of a particular locality', but also '[a] person who is attached by his occupation, function, etc. to some particular place or district'.[32] For Arjun Appadurai, the sense of being local, or belonging to a locality, emerges primarily from relations between people; a locality is a structure of feeling, rather than a geographical space.[33] In the neighbourhood around Wellington Street, the presence

---

[28]   Michael Slater, *Charles Dickens* (New Haven, CT: Yale University Press, 2009), 134; 420.

[29]   Charles Dickens, *David Copperfield*, ed. Nina Burgis (Oxford: Clarendon Press, 1981; 1st publ. 1849–50), 245.

[30]   Davis and Emeljanow, 179.

[31]   1851 census, HO107/1511, ff. 118–211, accessed 15 July 2011 online via http://www.ancestry.co.uk/.

[32]   First used in this sense in 1835.

[33]   Arjun Appadurai, 'The Production of Locality', in *Modernity at Large: Cultural Dimensions of Globalization*, 178–99 (Minneapolis: University of Minnesota Press, 1996), 179.

of close-knit networks within geographical proximity meant that both contributed to the construction of locality. Therefore, despite their undoubted national and international links, activities, and interests, the networks of Dickens, Reynolds, and Mayhew can be said to be, at least partly, 'local' ones.

Local connections to the theatres are evident from the London Post Office Directories, which reveal that theatrical service professions grew up around the theatres. An article in *London Society* points out that 'it is not alone the actors, whose persons we are familiar with on the stage, who are enabled to live and bring up their families' but a whole other group of workers 'whom we never see, and whose existence many do not even suspect', who are both essential to the theatres and dependent upon them. As well as backstage workers like the scene painters, carpenters, and scene shifters, there are those employed outside the theatre

at their own homes, costumiers, tailors, shoemakers, hosiers, wigmakers, jewellers, upholsterers, armourers, printers, draughtsmen, engravers, and billstickers.

These artists and artisans devote themselves exclusively to theatrical work [not] suitable for the streets. Generally speaking, the theatrical hosier's hose are all particoloured, the theatrical shoemaker's shoes all red-heeled, the theatrical jeweller's jewels all glass and tinfoil, the theatrical armourer's armour all white iron and blue paint. Their craft is thus confined exclusively to theatrical work, and their art aspires to produce nothing which will stand the test of the light of day. It is, in fact, a branch of manufacture and trade called into existence and operation solely by the requirements of the theatre.[34]

The article suggests there are 'a total of 12,000 persons deriving their income from theatrical employment'.[35] Several of these worked on the three sections of Wellington Street or on the surrounding streets.

If Mayhew turned left out of his office at 16 Upper Wellington Street he could stroll to the Lyceum; if he turned right out of his office, he could walk up Bow Street to Covent Garden Theatre. On his way, he would have passed a number of small businesses which serviced the local theatres and entertainment venues. On Upper Wellington Street, four doors up from the office of *London Labour,* was the shop of Abraham Haigh, the theatrical hosiery maker, while immediately opposite was William Goodwin, music seller and copyist.[36] The struggle by most theatres to make ends meet in this period seems to have had an effect on Haigh's family business: on Wednesday, 3 August 1842 he was ordered to come before a court in Portugal Street, Lincoln's-Inn Fields, as an insolvent debtor, but business must have picked up as he was still at number 12 in 1853, although he was sharing the premises with a tailor.[37] In 1854 his son David Haigh was issued with a court

---

[34] 'The Cost of Amusing the Public', *London Society*, April 1862, 193–4.

[35] 'The Cost of Amusing the Public', 195.

[36] *Watkins's Directory* (1852), 1852; 1851 census, HO107/1511, f. 119, accessed 15 July 2011 online via http://www.ancestry.co.uk/.

[37] 'Insolvent Debtors', *Jurist*, 6 July 1842, 245.

summons for failing to pay rates to the parish collector.[38] Bow Street itself was 'the centre of the theatrical world of London', according to Mary Elizabeth Braddon, who declared that 'the street is redolent of the footlights':

> In this street the dramatic agents have their offices, and to those offices flock all classes of the theatrical profession, from the provincial Macready who is only waiting to get an innings in order to set the town in a blaze, and who enters the official chamber with a pompous tragedy stalk, to the timid aspirant for dramatic fame who has never yet set foot upon a public stage.[39]

S.G. Fairbrother, of 31 Bow Street, printed playbills for the Lyceum from 1847.[40]

In the other direction, on Wellington Street (South), a lithographer called G.E. Madeley had a business at number 3.[41] The theatres brought him work, too. In 1835, he published a lithograph of Charles Mathews in costume,[42] and on another occasion he printed an image of the actor Frank Matthews, who worked with Madame Vestris at the Olympic and was later to appear as Dr Jeddlar in Albert Smith's adaptation of Dickens's *The Battle of Life* for the Lyceum. The theatres brought business to other families on the three sections of Wellington Street. Charles Bielefeld's *papier mâché* designs ornamented the insides of many public buildings, but were also used by at least one local theatre manager.[43] Dickens's close friend, the actor-manager Macready, managed both Covent Garden (1837–39) and Drury Lane (1841–43), where he 'proved to be as distinguished a manager as he was an actor'.[44] R.H. Horne (who had worked for Dickens on the *Daily News*, and subsequently got a staff job at *Household Words*) paid a visit to Bielefeld's premises in Staines and at 15 Wellington Street North, and declared in an article for *Household Words*:

> the works are not only carried on with the best skill and promptitude, but are of singular variety. This latter quality may be estimated when I mention that, among other 'old friends', the mask of Polyphemus, when 'Acis and Galatea'

---

[38]   City of Westminster Archives Centre SML/0452/6/6. For a useful account of the difficulties faced by theatre managers in this period, see Booth, 27–30.

[39]   M.E. Braddon, *Rupert Godwin*, 2 vols (Leipzig: Bernhard Tauchnitz, 1867), 1: 187–8.

[40]   See playbills in V&ATA Box 1383: Lyceum 1847.

[41]   *Kelly's POD* (1843), 446, and (1853), 555.

[42]   'A Portrait of John Liston, (1776–1846) and Charles Mathews, (1776–1835)', lithographed and published by G.E. Madeley, 3 Wellington Street, Strand. City of Westminster Archives Centre Theatre Collection, Box 2, No. 259; 'Mr. F. Mathews of Madame Vestris's Royal Olympic theatre as Sir Anthony Allsides', printed by G.E. Madeley, 3 Wellington Street, Strand. City of Westminster Archives Centre Theatre Collection, Box 3, No. 19.

[43]   See C.F. Bielefeld, *On the Use of Improved Papier Mâché in Furniture, in the Interior Decoration of Buildings, and in Works of Art*, 2nd edn (London: C.F. Bielefeld, 1850).

[44]   Booth, 42.

was produced so exquisitely by Mr. Macready, was modelled in this department; the anxious manager coming frequently himself to inspect and give instructions during the progress of that one-eyed countenance.[45]

Horne was part of Dickens's amateur theatrical troupe, and an avid fan of Macready; it is no surprise that his eye was caught by the theatricality of Bielefeld's designs.[46]

The experience of evening entertainments around Wellington Street between 1843 and 1853, then, was shaped by work done by interlinked local networks. These networks enjoyed as well as produced local entertainments, and made use of the services of local businesses. Members of the local print networks were late workers, just like the theatre workers, so they were on the spot to enjoy the entertainments in and around Wellington Street, and their working routines coincided with the late hours of the theatres. Dickens and the staff of *Household Words*, for example, would work late at 16 Wellington Street North at least once a week:

> Each week's issue was printed on the Wednesday, and on the following day [Dickens] and Wills and others met at five for the weekly editorial conference which might go through dinner and into the evening. It was at this meeting that most of the articles were chosen (characteristically Dickens managed to work three weeks ahead of publication), but it was Dickens himself who decided upon the order in which they would appear.[47]

The late working hours of those who contributed to the print trade on Wellington Street and nearby meant that, as they sat in their offices, they would have heard the sounds of the Lyceum Theatre's evening routine. Under Madame Vestris's management, the Lyceum box office closed at six o'clock pm; the doors opened at six-thirty; performances began at seven o'clock and lasted until about eleven-thirty. Under the Keeleys' management, half-price entry was allowed at nine o'clock pm.[48] Between eight and nine in the evening the ham sandwich-seller interviewed by Mayhew stood outside the theatre doors to catch customers emerging for a break or just arriving. He explains to Mayhew that 'the Lyceum was good, when it was Mr. Keeley's. I hardly know what sort my customers are, but they're those that go to the theaytres [*sic.*]: shopkeepers and clerks I think. Gentlemen don't often buy of me [*sic.*]'.[49] The *Morning Post*'s report of the fire at Bielefeld's works

---

[45]   [Horne], 'The Pasha's New Boat', *HW*, 22 November 1851, 213. For more on *papier mâché* objects in this article, see Catherine Waters, *Commodity Culture in Dickens's Household Words: The Social Life of Goods* (Aldershot: Ashgate, 2008), 122. For more on Horne and Bielefeld, see Chapter 4.

[46]   For a detailed discussion of Horne's part in Wellington Street's networks and Dickens's acting troupe, see Chapter 4.

[47]   Ackroyd, *Dickens*, 622–3.

[48]   Timings taken from playbills in V&ATA, Lyceum Collection.

[49]   Henry Mayhew, *London Labour and the London Poor*, 3 vols (London: Office of London Labour and the London Poor, 1851–52: 178.

in 1854 (see Chapter 1) makes clear that even at around ten o'clock at night, when the fire started, the Strand was so crowded that there were soon 'dense masses of spectators' enjoying the spectacle, as if it was a night at the Lyceum itself.[50] The newspaper's printers, meanwhile, were still hard at work. An 1853 article by Dickens for *Household Words* on the importance of the imagination reveals his awareness of the routines of the Lyceum:

> Even as we write in our common-place office, we behold from the window, four young ladies with peculiarly limp bonnets, and of a yellow or drab style of beauty, making for the stage-door of the Lyceum theatre, in the dirty little fog-choked street over the way. Grown up wisdom whispers that these are beautiful fairies by night, and that they will find Fairy Land dirty even to their splashed skirts, and rather cold and dull (notwithstanding its mixed gas and daylight), this easterly morning. But, we don't believe it.

The view out of his office window tells Dickens, as he communicates to his imagined network of readers through his article, that he is part of a network of people who work with 'fancies' and the imagination to preserve 'the eye and mind of childhood'.[51]

The printers of the *Morning Post*, the staff of *Household Words*, and the street sellers were not the only locals accustomed to working into the evening. Some of the booksellers may have had workshops and binding rooms over their premises, as well as shops; a story in *All The Year Round* describes '[t]he blackened floor, crowded with piles of reams of paper' of one such binding-room.[52] An article for the *Dublin University Magazine* describes how after dark, 'lights gleamed from the window of William Chambers's small printing-room, whence issued also the wheasy [*sic.*] sounds of his ever-toiling press'.[53] Thackeray's famous description of the premises of a newspaper in the 1840s in *Pendennis* (1850) makes much of the fact that the newspaper workers keep late hours:

> Reporters were coming out of the place, or rushing up to it in cabs; there were lamps burning in the editors' rooms, and above where the compositors were at work: the windows of the building were in a blaze of gas.[54]

Theatre-critics (Forster's early role at the *Examiner*) would arrive at the newspaper offices after the theatres closed.[55] It was not just the reporters who kept the

---

50   'Destruction of Bielefeld's Papier Mache Works', *Morning Post*, 10 March 1854, 5.

51   [Charles Dickens], 'Where we stopped growing', *HW*, 1 January 1853, 362.

52   'The Real Murderer', *All The Year Round*, 2 January 1864, 448.

53   'William and Robert Chambers', *Dublin University Magazine*, February 1851, 177.

54   William Makepeace Thackeray, *The History of Pendennis*, ed. John Sutherland (Oxford: Oxford University Press, 1994), 390.

55   Tracy C. Davis, 'Amelia Chesson Enters the Fourth Estate: "She must, therefore, be considered a pioneer in lady journalism"'. Paper presented at the annual conference for the British Association for Victorian Studies, University of Birmingham, 1–3 September 2011.

cab-drivers occupied all evening. Evenings on Wellington Street were busy with both local workers and visitors to the theatre: those who worked on the street, and those who came in search of 'Fairy Land'.

Evening entertainments in the Strand neighbourhood enabled members of the local print networks to rub shoulders with visitors to the area; the local face-to-face community met those who belonged to the wider public. One of the most well-documented examples of nineteenth-century theatregoing is, of course, Dickens:

> Dickens's playgoing [...] spanned the gamut of West End taste. He wrote on one instance to an actor, William Mitchell, [...] that he had been 'a very staunch admirer' and had seen him at the Queen's, Covent Garden, the Strand, and the St James's in the 1830s, in plays as various as a burletta by Henry Mayhew, a burlesque opera by Gilbert à Beckett, a military spectacle by Planche, and J.T. Haines's farce *A House Divided* [...]. When he was staying at the offices of *All The Year Round* by himself in 1860, he wrote to say that he was 'taking a stall at a Theatre every night,' including the Christmas pieces at Covent Garden and the Lyceum. On the occasions he didn't accompany his family [...] he went with Clarkson Stanfield, Mark Lemon, Daniel Maclise, Wilkie Collins, or John Leech, all of whom were his artistic or journalistic friends, to see plays.[56]

Dickens was not the only writer with connections to Wellington Street who spent evenings as an audience member in the theatres around the Strand. The theatre was one of the few places on Wellington Street where male and female writers and editors met and mingled. In 1864, G.H. Lewes went with George Eliot to see Kate Bateman in *Leah, the Forsaken* at the Adelphi, a play which Anthony Trollope also saw that year:

> At that performance they would probably have met George Augustus Sala, together with Horace and Augustus Mayhew and Charles Kenney: Sala maintained that they went 'at least three times a week to the stalls at the Adelphi for the express purpose of weeping bitterly over the woes of the persecuted Hebrew maiden.'[57]

As we saw in the Introduction, Dickens and Forster went with Elizabeth Gaskell to the Lyceum in 1854.[58] Montagu Williams, a barrister and writer for *Household Words*, went to the Lyceum when it was under the management of the Keeleys, and later of Madame Vestris and Charles Mathews.[59]

Women like Eliza Vestris and Mary Keeley were crucial to the development of the West End, as Jacky Bratton has demonstrated. However, networking in the

---

[56] Davis and Emeljanow, 188.

[57] Davis and Emeljanow, 188.

[58] James A. Davies, *John Forster: A Literary Life* (Leicester: Leicester University Press, 1983), 92.

[59] Davis and Emeljanow, 188.

Wellington Street neighbourhood involved a very homosocial community.[60] For the male writers and editors, an evening was not necessarily spent wholly at the theatre. Prostitutes solicited for business in the theatre foyers and auditoriums, and retired with their customers to rooms nearby.[61] Apart from brothels, after a visit to the Lyceum they could go on to one of the many taverns, coffee houses, or supper rooms close by, often advertised in guidebooks to London – evening venues where locals and tourists might rub shoulders.[62] Particularly popular were Ries's Cigar Divan at 101–2 Strand, the Cider Cellars on Maiden Lane, Evan's supper rooms in Covent Garden (renamed 'The Cave of Harmony' by Thackeray in *The Newcomes*, 1853–55), and the Coal Hole, also on the Strand.[63] As Jerry White describes it:

> the district north and south of Fleet Street and the Strand, including Covent Garden [...] was *the* London bohemia, where Fleet Street was properly renamed 'the Street of Drink'. Here, the newspaper, magazine and publishers' offices lay just a raised glass away from the pubs and clubs of literary London. They were legion. The Garrick's Head, Bow Street, where the literary men and 'theatricals' formed the Rationals Club in the late 1830s. The Wrekin Tavern, Broad Court (off Bow Street), where an 'ordinary' was held for 'choice spirits' in the 1840s. The Shakespeare's Head, Wych Street, run in 1840–1 by Mark Lemon, but with Grub Street links, like all of these places, long before and for some years after. Clunn's Hotel, Covent Garden Piazza, where the Fielding Club, later Our Club, dined on Saturday evenings in the 1850s with Thackeray and John Leech, the artist, among the company. And other favourite pressmen's pubs around mid-century included the Old Dog, Holywell Street, the Coach and Horses and Edinburgh Castle, Strand, the Sheridan Knowles, Brydges Street, and any number in Fleet Street itself, like Peel's Coffee House, the Green Dragon, the Cock, and of course the Cheese.[64]

Renton Nicholson's late-night venue, the Garrick's Head and Town Hotel, at 27 Bow Street, drew poets, actors, and MPs to its 'Judge and Jury Society' nights in the 1840s, where cross-dressing and bawdy jokes ensured a lively evening's

---

[60]   Bratton, *The Making of the West End Stage*, 86; see also Tracy C. Davis, 'Amelia Chesson Enters the Fourth Estate'. For a queer reading of male homosociability in the eighteenth- and nineteenth-century novel, see Eve Kosofsky Sedgwick, *Between Men: English Literature and Male Homosocial Desire* (New York: Columbia University Press, 1985). For an excellent discussion of mid-century clubland, see Barbara Black, *A Room of His Own: A Literary-Cultural Study of Victorian Clubland* (Ohio: Ohio University Press, 2012).

[61]   Tracy C. Davis, 'Actresses and Prostitutes in Victorian London', *Theatre Research International* 13 (1988): 226–7.

[62]   See *Cruchley's Picture of London* (1844 and 1851), and *Gilbert's Visitor's Guide to London* (London: James Gilbert, 1851).

[63]   Ashton, 3–4.

[64]   White, 246.

entertainment. Nicholson also found notoriety as the writer of *Dombey and Daughter*, in imitation of Dickens.[65]

Male sociability between members of the Wellington Street community revolved around clubs, late-night retreats for late-night workers in journalism and the theatre, but also for those who had just been in to see a play.[66] Quite apart from the Garrick with its clubhouse, there were a succession of informal drinking and dining societies running amongst local writers and editors, where journalists and novelists rubbed shoulders with dramatic authors and critics. Jerrold, Lemon, Cruikshank, Mayhew, and others were part of the Rationals Club in the 1830s, which met first at the Garrick's Head in Bow Street on Saturday afternoons before moving on later in the evening to the Wrekin in Broad Court (between Bow Street and Drury Lane). Part of the entertainment was a system of fines for offences like 'starting a discussion on the immorality of one's soul before two o'clock in the morning'.[67] In 1847, Jerrold tried to get Dickens to join the Museum Club, which was started by Forster, Macready, and friends 'for literary and artistic men'.[68] It was used for networking and job-hunting as well as socializing, and had premises in Henrietta Street, Covent Garden.[69] These were open all day but came alive in the evenings, when 'a considerable number used to meet [...] for talk and smoke in an upper room', with Jerrold as their 'kind of chief'.[70] The publisher George Smith loved these entertaining gatherings:

> The wit was brilliant, the jokes abundant, the laughter uproarious [...] often I came away [...] with sides that were literally sore with laughter [...] [G.H.] Lewes had a wonderful gift for dramatic representation [...] Jerrold's flow of wit was unfailing, his repartee was of lightning-like swiftness.[71]

As Russell Stephens has shown, 'for all its apparent size the world of the dramatic author was a close one', and it was interlinked with the networks of writers and editors precisely because men like Jerrold and Mayhew had a foot in both camps.[72]

---

[65]   G.C. Boase, 'Nicholson, Renton (1809–1861)', revised K.D. Reynolds, *DNB*, accessed 11 August 2012 online via www.oxforddnb.com.

[66]   See Bratton, *The Making of the West End Stage*, 101–7, on the tribalism of London clubs.

[67]   Michael Slater, *Douglas Jerrold: 1803–1857* (London: Duckworth, 2002), 222.

[68]   Ibid.

[69]   David Masson, *Memories of London in the Forties*, arranged for publication and annotated by his daughter Flora Masson (London: Blackwood, 1908), 212–13.

[70]   Ibid., 213. This description of Jerrold as a 'chief' highlights the tribalism emphasized by Phiz's son's account of print networks at mid-century (see Introduction).

[71]   George Smith, quoted from Smith's MS. in the National Library of Scotland in Slater, *Douglas Jerrold*, 223.

[72]   John Russell Stephens, *The Profession of the Playwright: British Theatre 1800–1900* (Cambridge: Cambridge University Press, 1992), 12–13.

Jacky Bratton has analyzed the 'imaginary land' of 'Bohemia', which 'was a notable feature of the mid-century', particularly amongst the younger men in Dickens's circle, like Sala, Yates, and Smith.[73] Bratton argues that Bohemia was gendered as a specifically male space which excluded the many women who, as actresses, playwrights, reviewers, and managers, contributed to the economy of the West End stage.[74] For Bratton, this was because of anxieties about the role of the hack writer and playwright when compared with Carlyle's heroic 'man of letters' who produced novels, poetry, and history; she suggests that this cultural anxiety explains why Dickens prioritized novels and journalism over 'his wide and important stage work'.[75] Bratton's argument is convincing. But 'Bohemia' was also a sign which could be deployed to draw together men from many different origins and backgrounds into 'locals' of this particular network and of this particular cultural space. It is no coincidence that the image they chose, Bohemia, was a geographic one, of an imagined country and a symbolic neighbourhood. In a city of wanderers and migrants where few people were truly 'local', interlinked print and entertainment networks worked hard to create a sense of male belonging; contemporary memoirs are keen to present their world as one of community. There was also an economic imperative to use networks to secure work in a difficult market.[76] Tribalism involved fierce competition as much as (and perhaps more than) it did friendly assistance.[77] These were networks for which the theatre audience, although drawn from outside the face-to-face community as well as from within it, played an important role.

The Writer-as-Showman, Adaptation, and the 'Real' Public

The dialogue between the literary, journalistic, artistic, and theatrical worlds is mirrored by their physical proximity on Wellington Street, and shows that they were not separate and isolated fields, but ones in which the same people participated in interlocking networks. Therefore, audiences of visual entertainments (whether of dramas, burlesques, panoramas, exhibitions, or street musicians) provided

---

[73]   Bratton, *The Making of the West End Stage*, 6.

[74]   Ibid., 6–7. For a full discussion of the daily working lives of Victorian actresses and the trope of the actress-as-prostitute, see: Tracy C. Davis, *Actresses as Working Women: Their Social Identity in Victorian Culture* (London: Routledge, 1991); Katherine Newey, *Women's Theatre Writing in Victorian Britain* (Basingstoke: Palgrave Macmillan, 2005); Kerry Powell, *Women and Victorian Theatre* (Cambridge: Cambridge University Press, 1997).

[75]   Bratton, *The Making of the West End Stage*, 88.

[76]   Joanne Shattock, 'Professional Networking, Masculine and Feminine', in 'Victorian Networks and the Periodical Press', ed. Alexis Easley, 128–40, special issue, *Victorian Periodicals Review* 44, no. 2 (Summer 2011). Dramatists in the 1840s and '50s were particularly poorly paid. See Stephens, *The Profession of the Playwright*, 19; 25.

[77]   See Antonia Harland-Lang, 'Thackeray and Bohemia', PhD diss., University of Cambridge, 2010, 223–4.

writers of all kinds with an encounter with their 'real' public. Martin Meisel's *Realizations* has established the ways in which the relationship between serial narratives, illustrations, and drama were understood differently in the nineteenth century, as 'the burgeoning collaborative form of serial illustrated fiction' begged the question, 'who was illustrating whom?'[78] Meisel points to Cruikshank's famous claim that he was more the 'author' of several of Ainsworth's and Dickens's novels than the respective writers themselves.[79] Meisel uses this as evidence that drama, painting, writing, and illustrating were not operating in separate spheres, but in an 'intricate web of local connections that show the arts to be one living tissue'.[80] Meisel's phrase 'local connections' is a particularly interesting one; he is using it metaphorically, but it could be pushed further to consider the wealth of social and business connections between artists, dramatists, theatre managers, and writers in and around Wellington Street in the 1840s and '50s. Meisel shows that Cruikshank's and Phiz's illustrations were 'realised' on stage, but does not develop this further.[81] More recently, Deborah Vlock has challenged the model of the reader as a solitary individual and reading as a private, disciplining activity.[82] Vlock uses the influence of popular theatre on Dickens to argue that novel reading in the nineteenth century occurred within the context of the 'imaginary text', which was made up of archetypes from stage and page.[83] She sees readers as audience members too, and reading as a public activity, particularly because genre and disciplinary divisions

> did not in fact exist with much integrity in the nineteenth century. Novels and theatrical entertainments, novels and journalistic prose, novels and poetry constantly slipped in and out of mutual embrace.[84]

Vlock is more interested in text than illustrations, however. What neither Meisel nor Vlock consider fully are the material connections between audience and reader. These connections are embodied by the pages of the periodicals published in and around Wellington Street, and in the physical presence on the street of Lacy's theatrical bookshop and the Lyceum itself.

The connection between drama, fiction, and journalism was expressed in the period through the trope of writer-as-showman. *Punch* got round the problem of the involvement of multiple personalities with the venture by 'the magazine's central

---

[78]   Martin Meisel, *Realizations: Narrative, Pictorial and Theatrical Arts in Nineteenth-Century England* (Princeton, NJ: Princeton University Press, 1983), 248.

[79]   Ibid., 247.

[80]   Ibid., 3.

[81]   Ibid., 251–82.

[82]   Deborah Vlock, *Dickens, Novel Reading, and the Victorian Popular Theatre* (Cambridge: Cambridge University Press, 1998), especially 2–4.

[83]   Ibid., 6.

[84]   Vlock, 10.

Figure 3.6   Illustration for 'Prologue', *Punch* 5, 1843, 1. The periodical was
               still based at 13 Wellington Street (South) until January 1844 (see
               Chapter 1). Reproduced with the permission of Senate House
               Library, University of London. PR [Z-Punch].

organising conceit of presenting "Mister Punch" as its author and spokesman'.[85]
In this way, the *Punch* writers were sheltered by anonymity and ventriloquized
their opinions through the mouthpiece of Mister Punch, although in practice their
identities were well known (Figure 3.6).[86]

   This connection of writer to performer, or rather to theatrical manager (reduced
to small scale for satirical effect), was reused by others with connections to the
Punch circle. *Puppet-Show* (which, as we have already seen in Chapter 1, was
a rival to *Punch* established by Henry Vizetelly in 1848 at 11 Wellington Street
North) made the trope explicit. *Puppet-Show* declared in the opening address to
the reader of the first number, in March 1848, that 'THE "SHOWMAN" presents
his compliments and his portrait to the British Public, and introduces himself as
a person who intends exhibiting the PUPPETS of the day in their true light'.[87]
This portrait turns out to be that of a weary-looking puppetmaster, clutching a
collection of puppets held against a backdrop of St. Paul's, who rests his head on
one hand as if worn out by the vanities of this world (Figure 3.7). To enforce the
point, the masthead of *Puppet-Show* depicts the same figure of the Showman, who
wields his puppets as he acts as a stand-in author for the satirical sallies of Angus
B. Reach and other contributors (Figure 3.8).

   In the fourth number, an engraving of a puppet theatre introduces a satirical
poem which likens all the world to a small stage of marionettes, and ends with the
exhortation that the reader 'Learn to look behind the curtain, | Wisest he that still
enquires, | When he acts for self or others, | Whose the hand that pulls the wires.'[88]

---

[85]   Patrick Leary, *The Punch Brotherhood: Table Talk and Print Culture in
Mid-Victorian Britain (London: British Library, 2010), 3.
[86]   Ibid., 13. 'Ventriloquism' is first recorded in the *OED* in 1797.
[87]   'Our Name and Address', *Puppet-Show*, 18 March 1848, 1–2.
[88]   'The Puppet-Show', *Puppet-Show*, 8 April 1848, 25–6.

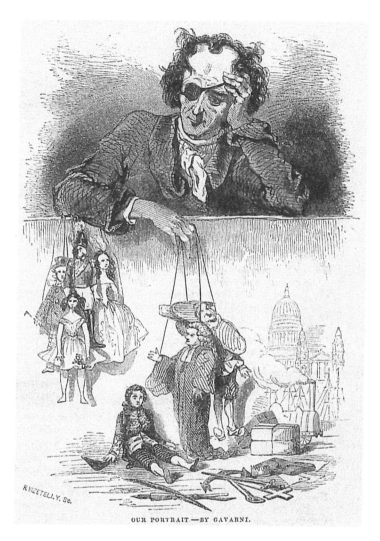

OUR PORTRAIT—BY GAVARNI.

Figure 3.7   *The Portrait of the Showman, Puppet-Show*, 18 March 1848, 1.
Reproduced with the permission of Senate House Library,
University of London. PR [Z-Puppet].

Figure 3.8   The masthead of *Puppet-Show*, 1848. Taken from *Puppet-Show*, 18
March 1848, 1. Reproduced with the permission of Senate House
Library, University of London. PR [Z-Puppet].

In June of the same year, another of the *Punch* circle, W.M. Thackeray, wrote a
preface for the 1848 volume edition of *Vanity Fair* called 'Before the Curtain'. In
this preface, Thackeray depicts 'the Author' as 'the Manager of the Performance'
and the characters of the novel as both autonomous 'actors' about to go on stage
and 'Puppets' dancing to his tune:

> What more has the manager of the Performance to say? To acknowledge the
> kindness with which it has been received in all the principal towns of England
> through which the show has passed, and where it has been most favourably
> noticed by the respected conductors of the public Press, and by the Nobility and
> Gentry. He is proud to think that his Puppets have given satisfaction to the very
> best company in this empire […].
>   And with this, and a profound bow to his patrons, the Manager retires, and
> the curtain rises.[89]

Fiction, journalism, and the 'show' are intertwined.

The trope of writer-as-showman was not a new one. On the Vignette Title of
the 1836 'First Series' of *Sketches by Boz*, Boz and Cruikshank are shown in a hot
air balloon as if about to ascend over London and provide a bird's-eye view of the
community.[90] This is Boz-as-showman, a spectacle himself in a city of spectacles.

---

[89]   William Makepeace Thackeray, 'Before the Curtain', in *Vanity Fair: A Novel
without a Hero*, ed. J.I.M. Stewart (London: Penguin, 1998; 1st publ. 1848), 34. This novel
was published by Bradbury and Evans in Bouverie Street, off Fleet Street, who owned
Punch from 1843 and also published *Household Words*.

[90]   Jeremy Tambling makes the same point in *Going Astray: Dickens and London*
(Harlow: Pearson Longman, 2009), 23. For more on Cruikshank's illustrations to *Sketches
by Boz*, see J. Hillis Miller, 'The Fiction of Realism: Sketches by Boz, Oliver Twist, and

Elaine Freedgood shows how the early Victorian balloonist was a figure who was perceived as very much an individual and a free agent, and so the depiction of Boz as a balloonist emphasizes his freedom to roam and his unique ability to observe (Figure 3.9).[91]

Boz hereby tacks his name onto the already 'well-earned reputation' of Cruikshank, and offers their joint venture as a way of helping readers by providing them with a comprehensive overview of the panorama of the city. This is Boz-as-guide as well as Boz-as-showman, who has brought together the fragmented parts of the city and the fragmented individual sketches into a coherent volume.[92] But the image also portrays Boz as a figure to be looked at in his turn, an entertainer for bourgeois readers. This is made clear in the illustration by the middle-class figures waving the balloon off, like the spectators at the balloon ascent in the sketch 'Vauxhall-gardens by Day'.[93] Boz is set up here as much as a showman as a writer.

The material links between readers and audiences were demonstrated on Wellington Street by the presence of Thomas Hailes Lacy's theatrical bookshop, next to *Household Words* and only nine doors down from where Mayhew opened his office in 1851. This shop, like the Lyceum, was another important site in nineteenth-century theatrical history. Lacy was on Wellington Street between 1849 and 1857 before moving his shop to 89 Strand, opposite Southampton Street.[94] Lacy was very successful, if not well liked; he bought out the lists of competitors like John Duncombe and became the definitive publisher of cheap editions of plays. Lacy bought cheap copyrights from impoverished dramatists, and was twice prosecuted for unauthorized adaptations of copyright novels.[95] F.C. Burnand, a young playwright in the 1860s, showed his distaste for the

---

Cruikshank's Illustrations', in *Dickens Centennial Essays*, ed. Ada Nisbet and Blake Nevius (Berkeley: University of California Press, 1971), 85–153.

[91]   Elaine Freedgood, 'Groundless Optimism: regression in the service of the ego, England and Empire in Victorian ballooning memoirs', in *Victorian Writing About Risk: Imagining a Safe England in a Dangerous World* (Cambridge: Cambridge University Press, 2000), 83.

[92]   Ibid., 88.

[93]   Charles Dickens, 'Vauxhall-gardens by Day', in *Sketches by Boz and Other Early Papers 1833–39*, vol. 1 of *Dickens' Journalism*, ed. Michael Slater (London: J.M. Dent, 1994), 127–32. For a report of a balloon ascent by Mr Green just before the publication of this sketch, see 'The Late Grand Balloon Ascent. – Mr Green's Own Account', *London Dispatch*, 17 September 1836, 1.

[94]   *Kelly's POD* (1851), 555; Stephens, 130–31.

[95]   Stephens, *The Profession of the Playwright*, 99; 130. Stephens notes that *Lacy's Acting Edition of Plays*, begun in 1850, was the most prominent series of drama for the masses and 'ran to over 100 volumes, covering 1,485 plays' (131). After he retired, Lacy's stock was transferred to Samuel French, still a leading publisher of acting editions.

Figure 3.9   The Vignette Title of the 1836 'First Series', *Sketches by Boz*.
George Cruikshank. Reproduced by courtesy of Charles Dickens
Museum, London.

bookseller in his description of Lacy in 'dirty shirt sleeves', 'muddling about with books and papers in a very ill-lighted and grimy shop'.[96]

The shop is mentioned in an 1854 article for *Household Words* with no word of explanation; Lacy's establishment was so well known that no further context was needed. The article laments the lost world of Grand Opera at Haymarket and the hostile invasion of Italian music into the local world around Wellington Street of 'bygone English worthies' (either dead or retired) like Siddons, Kean, Kemble, and Macready:

> alas [...] The Grand Opera exists no more. I know there is an establishment in the vicinity of Covent Garden [...] where the best operas are given by the best singers and instrumentalists. But I cannot call it THE Opera. It can never be more to me than Covent Garden Theatre – the conquered, but never to be the naturalised domain of Italian music. The ghost of Garrick jostles the ghost of Farinelli in Bow Street, and, from Mr. Lacy's shop in Wellington Street, the indignant voices of Colman, Sheridan, Kenny, and O'Keefe, seem to be crying to Bellini and Donizetti, Meyerbeer and Mozart, 'What do ye here?' What have the traditions of maestri and macaroni, violins and Vellutis, bassi and ballet girls, have to do with a locality hallowed by the memory of the Great Twin Brethren, the two mighty English theatres of Covent Garden and Drury Lane?[97]

The 'foreign', epitomized here by 'Italian music', is a threat to what is conceived of as a specifically English, specifically local area of London. Lacy published playtexts of Dickens adaptations, as well as of plays by *Punch*-ites like Gilbert à Beckett, Shirley Brooks, Mark Lemon, and Douglas Jerrold, as well as G.H. Lewes (under his pseudonym Slingsby Lawrence) and Edmund Yates, friend of Dickens and Sala and contributor to *Household Words*.[98] Several of these plays were performed at the Lyceum itself, as I shall discuss later. The Lacys were the living epitome of the links between stage and page: Thomas also wrote or co-wrote and published several of his own plays, and his wife, Frances, acted in Madame Vestris's company at the Olympic between 1840 and 1843.[99] Lacy's shop was not the only place on Wellington Street where playtexts were sold, however.[100] At the Lyceum itself, printed copies of plays taken from the prompt book were for sale, 'Printed and Published by W.S. Johnson, "Nassau Steam Press", 60, St. Martin's

---

[96]   F.C. Burnand, *Records and Reminiscences, Personal and General*, 2 vols (London: Methuen, 1904), 1: 368.

[97]   'The Musical World', *HW*, 29 July 1854, 561–2.

[98]   See the Victorian Plays Project, based at the University of Worcester and compiled by Prof. Richard Pearson, Dr Kate Mattacks, and Dr Heike Bauer, for a useful digital archive of *Lacy's Acting Edition of Plays* (1848–73), accessed 6 October 2011 online via http://victorian.worc.ac.uk/modx/.

[99]   John Russell Stephens, 'Lacy, Thomas Hailes (1809–1873)', *DNB*, accessed 11 August 2012 online via www.oxforddnb.com.

[100]   John Dicks, Reynolds's business partner, brought out plays under *Dick's Standard Drama* from 1875 (Stephens, *The Profession of the Playwright*, 131).

Lane'.[101] The same printer also produced the Lyceum's playbills, until Madame Vestris and Charles Mathews took over management and used S.G. Fairbrother of 31 Bow Street as their playbill printer. Lacy later took over Fairbrother's stock of playtexts.[102]

Further links between stage and page were created by the fact that between 1843 and 1853, several of the writers and editors with connections to Wellington Street wrote for audiences at the Lyceum almost as much as they wrote for readers of their fiction, their periodicals, or their newspapers. Angus B. Reach, who wrote for *Puppet-Show*, among other periodicals, wrote a comedy called *Which Mr. Smith?* for the Lyceum in 1846; in 1852 a song written by Reach was performed by Henry Russell during an evening of emigrant songs, delivered along with 'panoramas of negro life'.[103] Albert Smith, who co-edited *The Man in the Moon* with Reach, was married to a daughter of Mr and Mrs Keeley.[104] Smith was a relatively prolific contributor to the Lyceum's repertoire; he wrote a prologue to the Lyceum's adaptation of *Martin Chuzzlewit* (written by Edward Stirling) when Dickens refused to do so himself, he dramatized Dickens's Christmas Books with express permission from Dickens (these were the only 'authorised' adaptations), and he wrote or co-wrote a number of burlesques and extravaganzas for the Lyceum's stage.[105] In 1850 he took part in a benefit night for Madame Vestris, and in that same year he wrote *Novelty Fair: Or, Hints for 1851*, a review about the Great Exhibition.[106] Smith went on to achieve great popularity with his own shows, which were one-man visual entertainments about foreign travel. Albert Smith's brother Angus later managed Dickens's reading tours.[107] The Keeleys' other son-in-law was Montagu Williams, who not only contributed to *Household Words* but also wrote and adapted plays and farces, along with F.C. Burnand.[108]

---

[101]   Imprint from British Library copy of Albert Smith, *The Drama Founded on the New Christmas Annual of Charles Dickens, Esq., Called The Battle of Life, Dramatised by Albert Smith, Esq., (Member of the Dramatic Author's Society,) From early Proofs of the Work, By the Express Permission of the Author* (London: W.S. Johnson, [1846]).

[102]   See playbills, V&ATA Box 1381: Lyceum 1845; Box 1383: Lyceum 1847.

[103]   See playbills, V&ATA Box 1382: Lyceum 1846; Box 1400: Lyceum April–Sept 1852.

[104]   Peter H. Hansen, 'Smith, Albert Richard (1816–1860)', *DNB*, accessed 11 August 2012 online via http://www.oxforddnb.com.

[105]   V&ATA Box 1380: Lyceum 1840–44; See *The Pilgrim Edition of the Letters of Charles Dickens*, ed. Madeline House, Graham Storey, and Kathleen Tillotson, 12 vols (Oxford: Clarendon Press, 1965–2002), 4: 150–51; V&ATA Box 1381: Lyceum 1845. Smith and Dickens became great friends, and shared a love of the Alps.

[106]   See V&ATA Box 1393: Lyceum July–Dec 1850 and Box 1394: Lyceum Jan–Feb 1851.

[107]   Peter H. Hansen.

[108]   Joseph Knight, 'Keeley, Robert (1793–1869)', rev. Nilanjana Banerji, *DNB*, accessed 11 August 2012 online via http://www.oxforddnb.com.

Others of Dickens's and Jerrold's networks also wrote for the Lyceum audiences alongside writing for readers of fiction and newspapers. Mark Lemon, one of Dickens's amateur players, and Gilbert à Beckett, a school friend of Douglas Jerrold, co-wrote *Open Sesame; or, a Night with the Forty Thieves* and *Aladdin; or the Wonderful Lamp* for the Lyceum; such extravaganzas must have been what led Dickens to describe the Lyceum as 'Fairy Land' in *Household Words*.[109] Shirley Brooks was another member of these networks who could turn his hand to multiple genres. Brooks did illustrations for a work by Smith, wrote for the *Morning Chronicle* from 1848 to 1852 and *Punch* from 1851 (he took over from Lemon as editor of *Punch* in 1870), and found success as a dramatist.[110] His drama *The Creole, or Love's Fetters* and his comedy *Anything for a Change* were performed at the Lyceum in 1847 and 1848, respectively, and he wrote his own dramatic tribute to the Great Exhibition, *The Exposition,* for the Strand Theatre; it was published by T.H. Lacy.[111] Networking often involved publishing positive 'puffs' for friends: *Puppet-Show* gave an unusually favourable notice of *Anything for a Change* as 'witty, sparkling, and amusing'.[112] Douglas Jerrold and his son W. Blanchard Jerrold both had plays put on at the Lyceum between 1843 and 1853, at the same time that they were writing fiction and journalism.[113] G.H. Lewes visited the Lyceum as a reviewer for the *Leader* and wrote several plays for its stage as Slingsby Lawrence. These included the highly popular *The Game of Speculation* and, with Charles Mathews, *A Chain of Events* and *A Strange History,* both of which were published by Lacy.[114]

There were other links between those who wrote for audiences and those who wrote for readers. Dickens's friend Clarkson Stanfield ('Stanny'), the scene painter and illustrator, worked on Dickens's Christmas books as well as on an authorized adaptation of *The Chimes* at the Adelphi, along with Leech, Maclise, and Doyle.[115] Deborah Vlock has joined a long line of critics who agree that the comic performances of Charles Mathews, Sr., the manager's father, influenced Dickens's comic characters, and Charles Dickens, Jr., edited the biography

---

[109]   [Dickens], 'A Detective Police Party', 409. For playbills of Lemon and à Beckett's collaborations, see V&ATA Box 1380: Lyceum 1840–44.

[110]   G.C. Boase, 'Brooks, Charles William Shirley (1816–1874)', rev. H.C.G. Matthew, *DNB*, accessed 11 August 2012 online via http://www.oxforddnb.com.

[111]   V&ATA Box 1385: Lyceum April–July 1848; Victorian Plays Project, play list accessed 7 October 2011 online via http://victorian.worc.ac.uk/modx/index.php?id=32.

[112]   'Editor's Box', *Puppet-Show*, 17 June 1848, 107.

[113]   These were *The Prisoner of War* and *Cool as a Cucumber*, respectively. V&ATA Box 1381: Lyceum 1845; Box 1395: Lyceum Mar–April 1851.

[114]   V&ATA Box 1398: Lyceum Sept–Dec 1851 and Box 1400: Lyceum April–Sept 1852; Victorian Plays Project, play list accessed 7 October 2011online via http://victorian.worc.ac.uk/modx/index.php?id=32.

[115]   Pieter van der Merwe, 'Stanfield, Clarkson (1793–1867)', *DNB*, accessed 11 August 2012 online via http://www.oxforddnb.com; H. Philip Bolton, *Dickens Dramatized* (London: Mansell, 1987), 269.

of Charles J. Mathews.[116] In York Street, which bisects Wellington Street, the theatrical periodical *The Curtain* drew together many of the 'popular writers' of the day, including Reach, Smith, and Horace Mayhew (brother of Henry). Listed on the cover of the number for 13 July 1847 alongside these names is Charles Kenney, who worked with Albert Smith on extravaganzas for the Lyceum.[117]

The writers and editors of Wellington Street often had links with other theatres, too. Henry and Augustus Mayhew both also wrote for the stage; their brother Horace was a longstanding sub-editor of *Punch* and wrote a play too, while Edward Mayhew wrote a book about theatre practice.[118] The *Punch* writers collaborated on *Punch's Pantomime,* which was performed at Covent Garden Theatre and published from the *Punch* office while the periodical's headquarters were still at 13 Wellington Street (South).[119] Douglas Jerrold and Gilbert à Beckett co-managed the Queen's Theatre in the 1830s, and Dickens was first professionally involved with à Beckett when they were both writing for the St. James's Theatre.[120] The Strand Theatre was co-managed by Douglas Jerrold (who came from a theatrical family himself) and his father-in-law, W.J. Hammond, in the 1830s. When it was renamed Punch's Playhouse briefly for a year from April 1851, this was in tribute to Jerrold himself, who was brother-in-law to the new manager, William Copeland (as well as father-in-law to Mayhew).[121] More broadly, writers connected to Wellington Street had a large influence on London drama in the 1840s and '50s, as it was not just Dickens who had his famous works adapted for the stage. Reynolds, Jerrold, and Mayhew all had their most well-known London writings turned into popular plays.[122]

All these biographical connections show that the world of the writer and the world of the theatre were not separate, but were bound up together in the same

---

[116] *The Life of Charles James Mathews: Chiefly Autobiographical, with Selections from his Correspondents and Speeches*, ed. Charles Dickens, Jr., 2 vols (London: Macmillan, 1879).

[117] Front cover of *The Curtain*, 13 July 1847. V&ATA Box 1382: Lyceum 1847; Kurt Gänzl, 'Kenney, Charles Lamb (1821–1881)', *DNB*, accessed 11 August 2012 online via http://www.oxforddnb.com.

[118] Deborah Vlock, 'Mayhew, Horace (1816–1872)', *DNB*, accessed 11 August 2012 online via www.oxforddnb.com; Edward Mayhew, *Stage Effect: or, the Principles which Command Dramatic Success in the Theatre* (London: C. Mitchell, 1840).

[119] The Writers of Punch, *Punch's Pantomime: or, Harlequin King John and Magna Carta* (London: Punch Office, 13 Wellington Street, Strand, 1843).

[120] Arthur William à Beckett, *The à Becketts of 'Punch': Memories of Fathers and Sons* (Westminster: Archibald Constable, 1903), 55.

[121] Raymond Mander and Joe Mitchenson, *The Lost Theatres of London* (London: Rupert Hart-Davis, 1968), 391; Stirling, *Old Drury Lane: Fifty Years' Recollections of Author, Actor, and Manager*, 2 vols (London: Chatto and Windus, 1881), 1: 195.

[122] G.W.M. Reynolds's *Mysteries of London*, Henry Mayhew's *London Labour and the London Poor*, and Douglas Jerrold's *History of St. Giles and St. James* were all adapted for the stage by several dramatists. For more on this, see Tony Williams, *The Representation of London in Regency and Victorian Drama.*

sphere, epitomized by pirated theatrical adaptations of fiction. Such adaptations were an open recognition that audiences were made up of current, prospective, and past readers (especially in the West End theatres, where audience literacy was likely to be higher on average than in the poorer theatres). Later in the century, Sala commented on an adaptation of a novel by the journalist, novelist, and dramatist Edmund Yates, a protégé of Dickens and of Albert Smith, whose father managed the Adelphi Theatre until 1842:[123]

> You have a series of segregated 'flashes' of the novelist's scenes and characters, and of his real purpose and intent, but a well-linked chain of narrative or action is generally past hoping for. Mr. Edmund Yates has not suffered more in this respect than has his illustrious Master in Letters. There is scarcely one novel of Charles Dickens that a real Dickensian scholar can listen to, as a play, with common patience.[124]

The adapter becomes a privileged type of reader, who can share (or inflict) their reading upon others. H. Chance Newton described the way he and another hack dramatist for the Britannia Theatre in Hoxton, Colin Hazlewood, raided publications such as the *London Journal* and *Reynolds's Miscellany* for suitable material:

> Hazlewood, or one of us working with him, would run through these periodicals, jotting down the main incidents in the stories thereof, and scissoring out here and there sundry axioms, aphorisms, and moral sentiments, and so forth [...]. [Later] he or his assistants would take down from the shelf sundry envelopes containing these aphorisms, such as 'Ambition is', etc., or 'Kindness of the heart', etc. and so forth, and would pop these moral, patriotic, and other reflections into the play-script then under way.[125]

One can see why such butcherings did not always go down well with authors. However, then, as now, such adaptations were good publicity and served to keep the writer in the public eye. Robert L. Mack points out that some critics have suggested that Lloyd's 'Salisbury School' writers may well have come to some arrangement with the cheap theatre managers about the adaptation of their fiction, aware that they had no protection from piracy under copyright law.[126]

---

[123] E.H. Yates, *Edmund Yates: His Recollections and Experiences*, 3rd edn, 2 vols (London: Richard Bentley, 1885), 1: 7.

[124] George Augustus Sala, *Echoes of the Year Eighteen Hundred and Eighty-Three* (London: Remington, 1884), 392.

[125] H. Chance Newton, *Crime and the Drama: or Dark Deeds Dramatized* (London: Stanley Paul, 1927), 203–4. Such 'scissoring' recalls attacks on so-called 'cut and paste journalism' throughout the first half of the nineteenth century.

[126] Robert L. Mack, *The Wonderful and Surprising History of Sweeney Todd: The Life and Times of an Urban Legend* (London: Continuum, 2007), 202.

Plagiarism and imitation were threats to artistic integrity, but also evidence of networks connected by print as well as by physical proximity.

Dickens took some measure of control over this problem by authorizing adaptations of some of his texts and then involving himself in the production. In his accounts of rehearsals for *The Battle of Life,* the writer really has become a showman:

> Keeley and his wife are making great preparations for producing the Christmas story; and I have made them (as an old Stage-manager) carry out one or two expensive notions of mine about Scenery and so forth [...]. If you will look into the [Lyceum] on the morning of the 17th 18th or 19th of next month, between the hours of 11 and 4, you will find me, in a very hot and dusty condition, playing all the parts of the piece, to the immense diversion of all the actors, Actresses, Scene shifters, carpenters, Musicians, chorus-people, tailors, dress-makers, scene painters, and general ragamuffins of the Theatre.[127]

By December, Dickens wrote to his wife:

> I really am bothered to death by this confounded *dramatization* of the Xmas Book. They were in a state so horrible at Keeley's yesterday (as perhaps Forster told you when he wrote) that I was obliged to read the book to them this morning.[128] I have just finished. They all cried very much, and seemed honestly moved [...]. At 8 tonight, we have a Rehearsal with Scenery and band, and everything but dresses. I see no probability of escaping from it before 1 or 2 o'clock in the morning. And I was at the Theatre all day yesterday. Unless I had come to London, I do not think there would have been much hope of the Version being more than just tolerated – even that, doubtful. All the actors bad. All the business frightfully behind-hand. The very words of the book confused in the copying into the densest and most insufferable nonsense. I must exempt, however, from the general badness, both the Keeleys [...]. [Their scenes are] quite perfect, even to me.
>
> The small manager [Robert Keeley], Forster, Talfourd, Stanny and Mac, dine with me at the Piazza [Coffee House, Covent Garden] today, before the rehearsal [...].
>
> Christmas Book published today – 23,000 copies already gone!!! Browne's plates for the next Dombey, much better than usual.[129]

Stage work, publishing, and illustration all occupy Dickens's mind in this letter, symbolized by his guests for dinner at the Piazza. The care he takes suggests that he knew this play was more than just an adaptation for current readers, but was

---

127   Charles Dickens, letter to W.W.F. De Cerjat, 27 November 1846, *Pilgrim*, 4: 662–3. This collaboration took place before *Household Words* was established.

128   This took place at Forster's house, 58 Lincoln's Inn Fields, about 15 or 20 minutes' walk from the theatre. See *Pilgrim*, 4: 681.

129   Charles Dickens, letter to Mrs Charles Dickens, 19 December 1846, *Pilgrim*, 4: 680–81.

also an advertisement for new ones and a way of reaching illiterate Lyceum-goers. Dickens also had his literary 'brand' to protect. This was not unprecedented: Dickens attended the rehearsals of Albert Smith's dramatization of *Cricket on the Hearth*, and declared afterwards that 'I took great pains with the "getting up" of the little piece: to the end that I might be slaughtered as gently as possible'.[130] Stirling made much of Dickens's appearance at rehearsals for his own adaptation of *Christmas Carol*:

> 1845. – Engaged to manage the Adelphi for Gladstone. Among the many dramas that I produced and wrote, ranked first Dickens's 'Christmas Carol', dramatized by his sanction. Dickens attended several rehearsals, furnishing valuable suggestions. Thinking to make Tiny Tim (a pretty child) more effective, I ordered a set of irons and bandages for his supposed weak legs. When Dickens saw this tried on the child, he took me aside:
> 'No, Stirling, no; this won't do! Remember how painful it would be to many of the audience having crippled children'.[131]

Dickens shows here that he has a definite sense of his 'real' audience; they were a gateway to his 'real' readers and to those audience members who could not read text, but could decipher a play.

Readers and audiences, then, were bound up together in the minds of writers, dramatists, and theatre reviewers. Dickens declared that 'every writer of fiction, though he may not adopt the dramatic form, writes in effect for the stage'.[132] Jacky Bratton argues that:

> Dickens's work is [...] one of the major foundations of the modern West End. Unwilling to confine himself to the impecunious Bohemian subworld of the career dramatist, but utterly unable to leave the theatre alone, the greatest Victorian author wrote for the stage only indirectly, but his work is nevertheless radically part of it. In literary terms, Dickens is the lost leader, the major modern dramatist sought for in vain by Macready and his supporters.[133]

Albert Smith's prologue to Stirling's authorized *Martin Chuzzlewit*, delivered by Mrs Keeley, invokes the presence of Dickens and his characters across his many other narratives:

> We owe this story of the present hour
> To that great master hand, whose graphic power
> Can call up laughter, bid the tear-drop start,
> Or find an echoing chord in every heart.

---

[130] Charles Dickens, letter to the Rev. Edward Taggart, 22 December 1845, *Pilgrim*, 4: 453.

[131] Stirling, *Old Drury Lane*, 186–7.

[132] *The Speeches of Charles Dickens*, ed. K.J. Fielding (Oxford: Clarendon Press, 1960), 262.

[133] Bratton, *The Making of the West End Stage*, 180.

Whom we have learned to deem an household friend,
Who, 'midst his varied writings never penn'd
One line that might his guileless pages spot,
One word that 'dying, he would wish to blot'.

We know there is around his simple name
A prestige thrown, your sympathies to claim;
But our poor playwright, feeling well his task,
Has sent me forth your clemency to ask.
And some old friends, selected from the rest,
Of human kind the sweetest and the best,
Crowd forth, your patient hearing to implore,
Presuming on the fellowship of yore.

These include, in chronological order, Mr Pickwick, Oliver Twist, the Cheeryble brothers from *Nicholas Nickleby*, Dolly Varden from *Barnaby Rudge*, and Tiny Tim. The cast of *Martin Chuzzlewit* are then positioned as the newest members of this imaginary troupe:

The others are to come. In anxious state
Behind the scenes your fiat they await.
Be satisfied, for yours and their behoof,
They'll do the best they can; now to the proof.[134]

'Graphic', during this period, carried the meaning both of '[o]f or pertaining to drawing or painting […], engraving, etching, etc.; also, the techniques of production and design involved in printing and publishing', and of '[p]roducing by words the effect of a picture; vividly descriptive, life-like' (*OED*). Dickens, the author of the original serial narrative, is evoked here as a kind of pictorial artist and stage manager, as well as a writer. His word-pictures, themselves realized in Phiz's illustrations, are what lead to the stage play. This play is itself characterized as 'life-like', depicting '[t]he romance of common life'. It is 'of the present hour' because it is contemporary and up to date, as well as because it is about to be performed. Therefore, 'the great master hand' of Dickens – compared with whom Stirling is merely 'our poor playwright' – is a 'household friend' (*Household Words* and the 'Preliminary Word' drew on tropes already used in relation to Dickens; see Chapter 1). The audience of the play and the reader of the review are drawn into an imagined community where a writer they have never met, and characters who are not real, are 'old friends' to them and to the other strangers in the audience, or other unknown readers whose homes (in both cases) may be far away. The audience is a community precisely because it is conceived of as an audience of readers, or at least of those familiar with Dickens's characters, with whom the characters have 'fellowship of yore'. These readers are addressed by a fellow reader of Dickens – Smith – whose words

---

134   V&ATA Box 1380: Lyceum 1840–44, 'Lyceum Theatre', *ILN*, 13 July 1844, 32.

are the prologue to the work of a very privileged reader, as the playbill made the audience aware that Stirling had early access to the serial's proof-sheets.[135] Audience, actors, characters, readers, illustrators, and writers are all connected by this performance.[136] Fiction becomes a way of bringing people together from many different places into one, small, localized network, symbolized by the theatre audience.

Readers and audiences are considered synonymous by the reviewer of *Martin Chuzzlewit*, too, in the *Illustrated London News*. The illustration chosen for the review (Figure 3.11) is of a scene in the play that is taken directly from the plate *Mr Pecksniff announces himself as the shield of Virtue* (Figure 3.10). In this plate by Phiz, Pecksniff is acting the part of the faithful friend, as well as acting out a standard melodramatic stance, as the reader is alerted to by the capital on 'Virtue'.

Note the identical pictures on the wall in both images, the faithful reproduction of Pecksniff's and Mark Tapley's costumes from the original plate, and the copy of Pecksniff's bust in the stage set, taken from Phiz's first plate for *Martin Chuzzlewit* the serial. The review offers an illustration which works just as much as a visual reminder of the serial as a visual anticipation of the play. It links the play to illustrations of the serial displayed in bookshop windows. It also offers a reader of *Martin Chuzzlewit* the serial a promise of an authentic dramatization which is faithful to the complete reading experience of following the text and the illustrations.

Many critics have noticed that adaptations of illustrated serial novels often contained *tableaux vivants* taken from the illustrations to the original text.[137] What is interesting about Stirling's adaptation of *Martin Chuzzlewit*, however, is that he seems to have structured his dramatization more around Phiz's illustrations than on Dickens's text. Stirling cuts all the American scenes from his adaptation, presumably for ease of representation, and so none of Phiz's American plates are realized on stage. Episodes shown in the plates for Chapters II–VI are either cut or compressed to speed up the action, although the comic scene of the dinner at Todgers's remains. With these notable exceptions, however, 22 of the 38 plates done by Phiz are used for scenes in Stirling's play, which has only five scenes that

---

[135] Playbill for *Martin Chuzzlewit*, V&ATA Box 1380: Lyceum 1840–44.

[136] Mathews tried to create a different type of intimacy with his audience in his closing address of the Lyceum's season in August 1849, where he candidly confessed that he had been losing money for two months and that the hot summer had not helped the box office, but finished by saying that he hoped the company would achieve the same average amount of success in the next season, to enable the theatre to make money the next year. The reviewer falls in line with this appeal to community spirit, declaring that 'the manager's efforts have always been so well directed, that his success is that of a public cause' (V&ATA Box 1389: Lyceum Aug–Dec 1849, 'The Theatres', *ILN*, 4 August 1849, 74).

[137] See Meisel and Bolton, for example.

Figure 3.10   *Mr Pecksniff announces himself as the shield of Virtue, Martin Chuzzlewit*, chp. XLIII. Phiz (Hablot K. Browne). Reproduced with the permission of Senate House Library, University of London. [S.L.] I [Dickens–1844].

Figure 3.11   Scene from *Martin Chuzzlewit* at the Lyceum Theatre, *ILN*, 13 July
1844, 32. V&ATA Box 1380: Lyceum 1840–44. © Victoria and
Albert Museum, London.

are not drawn directly or indirectly from Phiz's illustrations.[138] The play staged a
visual memory of the serial; even the font on the playbill replicated the font on the
cover of the monthly parts (see Figures 3.12 and 3.13). Furthermore, for an early
audience member who approached the novel after seeing the play (which must
have happened, given that the adaptation appeared so quickly after the publication
of the final number), the reading experience would have incorporated a visual
memory of the play.

---

[138]   Edward Stirling, *Martin Chuzzlewit!: A Drama in Three Acts. Adapted From C.
Dickens, Esq. Celebrated Work, by Edward Stirling, Esq.*, vol. 50 of Duncombe's Edition [of
British Theatre] (London: John Duncombe, [n.d.]); E. Stirling, *Martin Chuzzlewit* (act 1),
Lord Chamberlain's Plays collection, British Library manuscripts Add. 42976 ff. 516–
535b; Charles Dickens, *Martin Chuzzlewit*, ed. Margaret Cardwell (Oxford: Clarendon
Press, 1982). Further references will be to this Clarendon edition and will be given after
quotations in the text. The adaptation for the New Strand Theatre, in contrast, opens not
like Stirling's play – and the novel – with the Pecksniff household, but with an invented
scene at the bar of the Dragon with Tom Pinch, John Westlock, and Mrs Lupin (C. Webb,
Martin Chuzzlewit, Lord Chamberlain's Plays collection, British Library manuscripts Add.
42976 ff. 536–638).

Figure 3.12   Playbill for *Martin Chuzzlewit*, V&ATA Box 1380, Lyceum,
1840–44. © Victoria and Albert Museum, London.

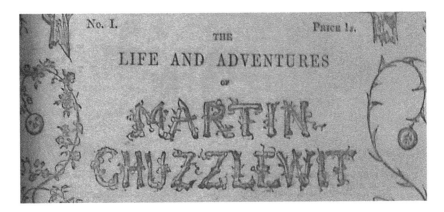

Figure 3.13   Phiz (Hablot K. Browne), cover for monthly parts, 1843.
Reproduced with the permission of Senate House Library,
University of London. [S.L.] I [Dickens–1844].

Smith reclaimed Dickens's ownership of his own words by adapting the
Christmas books from the original text almost to the letter, as if Dickens was
the ventriloquist speaking through him.[139] The reviewer of Smith's adaptation
of *Cricket on the Hearth* for the *Illustrated London News* agreed with the *Times*
that 'it would almost appear, as the *Times* remarked, that Mr. Dickens had its
representation at this house in his eye when he wrote the work'.[140] As Malcolm
Morley puts it, 'it was done purposely [...]. The task of adaptation needed little

---

[139]   When an enthusiastic audience demanded that Dickens take a bow after the first
performance of *The Battle of Life*, Smith took it in Dickens's place (V&ATA Box 1382:
Lyceum 1846, 'Lyceum Theatre', *ILN*, 26 December 1846, 413); see Albert Smith, *The
Drama Founded on the New Christmas Annual of Charles Dickens*.

[140]   V&ATA Box 1381: Lyceum 1845, 'The Theatres', *ILN*, 27 December 1845, 413.

more than taking the dialogue and using it in the sequence provided by the author.'[141] With *The Battle of Life*, as with *Cricket*, 'the pattern provided by Dickens largely prepared the ground for a stage version, each of the three parts into which the text is divided being material for an act [...]. [Dickens] had the theatre in mind when he planned the tale'.[142] The defence against plagiarism required a different conception of the imagined community of readers: in the Christmas books, Dickens's readers were always an audience.

Of course, the page and the stage had essential differences. The Lyceum produced an adaptation of Jerrold's popular comic series for *Punch*, *Mrs Caudle's Curtain Lectures*, in 1845. The review in the *Illustrated London News* suggests that the Keeleys misread Jerrold's series, and could not translate comic humour from printed page to stage; or rather, that the humour is different:

> Dramatic writers have yet to understand clearly the difference between the humour that appeals to the eye in a comic periodical, and that which speaks to the ear in a large audience. Some of *Mrs Caudle's* drollest bits, although given with that careful perception which distinguishes Mr Keeley's acting, failed to raise the slightest ruffle of laughter. And the spirit of the lectures was somewhat misunderstood by the adapter. *Caudle* is not a sot, but a victim; the sympathies of the listener should go with him entirely [...]. The humorous graphic detail which affords such amusement in the reading produces only *ennui* on the stage.[143]

'The absence of action and situation' fails to work on the stage, however well written and acted a piece may be. If audiences also contain readers, then a stage adaptation can fail because it comes across as a *mis*-reading.

Dickens took a curtain call at the first night of his play *The Village Coquettes* (1836). As Douglas-Fairhurst points out in *Becoming Dickens*, 'the curtains of the St. James's Theatre were green, as were the covers of Pickwick, so in coming onstage, Dickens would have looked strangely like the author himself emerging from his writing'.[144] The play was reviewed by Forster for the *Examiner*, and the curtain calls annoyed Forster, who considered it demeaning for a writer – however popular – to be paraded as spectacle, exhibited as 'the real living Boz'. The audience was unhappy, however, because Dickens failed to look like either the Boz they had envisaged or any of the Pickwick characters.[145] For a writer, revealing yourself as the showman was a risky business; the public were not your

---

[141]   Malcolm Morley, "The Cricket on the Stage", *Dickensian*, 48, no. 301 (Winter 1951/2): 17. See also Philip V. Allingham, "The Costuming and Set Design of Plays Adapted from Dickens's Christmas Books: Realisations of the Illustrations", in *Victorian Web*, accessed 1 November, 2011 online via http://www.victorianweb.org/.

[142]   Malcolm Morley, '*The Battle of Life* in the Theatre', *Dickensian* 48, no. 302 (Spring 1952): 76–7.

[143]   V&ATA Box 1381: Lyceum 1845, 'The Theatres', *ILN*, 19 July 1845, 42.

[144]   Robert Douglas-Fairhurst, *Becoming Dickens: The Invention of a Novelist* (Cambridge, MA and London: Belknap Press of Harvard University Press, 2011), 231.

[145]   [John Forster], 'Theatrical Examiner', *Examiner*, 11 December 1836, 792.

friends, no matter how much you addressed them as if they were. What a writer needed was both familiarity and distance. Dickens was visible in the window of 16 Wellington Street North, but this was only a short step away from his public humiliation as an 'exhibit' in the window of Warren's Blacking Factory as a boy.[146] Exhibiting oneself publicly as a 'showman' carried dangers when the print networks of Wellington Street and its neighbours were small enough not to be anonymous.[147]

Anonymity, Mayhew, and the Drama of the Streets

In 1852, Angus B. Reach was banned from spending any more evenings at the Lyceum because Vestris and Mathews mistakenly thought he had written a particularly critical review of its run for the *Morning Chronicle*. Their private spat was conducted publicly in print, through notices pinned up in the theatre and articles in the *Chronicle* (Figure 3.14).[148] Yet the fact that Reach was banned shows that Vestris and Mathews, and others at the Lyceum, knew full well who Reach was and were well able to recognize him if he came though the theatre's doors. Reach has 'chosen to throw off the character of anonymous enemy'; he has forfeited the right to be part of the in-crowd of 'Friends and Patrons' and is even charged with having no friends at all. In the tussle for supremacy between theatre manager and critic, print network and entertainment network, the manager has won: all passersby on Wellington Street would have seen the notice with Reach's name in large capitals, whereas his negative review is consigned to the attention only of 'those [...] who take an interest in such matters' (Figure 3.14). The suggestion is that the real public, made up of audience members and passersby, is actually larger that the imagined readership of the offending newspaper. The face-to-face network is characterized by Mathews the theatre manager as more important than the imagined network.

The West End theatre was romanticized in fiction as a site of coincidence and connection, where the anonymity supposedly found within the metropolitan crowd is stripped away by 'the many strange coincidences which life in the city creates', as Peter Ackroyd (rather lyrically) puts it.[149] Douglas Jerrold's popular novel *The History Of St. Giles And St. James* (serialized in *Douglas Jerrold's Shilling Magazine* 1847–49 and re-issued in two volumes in 1851) was premised on the connections and links between the worlds of the poor boy, St. Giles, and the

---

[146]   I am grateful to Richard Pearson for this point.

[147]   See Linda M. Shires, 'The Author as Spectacle and Commodity: Elizabeth Barrett Browning and Thomas Hardy', in *Victorian Literature and the Victorian Visual Imagination*, ed. Carol T. Christ and John O. Jordan (Berkeley: University of California Press, 1995), 198–212, on the simultaneous attraction and aversion to becoming a spectacle.

[148]   This led to the issue of press privileges and the independence of reviews to be debated in the 'The Press and the Theatres', *ILN Supplement*, 29 January 1853.

[149]   Ackroyd, *London*, 284.

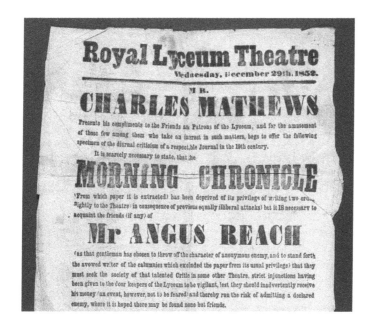

Figure 3.14   Public notice, Royal Lyceum Theatre, 29 December 1852.
              V&ATA Box 1401: Lyceum Oct–Dec 1852. © Victoria and Albert
              Museum, London.

rich boy, St. James. An early scene hammers home this point when all the main
characters so far introduced end up congregated on Bow Street after they emerge
from an evening spent at Covent Garden Theatre. Far from this being a happy
meeting, however, it results in both the marquis's family and the family of Jem the
linkman witnessing that '[y]oung St. Giles was the robber of young St. James'.[150]
These new theatres, recently built public spaces in the heart of the city, exist in
an uneasy, even paradoxical relationship with the known networks of the locality.
The theatre in this period mediates and negotiates between a public space designed
for a wider, more literate public and a more secluded world of coterie. This creates
an uneasiness in the representations of moments of encounter at the theatre.

   Often this kind of meeting and moment of recognition is the last thing in the
world that a character desires. David Copperfield, drunk after hosting his very first
dinner party in his new London lodgings, bumps into Agnes at the theatre while
out with Steerforth and his cronies and recalls this with horror as he nurses his
hangover the next morning (*David Copperfield*).[151] In *Bleak House*, Esther is made

[150]   Douglas Jerrold, *The History of St. Giles and St. James*, in *The Works of Douglas
Jerrold*, ed. W. Blanchard Jerrold, 4 vols (London: Bradbury & Evans, 1863–64; 1st publ.
1847–49, 1st volume edition 1851), 1: 41.
[151]   Charles Dickens, *David Copperfield*, ed. Nina Burgis (Oxford: Clarendon Press,
1981; 1st published 1849–50), 309–10.

to feel 'ridiculous' and 'uneasy' when the rejected Mr Guppy takes to following her to the theatre and staring at her, instead of at the stage, during a performance:

> from that time forth, we never went to the play, without my seeing Mr. Guppy in the pit [...]. If he were not there when we went in, and I began to hope he would not come, and yielded myself for a little while to the interest of the scene, I was certain to encounter his languishing eyes when I least expected it, and, from that time, to be quite sure that they were fixed upon me all the evening [...].
>
> So there I sat, not knowing where to look – for wherever I looked, I knew Mr. Guppy's eyes were following me – and thinking of the dreadful expense to which this young man was putting himself, on my account.[152]

We know we are in the realm of comedy, not tragedy, when we reach that last sentence, but the unsettling reversal of order remains. Esther herself has become the 'scene', rather than the play, as shown by the orientation of Phiz's drawing (Figure 3.15). Less comically, when Pip goes to watch Mr Wopsle perform at a theatre in Greenwich, he learns to his great unease that the villain, Compeyson, sat behind him 'like a ghost' during Wopsle's performance.[153]

Richard Markham works as a playwright under an assumed name to earn money in *Series I* of *Mysteries of London*, but is undone when he is unable to resist the acclaim of the audience and goes on stage to take a bow. At first, the theatre seems to be an impersonal place full of unfamiliar faces, an audience of anonymous strangers who could have come from anywhere in order to enjoy a night at a London play:

> Richard was dazzled by the glare of light, and for some time could see nothing distinctly.
>
> Myriads of human countenances, heaped together, danced before him; yet the aspect and feature of none were accurately delineated to his eyes. He could not have selected from amongst those countenances, even that of his long-lost brother, or that of his dearly-beloved Isabella, had they been both or either of them prominent in that multitude of faces.
>
> And Isabella *was* there, with her parents – impelled by the curiosity which had taken so many thither that evening.
>
> Her surprise, and that of her father and mother, may therefore well be conceived, when, in the author of one of the most successful and beautiful dramatic compositions of modern times, they recognised Richard Markham![154]

---

[152]   Charles Dickens, *Bleak House*, ed. Stephen Gill (Oxford: Oxford University Press, 1996; 1st publ. 1852–53; reissued 2008), 184. Further references are to this edition and appear parenthetically in the text.

[153]   Charles Dickens, *Great Expectations*, ed. Margaret Cardwell (Oxford: Clarendon Press, 1993; 1st publ. 1860–61), 384.

[154]   G.W.M. Reynolds, *The Mysteries of London, Series I*, 2 vols (London: George Vickers(?), October 1844–26 September 1846), 1: 276.

Figure 3.15   *Mr. Guppy's Desolation, Bleak House*, chp. XIII. Phiz (Hablot K. Browne). Reproduced with the permission of Senate House Library, University of London. [S.L.] I [Dickens–1853] copy 1.

Yet any illusion of safety in anonymity within the city is swept away by Reynolds within a few lines. Richard is immediately recognized by a member of the audience as 'Richard Markham who was condemned to two years' imprisonment for forgery!'; among the witnesses to this denunciation are the two young women who are in love with Richard, 'Mary-Anne and the faithful Isabella!', who both happen to be in the theatre that night.[155] The theatre comes to stand for the experience of the crowded, brightly lit metropolis itself, as the illusion of modernity and anonymity is slowly punctured by the way individual faces start to stand out from the crowd, and the face-to-face community is revealed as still there, hiding behind the surface.

The disorientating collision between the local and the strange, the familiar and the unfamiliar, is used by Mayhew to destabilize his readers' way of looking at the people of the metropolis in *London Labour*.[156] As I noted in the Introduction, comparisons have often been drawn between the writing of Dickens and Mayhew, and Douglas-Fairhurst has compared Mayhew with Reynolds.[157] As Humpherys points out, 'in 1845 Dickens and Mayhew were close enough for the latter to take part in the novelist's amateur theatrical *Every Man in His Humour*: Mayhew played Knowell [...], [but] after 1845 there is no indication of a continuing association between the two men'. Humpherys speculates that this could have been due to professional rivalry when Dickens was attempting to launch *Household Words*, or because of some sort of quarrel over an issue, such as occurred between Dickens and Jerrold over capital punishment (see Chapter 1). Dickens's failure to refer to *London Labour*, as Humpherys suggests, could also have been 'an effort to hide the fact that he used details from it in a few instances, if in fact he did'.[158] Yet the proximity of their offices in 1851–52 raises the probability that Dickens and Mayhew were well aware of each other, and may even have passed each other on the street. Mayhew was certainly just as surrounded by 'Fairy Land', and just as

---

[155]   Ibid.

[156]   The Wellington Street serial edition was not the first, nor the only, edition of the text; for a good account of the complicated publication history of *London Labour*, see Anne Humpherys, *Travels into the Poor Man's Country: The Work of Henry Mayhew* (Athens, GA: The University of Georgia Press, 1977). As Bernard Taithe explains, 'the 1851 edition is not the only one valid for the reader of Victorian literature, but it is the only one published under Mayhew's sole editorship and control. Later editions were certainly also widely read but not by the same people and not in the same way. The difference in price between the cheap editions of 1851, or even 1865, and the edition of 1861 and 1862 in hardcover volumes was significant. Moreover, reading [*London Labour*] as a serial, published over two years, was quite different from reading a bound, multi-volume book'; Bernard Taithe, 'Part I', in *The Essential Mayhew: Representing and Communicating the Poor*, ed. Bernard Taithe (London: Rivers Oram Press, 1996), 19.

[157]   See Humpherys, *Travels*; Taithe, 'Part I', 7; Robert Douglas-Fairhurst, 'Introduction', in *London Labour and the London Poor: a Selected Edition*, ed. Robert Douglas-Fairhurst (Oxford: Oxford University Press, 2010), xxxviii.

[158]   Humpherys, *Travels*, 179–80.

much a point of connection between literary, journalistic, and theatrical networks, as Dickens was.

The tension between familiarity and distance, the local and the strange, emerges in the theatrical style of Mayhew's interviews. As Joachim Schlor notes, '[m]any writers describe the city streets as stages, as theatre stages even'.[159] Mayhew goes one step further: he did not just go out and describe the poor and their environment; he got them to do that for him, so that they perform for the reader.[160] The theatricality inherent in these first-person narratives was quickly spotted by the hack dramatists, and adaptations of *London Labour* were popular at the cheaper theatres in the 1850s.[161] Mayhew himself dramatized his work, staging *Mr Henry Mayhew's Curious Conversazione* in 1857, in which he impersonated several urban 'types'.[162] One way in which this theatricality emerges onto the pages of *London Labour* is through its relationship, as Robert Douglas-Fairhurst suggests, to the dramatic monologue. This nineteenth-century form, made famous by the works of poets such as Browning (firstly in *Dramatic Lyrics*, published in 1842) and Tennyson, 'is one carefully situated between theatrical speech and the quieter reflections of print', and Douglas-Fairhurst shows that *London Labour* shares several features with Tennyson's and Browning's poetic versions of the dramatic monologue.[163] Mayhew's interview technique evolved during his *Morning Chronicle* days into a kind of showman's ventriloquism, 'a new form of reporting, a fusion of himself, through his questions, and the respondent, whose answers were reported in the first person, in a long interrupted monologue, with the questions absorbed into the replies'.[164] This technique allows for both familiarity and distance between interviewer and subject. The interviewer is absorbed into the voice of the interviewee, so there is less of a mediating voice between the words of the informant and the conclusions drawn by the reader. However, at the same time the informant is made to speak as if unprompted, like a strange exhibit.

---

[159]   Joachim Schlör, *Nights in the Big City: Paris – Berlin – London 1840–1930*, trans. Pierre Gottfried Imhof and Dafydd Rees Roberts (London: Reaktion Books, 1998; 1st publ. in German, 1991), 241.

[160]   This is not to accuse Mayhew of simply adding to 'the endless search after romantic vignettes of the poor'; Eileen Yeo is right to point out the difference between Mayhew and the 'purple passages and theatricalising of work people' found in the popular 'London low life' genre. Rather, it is to recognize that Mayhew's project brought writer, readers, and informants into a network bound together by print. See Eileen Yeo, 'Mayhew as Social Investigator', in *The Unknown Mayhew: Selections from the Morning Chronicle 1849–1850*, ed. E.P. Thompson and Eileen Yeo, 2nd edn (Harmondsworth: Penguin, 1984), 109.

[161]   See Tony Williams on such adaptations, 117–52.

[162]   Harland-Lang, 211–12.

[163]   Douglas-Fairhurst, introduction to Mayhew, *London Labour*, xxxiii–iv. Quotations from this work will be cited parenthetically in the text.

[164]   Humpherys, *Travels*, 40. Although, as Humpherys points out, the early pages of volume I are mostly written in Mayhew's narrative voice. See *Travels*, 74.

This reinforces Mayhew's introductory remarks about the strangeness of the world of London's poor. For all that the street-folk are visible in and around Wellington Street and its environs every day and evening, they might as well be as far away as 'darkest Africa' (*London Labour*, Preface: iii). At the same time, paradoxically, Mayhew the middle-class Bohemian's identification with his interviewees as he melds his voice with theirs – 'the implicit attraction street life held for him' – creates a link between the reader and people 'whom the public has less knowledge of than of the most distant tribes of the earth' (*London Labour*, Preface: iii).[165]

Mayhew's imagined national network of correspondents, readers, and informants was an extension of the essentially dialogic nature of running a periodical, and of the interlinked local world of Wellington Street. This is revealed through a study of the 'Answers to Correspondents' section of *London Labour*, printed on the front and back wrappers of each weekly number, which grew and developed as the weeks progressed.[166] Here, readers from around the country wrote in to challenge or support Mayhew's work, and Mayhew shared his theories on labour and on political economy. The letters also allow the voices of *London Labour*, Mayhew's interviewees, to speak again to the readers and to enter into a kind of dialogue with them (albeit one still mediated through Mayhew's editorial choices).[167] Taithe sees it as Mayhew 'enlarging his team' by recruiting his readers as providers of information, and this is definitely part of the story.[168] At one point, Mayhew asks for someone to come to the office at number 16 and audit accounts of monies distributed to the poor.[169] But Mayhew's interest in reader contributions might also have emerged from an understanding of print production as a collaborative and network-based business.

Mayhew did not work alone: Augustus Mayhew, Richard Knight, and Henry Wood helped Mayhew with transcribing interviews and finding suitable informants, while Volume 3 was mostly written by Horace St. John.[170] In 'Answers to Correspondents', Mayhew asks readers to send all donations to John Howden (Mayhew's publisher) at the office.[171] In his years at the *Punch* table, Mayhew would have been well used to the practice of publishing as a process and the

---

[165]   Humpherys, *Travels*, 79.

[166]   This is often incomplete or missing from bound editions of the 1850–52 serial. The best reproduction of 'Answers to Correspondents', gleaned from several different surviving copies, is in Part II of Taithe, 'Part II: Answers to Correspondents', 85–251.

[167]   The readers of *London Labour* are willing and able to challenge Mayhew's opinions and conclusions. For example, Mayhew conducts a long-running and strongly worded argument with a reader called 'W.H.' over political economy, and the occupants of the lodging house on Charles Street, Drury Lane, complain that it is not 'low' because they have a library and take *Household Words* (Taithe, ed., 'Part II: Answers to Correspondents', 172; 147).

[168]   Taithe, 'Part I', 24.

[169]   Taithe, ed., 'Part II: Answers to Correspondents', 166.

[170]   Yeo, 67–9; Taithe, 'Part I', 19.

[171]   Taithe, ed., 'Part II: Answers to Correspondents', 134–5.

printed periodical as a product which emerged out of discussion and dialogue.[172] There are moments when Mayhew's serial provides a glimpse of a very local print community. The three volumes of *London Labour* were dedicated by Mayhew to Douglas Jerrold, his father-in-law, ex-Punch colleague, and occupant three years previously of offices at 17 Upper Wellington Street for *Douglas Jerrold's Weekly Newspaper.* After the *London Labour* office moved to 16 Upper Wellington Street, *London Labour* advertised a pamphlet by William Tweedie.[173] Tweedie, as we have seen, has an address at 11 Wellington Street North in the 1852 *Post Office Directory* and is registered as resident at 18 Upper Wellington Street on the 1851 census.[174]

This networked world of the London print economy affected Mayhew's perception of the imagined network of his readers. Communication through 'Answers to Correspondents' offers to the reader a way of participating in Mayhew's project and in Mayhew's network.[175] The national perspective given by the readers in 'Answers to Correspondents' complicates the specificity of London in *London Labour*, as Taithe points out.[176] Mayhew made use of a national network of retailing; *London Labour*, 'published every Saturday, was sold in railway stations in London and in the provinces, Ireland included'.[177] The remoteness of London for many of its readers is revealed by one reader's suggestion that Mayhew should provide a map of London for provincial readers, to aid their mental mapping of the text.[178] But the correspondents' letters reveal a nationwide network of readers. An Oxfordshire reader writes in to say how useful *London*

---

[172] See Leary; Black, 112–46. This was very different to Dickens's approach to editing, where the governing persona and voice always had to be that of Dickens himself and '[t]he illusion of consensus was to be staged, [...] created by Dickens's systematic imposition of his own values and practices on the writings of his contributors' (Juliet John, *Dickens's Villains: Melodrama, Character, Popular Culture* (Oxford: Oxford University Press, 2001), 91–2.

[173] Taithe, ed., 'Part II: Answers to Correspondents', 206.

[174] *Kelly's POD*, 557; 1851 census, HO107/1511, f. 122, accessed 15 July 2011 online via http://www.ancestry.co.uk/. This was before he probably moved to 337 Strand, his publishing imprint address from 1852. See, for example, British Library catalogue items 4406.c.30. and 8435.a.35.

[175] Taithe, 'Part I', 27. This network is one that includes the voices of the street-poor and the working-class. Often they are soliciting financial aid. A poor harp-player writes in to beg for help; a shopkeeper writes in after his premises are destroyed by fire; a young Jewish man from Holland writes in looking for a job as a tutor (Taithe, ed., 'Part II: Answers to Correspondents', 99; 119; 243). Mayhew vouches for both of the latter, almost as if he is introducing his acquaintances to the reader. Readers themselves joined in: one reader visited the poor poet and wrote in to say that the man was just like his picture and in real need (Taithe, ed., 'Part II: Answers to Correspondents', 159). Reader reaches out to reader, almost over and above the head of Mayhew.

[176] Taithe, 'Part I', 32.

[177] Ibid., 18.

[178] Taithe, ed., 'Part II: Answers to Correspondents', 103.

Labour is for the whole country, not just for London, and furnishes him with information about labour conditions in Oxfordshire.[179] Another reader writes in with information on conditions in Edinburgh, while a lady sends a description of the popularity of magic lantern shows for the poor in her country parish.[180] Mayhew publishes letters from the Manchester Bolt Makers, the Derby Anti-Truck Society, and a letter about the Liverpool Benevolent Society for Reclaiming Unfortunate Females.[181] The imagined community of readers is presented as in fact a very intimate, dialogic network of shared interests and concerns.

Mayhew's showmanship as a writer, stage-managing the scene, worked to create an impression for the reader and for his interviewees of participation in a local, face-to-face network. However, this was not necessarily a positive experience for Mayhew's informants, whose performances in print sometimes ended their anonymity in the streets. Robert Douglas-Fairhurst has pointed out that the street sellers of *London Labour* sometimes have a tendency to describe their own lives like characters from the popular stage. One sees his point that '[i]t is hard to believe that a vagrant would say "To tell you the truth, I loved a roving, idle life" [...] unless he heard the coins chinking in his interviewer's pocket'.[182] Early and mid-Victorian iconography frequently fitted the poor into stereotypes drawn from the stage.[183] Figure 3.16, a sketch of a scene on Bow Street, places the costermonger, the Punch and Judy show, and the much grander stage of Covent Garden Theatre in the same urban and visual space. The costermonger is a spectacle to be observed, part of the street theatre of the metropolis, just as the street sellers found their way onto the urban stage (Figure 3.17). Readers here are consciously cast as spectators, as if in an audience.[184]

Readers were an audience for Mayhew, too, and he saw writing as 'visionary drama'.[185] Mayhew's serial allowed his street folk to perform poverty publicly; his writing made the unfamiliar world of the London street sellers more familiar,

---

[179]   Ibid., 187.

[180]   Ibid., 122; 157.

[181]   Ibid., 158; 209; 223.

[182]   Douglas-Fairhurst, introduction to *London Labour,* xxix.

[183]   See Vlock, 19.

[184]   This lithograph was published by that member of the radical metropolitan underworld, John Duncombe (see Chapter 1). Duncombe was also well known for his theatrical publications, including lithographs of popular actors and actresses, and a periodical, *The Mirror of the Stage,* which counted as its contributors Douglas Jerrold and Samuel Laman Blanchard. See John Drew, 'Blanchard, [Samuel] Laman (1803–1845)', *DNCJ,* 61, and Michael Slater, 'Jerrold, William Douglas (1803–1857)', *DNCJ,* 318.

[185]   Henry Mayhew, 'Preface', in *The Upper Rhine: The Scenery of its Banks and the Manners of Its People. Illustrated by Birket Foster. Described by Henry Mayhew* (London: George Routledge & Co., 1858), v–vi. Bernard Taithe makes a similar point in *The Essential Mayhew,* 14–15. Of course, such comparisons of writing with painting or illustration are inevitable in a book where the prose writer is given second billing to the artist on the title page.

Figure 3.16   *Covent Garden Theatre; The Costardmonger.* From Luke Limner's
London Cries and Public Edifices, 1847. © The British Library
Board, 1303.a.28, facing page 12.

Figure 3.17   *Come buy my oranges*. Lithographed cover to sheet music of a popular stage song, engraved by T.H. Jones, published by John Duncombe, 1855. The Bodleian Libraries, The University of Oxford, John Johnson Collection: Actors, Actresses and Entertainers 5 (38).

puncturing the anonymity of the metropolis. At the same time, it emphasized the exoticism of the local as it chronicled the colourful details of the lives of its unnamed subjects. In *London Labour* the 'foreign' is found strangely close and nearby, while at the same time the familiar and everyday sight of street traders looks suddenly as strange and exotic as any Lyceum burlesque. In the pages of *London Labour* the reader enters not a 'Fairy Land', but one where struggles worthy of melodrama are revealed uncomfortably as taking place just down the street and right under the nose of the reader. As Thackeray's review of *Morning Chronicle* letters for *Punch* expressed, 'you and I [...] we have had hitherto no community with the poor, [until Mayhew] travels into the poor man's country for us, and comes back with his tale of terror and wonder'.[186] What is remarkable, for Thackeray, is that 'the poor man's country' is all around him in the metropolis. Reading Mayhew's work in print allows people like Thackeray to feel 'community with the poor', but it also destabilizes his sense of how well he knows London. Mayhew's reports made the local seem foreign and the strange seem familiar, as if the extras of a play stepped forward to take centre stage, in what Tony Williams calls 'a fundamentally dramatic experience for his readers'.[187]

The anonymity of writers or performers, however, could not survive an entrance onto the stage. The Crippled Street-seller of Nutmeg-graters wrote in to *London Labour* to thank Mayhew for the monies forwarded to him, but adds: 'I am gazed at in the street with astonishment; and observations made in my hearing with respect to the Exact Likeness of the portrait.'[188] Because the publication exhibited his portrait, his face is known to strangers, and this means that he is aided with public donations. However, he has also lost his anonymity and become a well-known local 'exhibit', whom strangers think they know. Mayhew himself was concerned about the anonymity of readers in 'Answers to Correspondents'. He asks that names of correspondents be provided, 'as a guarantee of respectability and good faith':

> MR. MAYHEW (for obvious reasons) never prints the names of those from whom he receives his information, but leaves the public to look to him alone as the person responsible for the truth of the statements here published; it is therefore necessary for his own credit sake [*sic*.], that he should be furnished with the means of checking the credibility of his informants, before pledging himself to the authenticity of any facts with which they may supply him. All anonymous communications will henceforth be unattended to.[189]

Mayhew is both the public face of *London Labour* and the centre of a private network of communications. His cautious, multi-claused sentences here register

---

[186] [W.M. Thackeray], 'Waiting at the Station', *Punch*, 9 March 1850, 93.
[187] Tony Williams, 118.
[188] Taithe, ed., 'Part II: Answers to Correspondents', 134.
[189] Ibid., 89.

his uneasiness, as larger networks of readers and distribution collide with smaller local networks of coterie.

Public notoriety was problematic; the existence of face-to-face networks was not necessarily a comfortable aspect of city life, especially when personal relationships found their way into print. Edmund Yates found this to his cost in 1858 when he was expelled from the Garrick Club after Thackeray accused Yates of publishing private conversations in a gossip column for *Town Talk*.[190] Mayhew published his own portrait, as well as portraits of his interviewees, in *London Labour*, and despite journalistic anonymity the identities of many writers were open secrets. As Laurel Brake points out, 'anonymity or related styles of signature (pseudonyms or initials) officially prevailed, although the publication context often undermined the testimony of the letterpress': the names of contributors to the Wellington Street newspaper the *Leader* were used on public advertising placards, 'placarded at every railway station, for everyone to see who likes'.[191] Staff at the *Leader* were lampooned in Edward Whitty's 1857 novel *Friends of Bohemia: Or, Phases of London Life*, which brought gossip about the private lives of Thornton Leigh Hunt and G.H. Lewes into public print by referencing the sharing of spouses.[192] In the cheap press, the newspaper *Paul Pry* published what purported to be private gossip in a column called 'Paul Advises':

> Mrs. C.H. G–n, of Upper Wellington street, Covent garden (*Jerrold's Weekly News*), to behave a little more courteously to those about her. Does she remember before she was married she was a poor book folder? You are on the brink of having no house over your head, for the turn of a straw would do it, little as you may think of it.[193]

Whoever Mrs. G–n was from the *Jerrold's Weekly News* office, her unfortunate brush with *Paul Pry* placed her at the very crossover point between private networks of local knowledge and public networks of print.

Even in the 'modern abstraction' of the city, as Mary Poovey puts it, where global crowds mingle and everyone should be a stranger, an older sort of community where everyone knows each other is imagined to exist.[194] If anonymity did not exist in the way they might have expected for those who participated in the print networks, whether they were an integral part of its local coterie or separated from it by class or geography or gender, then becoming part of the 'local' community

---

190   Leary, 94.

191   Anon., 'The Social Regeneration School', [Church] *Guardian*, 5 November 1851, quoted in Laurel Brake, '"Time's Turbulence": Mapping Journalism's Networks', in 'Victorian Networks and the Periodical Press', 122–3.

192   Harland-Lang, 216.

193   'Paul Advises', *Paul Pry: The Reformer of the Age*, 5 March 1849, 3.

194   Mary Poovey, 'The Production of Abstract Space', in *Making a Social Body: British Cultural Formation, 1830–1864*, 25–54 (Chicago: University of Chicago Press, 1995).

was not a way of integrating incomers safely; rather, the 'local' contained an element of threat. Dickens was accused of ignoring one of his early employers at the solicitors Ellis and Blackmore when Blackmore spotted the now-famous young author at Covent Garden Theatre after a performance of *Fra Diavolo*.[195] Print culture built upon, and made use of, already established discourses of the face-to-face community, or tribal village, and the print networks in and around Wellington Street attest to the persistence of many of the ways of operating which developed in the early modern and eighteenth-century print world of London. London grew rapidly in the nineteenth century, especially after 1851.[196] However, Mayhew and others could still bump into people they knew on evenings out in Wellington Street, and this lack of anonymity carried its own risks.

The links between text, illustration, and visual representation capture a sense of the range of different types of 'reading' possible along the scale of literacy to illiteracy. But they also reveal the multiple ways in which audiences and readers viewed the city and made sense of their own place within it. This chapter has shown that when local contexts and networks are intertwined with larger, potentially national or even global ones, the result can be profoundly unsettling. Wellington Street was located at the heart of an imperial metropolis, not just a national capital, and the print networks of Wellington Street did not operate in isolation of that colonial context. Wellington Street exported both its publications and its print networks to colonial Melbourne, and played a part in imperial networks of print. The collision between the strange and the familiar in mid nineteenth-century Melbourne's print culture played out as an enabling cultural tension between the world of Wellington Street, London, and the world of Collins Street, Melbourne, as the next chapter will show.

---

[195] Douglas-Fairhurst, *Becoming Dickens*, 313.
[196] White, 68; 77.

Chapter 4
Night: 'The Compass of the World and They That Dwell Therein'

Investigating the links between London and Melbourne print culture at mid-century, and proposing that Collins Street, Melbourne, owed much to Wellington Street, London

'Tis always morning somewhere in the world.
—R.H. Horne, *Orion*, Bk. III, Canto 2, l. 43
(London: J. Miller, 1843)

Rats, stray animals, stray drunks, and someone sleeping in a doorway in an otherwise deserted street: Figure 4.1 below, published around 1857, could be a scene from Wellington Street in the dead of night. In fact, it is from a

Figure 4.1   Henry Heath Glover, *1 o'clock, a. m.*, in *12 Hours Road Scraping in Melbourne, c.* 1857. La Trobe Collection, State Library of Victoria. Reproduced by permission of the State Library of Victoria.

book of street scenes in Melbourne, *12 Hours Road Scraping in Melbourne. Scraped from the Streets. - and Sketched in Stone*, by Henry Heath Glover, held in the La Trobe Collection in the State Library of Victoria. The 24-hour rhythms of the print day were global as well as local. Once night fell on Wellington Street, the sun was rising on the other side of the globe in the Australian colonies (as the line from R.H. Horne's poem that heads this chapter suggests). In London, printers and editors worked late, journalists filed last-minute theatre reviews, and dramatists staggered home from Evans's Supper Rooms; meanwhile, in Melbourne, morning in the city was just underway.

Melbourne and London make an illuminating comparison, as Asa Briggs's *Victorian Cities* showed.[1] Glover's book was published by Edgar Ray & Co. from 23 Collins Street East, Melbourne. Collins Street was the home of *Melbourne Punch*, started in 1855 at 66 Collins Street East as a self-conscious 'child' of London *Punch*, which had an office at 3 Wellington Street (South) before it moved a few hundred yards away to just off Fleet Street by 1845.[2] *Melbourne Punch* was not the only Wellington Street export; one of *Melbourne Punch*'s key contributors was R.H. Horne, who emigrated to Melbourne in 1852 during the gold rush. As we have seen, Horne was one of the staff of *Household Words*, at work at 16 Wellington Street North.[3] This geoproximity to Dickens meant that Horne became part of Dickens's circle, and Horne made use of his new Wellington Street connections. Horne was very much a part of Dickens's face-to-face print network.[4] Furthermore, Horne used Wellington Street as the inspiration for some of his writing for *Household Words*, particularly his visit to Bielefeld's *papier mâché* factory at number 15 that I mentioned in Chapter 3. Horne took this conception of face-to-face networks with him to Melbourne. Horne's expectations of how print culture should function in Melbourne were born partly in the climate of the neighbourhood in and around

---

[1]   Asa Briggs, *Victorian Cities*, 2nd edn (Harmondsworth: Penguin, 1968).

[2]   *Robson's London Directory, Street Key, and Royal Court Guide, For 1843,* 24th edn (London: Bowtell, 1843). WCA microfilm collection, London Directories/1843/ vol 201, 312; *Kelly's London Post Office Directory* (London: W. Kelly, 1843–53, WCA microfilm collection, London Directories/1843–53 (1843), 446; Patrick Leary, *The Punch Brotherhood: Table Talk and Print Culture in Mid-Victorian Britain* (London: British Library, 2010), 147. The *Punch* office moved to 194 Strand in January 1844, before moving to the Bradbury & Evans office at 92 and finally 85 Fleet Street in 1845–46. There were other imitations of *London Punch* in the Australian colonies: see Lurline Stewart, *Australian Periodicals With Literary Content 1821–1925: An Annotated Bibliography* (Melbourne: Australian Scholarly Publishing, 2003).

[3]   See Percy Fitzgerald, *Memories of Charles Dickens: with an Account of 'Household Words' and 'All the Year Round' and of the Contributors Thereto* (Bristol: J.W. Arrowsmith; London: Simpkin, Marshall, Hamilton, Kent & Co., 1913), 125–6; Anne Blainey, *The Farthing Poet: A Biography of Richard Hengist Horne 1802–84, A Lesser Literary Lion* (London: Longmans Green & Co., 1968), 179; Cyril Pearl, *Always Morning: The Life of Richard Henry 'Orion' Horne* (Melbourne: F.W. Cheshire, 1960), 108.

[4]   Anne Blainey, 180–83; Pearl, *Always Morning*, 108–22.

Wellington Street, with its evening gatherings of literary, artistic, and theatrical friends and colleagues for both business and pleasure.

This chapter uses the relationships between Horne and Dickens, and Marcus Clarke and Dickens (as well as Mayhew and Sala), to argue that the networks of Wellington Street gave life to print networks on the other side of the globe. In his article on Bielefeld's Wellington Street business, published in November 1851, Horne also commented on how Bielefeld's new invention of large *papier mâché* slabs, suitable for construction projects, was not only destined for London use:

> I understand that [...] Mr. Bielefeld intends to turn his invention of these great slabs (which by new machinery he can manufacture of the size of an ordinary cottage wall, all in one piece) into house-building. By these means a complete house may be sent out to Australia, or elsewhere, all in flat pieces, occupying a comparatively trifling space in stowage; and on its arrival at its destination, the whole can be screwed together in a few hours.[5]

Work which originated in Wellington Street played a part in building – quite literally – the colonial city of Melbourne. According to the *Illustrated London News*, Bielefeld constructed a set of prefabricated buildings (including a church, a villa, and cottages) for a Mr Seymour, who planned to emigrate; the smaller houses could be put up in four hours[6] (Figure 4.2). Whether Mr Seymour and his prefabricated village made it to Australia is not known, and none of Bielefeld's *papier mâché* houses survive, but according to the architectural historian Miles Lewis:

> at least two papier mâché buildings by Bielefeld were built in Geelong, and two other papier mâché houses, probably his, in East Melbourne. At the Melbourne Exhibition of 1854 there were shown 'Patent Composition Boards, suitable for roofing, lining, &c, and adapted to the colony', which sound suspiciously like the unused components of papier mâché houses.[7]

London entrepreneurship, ingenuity, and paper built part of the city of Melbourne, as prefabricated forms emigrated from the Old World to the New. This was not just true of prefabricated buildings. Elements of London's print culture, like

---

    [5]   [R.H. Horne], 'The Pasha's New Boat', *HW*, 22 November 1851, 213.

    [6]   'A Papier Mâché Village For Australia', *ILN*, 6 August 1853, 80. The buildings were on show at Staines, where Bielefeld opened a new factory. They were constructed from Bielefeld's 'Improved *Papier Mâché*', which used steam technology to produce hard-wearing, grainless panels made in one mass from paper and pressed rag, waterproofed with Bielefeld's own special method; the cottages were designed to be clad externally in plain or corrugated iron, which could then be galvanized (John Timbs, *The Year-Book of Facts in Science and Art* [London: David Bogue, 1854]. See also 'Minor Topics of the Month', *Art Journal*, June 1857, 198–9, and 'Miscellanea', *Builder*, 7 May 1853, 299).

    [7]   Miles Lewis, '11.02 Paper & Papier Mâché [2008 edition]', in *Australian Building: A Cultural Investigation*, 2008, accessed 30 April 2012 online via http://www.mileslewis.net/australian-building/.

Figure 4.2   *Papier mâché* cottage. [Charles Frederick Bielefeld,] *Portable*
                Buildings, designed and built by Charles F. Bielefeld, Patentee
                (London: C.F. Bielefeld, 1853). Plate 8. Reproduced by permission
                of Miles Lewis.

Bielefeld's designs, shipped themselves out to Melbourne to be put up in the
colony. *Melbourne Punch* was another prefabricated export set up quickly and
efficiently upon arrival overseas. Writers, periodicals and newspapers from
Wellington Street found their way to Melbourne, and print culture networks based
on Wellington Street were reproduced by Melbourne immigrants like Horne and
Marcus Clarke. Such complex relations between colonial and metropolitan print
culture demand a more nuanced and careful scrutiny than is allowed by Benedict
Anderson's somewhat generic idea of 'print capitalism'.

     This chapter argues that, because the print networks of the three sections
of Wellington Street were reinforced by strong ties of physical proximity, they
had the background strength to sustain themselves when these networks became
'virtual' (to use Appadurai's term) and transnational and to be replicated abroad.
1850s and '60s Melbourne was a city where emigrant writers like Horne
(9 years older than Dickens) and Clarke (34 years younger than Dickens) wanted
to replicate the energetic success of Dickens and his circle. At the same time,
they were troubled by the enormous cultural weight of those who belonged to
the networks of Wellington Street. This ambivalence, what Andrew McCann
calls 'the realities of cultural transportation and dislocation', was, I argue, often
approached through embodied images of a parent-child relationship, as well as

images of the body of the writer and the body of their imagined reader.[8] It was not a reactionary ambivalence; rather, it provided an enabling cultural tension. Writers and editors in colonial Melbourne used the cultural capital of the Old World to breathe vigorous life into the print culture of the New. In the space of two decades, Melbourne went from a small settlement to a lively literary hub. Of course, much of this growth was driven by the presence of the gold fields. However, the first section of this chapter shows that the transplanting of prefabricated brands like *Punch*, and of celebrities like Horne, played a significant role in this dramatic transformation. The second section argues that in his book *Australian Facts and Prospects: to which is prefixed The Author's Australian Autobiography*, Horne envisaged Britain and its colonies, and more specifically London and Melbourne, as inextricably linked, part of what Appadurai calls the same 'locality'.[9]

The difficulties faced by literary emigrants to Melbourne suggest that the transplanting of London print culture to the 'New World' was no easy task.[10] Wellington Street was not rebuilt identically in Melbourne. Indeed, physically Collins Street was much more like Fleet Street or the Strand than Wellington Street; it was (and still is) longer, broader, and more fashionable (Figure 4.3).[11] However, the Old World print culture could be used to start something new: as night fell on Wellington Street, on the other side of the world on Collins Street it was morning.[12] The final section of this chapter argues that Marcus Clarke (part of

---

[8] Andrew McCann, *Marcus Clarke's Bohemia: Literature and Modernity in Colonial Melbourne* (Carlton, Victoria: Melbourne University Press, 2004), 19. Simon Sleight uses mid- to late-nineteenth-century Australian cartoons to discuss metaphors of youthfulness and issues of embodiment in British-Australian imperial relationships. I am indebted to his insights for much of my discussion of *Melbourne Punch* cartoons. See Simon Sleight, 'Wavering between virtue and vice: constructions of youth in Australian cartoons of the late-Victorian era', in *Drawing the Line: Using Cartoons as Historical Evidence*, ed. Richard Scully and Marian Quartly (Melbourne: Monash University ePress, 2009), 5.1–5.26, and Simon Sleight, *Young People and the Shaping of Public Space in Melbourne, 1870–1914* (Farnham: Ashgate, 2013).

[9] R.H. Horne, *Australian Facts and Prospects: to which is prefixed The Author's Australian Autobiography* (London: Smith, Elder & Co, 1859). Further references are to this edition, hereafter abbreviated as *Australian Facts*, and appear parenthetically in the text.

[10] Poverty and disenchantment were as common as financial and social success: Horne and his colleague William Howitt both returned to England eventually.

[11] By the second half of the nineteenth century, 'doing the block' on Collins Street was the fashionable place to promenade. See Andrew Brown-May, *Melbourne Street Life: The Itinerary of Our Days* (Kew, Victoria: Australian Scholarly Publishing, 1998), 58.

[12] Geoffrey Blainey's *The Tyranny of Distance: How Distance Shaped Australia's History*, 2nd edn (South Melbourne, Victoria: Sun Books, 1983; 1st publ. 1966) is interested in core-periphery relations, and argues that 'distance was a central factor in Australia's history' (Preface). While this is undoubtedly true, increasingly the dichotomy of core (or metropole) and periphery has been challenged; historians like Catherine Hall and Sonya O. Rose have argued that the culture of the British Empire's periphery influenced the metropolitan core (see Catherine Hall and Sonya O. Rose, 'Introduction: being at home

Figure 4.3   *Collins Street looking east from the Wesleyan Chapel, Melbourne,*
             1857. Engraved by J. Tingle. Published by Sands and Kenny.
             Reproduced by permission of the State Library of Victoria.

the young clique of rising Melbourne writers that formed around the established
figure of Horne) built upon the work of Wellington Street occupants Dickens,
Mayhew, and Sala to reappropriate urban sketch-writing for Melbourne and to talk
back to Wellington Street from Collins Street. When Clarke reached Melbourne in
1863, only 28 years after the city's foundation, Melbourne already possessed print
networks to rival Wellington Street's.[13] Clarke used the cultural tension between
Old and New to bring new and imaginative resonances to his urban sketches
of night-time Melbourne, and to connect colonial and metropolitan readers and
writers into an imagined network of print.

---

with the Empire', in *At Home With the Empire: Metropolitan Culture and the Imperial
World*, ed. Catherine Hall and Sonya O. Rose [Cambridge: Cambridge University Press,
2006], 1–31). Also in the 1960s, Louis Hartz argued that Australia is a 'fragment' of Britain,
and that the political development of new societies is largely determined by the cultural
heritage brought by the first settlers (see Louis Hartz, with contributions by Kenneth D.
McRae and others, *The Founding of New Societies: Studies in the History of the United
States, Latin America, South Africa, Canada, and Australia* (New York: Harcourt, Brace &
World, 1964). Hartz's ideas were critiqued by John Hirst in J.B. Hirst, 'Keeping colonial
history colonial: The Hartz thesis revisited', *[Australian] Historical Studies* 21, no. 82
(April 1984): 85–104; the debate, while not pressing, is still active in Australian Studies.
    [13]   For details of the rapid growth and expansion of Melbourne, see Briggs, 278.

The Emigrant's Body: R.H. Horne and *Melbourne Punch*

Despite the vast distance between Wellington Street and Collins Street, emigration did not create a cultural separation between the two neighbourhoods. The print culture of Wellington Street travelled with the body of its emigrants. Horne described the new colony as the child of the 'mother country', as if Melbourne was still tied to London by an invisible umbilical cord made out of print. Not only was Horne a contributor to *Melbourne Punch,* but, according to Marjorie J. Tipping, he was a member of the group – which included Frederick Sinnett, James Smith, N. Chevalier, and James Stiffe – that met to plan its issues.[14] When it was founded, *Melbourne Punch* depicted writing and publishing as a very personal business. In *Melbourne Punch*, print culture itself becomes like a family whose members may emigrate overseas but who remain connected in an imagined community. London print culture could emigrate just as London writers and booksellers emigrated, and so writers and their readers across the Empire could be linked. Emigration created new print-producing networks in 1850s Melbourne, but this did not mean that Melbourne networks considered themselves to be separated from London networks.

The emigrant's body carried the community of Wellington Street with it, whether it was the literal, physical bodies of Horne and his colleague William Howitt upon their arrival on the 'Kent', or the personified body of Melbourne Punch jn. on his fictional 'arrival' on board the 'Marco Polo'. In 1855, the following notice was published in the *Argus*, one of the two main Melbourne daily papers, published at 76 Collins Street East:

> MELBOURNE PUNCH, JN., Esq. begs to announce that having emigrated to the City which bears his name (both he and the city were named in compliment to a late illustrious Whig Nobleman), he has determined to issue a WEEKLY PERIODICAL of a highly interesting and instructive character. The first number will appear on or before Thursday, the 2nd of August.
>
> As it would ill become the modesty of youth to vaunt untested excellence, Mr. Punch, Junior, contents himself with observing that his Periodical will be in all respects superior to everything of the kind hitherto attempted in the universe. Printed and published (for the proprietors) by Edgar Ray, at the *Auction Mart, Daily Advertiser* Office, 66 Collins-street east, Melbourne.
>
> Price 6d. Subscriptions 6s. per quarter in advance.[15]

This mimicked the reports published in Melbourne's newspapers which marked the arrival of noteworthy emigrants.

The first number of *Melbourne Punch* carried a cartoon of Mr Punch jn.'s triumphant arrival in Melbourne, as its founding editors worked to create a 'body' for their personified periodical (Figure 4.4). Here, *Melbourne Punch* trades on itself as a transplanting of London print culture. Above the cartoon of Punch's

---

[14] Marjorie J. Tipping, 'Sinnett, Frederick (1830–1866)', *Australian Dictionary of Biography*, accessed 25 January 2012 online via http://adb.anu.edu.au/.

[15] 'Miscellaneous', *Argus*, 9 July 1855, 7.

Figure 4.4   *Departure of Mr. Punch from Gravesend; Arrival of Mr. Punch in Australia*, MP, 1, 1856, 1. Reproduced by permission of the Library for the Institute of Historical Research, University of London.

arrival in Melbourne is the depiction of his departure; we see Melbourne Punch as a member of the Punch 'family', 'son of the celebrated Mr Punch, of Fleet-street', previously of Wellington Street (South). Note how the low-key family scene of departure at the top becomes a grand state welcome at the bottom. The reader is asked to infer from the cartoon that Punch jnr. will go on to great things in the colony, even as they are asked to enjoy its mockery of the expectations of gold-rush emigrants.[16] London print culture is used to bolster Melbourne's fledgling papers and periodicals, even to the extent of the spoof reports from the *Times* and the *Argus* (on Punch's departure and arrival, respectively) laid side by side and so given equal status and weight. A review in the *Argus* of this first number noted that 'the title-page represents Mr. Punch, Jun., as seated in his chair of office. The well-known features of his sire may be traced in his physiognomy. [...] The whole figure is significant of vigorous youth'.[17] This carries a dual meaning, as the 'well-known features' of Mr. Punch could be both the resemblance of the cartoon son to his cartoon father and the resemblance of the layout and typeface of *Melbourne Punch* to its Wellington Street 'parent'. The body of the emigrant and the materiality of the printed page are linked; the 'vigorous youth' of the new venture is used both to link *Melbourne Punch* to, and to differentiate it from, the London version.

Where Mrs Punch comes from, in the cartoon of the Punch family, is not clear. There is a strong male bias in the cartoons discussed in this chapter. However, Simon Sleight points out that in late-Victorian cartoons depicting the relationships between Britain and 'Young Australia', 'whilst Britannia and John Bull are depicted fairly consistently [...], Australia (or Victoria) is drawn in multiple guises [...] and either male or female'.[18] The image of the parent in this discourse is also not always a father; Horne writes of Britain as the 'mother-country' (*Australian Facts*). Horne's and Clarke's print networks were overwhelmingly male, in a city where males outnumbered females by almost two to one in 1854.[19] As wives and mothers, women are usually a strong part of the emigration narrative. One of the few accounts of early Melbourne by a woman, Ellen Clacy, plays upon this to justify her entry into a male-dominated literary market:

> It may be deemed presumptuous that one of my age and sex should venture to give the public an account of personal adventures in a land which has so often been descanted upon by other and abler pens; but when I reflect on the many mothers, wives, and sisters in England, whose hearts are ever longing for information representing the dangers and privations to which their relatives at the antipodes are exposed, I cannot but hope that the presumption of my undertaking may be pardoned.[20]

---

16   I am grateful to Ian Henderson for this point.
17   'Melbourne Punch', *Argus*, 3 August 1855, 5.
18   Sleight, 'Wavering between virtue and vice', 5.19.
19   Brown-May, *Melbourne Street Life*, 60.
20   Mrs Charles Clacy, *A Lady's Visit to the Gold Diggings of Australia in 1852–53. Written on the Spot* (London: Hurst and Blackett, 1853), 1–2.

Clacy positions herself as the informant for the women who, like Horne's wife, were left behind when the men headed to the gold fields. However, Clacy's disclaimer highlights the fact that Melbourne publishing and Melbourne print networks, like their Wellington Street counterparts, were a homosocial world.

The notice in the Sydney *Empire* which announced the arrival of Horne and Howitt played up their 'Old World' connections, like the spoof report of the arrival of *Melbourne Punch*. It portrayed the two men as carriers of London print culture, although, interestingly, their contributions to *Household Words* are not thought worthy of mention:

> The ship Kent, which arrived at Melbourne two or three weeks ago, brought to that colony two gentlemen who have earned for themselves a distinguished rank in the world of literature [...]. We have not heard what are the ostensible objects of their voyage; but it may be fairly presumed, that the gentleman to whom we now particularly allude have in contemplation literary works on the social state and mineral developments of Australia; and it is a gratifying circumstance, that talents of such high order and so peculiarly suited to such performances, should be employed in making this noble country better known to the people of England. The name of William Howitt, or of R.H. Horne, on the title page of a work descriptive of our Australian cities [...] would ensure the attention of the British public [...]. As it may be safely calculated that these gentlemen will shortly visit our metropolis, we have extracted from a work, recently published in London, the following brief notices of their literary antecedents.[21]

There is a strange tension in evidence here between pride in the resources and energy of the youthful colony (Melbourne was founded in 1835) and awed fetishization of the 'literary world' of London and the 'Old Country'.[22] Horne's symbolic status as a literary celebrity in the *Argus* report comes not just from his 'talents of such high order' and the work of his own pen, but the fact of his perceived 'distinguished rank in the world of literature'. This sense of Horne's (and Howitt's) participation in a specific 'world' may have been bolstered by

---

[21]   'Our First Literary Arrivals', *Empire*, 8 October 1852, 1490. It is fortunate that the *Empire* was not aware of Horne's real motive for emigration, as expressed in his *Australian Autobiography*: 'But what brought me here? Was it a view to literature, science, art? Nothing of the kind. I did not come out as a philosopher, author, tourist, adventurous merchant, or speculator. I came out simply to dig for gold' (*Australian Facts*, 2).

[22]   Arthur Angel Phillips, in a foundational text for Australian nationalist criticism, called this fetishization 'The Cultural Cringe'. For an interesting discussion of Trollope's relationship to Phillips's idea of the 'Cringe', see Ian Henderson, 'Trollope in Australia: Gentlemen, the Cringe', paper (supplied by the author) presented at the Second Commodities and Culture in the Colonial World Workshop, 'Commodities and Affect', Centre of Advanced Study in English, Jadavpur University, Kolkata, India, 12–14 January 2011. Also presented at English/MCAS panel discussion, King's College London, 28 March 2011. As Henderson points out, Phillips linked the response of the reader to the effect of reading on the posture of the reader's body.

Horne's participation in the networks which operated on and around Wellington Street in the 1840s and 1850s.[23]

Horne's appointment to *Household Words* in 1850 as a staff writer brought him to Wellington Street and to the very heart of Dickens's network:

> he entered into the congenial society of Dickens's own group, a group almost as vigorous as its leader. There were Jerrold and Robert Bell who had remained his friends [...], the artists Daniel Maclise, Clarkson Stanfield, Frank Stone, Augustus Egg, his colleague on *Household Words* William Henry Wills, and there was Dickens's closest friend John Forster. [...] Dickens liked Horne. They got on well, if not closely or intensely, and Horne could be good company [...]. They accepted Horne readily, and he for his part was delighted and intoxicated to be accepted into one of the most dynamic, if not intellectual, of literary groups.[24]

Dickens's editorial sanctum was on the first floor at 16 Wellington Street North; elsewhere in the building was the sub-editor Wills, while Horne shared an office with John Dickens (see Figure 1.10).[25] Despite his unpopularity with Wills, Horne took part in the evening editorial staff meetings at number 16, and joined in the evening gatherings of Dickens's friends at the office and at dinners at Tavistock House. As I noted in Chapter 3, Horne was also a member of Dickens's amateur dramatics troupe, and performed with Forster, Lemon, Lewes, and other Wellington Street editors at Devonshire House before the Queen. Dickens was very critical of Horne's performance that evening, confiding in a friend that Horne was 'between ourselves (I speak seriously) the very worst actor the world ever saw, and [...] must not on any account be entrusted with more words than he has already'.[26] G.H. Lewes's review for the *Leader*, however, more generously allowed that 'there was some good acting, notably R.H. Horne's'. Horne later reminisced about 'the "unreserved hilarity" of their supper parties' between performances.[27] Horne knew Macready and Forster in his own right in the 1830s, and first knew the Howitts through his mother; Anne Blainey suggests that 'Horne may have lent money [to establish *Howitt's Journal*]; certainly he gave time and creative effort', as '[m]uch of his work was to appear in *Howitt's Journal* in the following two years [1846–48]'.[28] Perhaps it was at the Howitt's house in Clapton that Horne first met Dickens; either way, in 1846 Horne was taken on as Ireland correspondent for the *Daily News*, and so joined a distinguished list of contributors including *Punch*-ites

---

[23]   A similar argument could be made about Howitt; however, this chapter chooses to focus on Horne because of his impact on Melbourne literary life and his connection with *MP*. Horne stayed in Australia until 1869, much longer than Howitt, who left in 1854.

[24]   Anne Blainey, 180–81.

[25]   See Fitzgerald, *Memories of Charles Dickens,* 125–6; Anne Blainey, 179; Pearl, *Always Morning*, 108.

[26]   Anne Blainey, 183.

[27]   Pearl, *Always Morning*, 122.

[28]   Anne Blainey, 78; 165.

Lemon and Jerrold.[29] Horne collaborated with Jerrold and Angus B. Reach on the foundation of the Whittington Club, and Horne contributed to *Douglas Jerrold's Shilling Magazine*.[30] When Horne arrived in Melbourne, aged 49, he carried with him immense cultural capital.

As a representative of the culture of the 'mother country', then, Horne's influence upon the younger literary arrivals to Melbourne was considerable, although not always, perhaps, because of the poetry which Horne persisted in producing.[31] Cyril Pearl argues that by the 1860s,

> his Australian writings had no roots in Australia. [...] He felt no kinship with his new home [...]. But although he added nothing to Australian literature with his pen, Horne seems to have been a valuable stimulus to the younger writers of his circle.[32]

The son of George Gordon McCrae, in his memoirs, was more complimentary about Horne's literary status than his biographers:

> RICHARD HENGIST HORNE: a strong-brained man, with a body to match, divided his life between intellectual effort and worldly adventure. He spent seventeen years in this country, during which time he became, step by step, commander of a gold escort, Commissioner of the Crown Lands, and territorial magistrate.
>
> His literary reputation rose at least two pairs-of-stairs above that of any of his contemporaries; while, in England, he had grown to be almost within the aura of the really great.[33]

McCrae characterizes Horne as a vigorous man of action, in the mould of Carlyle's heroic man of letters. McCrae gives a generous estimate of Horne's position in London's, as well as in Melbourne's, print culture, although he does reveal how much of the esteem in which Horne was held in Melbourne came from Horne's association as the embodiment of the literary world of the Old Country.

---

[29] Pearl, *Always Morning*, 93.

[30] Anne Blainey, 209; 165; Monica Fryckstedt, 'Douglas Jerrold's Shilling Magazine', *Victorian Periodicals Review* 19, no. 1 (Spring 1986): 5–6.

[31] Horne was best known as a poet, the author of *Orion*, which sold for the low price of a farthing on Horne's insistence, when it was published in 1843, in a noble attempt to ensure wider access to epic poetry. For further discussions of Horne's work in the 1840s, see Paul Schlicke, 'Hazlitt, Horne, and the Spirit of the Age', *Studies in English Literature* 45, no. 4 (Autumn 2005): 829–51; Pearl, *Always Morning*; and Anne Blainey. For Horne's own comments on his failure to make money from poetry, and his disinclination to concentrate on prose, see *Australian Facts*, 2.

[32] Pearl, *Always Morning*, 225. Pearl chooses to ignore *Australian Facts*, which perhaps made more impact in London than in Melbourne, given that it was published in the metropolis.

[33] Hugh McCrae, 'My Father and My Father's Friends', in *Story-Book Only* (Sydney and London: Angus and Robertson, 1948; 1st publ. 1935), 31.

Despite his many hardships along the way, and his eventual disenchantment with Australia and return to England, what emigration allowed Horne to achieve was status in Melbourne as the kind of literary lion that he never managed to become in London. Horne would have found resonances with the heroic speech Mrs Micawber puts into the mouth of Mr Micawber before they leave for Australia: 'Enough of delay: enough of disappointment: enough of limited means. That was the old country. This is the new. Produce your reparation. Bring it forward!'[34] According to Anne Blainey's biography of Horne:

> there was a certain strain in his relations with Dickens. Even for so hero-worshipping a nature as Horne's it was not entirely possible to feel unmixed admiration for a genius nine years his junior who had climbed to fame through the very public and the very society that had turned Horne down. This uneasiness, of which Dickens, too, seemed somewhat aware, ran through most of their communications.[35]

In Melbourne, Horne could aspire to the status of Dickens, as the influential focal point of a print network. As the Scottish-Australian educator and journalist Alexander Sutherland argued in 1888, Horne

> stirred up his young companions, who formed a little clique, to think of literature as an aim worth striving for, and in the midst of an utterly Bohemian life, he had a reckless devotion to art that had an unmistakeable influence.[36]

This clique included Marcus Clarke and George Gordon McCrae, and possibly also Henry Kendall and Adam Lindsay Gordon.[37] According to Anne Blainey, after the publication in 1864 of Horne's lyric drama *Prometheus*, he had become 'indisputably the literary celebrity of Melbourne', and was 'now recognised as Melbourne's official literary spokesman' and honorary Poet Laureate, a role which Horne relished. In Dwight's bookshop in Bourke Street, owned by Horne's colonial

---

[34]   Charles Dickens, *David Copperfield*, ed. Nina Burgis (Oxford: Clarendon Press, 1981; 1st publ. 1849–50), 692–3.

[35]   Anne Blainey, 181. Disenchantment with this network pushed Horne to leave. According to Anne Blainey's biography, 'soon after Horne had joined the magazine, Wills had accused him of not pulling his weight', although he was unable to produce any evidence. Dickens reprimanded Wills, but 'the atmosphere remained uneasy'. The gold rush coincided with work and marriage troubles, and when 'Horne learned, inadvertently, the news of Howitt's departure from his publisher', he determined to seek his fortune in the colony of Victoria, in Australia (Anne Blainey, 190; 191).

[36]   Alexander Sutherland, *Victoria and Its Metropolis, Past and Present*, 2 vols (Melbourne: McCarron & Bird, 1888), 1: 498. Compare Anne Blainey, 233: 'How far Horne influenced this earliest Australian literary movement is doubtful.'

[37]   Anne Blainey, 232–3; Pearl, *Always Morning*, 231. See also 'HORNE, R.H. (Richard Henry) (1802–84)', in *The Oxford Companion to Australian Literature*, ed. William H. Wilde, Joy Hooton, and Barry Andrews, 2nd edn (Melbourne and Oxford: Oxford University Press, 1994), 380.

publisher, the young literary men of Melbourne gathered for hard drinking and boisterous practical jokes. Anne Blainey states:

> Horne was said to be the leader: a living symbol of the Old World's Romantic Literature [...] a man much lionised by those who hung around the literary fringes and won vicarious notoriety by recalling later the figure in the cloak and corkscrew curls [...]. He was even fêted occasionally, to his intense delight.[38]

Horne represented himself this way, too: he declared that 'I had many invitations, and received many kindnesses from persons to whom I had no other introduction than the knowledge of my literary position in the old country' (*Australian Facts*, 23). For his companions, Horne provided a physical link with the culture of 'home'; a conversation with Horne was one remove away from a conversation with Dickens or Jerrold.

Melbourne Punch had a very different relationship to cultural capital. The periodical claimed a tongue-in-cheek position as its own species of literary lion, offering a spoof prize for a suitable laudatory address:

> Mr. PUNCH, JUN., being altogether free from those petty jealousies, that are so apt to disfigure the characters of literary men, determined that his brother journalists of Melbourne – (Mr. Punch never disowns poor relations) should have occasion to rejoice over the birth of the present periodical. Accordingly he offered
>
> A Reward of One Thousand Pounds,
>
> and a certificate of merit, for the best prefatory address that should be forwarded to him. Having rejected a considerable number, Mr. Punch was at a loss to which of three competitors to assign the plan. [...] Mr. Punch at length determined that it would be unfair and invidious to give the thousand pounds to any one of the three and he therefore withholds that portion of the reward altogether. A certificate of merit, will however, be presented on application, to each of the writers [...].[39]

The phrase 'brother journalists' raises the possibility that Melbourne print culture might be a harmonious family, but this is undercut by the reference to *Melbourne Punch*'s competitors as 'poor relations'. *Melbourne Punch*'s claim to status, however, comes from its own membership of the Punch 'family', and the way it has hijacked the *Punch* brand. This form of plagiarism ('brandjacking', as Adrian Johns tells us it is called) gives an air of both assurance and anxiety to the early numbers of *Melbourne Punch*.[40] Cultural capital is invested in the *Punch* name.

---

[38]   Anne Blainey, 232–3. See also 'DWIGHT, Henry Tolman (?1823–71)', in *The Oxford Companion to Australian Literature*, 380.

[39]   'Competition for a laudatory address', *MP*, 1 (1856), 2.

[40]   Adrian Johns, *Piracy: the Intellectual Property Wars from Gutenberg to Gates* (Chicago: University of Chicago Press, 2009), 2–3. There was no business link between the two *Punches*; *Melbourne Punch* was an imitation, not a franchise.

The periodical makes use of its London 'parent', while also aggressively asserting its own worth. It is 'Mr PUNCH,' – 'JUN'.

Horne himself commented on what he saw as the curious state of the colony and its colonists: in Horne's eyes, Victoria and its colonists were young in years, but carried much of old world traditions, prejudices, and ideas with them (*Australian Facts*, 197–98). *Melbourne Punch* advertised itself as an embodiment of how print culture could use old forms to produce new versions, while Horne was valued because he was a living example of the old literary world. In Figure 4.5, from *Melbourne Punch*, the youthfulness of Melbourne's up-and-coming commercial enterprises is emphasized through the figures of street boys, but in the background the sign 'PUNCH JUNIOR' reminds us that the new world has been born out of the old. In this figure, Settler barter culture is shown as dying out. *Melbourne Punch* stands for capital and modern commerce, not just culture. The street boys embody the energetic and possibly unruly forces of 'Young Australia'.[41] However, in using such a physical and material understanding of cultural capital, 1850s Melbourne print culture could not escape Old Europe. The 'body' of the emigrant – whether in physical or material form – may have travelled the world, but Collins Street made effective use of its links with Wellington Street.

Horne and the Print Networks of London and Melbourne

By maintaining cultural ties to London print culture, Melbourne print culture in the 1850s constructed an image of physical proximity to London despite the vast distances between London and Melbourne (still about four months' sailing at mid-century),[42] just as much as it emphasized its evident differences from London. London and Melbourne were mapped onto each other, and Melbourne print culture strove to use its 'parent' model to assert its continued place in the cultural 'conversation' with London. This was particularly important in a period when Melbourne periodicals and newspapers competed with London imports for readers. This desire continued into the 1860s with the new generation of Melbourne writers and journalists, but it is already in evidence from the 1850s in the way Melbourne periodicals mimicked the titles of their London forebears. It can also be seen in the personal and professional connections between the networks established in and around Wellington Street and those which emerged in Melbourne, with a

---

41   See Sleight, 'Wavering between virtue and vice', 5.4.

42   For sailing times, see J.R. McCulloch, *A Dictionary, Practical, Theoretical, and Historical, of Commerce and Commercial Navigation*, ed. Hugh G. Reid, rev. edn (London: Longmans, Green & Co., 1875). For a discussion of sailing times and conditions at mid-century, see Geoffrey Blainey, 161–4. For the effects of the gold rush, see Geoffrey Blainey, pages 178 and 197. On comparisons between London and Melbourne in nineteenth-century journalism and literature, see Kylie Mirmohamedi and Susan K. Martin, *Colonial Dickens: What Australians Made of the World's Favourite Writer* (Melbourne: Australian Scholarly Publishing, 2012), 51–70.

YOUNG AUSTRALIA COMMERCIAL OPERATIONS.

Fruit Merchant.—Here, Jem, I'll Trade with you for some of them Punches for Dates. I aint got no cash just now.

News Agent.—Can't sell for nothing but cash (running off).
Here you are, Melbourne Punch, only sixpence.

Figure 4.5   *Young Australia Commercial Operations, MP*, 1, 1856, 22.
              Reproduced by permission of the Library for the Institute of
              Historical Research, University of London.

focal point at the *Melbourne Punch* office in Collins Street. Despite the lure of a new start in a new country, Horne and his *Melbourne Punch* colleagues show that members of print culture networks in colonial Melbourne not only retained ties to London print culture, but considered themselves to be, in some way, still part of that London world.

Even in the more nationalist 1880s, as Graeme Davison and David Dunstan show, comparisons with London were a popular trope of writing about Melbourne throughout the century.[43] Davison and Dunstan describe John Freeman's *Lights and Shadows of Melbourne Life* (1888) as 'a hybrid creation, with stock London

---

[43]   And other European cities too, especially Paris. See Graeme Davison, 'The European City in Australia', *Journal of Urban History* 27 (2001): 781–2. For Freeman, see Graeme Davison and David Dunstan, '"This Moral Pandemonium": Images of Low

"scenes" and "characters" only loosely clothed in colonial garb. As such it is hard to accept *Lights and Shadows* as an authentic portrait of Melbourne life'. In the 1870s, *Melbourne Punch* contributor John Stanley James used Dickens and Cruikshank – collaborators on *Sketches by Boz* – as reference points for his sketches of Melbourne poverty, published in the *Argus*.[44] But this impulse is particularly evident in 1850s and 1860s Melbourne print culture, and is exemplified by the ties between the communities of Wellington Street and Collins Street at mid-century. Andrew Brown-May positions late nineteenth-century Melbourne as 'a precinct of the global city', as part of what he sees as a growing transnational municipal community.[45] However, in the 1850s and even into the 1860s, the neighbourhoods of Wellington Street and Collins Street were already linked. This sense of a cultural and physical connection to the 'mother country' is expressed in Horne's book on Australia, *Australian Facts*.

Before he had even embarked at London's docks, the material connections between Wellington Street and the colony were already right before Horne's eyes. Australia was on everyone's mind and in everyone's paper because of the gold rush; what Horne called 'the London fever of that day' meant that '[g]o where you will, everybody appears to be going "off to the Diggings"'.[46] The proximity of Wellington Street to the Thames, its shipping, and the docks downriver would only have increased Horne's awareness of the burgeoning Empire. Robert L. Mack calls nineteenth-century Fleet Street

> the global epicentre not only of national news [...] and significant foreign affairs, but a street into which all the gossip and hearsay of the wider world seemed inevitably to tend [...]. [By the time] the river's edge came into view of any approaching ship, [news and gossip] were likely already to have leapt from the vessel, and so begin to make the short sprint to Fleet Street and thence to the rest of the country.[47]

Life', in *The Outcasts of Melbourne: Essays in Social History*, ed. Graeme Davison, David Dunstan, and Chris McConville (Sydney: Allen & Unwin, 1985), 43.

44   See especially John Stanley James ('the Vagabond'), 'A Night in the Model Lodging House', *Argus*, 15 April 1876, 5.

45   Andrew Brown-May, 'In the Precincts of the Global City: The Transnational Network of Municipal Affairs in Melbourne, Australia, at the End of the Nineteenth Century', in *Another Global City: Historical Explorations into the Transnational Municipal Movement, 1850–2000*, ed. Pierre-Yves Saunier and Shane Ewen (Basingstoke: Palgrave Macmillan, 2008), 19–34.

46   *Australian Facts*, 2; 'Off to the Diggings!', *HW*, 17 July 1852, 405. Ten years after Horne left *Household Words*, Dickens wrote: 'He would probably have remained associated with my Journal to this day, if he had not, in the time of the Gold Fever, been seized with visions of Emigration' (Charles Dickens, letter to Robert Bell, 1 February 1862, in *The Pilgrim Edition of the Letters of Charles Dickens*, ed. Madeline House, Graham Storey, and Kathleen Tillotson, 12 vols (Oxford: Clarendon Press, 1965–2002), 10: 29.

47   Robert L. Mack, *The Wonderful and Surprising History of Sweeney Todd: The Life and Times of an Urban Legend* (London: Continuum, 2007), 86.

Such a description also holds good for the nineteenth-century Strand neighbourhood. In 'Down With the Tide', written by Dickens for *Household Words* and published in February 1853, Dickens describes night-time on the Thames as he sits in a police galley, when '[e]very colour but black seemed to have departed from the world.' Dickens starts at Waterloo Bridge, just below Wellington Street (South), and then rows down to below London Bridge, where he sees 'tiers of shipping, whose many hulls, lying close together, rose out of the water like black streets. [...] Nothing seemed awake but a dog here and there'.[48] These mighty ships brought goods and passengers, as well as news, from around the colonies and the globe. Britain's international connections were distant, yet present, in the metropolis.

Elsewhere on Wellington Street, encounters between the local and the international took place. The Lyceum advertised a programme of emigrant's songs, while *Reynolds's Weekly News* trumpeted the perils of emigration for a depopulated Britain.[49] Horne collaborated with Mrs Chisholm on an article about life in Australia for *Household Words*.[50] He also collaborated with Dickens on an article about the Great Exhibition, an event which John Scott Russell (who had edited the *Railway Chronicle* from number 14) was instrumental in planning.[51] In 1850, Albert Smith's revue *Novelty Fair* played regularly at the Lyceum; along with Shirley Brooks's *The Exposition,* at the nearby Adelphi, *Novelty Fair* poked fun at the tension between nationalism and internationalism prevalent throughout discussion of the 1851 Great Exhibition, and throughout the Exhibition itself. It included a 'demonstration' of the telegraph, live on stage.[52] Horne's poem 'The Great Peace-Maker', published in *Household Words* in 1851, envisaged the telegraph as a way of uniting humanity across international boundaries, for 'nation knowing nation by the truth, – | By actual presence, and familiar words, | Spoken or written, henceforth will be slow | To see the red necessity of war'.[53] The phrase 'familiar words' recalls the famous tagline of *Household Words* itself; telegraphic networks and print networks alike will build 'human brotherhood [...] in distant hearts'.[54] London *Punch* advertised itself as a promoter of international friendship, with an image of all nations united by their shared (though separate) experience of reading the periodical. The cartoons surrounding the 'Prologue' to Volume 5

---

48   [Charles Dickens], 'Down With the Tide', *HW*, 5 February 1853, 481; 484.

49   V&ATA Box 1400: Lyceum April–Sept 1852; G.W.M. Reynolds, 'The Swelling Tide of Emigration', *RWN*, 17 October 1852, 1.

50   Anne Lohrli, *'Household Words' A Weekly Journal 1850–1859 Conducted by Charles Dickens, Table of Contents, List of Contributors and Their Contributions Based on the 'Household Words' Office Book* (Toronto: University of Toronto Press, 1973), 311.

51   Jeffrey A. Auerbach, *The Great Exhibition of 1851: A Nation on Display* (New Haven, CT: Yale University Press, 1999), 17. The title of this chapter comes from the epigraph to the Exhibition catalogue.

52   [Albert Smith], *Novelty Fair; or, Hints for 1851* (London: T.H. Lacy, [n.d.]), Act I, scene 3, 16.

53   [R.H. Horne], 'The Great Peace-Maker', *HW*, 14 June 1851, 276.

54   Ibid., 277.

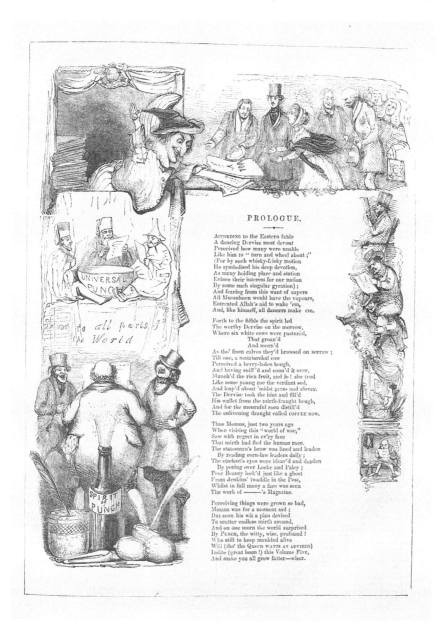

Figure 4.6   *Prologue*, London *Punch* 5, 1843. Reproduced with the permission of Senate House Library, University of London. PR [Z-Punch].

suggests that print culture can be a means of overcoming physical and cultural boundaries – but only if you buy *Punch* (Figure 4.6).

Despite the fact of Horne and his network's physical separation from London, they used print to create a cultural construction of physical proximity. Of course, the strangeness of Melbourne upon arrival, and the hardships to be faced by the unwary middle class emigrant, were emphasized in much emigration literature, including William Howitt's *Land, Labour, and Gold* (1855) and Horne's fictionalized accounts of his departure and journey to Melbourne, and vignettes of Australian life, written for *Household Words*.[55] Howitt recorded his shock upon arrival at a city where '[t]here is not the slightest shadow of a shade of any quay, wharf, or warehouse in the harbour, – no work of man, in fact, to facilitate the landing and stowage of goods'.[56] Howitt declared that '[a]t present, to use the language of the Chief justice in a pamphlet he has published on the gold fever, "It is a capital that is neither lighted, paved, nor drained"'.[57] Howitt was struck by the frantic activity in the streets, described in a flurry of breathless clauses:

> The number of drunken fellows which you see about the streets is something fearful; and their language is still more so [...]. Everybody gallops here, or at least goes at a canter – which they call the Australian *lope* [...]. The streets here, spite of the fine weather drawing off immense numbers daily to the diggings, are crowded with rude-looking diggers and hosts of immigrants, with their wives, their bundles, and their dogs. All down, near the wharves, it is a scene of dust, drays and carts hurrying to and fro, and heaps of boxes, trunks, bundles, and digging-tools. [*sic*][58]

Horne's description of his first lodgings in Melbourne also has a slightly shell-shocked tone:

> By the introduction and recommendation of my friend the Major, I was permitted, as a favour, to enjoy the little backroom of a two-roomed hovel, in which a woman and her daughter resided [...]. My 'look-out' was upon a narrow patch of yard all bestrewn with shattered things: loose firewood, fragments of old furniture, boxes, trunks, and rags of clothes and bedding, with a mad conglomerate on one side emitting typhoid odours. Broken palings pretended

---

[55]   As Shirley Walker notes, '[f]rom at least the 1850s there had been two clearly opposing perceptions of Australia: an optimistic and euphoric view as against a more realist, subversive one. This opposition became clear in the 1850s, the period of the great gold rushes, where the wave of euphoria which swept thousands of emigrants to Victoria was challenged by most, if not all, of those who came, saw, and reported'; Shirley Walker, 'Perceptions of Australia, 1855–1915', in *The Penguin New Literary History of Australia*, gen. ed. Laurie Hergenhan (Ringwood, Victoria and Harmondsworth: Penguin, 1988), 160.

[56]   William Howitt, *Land, Labour, and Gold or, Two Years in Victoria, with Visits to Sydney and Van Dieman's Land*, 2 vols (London: Longman, Brown, Green, and Longmans, 1855), 1: 6–7.

[57]   Ibid., 1: 13.

[58]   Ibid., 1: 35.

to divide this yard from the yards on each side; – one of these was all mud and cesspool, the other all wretchedness and squalor; the only conspicuous objects being heaps of broken ginger-beer bottles and a dead monkey. The back-yards of Melbourne at this period defy description in any such space as I can afford. This represented domestic civilization returning to chaos!

The two women were most insolent. Perceiving that their society was distasteful to me, they used to set the door between the two rooms ajar, and talk *at* me in subtle tropes and allegories with colonial finesse. Some people wanted to set themselves up as a sort of superfine over other people, who knew how the cat leaps as well as they; but all such people would soon be brought to humble pie with all their seven senses in this kolny [*sic.*], and be d-— to them. 'You must do this – (must we? – ah!) – and you ought to do that – (ought we? – oh!) – but the like of such chaps'll soon find out that here there's *no* must or ought. Jack's as good as his master'. (Australian Facts, 6–7)

This one backyard is made to stand for the whole colony of Victoria, which seems to Horne to be a degenerated 'chaos' of 'shattered things', himself, perhaps, included. The women's attitude towards Horne is a rejection of any idea of cultural capital from the Old World. Melbourne was undoubtedly a culture shock for Horne and Howitt.[59]

Even after the first shock of arrival, Melbourne was a startling place for the middle-class London immigrant. As well as the diggers from all over the world there was Melbourne's large and vibrant Chinatown, and small numbers of aboriginal Australians were visible in the young city. 'Melbourne was the city of mud', as Brown-May puts it, and in wet weather the inadequate footpaths meant that the streets were often impassable for pedestrians.[60] In 1856 the *Argus* reported that a man drowned in Spenser Street under 6 feet of water and mud; according to Brown-May, such drownings in the street were not uncommon.[61] Horne himself recalled seeing violent floodwaters sweep through the city (*Australian Facts*, 192). In the early 1850s, drovers were still permitted to herd cattle down the city streets between midnight and 8 am.[62] Melbourne streets at night 'presented anything

---

[59] The shock of arrival was a popular scene in colonial fiction. George Henry Haydon's novel *The Australian Emigrant* has echoes of Martin Chuzzlewit's arrival in Eden: '"Melbourne!" said Weevel, "– that Melbourne!! I have a plan of the town here;" and produced one from his pocketbook. "Pray point out the several churches marked on it. – Where is the custom-house? – Where the gaol? – Where the wharf? – Where is the government-house? – the barracks? – the police office? – and in short, where *is* the town?" "Easy", cried the skipper [...], "The shade of the largest trees left standing are our churches for the present [...]. That little crib, a short way up from the Yarra, is the custom-house [...]. The plan you are staring at, young man, is correct enough; only, it is what Melbourne is going to be – not exactly what is. I'll just give it five years", said the captain, prophetically.' G.H. Haydon, *The Australian Emigrant, A Rambling Story, Containing As Much Fact As Fiction* (London: Arthur Hall, Virtue, and Co., and W. Roberts, Exeter, 1854), 45–7.

[60] Brown-May, *Melbourne Street Life*, 32; 41.

[61] Ibid., 32.

[62] Ibid., 66.

but a pleasant aspect'; according to Ellen Clacy's account, 'owing to the want of lamps, few, except when full moon, dare stir out after dark'.[63] Howitt echoed many contemporary anxieties when he remarked that

> There is no denying that crime has already reached a height which is awful. The vast mass of rude fellows who flock here from all corners of the world, and then get extraordinary sums of money, such as they hitherto have had no conception of, makes this no wonder. Here, too, they mingle with the worst escaped convicts, and receive a *finish* to their education in all depravity.[64]

These were the characters feared by the nervous night-time pedestrian. Even in the 1860s, night-time in Melbourne was considered threatening to the 'respectable' citizen. The son of one of Horne's friends claimed that

> During the sixties Melbourne was a hefty city. Bourke Street, packed with foreign cafes, represented a cosmopolis by night. Fashionable women, accompanied by the bucks of the period, emerged from the Scandinavian Music Hall, among barrowmen selling oysters across gutters that frequently stank. There were brawls: doors flying open, drunkards crashing on the footpaths, figures silhouetted against squares of light, sailors with their doxies, constables in belltopper-hats, diggers, soldiers, ticket-of-leave men, and aboriginals.[65]

There is an emphasis on latent masculine aggression in these descriptions of the night-time streets of mid-century Melbourne.

The sanctum of the editor's office was not safe from this violence. In 1855, the editor and the publisher of *Melbourne Punch* were attacked by the irate target of one of *Punch*'s cartoons:

> On Thursday afternoon Mr. Bernal, formerly a Gold Commissioner, and who figured rather prominently in a caricature in that morning's *Punch*, called at *Punch*'s head-quarters, in Collins-street, where he met the reputed editor, Mr. Frederick Sinnett, and the publisher, Mr. Edgar Ray. After some conversation of a not over-amicable character […] Mr. Bernal proceeded to administer a dose of corporal chastisement […] assisted by a Mr. Candor […]. The result was that the *Punchites* got well 'punched', and as is generally the case with those who come off 'second best' in such encounters, they have applied for and obtained summonses against their assailants. The double charge of assault will be heard in the City Court this morning, when *Punch*, Junior, will have the honour of making

---

[63]   Henry Brown, *Victoria, As I Found It* (London: T. Cautley Newby, 1862), 45; Clacy, *A Lady's Visit*, 24.

[64]   Howitt, 35.

[65]   McCrae, 16. 'Ticket-of-leave' men were transported convicts who had completed a period of probation and been granted certain freedoms (such as seeking employment within a specified district, bringing their families over from Britain, etc.) as a reward for good behaviour.

a personal acquaintance with his very particular friend the Right Worshipful and a bench of magistrates.[66]

This report first appeared in the *Melbourne Herald*; given that the *Herald*'s office was on Collins Street, the staff there may well have heard the commotion at number 66. The magistrate ruled against *Punch*, which responded with satire (Figures 4.7a and b). On hearing of these events, Horne could have been forgiven if he had decided that life as an editor and writer in Collins Street was far removed from life at 16 Wellington Street North.

However, responses to colonial life were more complicated than that.[67] London and Melbourne were frequently aligned in language and rhetoric, and by what Wallace Kirsop calls the 'transplanting of skills and of ready access to key networks in London'.[68] London's print networks expanded into Melbourne and turned a local face-to-face community into a more 'virtual' one (in Arjun Appadurai's terms) that stretched the definition of what 'local' might mean.[69] Many London writers, booksellers, and publishers emigrated during the gold rush; some, like Horne and Howitt, went out for the diggings and then became disillusioned with prospects there. Others, particularly booksellers, headed to Melbourne specifically to make a new start in their chosen profession:

> Some, like E.W. Cole and J.S. Gotch, came from other occupations. Others, like Henry Tolman Dwight, claimed trade experience in London, but took such employment as photography before setting up in shops. However, such major figures as George Robertson, Samuel Mullen, William Charles Rigby, Adam Graham Melville, George Slater, Alfred James Smith and William Maddock had worked or been apprenticed in bookselling in Dublin, London, Edinburgh and the English provinces.[70]

Samuel Mullen's bookshop, opened in 1859 at 67 Collins Street East, later became a fashionable lending library like Mudie's in London.[71] Amongst Horne's circle,

---

[66] 'Punch in Trouble', *Empire*, 27 September 1855, 5. Reprinted from the *Melbourne Herald*, September 22, 1855.

[67] See Briggs, 295.

[68] Wallace Kirsop, 'Cole's Book Arcade', in *Worlds of Print: Diversity in the Book Trade*, ed. John Hinks and Catherine Armstrong (New Castle, DE: Oak Knoll Press; London: British Library, 2006), 32.

[69] Arjun Appadurai, 'The Production of Locality', in *Modernity at Large: Cultural Dimensions of Globalization* (Minneapolis: University of Minnesota Press, 1996), 189.

[70] Wallace Kirsop, 'Bookselling and Publishing in the Nineteenth Century', in *The Book in Australia: Essays Towards a Cultural and Social History*, ed. D.H. Borchardt and Wallace Kirsop (Clayton, Victoria: Australian Reference Publications in association with the Centre for Bibliographical and Textual Studies, Monash University, 1988), 31.

[71] Wallace Kirsop, 'From Curry's to Collins Street, or How a Dubliner Became the "Melbourne Mudie"', in *The Moving Market: Continuity and Change in the Book Trade*, ed. Peter Isaac and Barry McKay (New Castle, DE: Oak Knoll Press, 2001), 83.

(left) Figure 4.7a   An Editor's Room in Melbourne;   (right) Figure 4.7b   To Editors and Others

MP, 1, 1856, 69 and 73. Reproduced by permission of the Library for the Institute of Historical Research, University of London.

he was not the only emigrant with connections to the networks associated with Wellington Street. Horne sailed to Melbourne with William Howitt and his two sons on board the *Kent*; Howitt, his wife, and his daughter were also contributors to *Household Words*.[72] Godfrey Howitt, his brother, had a house at the east end of Collins Street, famous for its high walled garden.[73] Horne brought with him a letter of introduction to Captain Chisholm, who had an office on Swanstone Street (*Australian Facts*, 178). Captain Chisholm was the husband of Caroline Chisholm, whose article 'Pictures of Life in Australia' had been edited by Horne.[74] Caroline Chisholm became known as the 'Emigrant's Friend' for her promotion of emigration schemes though her Family Colonisation Society; she is widely considered the model for Mrs Jellyby in *Bleak House*.[75] It was the Chisholms who raised the subscription list for the colonial edition of *Orion* (the poem which made Horne's name in 1843), published by James J. Blundell, whose bookshop was at 44 Collins Street West.[76]

Horne's fellow contributors to *Melbourne Punch* had Wellington Street connections, too.[77] James Smith, contributor and editor 1857–63 had once worked with Jerrold, according to Horne biographer Anne Blainey. Butler Cole Aspinall, another contributor, had been friends with G.H. Lewes in London, while James Stiffe was the originator of one of London *Punch*'s most popular jokes, 'Advice to those about to marry – Don't'.[78] The unpaid contributor William à Beckett, later Chief Justice, was the elder brother of Gilbert à Beckett of London *Punch*; Gilbert was also in Dickens's acting troupe and had written for the Lyceum.[79] In Melbourne, Horne came across Charles Gavan Duffy, also a contributor to *Melbourne Punch*, whom he had first met in Ireland when Horne was Dublin correspondent for the *Daily News* and Duffy edited the *Nation* weekly paper. Duffy got Horne a job

---

[72]   Anne Blainey, 165.

[73]   Judith Buckrich, 'Collins Street', in *eMelbourne: The City Past and Present* (Encyclopedia of Melbourne Online), accessed 26 January 2012 online via http://www.emelbourne.net.au.

[74]   Lohrli, 311.

[75]   Joanna Bogle, 'Chisholm, Caroline (1808–1877)', *DNB*, accessed 11 August 2012 online via http://www.oxforddnb.com/.

[76]   Anne Blainey, 209. For Blundell, see Eri J. Schumaker, *A Concise Bibliography of The Complete Works of Richard H. Horne, 1802–1884* (Granville, OH: Granville Times Press, 1943), and 'Colonial Publications', *MP*, 1 (1856), inside front cover.

[77]   For a list of *MP* contributors, see Lurline Stewart, *Australian Periodicals*, 84–5. See also Marguerite Mahood, *The Loaded Line: Australian Political Caricature 1788–1901* (Carlton, Victoria: Melbourne University Press, 1973), and Mahood, 'Melbourne Punch and its Early Artists', *La Trobe Library Journal* 4 (October 1969), accessed 6 January 2014 online via http://www.slv.vic.gov.au/latrobejournal/issue/latrobe-04/t1-g-t1.html.

[78]   Anne Blainey, 209; Mahood, *Loaded Line*, 44; McCrae, 33. This joke is also attributed to Henry Mayhew.

[79]   See Chapter 3; Arthur William à Beckett, *The à Becketts of 'Punch': Memories of Fathers and Sons* (Westminster: Archibald Constable, 1903), 22.

during one of Horne's frequent penniless states.[80] All of these members of the Melbourne print networks were emigrants, rather than Australian-born.

As well as biographical links to the print networks of Wellington Street, Horne and his fellow contributors to *Melbourne Punch* had a similar way of working to their Wellington Street counterparts. The brawl in the *Melbourne Punch* office proves Marguerite Mahood's point that this was 'an urban community where everyone was more or less known to everyone else'.[81] What angered Sinnett's assailant was, according to the *Argus*'s report of the trial, that

> When he now went into the street, he was assailed by hundreds of ragged urchins, with 'There goes the man in *Punch!*' On passing an omnibus or carriage stand the cry was, 'There goes the man in *Punch!*' [...]. And even when he entered any shop in town, there, staring him in the face, was 'the man in *Punch!*' It was certainly very annoying to him.[82]

As Lurline Stewart puts it:

> these immigrants were not so much a cohesive group as members of smaller circles whose interests tended to overlap. They visited each other's homes or met at hotels and clubs. They joined the same societies and served together on councils and committees. They produced and edited periodicals and supported cultural movements and foundations, moving from one circle to another according to the particular interest of the time.[83]

This description could serve equally well for the networks which operated between the editors, writers, and theatre managers with links to Wellington Street. Those involved in print production and literary work 'were comparatively few in number and, in the records of their activities, the same names appear in different contexts as presidents and secretaries, editors and contributors', as they shared their enthusiasm for the 'pursuit of cultural activity'.[84]

Just as amongst Dickens's network, business and socializing went hand in hand. Horne was a founding member of the Garrick Club (which never had enough money for a clubhouse), set up in direct imitation of the London version, along with Nicholas Chevalier, Archibald Mitchie, and James Smith. All of these men worked on *Melbourne Punch*, while Horne had also been a fellow contributor to the same periodicals as key members John Shillinglaw and James Nield.[85] A similar group,

---

[80]   Anne Blainey, 209; Pearl, *Always Morning*, 93.

[81]   Mahood, *Loaded Line*, 53.

[82]   'Assault', *Argus*, 24 September 1855, 5.

[83]   Lurline Stewart, *James Smith: the Making of a Colonial Culture* (Sydney: Allen & Unwin, 1989), 7.

[84]   Ibid., 9.

[85]   Ibid., 45; Paul De Serville, 'Garrick Club', in *eMelbourne*, accessed 20 January 2012 online via http://www.emelbourne.net.au.

but which included younger writers, went on later to form the Yorick Club in the 1860s, with its clubhouse in part of the *Melbourne Punch* building:

> I think it was Marcus Clarke who first broached the subject of the Yorick Club to John Shillinglaw; John Shillinglaw to F.W. Haddon, editor of the *Australasian*. Prior to this, there had been gatherings of writers and artists at Nissen's Café in Bourke Street; but Clarke and Shillinglaw wanted a place to themselves [...] Accordingly, they leased an apartment next door to the *Argus* Office, at a pound a week; and [...] instituted a genuine club. They took unto themselves saddle-back chairs (made up of bundles of newspapers), and drank beer out of pint-pots; but, lest they should forget their mortality, Shillinglaw installed upon the hat rack a skull with a pipe between its teeth [...]. [On opening night] By six o'clock next morning half the revellers were asleep; and George Walstab, still sober, went the rounds, blackening their faces, in between the whiskers, with burnt cork.[86]

At the Argus Hotel and Dining Rooms on Collins Street, 'near the Argus Office', Smith and friends had a reserved round table where they met after the theatres closed.[87] The Theatre Royale, round the corner at 71–81 Bourke Street, was the favourite haunt of Clarke and his friends, immortalized in his sketch 'The Café Lutetia'.[88] As on Wellington Street, links of business, friendship, and marriage became interwoven. The first editor and co-publisher of *Melbourne Punch*, Frederick Sinnett, had a business partner called Archibald Mitchie, a friend of Horne's. Mitchie's daughter Isabella married the nephew of William à Beckett.[89] Lurline Stewart quotes Smith's account of his visit to Butler Cole Aspinall's first home as a guest of Aspinall and his wife, who lived in

> a little three-roomed cottage in Flinders-Lane, at which a drayman would now turn up his nose [...] we were terribly cramped for room, and the experiments in cooking of a raw Irish girl, who had been imported from Connemara, were of the most rashly adventurous character; but they were provocative of endless amusement [...] it was one of the merriest evenings I ever remember to have spent in Melbourne.[90]

---

[86]   McCrae, 19–20.

[87]   Advertisement inside front cover, *Melbourne Punch*, 1 (1856); Lurline Stewart, *James Smith*, 7.

[88]   McCann, 34. For a discussion of the fantastical elements of descriptions of this colonial Bohemia, see McCann, especially 30–32, 46, and 51. The name 'Theatre Royale' contains an echo of Wellington Street's 'Theatre Royal, Lyceum'. As in London and in Paris, the theatre and print districts overlap. See Graeme Davison, 'The European City in Australia', 781–2.

[89]   'Death Of Sir Archibald Michie', *Argus*, 23 June 1899, 6.

[90]   Lurline Stewart, *James Smith*, 7.

This is demonstrably not the modern metropolis which Smith left behind him, but it retains elements of that London life. The 'amusement' comes partly from this awkward juxtaposition.

Finally, the Collins Street networks, like the Wellington Street ones, were linked because they had to work in several publications to survive. In the 1850s and '60s, *Melbourne Punch* was surrounded on Collins Street by the *Argus* (and its weekly, the *Australasian*), the *Age* (and its weekly, the *Leader*), and the *Herald*.[91] Of his fellow contributors to *Melbourne Punch*, James Smith, William à Beckett, Charles Whitehead, and Butler Cole Aspinall all wrote on other publications to which Horne also contributed work.[92] Sinnett worked for both the *Argus* and *Melbourne Punch*.[93] Theatre work kept them going too: Marcus Clarke started as theatre critic for the *Argus*, was a prolific playwright, and married the actress Maria Dunn.[94] Furthermore, famous London figures with Wellington Street connections were evoked and discussed through literary lectures, visits, and obituaries: the assumption was that the Melbourne reader not only knew who these people were, but cared.[95] As Ken Stewart puts it:

> the goldrush immigrants joined with politically liberal resident literati of the professional classes, and with native-born writers like Daniel Deniehy and Henry Kendall, to establish or extend those networks of communication, exchange and support which gave readers and writers their literary bearings. They thought of their literary community as provincial and growing, no longer tiny and isolated.[96]

They were isolated neither from each other, nor from London.

A construction of cultural proximity to London was also evident in the way the Melbourne periodical and newspaper press replicated London titles.[97] As well as *Melbourne Punch* (1855–), Melbourne titles such as the *Melbourne Illustrated News* (October–November 1853), the *Australian Builder* (1859–61), the *Spectator* (July 1865–March 1867), the *Melbourne Leader* (January 1856–June 1957; simply the *Leader* from January 1862), and the *Melbourne Examiner* (July 1857–September 1864) evoked, if they did not directly imitate, their London predecessors (of which the latter three were all published from addresses on the three sections of Wellington Street). More direct influences existed: the

---

91   Judith Buckrich, 'Collins Street', in *eMelbourne*, accessed 26 January 2012.

92   See Lurline Stewart, *Australian Periodicals.*

93   Marjorie J. Tipping, 'Sinnett, Frederick (1830–1866)', *ADB*, accessed 25 January 2012 online via http://adb.anu.edu.au/.

94   *Cyril Hopkins' Marcus Clarke*, ed. Laurie Hergenhan, Ken Stewart, and Michael Wilding (North Melbourne, Victoria: Australian Scholarly Publishing, 2009), 165–9; Michael Wilding, *Marcus Clarke* (Melbourne and Oxford: Oxford University Press, 1977), 7.

95   See, for example, 'Lecture on Douglas Jerrold', *Argus*, 10 April 1858, 5.

96   James Smith, 'Old Melbourne', *Victorian Review* 9 (1883–84), 405, quoted in Ken Stewart, 'Journalism and the World of the Writer: The Production of Australian Literature, 1855–1915', in *The Penguin New Literary History of Australia*, 175.

97   Lurline Stewart, *James Smith*, 83.

Victorian Review (1860–61), published out of the *Melbourne Punch* office by Edgar Ray, was modelled on the *Army and Navy Gazette*; the *Melbourne Monthly Magazine* (May–November 1855) was modelled on *Blackwood's*; the *Australian Journal* (September 1865–April 1962) was modelled on the *Family Herald*; and the *Australasian Monthly Review* (March–April 1866) was modelled on the *Fortnightly Review*.[98] In the names of Melbourne's main dailies, the *Argus* and the *Age*, we hear the echoes of Wellington Street. In the *Post Office Directory* for 1844, 13 Wellington Street North (across the street from where Reynolds's office will be, and three doors down from the building which will contain *Household Words*) is listed as the office for the *Argus* weekly newspaper.[99] By 1844, this paper had already merged with its rival, the *Age*, to form the *Age and Argus*. Shirley Brooks was the editor of this short-lived paper (before it turned into *The English Gentleman* in 1845), around the same time that he first became involved with the *Punch* circle.[100]

A sense of separation was never likely to be immediate when so many of the gold rush colonists came not as settlers, but as prospectors, determined to stay only as long as it took to make their fortune and longing for the culture of 'home'. James Smith, who arrived in Australia from London in 1854, wrote in the *Centennial Magazine* in 1889 that 'Few of us regarded it as our permanent home. Everybody was going to 'make his pile' [and return to Britain]'.[101] Horne himself admitted that

> Never intending, when I left England, to remain in Melbourne, I had declined nearly all offers of letters of introduction. Several, however, had been sent to me, and I availed myself of the one addressed to Major Chisholm. To the kindness and candour of this gentleman, together with the accuracy of the information he gave me, I was indebted for the quiet shattering of those golden lottery-wheels, which so many of us had believed would lead to fortune. (*Australian Facts*, 4)

Smith's avowed goal was 'the transplantation of English ideas, principles, and modes of action'.[102] The word 'transplantation' evokes popular rhetoric of the Australian colonies as an empty land, devoid of any native population, a paradise

---

[98] See Lurline Stewart, *James Smith*, 89; 85; 90; 92. For details of nineteenth-century periodicals published in Melbourne, see Lurline Stewart, *Australian Periodicals*.

[99] *Kelly's POD* (1844), 514.

[100] David Haldane Lawrence, 'Age (1825–1843)', *DNCJ*, 8; Patrick Leary, 'Brooks, Charles William Shirley (1816–1874)', *DNCJ*, 81.

[101] Quoted in Lurline Stewart, *James Smith*, 7. See also Howitt's comments in *Land, Labour and Gold*, 37: 'Everybody talks of England as home. They are all going home someday. [...] All are in a sort of temporary exile, – the servants of mammon, that they may spend "golden earnings at home."'

[102] Lurline Stewart, *James Smith*, 7. Of course, Clarke's 1860s Collins Street was very different to Horne's and Smith's 1850s neighbourhood, as the original gold rush literary men worked hard at 'transplanting', in Smith's term, the kind of literary, theatrical, journalistic, and artistic world that they had left behind.

regained to which the prospector could bring the old world through reading and self-improvement:

> Even in these wide and tenantless plains we may equally recall our former intellectual avocation. The classical reminiscences of ancient strife may be vividly depicted. There is still the intrepidity of Xenophon, the terrible genius of Hannibal, Babylon in her gigantic splendour, and Rome in her ancient glory. In the higher avocations of our leisure hours, the warlike achievements of the Greeks […] may be transferred to the Southern Hemisphere.[103]

The conquering colonist could win victories over the land inspired by the classics; but even cheap periodicals were a useful weapon in the battle to turn Melbourne into 'the London […] of the Southern hemisphere'.[104]

However, the culture of the 'mother country' provided competition for the writers and editors of Collins Street, just as much as it was an essential reference point for their work. Imported books and periodicals from 'home' were big business. As Elizabeth Webby puts it, 'in early Australia, as in all colonial societies, the most important influence on the production of literature was the relationship with the parent culture'.[105] Webby notes that 'a surprisingly high number of the first settlers could read, and by 1890 adult literacy was almost universal'.[106] For Webby, reading became one of the ways in which the colonists proclaimed their continued participation in the cultural conversations of home:

> As early as February 1828 […] one of several short-lived local magazines, the *Austral-Asiatic Review*, was enthusing, 'The British nation is characteristically designated "*a reading People*"; and wherever they spread themselves – however distant from their native land their circumstances may carry them – their native attribute remains rather increased than diminished'.[107]

What the colonists wanted to read, however, were imported books and periodicals from 'home'. As Webby writes:

---

[103]   Committee of the Melbourne Mechanics Institute, *Port Phillip Patriot*, 17 February 1842. Quoted in M. Askew and B. Hubber, 'The Colonial Reader Observed: Reading in Its Cultural Context', in *The Book in Australia*, 113.

[104]   Mahood, 'Melbourne Punch and its Early Artists', 65. See also Frederick Sinnett's essay 'The Fiction Fields of Australia', *Journal of Australasia* 1, July–December 1856, which uses the dual meaning of 'cultivation' to argue that Australia can 'grow' its own literature, and draws many of its examples from Dickens's novels.

[105]   Elizabeth Webby, 'Writers, Printers, Readers: the Production of Australian Literature Before 1855', in *The Penguin New Literary History of Australia*, 113.

[106]   Elizabeth Webby, 'The Beginnings of Literature in Colonial Australia', in *The Cambridge History of Australian Literature*, ed. Peter Pierce (Cambridge: Cambridge University Press, 2009), 34.

[107]   Elizabeth Webby, 'Colonial Writers and Readers', in *The Cambridge Companion to Australian Literature*, ed. Elizabeth Webby (Cambridge: Cambridge University Press, 2000), 54.

Since all the material needed for printing had to be imported, it cost at least twice as much to print a book in Australia as in England. English publications also had the charm of the known amidst the unknown. A favourite vignette of writers describing bush life in mid-century was the squatter's table with its copies of *Punch* and the *Illustrated London News*. And, of course, imported books were believed to be of superior quality.[108]

Even antiquarian books were shipped out to be auctioned in colonies; London bookseller Edward Lumley sent a consignment of stock to Melbourne in 1856.[109] A Melbourne writer in the 1850s and '60s was much more likely to send their book to London for publication than to launch it locally: 'for much of the nineteenth century, and indeed afterwards, Australian readers were mainly interested in books by English authors and Australian authors were largely dependent on the English publishing industry', especially as, by the time Horne was trying to establish himself in Melbourne, 'it was possible to buy the latest English releases only four to six months after they had appeared in London'.[110] This cultural tension energized Melbourne's print culture. As with the *Punch* brand, connections with the London trade were both enabling and problematic for the writers and booksellers of Collins Street.

Of course, conditions gradually changed over the 1850s and '60s as men like Smith and his contemporaries developed more of a local market for periodicals as well as books and newspapers:[111]

> According to G.B. Barton, in 1866 the *Australian Journal* was circulating an average of 5500 copies weekly, including 1750 in New South Wales. This was at least equal to the circulation of English Magazines of a similar type and cost, again indicating [like the success of *Melbourne Punch*] that Australian readers were prepared to support local magazines if their contents and prices were competitive with the imported products.[112]

According to the *Dictionary of Commerce* for 1875, by the 1860s the number of printed books imported into Victoria from the UK was falling steadily. In 1865, 6,262 cwts or £71,068 worth of printed books were imported; two years later this had fallen to 5,721 cwts, or £61,938.[113] Despite prejudice against local productions,

---

[108] Webby, 'Writers, Printers, Readers', 114.
[109] Kirsop, 'Bookselling and Publishing in the Nineteenth Century', 21.
[110] Webby, 'Colonial Writers and Readers', 50; 54.
[111] Although Elizabeth Morrison shows that imported fiction from abroad was still hugely popular in the latter part of the century; see Morrison, 'Serial Fiction in Australian Colonial Newspapers', in *Literature in the Marketplace: Nineteenth-Century British Publishing and Reading Practices*, ed. John O. Jordan and Robert L. Patten (Cambridge: Cambridge University Press, 1995), 306–23.
[112] Webby, 'The Beginnings of Literature in Colonial Australia', 47.
[113] McCulloch, 882. The hundredweight (abbreviated cwt) is a unit of measure equivalent to 112 pounds (lb.) under the imperial system.

'commercial interests ensured that local newspapers flourished' and, given that newspapers carried sketches and fiction, they gave opportunities to local writers, paid for by advertising. The first edition of the first Melbourne newspaper, the short-lived *Melbourne Advertiser*, appeared on 1 January 1837, while the first Australian periodical, the *Australian Magazine*, appeared in Sydney in 1821; according to Lurline Stewart, 'close to 200 literary or partly-literary periodicals were produced in Melbourne in the nineteenth century'.[114] However, 'local writers and dramatists had to struggle to make a living in part because nineteenth-century Australian readers and audiences were so well provided for from overseas'.[115]

The writers and editors of 1850s Melbourne, then, experienced an acute double bind. To compete with popular imported print, they needed to show what was distinct about their own work and print culture. Yet to assert the value of that work, they sought to show that they were linked to their London counterparts; they wanted to share the same virtual neighbourhood as Dickens, Jerrold, Lemon, and Sala. These conditions affected Horne's prose work on Australia. Horne's only lengthy 'Australian' prose work, *Australian Facts*, which also includes the autobiographical fragment, compares London and Melbourne and emphasizes the hardships for literary emigrants and the necessity of the colony retaining links to the 'mother-country'. Horne's book is keenly aware of the separation from London's literary world occasioned by emigration. It is full of anxiety about the distance of time and space between London and Melbourne, and represents an attempt to construct through print an image of personal relationship and physical proximity between writer and reader. Yet in the end, Horne only succeeds in emphasizing the very physical and cultural separation that he fears so much.

First, Horne's 'Preface' opens the book with a bid to undo any sense of separation between author and reader:

> Touching the composition of these pages, the reader is requested to regard them, as far as he can, in the light of a long and careful letter, written in the familiar language of a far-off friend, and not as a systematic work. (*Australian Facts*, xii)

Horne places his work within the genre of emigrants' letters, although he sounds a note of caution, not of eager encouragement, to the prospective emigrant. The writer is positioned in the role of a 'friend', albeit a 'far-off' one, with the suggestion of intimacy, familiarity, and face-to-face acquaintance that this implies. The publishers themselves encouraged this sense of familiarity as a guarantor of authenticity for the work as a whole; their 'Advertisement' in the front states that the publishers decided to move the autobiographical fragment forward from the Appendix so that it appears before the main text of *Australian Facts*:

---

[114]   D.H. Borchardt, 'Printing Comes to Australia', in *The Book in Australia*, ed. Borchardt and Wallace Kirsop, 12; Lurline Stewart, *James Smith*, 83–4.

[115]   Webby, 'Colonial Writers and Readers', 55; 51. In Melbourne's 'cosmopolis', imports did not just include English-language publications, of course.

> They trust that this arrangement will be approved by readers in Australia, as
> well as by those in England, inasmuch as the Author's personal experience of
> Australian life, and his opportunities of observation, become a guarantee for
> the correctness of his statements on the subject of the Australian Colonies.
> ('Advertisement', *Australian Facts*, front matter)

However, though Horne's choice of language may aim to reduce the distance between Melbourne writer and London book-buyer, the realities of long-distance publishing intrude, persistently, on the text. Horne hopes that '[w]ishing to prevent mischief by taking advantage of an early mail, may entitle me to some slight indulgence for hasty shortcomings' (*Australian Facts*, x), and elsewhere he decides to leave out further details 'partly because it would occupy too much space' in his text, but presumably also in his mail packet. The *Australian Autobiography* in *Australian Facts and Prospects* itself ends abruptly with the bracketed statement: '[Having left this sketch to the last, as of least moment, the closing of the mail compels me to drop the pen.]' (43).

Horne also frames his book not just as an epistle to his reader, but as part of a conversation within metropolitan print culture. Horne is entering the emigration debate which raged throughout the London periodical and newspaper press in the 1850s, including through *Household Words* and *Reynolds's Weekly News*. His specific aim is that the book will correct the inaccuracies of Frank Fowler's 'off-hand, rollicking, and not-at-all-particular' account of Australia, *Southern Lights and Shadows*, for the benefit of families considering emigration (*Australian Facts*, xi). However, much as Horne attempts to position himself as someone very much still part of London print culture, who just happens to be in the colony, his refutation of Fowler's book in *Australian Facts* rests on his argument that membership in London's print networks is no guarantee of colonial success, as Melbourne is a very different world (55). Horne's view was probably jaundiced by his own struggles; by 1859 he had failed as a prospector and had not yet been taken up as a literary lion by Melbourne. However, he declares that membership in the knowable community of writers at home is little help to aspiring writers in the colony: newcomers will find it hard, the established writers were already known for doing other things well besides writing, and three relatives of popular British writers are doing badly – although, frustratingly, he does not choose to name names (45–63). Melbourne print culture as described here is not even an outpost of the London community, but a completely separate world with its own rules. Horne tries to depict Melbourne as 'the future London of the Southern hemisphere' (195), but his comparisons do not flatter either city. He informs us that although the number of prostitutes in Melbourne is similar to that in London, behaviour is worse than St. Giles or Covent Garden, and in a telling passage complains that the latest fashions from the Old World are worn and corrupted by prostitutes in the New World (89–90; 88). Degeneration, not new life through imitation, is his theme. It is not 'Old World' London that he finally chooses as a model for Melbourne's future, but 'New World' New York.[116] Despite Horne's professed wishes, cultural and physical separation between the Old and New Worlds is a fact of emigration.

Therefore, Horne fights against the realities of this separation in *Australian Facts* in ways which only serve to emphasize them. He declares that it is essential to have telegraphic communication with England 'long before' the telegraph goes across the bush, so that '[t]he three capitals of Australia will be brought within five minutes of London' (211), and quotes Bulwer Lytton that 'the sceptre of Queen Victoria is an electric rod' which connects the Old to the New country (213). Horne believes (or wants to believe) that two-thirds of Australians retain 'loyalty and affection' for the 'mother-country' (214), and asks whether, in dire need, 'is it not possible to change the seat of empire?' (218). He considers it too dangerous to move to India, but:

> here, in the heart of the Australasian group, would you find a virgin soil wherein to transplant the aged oak of British empire. Here, with no hostile tribes or sects intermingled with the populations, still less any armed nations hovering on shifty frontiers – here would you find 'bone of your bone and flesh of your flesh'; your own laws, religion, customs, food; a milder and more genial climate, and open arms to receive you. (*Australian Facts*, 219)

Again, the rhetoric of the empty land is used to argue that such 'transplanting' is possible. By now, however, even Horne cannot pretend that this is a solution to his problems:

> To such 'vain imaginings' are we prone at times, in exile or in absence, far across the seas. The misgiving pen, prompted by more sober reflections, hovers over these concluding pages, and prepares to cancel and cross them down. Kind reader, permit them to remain; [we should not] feel ashamed of the vigorous birth of our impractical hopes. [...] But for you, my fellow-sojourners in these colonies, the one substantial piece of advice I would offer – the only advice I have presumed directly to offer – the one exhortation, the one steadfast hope, may be comprised in this: For your own sake, even more than for *her* sake, never, of your own voluntary act, separate yourselves from the mother-country. (*Australian Facts*, 220)

For Horne, the sense of physical separation is all too real. Cultural proximity is the best that he can hope for; this may be a tenuous link, but one which must, in Horne's view, be maintained.[117]

---

[116]   American and Australian cities were often compared, too. For more on American emigration to Australia during the gold rush, see E. Daniel Potts and Annette Potts, *Young America and Australian Gold: Americans and the Gold Rush of the 1850s* (St. Lucia, Queensland: University of Queensland Press, 1974).

[117]   When he returns 'home' a decade later, in 1869, physical proximity is not even a solution: he is not welcomed back by Dickens. See Pearl, *Always Morning*, 229–30. Also, in 1859 *Household Words* was wound up and Dickens started *All the Year Round*. This new periodical moved to new offices at 11 Wellington Street North; in 1859 Wellington Street

Charles Lamb's essay 'Distant Correspondents' from the *London Magazine*, based upon a letter to a London friend now in Australia, wrestled with similar problems in the 1820s, 'staging his lost intimacy with his friend in a [...] public context':[118]

> I am insensibly chatting to you as familiarly as when we used to exchange good-morrows out of our old contiguous windows, in pump-famed Hare-court in the Temple. [...] My heart is as dry as that spring sometimes proves in a thirsty August, when I revert to the space that is between us; a length of passage enough to render obsolete the phrases of our English letters before they reach you.[119]

Even cultural proximity comes under threat for Lamb in this earlier period before faster communications, when the distances are so vast that written words become out of date. In *David Copperfield*, however, Mr Micawber's public letter to David in the *Port Middlebay Times* suggests that shared cultural experiences *can* connect networks across vast geographic distances, and cultural proximity can overcome physical separation. Micawber's letter is a glorious piece of comic satire by Dickens on the kinds of cultural tension expressed by Horne's book.[120] Like Horne's 'Preface', the letter is printed to be read by multiple unknown readers, but is addressed to an intimate friend. Micawber acknowledges that '[y]ears have elapsed, since I had the opportunity of ocularly perusing the lineaments, now familiar to the imagination of a considerable portion of the civilised world'; in other words, since he has seen David face to face. However, Micawber states that: '[y]ou are not unknown here [...] Though "remote", we are neither "unfriended", "melancholy", nor (I may add) "slow"'. David, the now-famous author, has friends in Port Middlebay who 'know' him through his works and look to him for 'entertainment', but also 'instruction'. However, Micawber, the fêted Magistrate and 'diligent and esteemed correspondent' of the *Port Middlebay Times*, may give due praise to David 'THE EMINENT AUTHOR', but he also asserts the ability of the writers and readers of Port Middlebay to contribute to the cultural conversations of the metropolis. They may be 'remote', but they are not 'slow'. Micawber reinvents himself as a successful public figure with more gusto than even David himself achieves; Dickens admires his creation even as he mocks him. The colony has something to teach the metropolis.

---

itself was renamed and renumbered. In both the landscape of London and the field of print culture, there was not a lot that was familiar for Horne to return to.

[118] Gillian Russell and Clara Tuite, 'Introducing Romantic Sociability', in *Romantic Sociability: Social Networks and Literary Culture in Britain, 1770–1840*, ed. Gillian Russell and Clara Tuite (Cambridge: Cambridge University Press, 2002), 19.

[119] Charles Lamb, 'Distant Correspondents', in *The Works of Charles and Mary Lamb*, ed. E.V. Lucas, 7 vols (London: Methuen, 1905), 2: 108.

[120] Charles Dickens, *David Copperfield*, ed. Nina Burgis (Oxford: Clarendon Press, 1981; 1st publ. 1849–50), 746–7. I am grateful to Ian Henderson for drawing this to my attention.

Horne finally decides that even if the Queen and her court uprooted to Melbourne, it could not reproduce London, because it does not have the history: 'the old black grandeur of London would be left behind' (*Australian Facts*, 197). Horne's ideal vision for the future of Anglo-Australian relations is for them to become like that of grown-up children and parents, with no resentment but no 'servile dependence' either (212). This metaphor of the parent in the 'Old World', the 'mother country', and the emigrant child of the 'New World' becomes more difficult, however, when the new writer is not only separated from their 'parent' influences by space and by emigration, but is at one remove from them anyway by youth and by time. Horne could at least claim friendship with Dickens, while *Melbourne Punch* started with contributors from the same generation as its London original. Marcus Clarke, on the other hand, was part of a younger set than Horne and arrived in Melbourne 10 years later. His sketches of Melbourne life, heavily influenced by Dickens, Jerrold, and Mayhew, as well as by the early work of the younger Sala, were written in the late 1860s, not the mid-1850s. Marcus Clarke wrestled with how to manage his relationship with a previous generation of writers separated from him by space and emigration, but also by the passing of years.

'Borrowed Metaphors and Stolen Thoughts': Marcus Clarke's Night-time

Marcus Clarke's Melbourne sketches were first published from Collins Street in the *Argus* and the *Age* and in their respective weeklies, the *Australasian* and the *Leader* (although his first comic piece, 'The Puff Conclusive', was published in *Melbourne Punch* on 19 November 1863, five months after his arrival in the colony).[121] In his avowal of the influence of writers linked to Wellington Street, like Henry Mayhew, G.A. Sala, Douglas Jerrold, and Charles Dickens, Clarke was a self-conscious 'child' of Wellington Street. As we have seen, Clarke ('the Peripatetic Philosopher') and Horne participated in the same networks in Melbourne. Clarke knew Collins Street well:

> Here is *The Daily Tickler* and *Weekly Chimes* office, with its front door placarded with caricatures by Joe Barrington, and its passageways thronged with eager moralists upon John Stewart Mill. Here is the *Peacock* office, with Chips the leader-writer airing his boot-heels in the passage as usual; there the Cassowary Club, with Oedipus Quackendrum writing *Punch* copy in the upper window. Underneath the Cassowary window stands ever open the door of the Iphiginia Café and dining rooms, where congregate from morning until evening the scandal-mongers of the metropolis. If a good thing is said at the Woolsack, you

---

[121]   Wilding, 5; L.T. Hergenhan, introduction to *A Colonial City: High and Low Life. Selected Journalism of Marcus Clarke*, ed. L.T. Hergenhan (St. Lucia, Queensland: University of Queensland Press, 1972), xxiv.

can be sure to hear it at the Iphiginia in thirteen minutes. Next to the Café is the Peacock hotel, with jolly Hans Breitman at the door.[122]

Clarke embraced the role of following in others' footsteps as he laid out how his 'Peripatetic Philosophy' will imitate the 'ancient *flâneurs*' of Athens and the Paris of Victor Hugo:

> There is much to be learnt from street life, and one's 'daily walks abroad' are instructive as well as amusing. To imitate the ancient peripatetics has long been my pleasure. I am a Bohemian [...]. I have passed into the *Cour Des Miracles*, and have been made free of its mysteries. I live, I walk, I eat, I drink, and philosophise. ('Peripatetic Philosophy', in *Colonial City*, 5; originally printed in *Australasian*, 23 November 1867)

Clarke inserts himself into a very male tradition. However, Clarke's own footsteps echo along very different streets. He cannot literally follow the *flâneurs* of 'Old World' Europe, as he is in Melbourne, on streets that have only just acquired gas lighting and paving and have not had time to acquire what Horne calls 'the old black grandeur of London' or of any other European metropolis. Clarke's sketches of the night-time haunts of the Melbourne poor, in particular, make use of his Wellington Street antecedents to re-appropriate their interest in the bodies of the poor, and the eye of the observing journalist, for the streets of Melbourne. Clarke's descriptions of night-time among the Melbourne poor evoke night-time scenes as witnessed by Mayhew and Sala, until Melbourne nights come to remind us of nights in and around Wellington Street. However, Clarke's prose is also full of anxieties about what it means to follow in a literary tradition and, more specifically, what it means to lay claim to a cultural inheritance from whose beginnings you are separated not only by years, but by thousands of miles of ocean.

In Harold Bloom's study *The Anxiety of Influence*, poetic influence involves a desperate struggle with the poet's predecessors, a tug of love and hate where the need to outdo the predecessor is as important as the desire to invoke them. For Bloom, poetic influence works through a tense, Freudian parent-child relationship:

> The profundities of poetic influence cannot be reduced to source-study, to the history of ideas, to the patterning of images. Poetic influence [...] is necessarily the study of the life-cycle of the poet-as-poet [...]. [We are] compelled to examine simultaneously the relations between poets as cases akin to what Freud called the family romance, and as chapters in the history of modern revisionism.[123]

---

[122]   Marcus Clarke, 'Down Camomile Street [Collins street]', in *Colonial City*, 303; *Weekly Times*, 17 January 1874. For ease of access, further references to Clarke's sketches are cited from *Colonial City*, edited by Hergenhan, and appear after long quotations in the text or as footnotes after short quotations. The date and place of first publication is also provided the first time a sketch is cited.

[123]   Harold Bloom, *The Anxiety of Influence: A Theory of Poetry*, 2nd edn (New York and Oxford: Oxford University Press, 1997), 7–8.

Because poetic influence involves such agonies of creativity on the part of the 'younger' poet, 'poetic influence need not make poets less original; as often it makes them more original, though not necessarily better'.[124] However:

> Poetic history [is] indistinguishable from poetic influence, since strong poets make that history by misreading one another, so as to make clear imaginative space for themselves.
>
> My only concern is with strong poets, major figures with the persistence to wrestle with their strong precursors, even to the death. Weaker talents idealize; figures of capable imagination appropriate for themselves. But nothing is got for nothing, and self-appropriation involves the immense anxieties of indebtedness, for what strong maker desires the realization that he had failed to create for himself?[125]

Marcus Clarke was, of course, a journalist and not a poet like Horne. A journalist does not have the same relationship to originality as a poet, and Clarke made no secret of his own literary influences. He drew upon the work of Sala and Mayhew for his own articles about the urban poor, but in order to do so he would at times both celebrate and deny his literary ancestors.

In 'To the Public', his preface to a collected edition of his early sketches and articles called *The Peripatetic Philosopher* (1869), Clarke mocks his awkward relationship with his literary and journalistic 'parents':

> How comes it, you not unnaturally ask, that this fellow thrusts himself into print, and publishes a preposterous book, full of stale jokes, and borrowed metaphors, and stolen thoughts, and hashed-up ideas of other people? How comes it that this miserable decoction of Thackeray, and Dickens, and Balzac, and George Sala, and Douglas Jerrold, and anybody else whose works are obtainable to be plagiarised, is shaken up in a half-crown bottle, with a gaudy label on it, and sold to me as 'Philosophy'? Is it not bad enough, you say, to see this impertinent fellow thrusting himself into print every week in the columns of the *Australasian*, and laughing at his superiors with all the insolence of anonymity? ('Preface: The Peripatetic Philosopher [1869]', in *Colonial City*, 1–2; originally printed in Clarke's *The Peripatetic Philosopher*)

Clarke delights in the role of iconoclast and of the detached and mocking observer of Melbourne high and low life. He positions himself in the tradition of writers who were able to take on that kind of work, but he also presents himself as the 'impertinent' youth who can laugh at the very tradition he wants to join. Immediately after this colloquial address to the reader, Clarke adds spoof 'Opinions of the Press':

> Thackeray without the sarcasm. – *Ballarat Courier*.

---

[124]   Ibid., 7.
[125]   Bloom, 5.

Douglas Jerrold without the wit. – *Ballarat Star*. ('Opinions of the Press [Marcus Clarke]', in *Colonial City*, 3); originally printed in Clarke's *The Peripatetic Philosopher*)

Clarke is anxious to head off accusations of plagiarism or unimaginative imitation, which could put him at a financial disadvantage; after all, he tells the reader that his motivation for publishing the book is 'simply because I think it will SELL'.[126] Yet implicitly, by invoking his European models, he raises his work to be judged on an equal footing with them, and as exceeding them. At the same time, Clarke relishes here the absurdity of using 'Old World' tropes for such a new city – a place where 'for some considerable time a large proportion of the population was not housed, but encamped under tents!'[127] – while still asserting that this is an important thing to do. Clarke's sketches of Melbourne low-life attempt, among other things, to address two big questions: what created the foundations for Melbourne print culture, and what makes it distinct from its European, and more specifically its London, parents?

These questions come to the fore in Clarke's sketch 'A Night at the Immigrants' Home', as night-time saw Clarke become 'the midnight wanderer of the streets':[128]

> I am going to tell you as plainly as I can how the minority of Melbourne inhabitants live. I will take you into their houses, their lodgings, their taverns – I will show you their pleasures and their pains – I will give you their histories, taken down from their own lips [...]. I do not pretend [...] that I can emulate in any way the excitements of M. Sue or pre-Raphaelite pruriency of the Ruskinian Reynolds; [...] the genius of Dumas *fils* or the accuracy of Mayhew. You can read as much and more of vice and crime in the pages of *London Labour and the London Poor* as you can possibly wish for, and if you expect to find anything of the kind here you will be disappointed. But I would beg you to take particular notice of one thing, which is this; – that whereas these books treat of the poor of London and Paris – people with whom you have nothing to do – the few simple facts which I have been at some trouble to collect, and the misery which I have in some measure experienced, exists *here*; that this Bohemia of mine is

---

[126] 'Preface', in *Colonial City*, 2.

[127] McCulloch, 881. For Horne's own experiences in Canvass Town, see *Australian Facts*, 23; for his fictionalized account, see [R.H. Horne], 'Canvass Town', *HW*, 18 June 1853, 361–7. Alan Mayne argues that slums were always 'products of discourse' which used certain tropes to fit urban centres into the established iconography of the 'modern city'. See Alan Mayne, *The Imagined Slum: Newspaper Representation in Three Cities 1870– 1914* (Leicester: Leicester University Press, 1993), 4. In this he follows on from Graeme Davison, who notes, in his introduction to *The Outcasts of Melbourne*, that descriptions of London's poor were a potentially misleading model to poverty in the very different conditions of new colonial cities (3). Asa Briggs argues that Melbourne's working-classes were well paid and better regarded than London's: 'There was poverty [...] but there was less hopeless destitution' (Briggs, 300).

[128] 'Taking Mine Ease In Mine Inn', in *Colonial City*, 147; *Australasian*, 3 July 1869.

just exactly within a stone's throw of your doors. ('A Night at the Immigrants' Home', 134; *Australasian*, 12 June 1869)[129]

'Bohemia', here, is both the same cultural space as Mayhew's Strand, and a very different one. Clarke draws a distinction between the Upper Bohemia of artists, writers, and journalists, and a Lower Bohemia of itinerant wanderers and real suffering. Upper Bohemia is the setting for Clarke's early Melbourne life, where '[t]he morning was spent in scribbling, the afternoon in tobacco, the evening in dinner, theatre, and gaslight. [...] I am sure we were often out of bed after the small hours'.[130] Lower Bohemia is the land of poverty which awaits the emigrant who can no longer find work.[131]

In 'A Night at the Immigrants' Home', Clarke repeatedly asks the reader to take on the body of the emigrant as 'Our Bohemian – in my person or yours, reader, – goes into the guardroom at the gate'.[132] Clarke makes use of the proprietorial 'our' again when he declares, '[b]ut our Bohemian – in your person or mine – has no such comfortable couch'.[133] This time, the emphasis is reversed and placed upon the reader, and the emigrant's body becomes more his than Clarke's. By addressing his reader directly, Clarke personalizes poverty; as he writes at the end of the sketch, '[i]t is only by applying these things to ourselves that we can realise them'.[134] In this way, Clarke's imagined community is widened to include his reader, who is also the reader (or potential reader) of Reynolds, Dickens, Sala, and Mayhew, as well as of Hugo and Sue. The sketch becomes not just a story of Melbourne poverty, but of 'Old World' poverty too. This is particularly true because Clarke is describing the Immigrant's Home – after all, it was the poor of Britain and Ireland who were most encouraged to emigrate. The reader is made aware of the bodies of all the other poor, from all the other streets, who press themselves into Clarke's text. Night-time in and around Wellington Street is used to bring together those who experience many other urban night-times into a chaotic imagined network.

Clarke is fascinated by the Bohemia of Paris as much as of London; with Victor Hugo as much as with Henry Mayhew. In Michael Wilding's words, 'he was one of the first internationalists in Australian writing', and McCann has commented on what he calls the 'citational quality of [Clarke's] sketches'.[135] However, it is clear

---

129 It is very likely that Clarke is referring to G.W.M. Reynolds here; as McCann writes, *Sketches by Boz* was one of the most 'visible and financially successful' models for Clarke's sketches, but 'George Reynolds's immensely popular *Mysteries of London* may also have been an influence' (McCann, 44).

130 Marcus Clarke, in Wilding, 6–7.

131 See Wilding's account of the deaths of Charles Whitehead, and Clarke himself, 8 and xxxix.

132 *Colonial City*, 135.

133 Ibid., 137.

134 Ibid., 141.

135 Wilding, 3; McCann, 59. See also 'A Cheap Lodging-House', in *Colonial City*, 167; *Australasian*, 31 July 1869.

that Clarke is eager to claim London as a reference point for the kind of cultural world he hopes to see established in Melbourne.[136] The pursuers of Melbourne serving-girls 'are men for whom the literature of Holywell-street has charms'; 'the Melbourne carman [...] is a better stamp of man than the London cabman'; 'Bourke-street at midnight is something very little better than the Haymarket (London) at two in the morning'.[137] For Clarke, literate and educated Melbourne is still interested in London conversations – and will be flattered by the assumption that it is still part of such conversations – including a dispute over the practice of theatre reviewing:

> Not long since the dramatic public chose to be furious with the critics [...]. From the *Athenaeum* to *Lloyd's* penny weekly, [theatre critics] all unite against their reviler [the public]. Anyone who knows what theatrical criticism is all over the world just now, will side with the attacking party. ('Dramatic Critics', in *Colonial City*, 13; *Australasian*, 21 December 1867)

'Anyone' includes, of course, Clarke's implied reader.

In the sketches of Melbourne low-life, this London is often Dickens's London.[138] For Clarke, this is not just because Dickens himself wrote about London, but because he encouraged others to do likewise. Clarke's long obituary of Dickens, written for the *Argus* in 1870, declared:

> Take Dickens from our literature, and we should lose half the humour of our essayists and journalists. He invented Albert Smith, Collins, Yates, Braddon, Sala and a host of others. They would never have written but for him. ('Charles Dickens', in *Colonial City*, 235; *Argus*, 18 July 1870)

According to Clarke, in Dickens we see 'our nineteenth-century existence, with its gambling, starving, pauper-burying, speculating, poisoning and swindling; [...] chancery suits, theatres, prisons, [...] banks, frauds on insurance companies'.[139] As Ken Stewart puts it, '[t]hese are, of course, the themes of his journalistic sketches of Melbourne'.[140] Night-time Melbourne is frequently a Dickensian night-time,

---

[136]   Clarke veered between accepting and hating his adopted city. Clarke wrote home to a friend, 'I was fond of Art and Literature, I came where both are unknown; I was conversant with the manners of a class, I came where "Money makes the gentleman"; I hated vulgarity, I came where it reigns supreme [...]. In a word I dread lest I become like others'. However, in another mood he could write that 'I am glad on the whole I came out'. Hergenham, introduction to *Colonial City*, xx–xxi.

[137]   'Arcadia in the Colonies', in *Colonial City*, 28; *Australasian*, 29 August 1868 and 3 October 1868; 'Carmen [Cabmen]', in *Colonial City*, 57; *Australasian*, 20 February 1869); 'Melbourne Streets at Midnight', in *Colonial City*, 101; *Argus*, 28 February 1868.

[138]   See Mirmohamedi and Martin, 51–70.

[139]   'Charles Dickens', in *Colonial City*, 235.

[140]   Ken Stewart, 'Britain's Australia', in *The Cambridge History of Australian Literature*, ed by Peter Pierce, 7–33 (Cambridge: Cambridge University Press, 2009), 27.

and Dickens becomes a shared reference point between Clarke and his readers. Clarke declares that 'Mr Montague Tigg would pale his ineffectual fires before one of our Australian promoters', while the first part of his sketch 'A Pawnbroker's Shop on a Saturday Night' owes a lot to 'The Pawnbroker's Shop' near 'Drury Lane' in *Sketches by Boz*, with its personified articles for sale, its counter-side view of the two clerks and the motley customers, and its description of the 'poor neighbourhood'.[141]

Dickens's characters are also used to link Clarke, his readers, and the Melbourne poor. An inmate of a cheap lodging-house describes a Melbourne lawyer as 'the Jaggers of Victoria!', and this reference starts a discussion of Dickens by the lodgers:

> An outcry of 'Who's he?' upon which the clerk repeats such part of the story of *Great Expectations* as bears upon that admirable lawyer. 'The story is by Dickens?' asked a swagman. He called the author of *Pickwick* 'Dickings', and proceeded to give the room an account of the novelist's early life which would certainly have astonished him could he have heard it. A fat, pulpy man, with a face like an underboiled pease-pudding, woke up to say that 'he knowed Dickings. He'd seen a play called *Barnaby Rudge*, what he wrote, and,' he added, with a tremendous oath, 'a – good play it was, I can tell yer!' ('A Cheap Lodging-House', in *Colonial City*, 167; *Australasian*, 31 July 1869)

The joke here is on the lodgers. Clarke allows himself and his readers a moment of superiority; they know the true facts of Dickens's life and works. However, Clarke recognizes the enjoyment of Dickens, or at least of Dickensian adaptations, by writer, reader, and subjects. Clarke's appreciation for Dickens colours his performance as a writer, just as it colours the performance of the swagman as an impromptu biographer. Clarke draws the outcasts of Melbourne into the imagined network of literary influence and inheritance.

We can see the influence of Mayhew's and Sala's wanderings around the night-time streets of London in Clarke's 'A Night at the Immigrants' Home'. Clarke tells the (male) reader:[142]

> if you would absolutely know what Bohemia means, you must shut up [your books], […] hire a 'loafer's' suit of clothes, leave your watch on the mantelpiece, and come with me. I will take you, Dante-like, on an excursion through a real Inferno. ('A Night at the Immigrants' Home', in *Colonial City*, 132)

---

[141] 'Sharebroking', in *Colonial City*, 18; *Australasian*, 9 February 1868; 'A Pawnbroker's Shop on a Saturday Night', in *Colonial City*, 108; *Argus*, 6 March 1868; Charles Dickens, 'The Pawnbroker's Shop', in *Sketches by Boz*, 186–93.

[142] For a discussion of female ramblers of the streets, see Deborah Epstein Nord, *Walking the Victorian Streets: Women, Representation and the City* (Ithaca, NY: Cornell University Press, 1995). For a discussion of the attractions of nocturnal visits to the slums in nineteenth-century journalism, see Seth Koven, *Slumming: Sexual and Social Politics in Victorian London* (Princeton, NJ: Princeton University Press, 2004).

Only a walking-tour will provide the necessary insights. Print culture, it is argued, will not help you to understand the realities of Lower Bohemia, although Clarke is himself, of course, using print to explain these realities to the reader. Clarke echoes Sala's invitation to *his* reader in Sala's 1851 article for *Household Words*, 'The Key of the Street'. Locked out of his lodgings (possibly his room in Upper Wellington Street) for the night, Sala sets out to describe how he wandered through the neighbourhood of the Strand at night-time:[143]

> Come with me, luxuriant tenant of heavy-draped four-poster – basker on feather-bed, and nestler in lawn sheets […]. Come with me, even workman, labourer, peasant – sleeper on narrow pallet – though your mattress be hard and your rug coarse. Leave your bed – bad as it may be – and gaze on those who have no beds at all. Follow with me the veins and arteries of this huge giant that lies a-sleeping. Listen while with 'the key of the street' I unlock the stony coffer, and bring forth the book, and from the macadamised page read forth the lore of midnight London Life.[144]

The body of the reader must 'travel' through the embodied city of London, imagined as a sleeping 'giant'. But it is also a 'book', where each street is a 'macadamised page'. For Sala, the city streets and its print culture are synonymous. Clarke's invitation, however, is like a critique of Sala's article. Clarke asks:

> Has it ever occurred to you, reader, what you would do if by some wild chance you were compelled to sleep out all night. It is possible you would walk about until morning, or go into some friendly public-house, and sit down on the bench there. But suppose you had to repeat this process every night. Suppose that you were too ragged and too miserable to be admitted into the glowing circle near the tap-room fire, what would you do then? That is another question, isn't it? ('A Night at the Immigrants' Home', in *Colonial City*, 133)

Clarke's reader must imagine a repetition of such dreadful nights. Sala is not forced to repeat the experience, nor does he ask the reader to; the article ends with his return to 'HOME and BED', just as 'work-away, steady-going London' awakes and begins to stir ('The Key of the Street', 572). Clarke makes an imaginative demand upon his reader that goes one step further than Sala's article does.

Clarke also uses the work of Sala's neighbour Henry Mayhew to provide a pedigree for his descriptions of the night-time experiences of the urban poor.

---

[143]   'The article describes a "nocturnal misadventure" in which Sala was accidentally locked out of his lodgings in Upper Wellington Street with only ninepence in his pocket, and had to walk the streets till seven o'clock the next morning'; Catherine Waters, *Commodity Culture in Dickens's Household Words: The Social Life of Goods* (Aldershot: Ashgate, 2008), 67.

[144]   [G.A. Sala], 'The Key of the Street', *HW*, 6 September 1851, 566. Further references are given parenthetically in the text.

London Labour and the London Poor is intrigued by where the street-folk of the metropolis spend the night. 'Of the Homes of Costermongers' and 'Of the Low Lodging-Houses of London', as well as 'Description of the Asylum for the Homeless', from the 1849 *Morning Chronicle* series, reprinted in the 1861 volume edition, find their echoes in 'A Night at the Immigrants' Home'. In this sketch, Clarke has a Mayhew-like focus on lists and bodily detail:

> At this moment of writing there are 68 helpless persons in the Home – 20 under
> 50 years of age, 18 under 60, 20 under 70, 9 under 80, and 1 under 90.
> A few particulars:–
> R.K., thirty years in the colony, aged seventy-two; old age.
> J.B., thirty-two years in the colony, aged sixty-four; rupture.
> J.W., one year in the colony, aged forty; broken leg.
> R.F., sixteen years in the colony, aged sixty; blind.
> J.W., thirty-eight years in the colony, aged sixty-two; chronic rheumatism.
> T.B., thirty years in the colony, aged eighty; giddiness in the head. ('A Night at
> the Immigrants' Home', in *Colonial City*, 140)

Like Mayhew in *London Labour*, Clarke uses this list to complement portraits of individuals. Although he relies more on his own descriptions than on first-person interviews, Clarke uses Mayhew's method of getting an individual person to stand for a type:

> Smart Bohemia, with a semi-fashionable coat, catches a word of the reporter's
> French and corrects pronunciation gravely. [...] Slinking Bohemia, of the true
> loafer's breed, sneaks up furtively and asks about 'telegrams'. [...] Stalwart
> Bohemia, in ragged sailor's jersey, looks a better stamp [...] ('A Night at the
> Immigrants' Home', in *Colonial City*, 136)

'Mark the faces', Clarke instructs as he asks the reader to interpret the lives of the inmates from their bodies, to construct a narrative of their lives and read it like a book.

Clarke also makes use of Mayhew's ethnographic approach to the urban poor. In *London Labour*, Mayhew announces that he is 'the traveller into the undiscovered country of the poor', 'supplying information concerning a large body of persons, of whom the public has less knowledge than of the most distant tribes of the earth', 'from the lips of the people themselves'. Mayhew divides people into two categories, 'the wanderers and the settlers – the vagabond and the citizen', although '[b]etween the two extremes, however, ethnographers recognize a mediate variety, partaking of the attributes of both' (preface to *London Labour*, iii). Clarke, too, adopts the tone of the sociologist in parts of his series on Lower Bohemia:

> The wide land of Lower Bohemia contains many races – gypsies, thieves,
> gamblers, vagabonds, and convicts, each of whom has a language of his own.
> [...] In this city, all these various tongues are fused and melted into a hideous

barbaric gabble, [...] – a mixed speech, which is fast becoming a language peculiar to the city, and is worth noticing. ('The Language of Bohemia', in *Colonial City*, 155; *Australasian*, 17 July 1869)

This is the ethnographic tone applied to the inhabitants of one's own city, of the type described by Buzard as 'metropolitan autoethnography' in his analysis of mid-Victorian English novels such as *Bleak House*:[145]

[T]he wilderness creates a race of men for herself, hardy, silent, keen, and quick-witted, hunters, trappers, dwellers in the deserts. Civilisation has its wilderness, which has given birth to a race of Ishmaelites, whose hand is against every man, and every man's hand against them. These men have no home, they wander. They tear their substance from between the paws of the law, and every now and then the law awakes and kills one or two. They are the Crusoes of society, the 'trappers' of the city-wilderness. Imagine a hunter of men instead of a hunter of beasts, a desert of locked doors instead of a desert of shadeless sand, a pavement instead of a prairie, a policeman instead of a Comanche, and you have your Bohemian. ('In Outer Darkness', in *Colonial City*, 169; *Argus*, 21 August 1869)

These Bohemian bodies, like their language, are wild, uncivilized, and untamed.

Mayhew's famous classifications for the urban poor, 'THOSE THAT *WILL* WORK, THOSE THAT *CANNOT* WORK, AND THOSE THAT *WILL NOT* WORK', are picked up on by Clarke in 'A Night at the Immigrants' Home'.[146] Mayhew keeps on classifying; he divides the street-folk into six categories in volume 1, and then divides the first category of street sellers into a further eight sections, several with their own subsections (*London Labour*, 1: 3). Clarke's own classifications ask the reader to make a direct intertextual link with the Wellington Street text:

My Bohemians may be divided into three classes. The criminal class, who won't work and will steal; the honest poor, who can't obtain work and won't steal; the diseased, the cripple, the maim, the halt, the blind, who cannot work and don't steal. The Bohemians live in various places. ('A Night at the Immigrants' Home', in *Colonial City*, 133)

This passage is also a direct imitation of Sala's well-known 'The Key of the Street':

---

[145]   James Buzard, *Disorienting Fiction: The Autoethnographic Work of Nineteenth-Century British Novels* (Princeton, NJ: Princeton University Press, 2005). See also Adam Hansen, 'Exhibiting Vagrancy, 1851: Victorian London and the "Vagabond Savage"', *Literary London: Interdisciplinary Studies in the Representation of London*, 2: 2 (September 2004), accessed 16 August 2012 online via http://www.literarylondon.org/london-journal/september2004/hansen.html.
[146]   Title page to *London Labour*.

> People who stop up, or out all night, may be divided into three classes: – First,
> editors, bakers, market-gardeners, and all those who are kept out of their beds by
> business. Secondly, gentlemen and 'gents', anxious to cultivate a knowledge of
> the 'lark' species, or intent on the navigation of the 'spree'. Thirdly, and lastly,
> those ladies and gentlemen who do not go to bed, for the very simple reason that
> they have no beds to go to. ([Sala], 'The Key of the Street', 566)

Note the way editors are part of the night-time landscape, as participants in the
nocturnal culture of print. All three writers are well aware of the short distance
from jobbing journalist to starving in the street; the divide between vagabond
and citizen, respectable or fallen woman, was not necessarily clear. Mayhew the
middle-class Bohemian melds his voice with his interviewee's, which suggests
'the implicit attraction street life held for him', and creates a bridge for the reader
between them and the London poor.[147] Clarke declared that 'the wonderful life of
the vagabond has for me a strange attraction'.[148] That this could be a dangerous
road was well known: Charles Whitehead, friend of Horne, Dickens, and Jerrold
and contributor to both *Household Words* and *Melbourne Punch*, died a pauper's
death in Melbourne Hospital in 1862, aged only 58.[149]

Where Clarke differs from his Wellington Street predecessors, however, is in
the very fact that he is aware of how he is following in a literary and journalistic
tradition of the 'Old World', a world that he has left behind. Clarke visualizes his
Bohemians in visceral, physical terms. For him, the Bohemian has one body, but
many parts:

> But to set down for you the component parts of this strange creature, to dissect
> for you the body of this hideous animal and lecture learnedly and loudly upon
> its anatomy would be but a dull task. ('Le Roi S'Amuse', in *Colonial City*, 141)

Instead of 'dissecting' this body of people in a scientific manner, Clarke tells
us that he 'will rather take you with me to see it, alive and suffering'.[150] This
Bohemian body has so many parts because it is not just made up of the Melbourne
poor. Clarke's Bohemian body reawakens all the bodies of the poor described and
discussed from Wellington Street. Clarke may tell the reader that 'this Bohemia of
mine is just exactly within a stone's throw of your doors', and 'you have nothing to
do' with the poor of Old Europe, but his choice of language in the Lower Bohemia
sketches reveals that the exact opposite is true.[151] The poor emigrants of the

---

[147] Anne Humpherys, *Travels into the Poor Man's Country: The Work of Henry
Mayhew* (Athens, GA: The University of Georgia Press, 1977), 79.

[148] 'Le Roi S'Amuse', in *Colonial City*, 141; *Australasian*, 19 June 1869. 'The
Vagabond' was, of course, the pseudonym of the Melbourne journalist and sketch-writer
John Stanley James (1843–96).

[149] Clive Turnbull, 'Whitehead, Charles (1804–1862)', *ADB*, accessed 23 March
2012 online via http://adb.anu.edu.au/.

[150] 'Le Roi S'Amuse', in *Colonial City*, 142.

[151] 'A Night at the Immigrants' Home', in *Colonial City*, 134.

Immigrant's Home, and their fellows who did not emigrate, find their way out of the neighbourhood of Wellington Street and into Clarke's sketches.[152] Connections are found not in physical proximity, but in proximity of metaphor, imagery, and language. Urban spaces are linked through the printed page and on the printed page.

Collins Street and Wellington Street both have their share of poor Bohemians; 'some of them gain a scanty pittance by selling newspapers, and can be seen any hour of the day propping up the walls of the newspaper offices, or standing under the *Argus* "verandah"', and Clarke's sketches of Lower Bohemia make their connections apparent.[153] By the time Horne was preparing to leave Melbourne, Australian print culture was much less Anglo-derivative. As Anne Blainey puts it, by the 1860s 'periodicals were more numerous and less imitative of their English counterparts'.[154] This chapter has argued that Melbourne print culture was helped to develop so quickly by the 'export' of prefabricated forms from the metropolis, both at the level of text – like *Melbourne Punch* and Clarke's sketches of night-time Melbourne – and based on exported working practices and networks. Metropolitan and colonial writers, editors, and readers are drawn together by these connections into a vast network of print.

For Andrew McCann, the 'netherworld' of Clarke's depiction of colonial Melbourne turns it into the ultimate Bohemia, but one which also becomes a space that is everywhere, 'a ubiquitous kind of urbanism, in which the Bohemian is always, but paradoxically, at home', the ultimate expression of the experience of modernity as a mode of dislocation.[155] The connections of the Collins Street networks to the Wellington Street ones add layers to this picture of dislocation and disconnection. In Clarke's sketches, in the words of *Bleak House*, Collins Street and Wellington Street are 'very curiously brought together' into something new. The bodies of the Old World and the New World slum-dwellers, sketch-writers, and readers are connected into a network of associations and influences that reveal the complicated relationship between London print networks and the networks of colonial Melbourne. This is a global village, and it is not just the Bohemian who is 'at home' in both night-time Melbourne and night-time London. However, it is an imagined network which complicates the boundaries between public and private communications, as David Copperfield finds when he reads Micawber's letter, addressed to him by his friend but contained within a foreign newspaper. This imagined network is invigorating, but also unsettling.

---

[152]   See Wilding on *His Natural Life* (1870–72): 'Clarke's antipodes is indeed the underworld: the world beneath Europe, the other side of the globe, [...] the underworld of English society that England preferred not to know about and to dispose of' (18).

[153]   'A Night at the Immigrants' Home', in *Colonial City*, 134.

[154]   Anne Blainey, 232–3.

[155]   McCann, 60.

Conclusion
'Very Curiously Brought Together' by *Bleak House*

Mr Dickens's genius is especially suited to the delineation of city life. London is like a newspaper. Everything is there, and everything is disconnected. There is every kind of person in some houses; but there is no more connection between the houses than between the neighbours in the lists of 'births, marriages, and deaths.' As we change from the broad leader to the squalid police-report, we pass a corner and we are in a changed world. This is advantageous to Mr Dickens's genius. His memory is full of instances of old buildings and curious people, and he does not care to piece them together. On the contrary, each scene, to his mind, is a separate scene, – each street a separate street.

> —Walter Bagehot, "Charles Dickens", in *The Collected Works of Walter Bagehot*, ed. Norman St John Stevas, 15 vols (London: The Economist, 1965–86), 2: 87.

Bleak House is a novel fascinated by links, one in which every coincidence is there to reveal a hidden connection. Characters move through the novel and learn their positions in this web of links as they go. They emerge as nodes on a vast and intricate network, which is centred on the metropolis but has implications beyond it.[1] This book has argued that important print networks in mid-Victorian London were reinforced by physical proximity on the three sections of Wellington Street and the surrounding neighbourhood. It has argued that these conditions of production led writers and editors to represent their imagined community of readers as members of an imagined network that could stretch across the Empire, where a close relationship between writer and reader could be replicated in print. I will finish by suggesting that Dickens's obsession with connections in *Bleak House* looks much less strange and implausible when viewed against the backdrop of his experiences of Wellington Street, where he set up *Household Words* the year before he began *Bleak House*.

In the novel, the ability to 'network' – that is, to see and to make use of connections – is crucial to survival, happiness, or success. *Bleak House* is just as

---

[1] James Buzard points out that these connections have more implications on a national scale than on a global one: Buzard, *Disorienting Fiction: The Autoethnographic Work of Nineteenth-Century British Novels* (Princeton, NJ: Princeton University Press, 2005). Jonathan H. Grossman reads the more international networks of *Little Dorrit* as a direct 'response' to *Bleak House*, in which a 'reconfigured internationalist view imagined around international simultaneity enters'. *Dickens's Networks: Public Transport and the Novel* (Oxford: Oxford University Press, 2012), 188; 176.

interested in failed connections, in disconnection, as it is in successful connections. Even characters like Sir Leicester Dedlock and Mr Tulkinghorn, who seem so sure of their 'place' in the system, are confronted with the violent realization that things are not as they read them. But it is also the readers who must learn this networked way of working, if they are to read the clues and anticipate the revelations of the links between the characters. In *Bleak House*, Dickens presents a city where absolute and permanent anonymity is not possible when everyone is connected to everyone else. James Buzard has declared that

> Such everything-is-connected arguments have only gone half the distance necessary to comprehend a novel in whose form the trope of the unforeseen-but-now-revealed-connection is matched by and even grounded in a trope of *disassociation* or disconnection.[2]

I do not wish to disagree with this, but it needs to be modified. Moments of failed connection are there for the reader to realize later, and with hindsight, how interconnected London really is. In *Bleak House*, Esther stands outside her father's 'dark door' and does not know it;[3] Jobling/Weevle lodges in Nemo's old room and puts Lady Dedlock's 'portrait' on the wall in 'the Galaxy gallery of British beauty',[4] but does not realize the connection that Mr Guppy (and by now the reader) has made. It is only gradually that the reader sees how all the nodes on the network link up.

Indeed, Walter Bagehot, in the quote which heads this Conclusion, describes Dickens as the ultimate writer about urban disconnection. Bagehot's London is one where social networks have broken down: '[e]verything is there and everything is disconnected'. Bagehot's vision of 'city life' in general, and London in particular, is one where 'there is no more connection between the houses than between the neighbours in the lists of "births, marriages, and deaths"'. Individuals are brought together by the coincidence of physical proximity, and little more, and the physical fabric of the city both produces and is a product of this disconnected city life. Bagehot maps the structure of a mid-nineteenth-century newspaper onto the streets of London; the movement of readers as they switch their attention from one type of article to another, or as they turn the page, is like the view of the city that pedestrians have as they move around the metropolis, so '[a]s we change from the broad leader to the squalid police-report, we pass a corner and we are in a changed world'. He invokes a London of socioeconomic contrasts between rich and poor, as Reynolds does in *Mysteries* and Mayhew does in *London Labour*. Bagehot argues that what he reads as the disconnected nature of London 'is advantageous to Mr Dickens's genius', because Dickens fills his writings with 'old buildings and curious people, and he does not care to piece them together'. For Bagehot, the

---

  [2]   Buzard, 114.

  [3]   Charles Dickens, *Bleak House*, ed. Stephen Gill (Oxford: Oxford University Press, 1996; reissued 2008; 1st publ. 1852–53), 68.

  [4]   Ibid., 470.

writings of Dickens reinforce his experiences of a disconnected city life, where any sense of a social network is difficult, if not impossible, to find.

Yet Bagehot's image of the reader is crucial here: the choice of layout in a newspaper has never been quite as random as Bagehot suggests. Different types of content did tend to appear on different pages in nineteenth-century newspapers: advertisements at the front or the back, the leader in the middle, theatre reviews towards the end. However, in newspapers with a clear theme (like the *Railway Chronicle*) or political slant (the *Times* or *Reynolds's Weekly Newspaper*), readers draw connections between different articles in a newspaper based upon their physical proximity on the page. The reader of *Bleak House* must learn this 'networked' way of reading, as London in this novel is not so much like a newspaper, but like the world of interconnected print networks with which I have shown Dickens to be so familiar. Different characters in *Bleak House* see different things; evidence is there for them to read, but the audiences are self-selecting. Sir Leicester is unable to read the scandal-sheet narrative of his wife's life; Esther is unable and unwilling to decipher the harsh realities of her birth and her mother's death until they are forced upon her; illiterate Jo cannot untangle the connection between the 'jolly servant' and Esther.[5] Through their struggles to comprehend the network effectively, the novel enacts the variety of readerships and levels of literacy in 1850s London.

The first number of *Bleak House* (Chapters 1–4) seems disjointed, but the majority of the most important connections on the network are there, ready for the reader to decipher – if they can. The key documents are already introduced: 'old Tom Jarndyce' (of Tom-All-Alone's) and the missing Jarndyce will,[6] and the portion of Nemo's 'original hand'.[7] The chapter about 'childless' Lady Dedlock, who looks out at the keeper's lodge where George and Phil later live,[8] is followed by the first chapter narrated by the motherless Esther, who has never heard her parents spoken of.[9] A few pages on, Lady Dedlock's history is hinted at by the response of Esther's supposed godmother to 'the sinful woman' in the Bible story: '[h]e that is without sin among you, let him first cast a stone at her!'[10] The reader swiftly learns that Miss Barbary is, in fact, Esther's aunt; Esther does not have parents only according to the 'law' – a hint that she does have some, somewhere. Finally, Mr Guppy pays Esther the compliment about her 'appearance'[11] that shows he has already started to become 'fixed and fascinated'[12] by Esther's face, a fixation which leads him to Lady Dedlock. The cultural historian James Donald has remarked that:

---

5   Ibid., 243.
6   Ibid., 14.
7   Ibid., 23.
8   Ibid., 18.
9   Ibid., 25.
10   Ibid., 28.
11   Ibid., 45.
12   Ibid., 101.

Dickens's London is a city of networks. In part, these are social, economic, or administrative: the railways of *Dombey and Son*, the dust heaps of *Our Mutual Friend*, the prisons of *Little Dorrit*. But they are also narrative networks. London becomes a space constituted by the possibility of the narration of its social relations. In *Bleak House*, the narrative moves beyond or behind the empirical reality of fog and bustle to unravel a hidden reality, the link between an aristocratic landowner and an impoverished crossing sweeper.[13]

The famous opening passage of *Bleak House*, referred to obliquely in the quote above, sets the tone for the rest of the first number and the rest of the novel: disconnected people who, in fact, turn out to be connected – by fog on the city streets, by the metaphorical fog of the legal process and the ongoing Jarndyce case, and by underlying social links.

Moments of disconnection in the novel come not from the essential nature of the city, but from those characters who fail to network correctly or attempt to drop out of the network altogether. Sir Leicester Dedlock fails to observe Lady Dedlock as clearly as Tulkinghorn, and fails to connect her agitation in Chapter 2 to the law-writer's letter; even at the end, he 'cannot bear to look upon her cast down from the high place she has graced so well'.[14] Mr Guppy connects Esther to the portrait of Lady Dedlock, but fails to connect Lady Dedlock to Nemo. Jo spreads disease, but in his feverish state he fails to articulate the connection he sees between Esther and Lady Dedlock, only able to cry, 'she looks to me like the t'other one'.[15] Richard fails to stick at any of the professions found for him by Mr Jarndyce through his network of contacts, unlike Allan Woodcourt, who accepts a house and a job and a wife from John Jarndyce in Chapter 64. Finally, Mrs Jellyby is an example of what is, in the novel's terms, a perverse kind of networker, with her eyes too fixed on 'the African project' and her networks of philanthropist correspondents to pay attention to her family networks at home.[16]

Those who recognize that they are connected to others on the social network which Dickens creates, and who successfully use their knowledge of these links to help others, are held up to the reader as the heroes of the narrative. As well as Allan Woodcourt and his benefactor Mr Jarndyce, Esther is, of course, the ultimate networker, the hub of all number of connections and the centre of any society in which she finds herself. Mrs Bagnet is also successful at spotting and making the most of connections; she uses these detective-like skills to reunite George and his mother, Sir Leicester's housekeeper. Set against Esther and Mrs Bagnet are the professional networkers: Mr Tulkinghorn, Smallweed, Inspector Bucket the professional detective, and the Lord High Chancellor as the embodiment of the Court of Chancery. Despite the importance of documents in *Bleak House*, it is

---

13   James Donald, *Imagining the Modern City* (London: Athlone Press, 1999), 2.
14   Dickens, *Bleak House*, 775.
15   Ibid., 430.
16   Ibid., 48.

the successful use of face-to-face connections to extract information which really undermines the anonymity of the city.

Because face-to-face contact is so important to the revelation of secrets and links in the novel, any desire for anonymity can be undermined by a character's own body. The likeness of Esther's face to her mother's is erased by her illness,[17] but Mr Guppy has already spotted it. Nemo tries to stay anonymous, but his real identity catches up with him because his 'hand' (-writing) is recognized by Lady Dedlock.[18] Lady Dedlock herself tries to find anonymity in two different disguises, but her hands and face betray her. First it is Jo who 'silently notices how white and small her hand is, and what a jolly servant she must be to wear such sparkling rings',[19] and then, when she tries to melt into the London crowds dressed as the brickmaker's wife, Inspector Bucket reads her movements correctly and 'the face' which Esther turns over is not that of Jenny, but 'my mother cold and dead'.[20] Despite the differing abilities of characters to read a situation correctly, ultimately there can be no secrets in such a tightly interconnected world.

Abler, Adams, and Gould's *Spatial Organization* ends with a plea: '[I]n our attempts to anticipate what the spatial structure of the future will be like, it is important that we pay close attention to existing metropolitan areas and the behaviour of people within them.'[21] As well as attending to the spaces of the present, we should take note of the city spaces of the past and their social networks. There is more work to be done on how such networks function on the ground, and on the ways in which networks established in the imperial metropolis enabled colonial print cultures to spring rapidly into life, prefabricated. This book has argued that print networks are reinforced by physical proximity within urban space, and that even across vast distances and between cities, print networks become virtual spaces where metropolis and colony, writer and reader are connected in a vast imagined network. In an era in which technological advances allow us greater virtual communication than ever before, we should not blind ourselves to the importance of face-to-face networks in the human imagination.

---

[17]   Ibid., 535.
[18]   Ibid., 23.
[19]   Ibid., 243.
[20]   Ibid., 847.
[21]   Ronald Abler, John S. Adams, and Peter Gould, *Spatial Organization: The Geographer's View of the World* (Englewood Cliffs, NJ: Prentice-Hall, 1971), 570.

Appendix

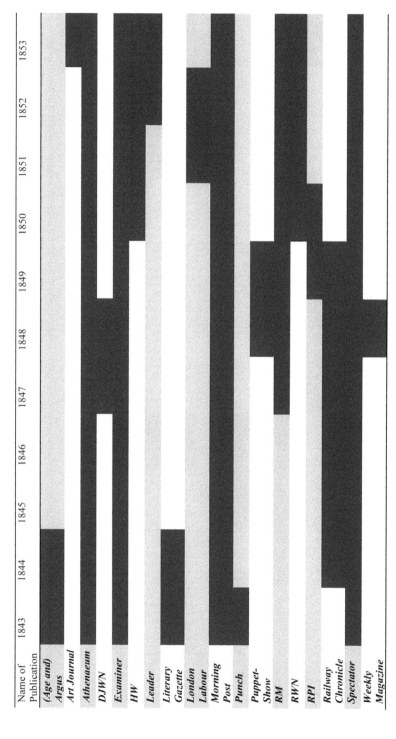

Figure A.1   Graph showing newspapers and periodicals discussed, with approximate dates of when their offices were on the three sections of Wellington Street, 1843–53.

Figure A.2   Graph showing writers with plays, or adaptations of their fiction, put on at the Lyceum Theatre, 1843–53.

Bibliography

Archive Resources

London, London Metropolitan Archives
London, City of Westminster Archives Centre
London, V&A Theatre Archives

Manuscripts

Stirling, E. *Martin Chuzzlewit* (Act 1), Lord Chamberlain's Plays collection, British Library manuscripts Add. 42976 ff. 516–35b.
Webb, C. *Martin Chuzzlewit*, Lord Chamberlain's Plays collection, British Library manuscripts Add. 42976 ff. 536–638.

City Guide Books, Directories, and Maps

Cruchley's New Plan of London, Improved to 1847. London: G.F. Cruchley, 1847.
Cruchley's Picture of London, 9th edn. London: Cruchley, 1844.
Cruchley's Picture of London, 16th edn. London: Cruchley, 1851.
Evans, Charles, *Grand Panorama of London From the Thames*, 1849; first published black and white. London: Vizetelly, 1845.
Gilbert's Visitor's Guide to London. London: James Gilbert, 1851.
Horwood, Richard. *Plan of the Cities of London and Westminster, the Borough of Southwark, and Parts Adjoining. Showing Every House*. 1792–99.
Jackson, Peter, ed. *John Tallis's London Street Views: 1838–1840. Together with the revised and enlarged views of 1847*. London: London Topographical Society and Nattali & Maurice, 1969.
Kelly's London Post Office Directory. London: W. Kelly, 1843–1853. WCA microfilm collection, London Directories/1843–53/vols 253–67.
Robson's London Directory, Street Key, and Royal Court Guide, For 1843, 24th edn. London: Bowtell, 1843. WCA microfilm collection, London Directories/1843/vol. 201.
Stanford, Edward. *Map of the School Board District of Westminster*. London: Stanford, 1879.
———. *Stanford's Library Map of London and its Suburbs*, 1st edn. London: Stanford, 1862.

Watkins's Commercial and General Directory and Court Guide for 1852. London: Longman, Brown, Green, and Longmans, 1852. WCA microfilm collection, London Directories/1852/vol. 57.

Newspapers and Periodicals Consulted

Argus (Melbourne)
Athenaeum
Bentley's Miscellany
Daily News
Douglas Jerrold's Shilling Magazine
Douglas Jerrold's Weekly Newspaper
Examiner
Household Words
Illustrated London News
Leader
Lloyd's Weekly London Newspaper
Lloyd's Weekly Miscellany
London Journal
Melbourne Punch
Morning Post
Paul Pry: The Reformer of the Age
Penny Magazine of the Society for the Diffusion of Useful Knowledge
Punch
Puppet-Show
Railway Chronicle
Reynolds's Miscellany
Reynolds's Political Instructor
Reynolds's Weekly Newspaper
Times
Weekly Magazine

Individual Newspaper and Periodical Articles Cited

Anonymous, 'A Papier Mâché Village For Australia'. *ILN*, 6 August 1853, 80.
———. 'Abolition of the Income Tax […] (from the Sun of Monday)'. *Freeman's Journal*, 11 March 1848, 3.
———. 'Advertisements and Notices'. *RPI*, 23 March 1850, 152.
———. 'Advertisements and Notices'. *RWN*, 12 May 1850, 8.
———. 'Advertisements Extraordinary'. *Man in the Moon*, 3, 1848, 1–58.
———. 'An Editor's Room in Melbourne'. *MP*, 1, 1856, 69.
———. 'Assault'. *Argus*, 24 September 1855, 5–6.
———. 'A Suggestion'. *MP*, 1, 1856, 82.

————. 'Bawds and Brothels. No. III. Louisa Stanley'. *Paul Pry: the Reformer of the Age*, 19 December 1849, 1–2.

————. 'Biographical Sketches of Eminent Living Authors – Mr G.W.M. Reynolds'. *London Journal*, 29 November 1845, 101.

————. 'Births'. *The Times*, 16 October 1846, 7.

————. 'Colonial Publications'. *MP*, 1, 1856.

————. 'Competition for a laudatory address'. *MP*, 1, 1856, 2.

————. 'Death Of Sir Archibald Michie'. *Argus*, 23 June 1899, 6.

————. 'Departure of Mr. Punch from Gravesend; Arrival of Mr. Punch in Australia'. *MP*, 1, 1856, 1.

————. 'Destruction of Bielefeld's Papier Mâché Works'. *Morning Post*, 10 March 1854, 5.

————. 'Dips into the Diary of Barabas Bolt, Esq.'. *Man in the Moon*, 3, 1848, 235–44.

————. 'Disturbances in Trafalgar Square'. *DN*, 8 March 1848, 3.

————. 'Editor's Box'. *Puppet-Show*, 17 June 1848, 107.

————. 'Editor's Box'. *Puppet-Show*, 24 June 1848, 115.

————. 'The Festival of Messrs Reynolds's and Dicks's Establishment'. *RN*, 11 July 1875, 1.

————. 'Fiction'. *Critic*, 20 November 1847, 326.

————. 'Fire in the Strand – Narrow Escape of the Adelphi Theatre'. *Morning Post*, 12 January 1846, 7.

————. 'Gothic Ornaments, drawn from examples executed in the Improved Papier Mâché'. *The Gentleman's Magazine: and historical review*, August 1835, 1.

————. 'The Great Open-Air Meeting in Trafalgar-Square. – Brutality of the Police'. *Northern Star*, 11 March 1848, 8.

————. '"Gretna Green," the "Daily News," and the "Express"'. *RM*, 27 November 1847, 46–7.

————. 'How to Save Two-Pence A-Week'. *Puppet-Show*, 18 March 1848, 8.

————. 'Insolvent Debtors'. *Jurist*, 6 July 1842, 245.

————. 'Lecture on Douglas Jerrold'. *Argus*, 10 April 1858, 5.

————. 'Literature of the Lower Orders'. *DN*, 2 November 1847, 3.

————. 'Literature of the Lower Orders'. *DN*, 9 November 1847, 2–3.

————. 'Lyceum Theatre'. *ILN*, 13 July 1844, 32.

————. 'Lyceum Theatre'. *ILN*, 26 December 1846, 413.

————. 'Meeting in Trafalgar-square'. *DN*, 7 March 1848, 4.

————. 'Melbourne Punch'. *Argus*, 3 August 1855, 5.

————. 'Minor Topics of the Month'. *Art Journal*, June 1857, 198–99.

————. 'Miscellanea'. *Builder*, 7 May 1853, 299.

————. 'Miscellaneous'. *Argus*, 9 July 1855, 7.

————. 'Mr. Punch, jun.'. *MP*, 1, 1856, 2.

————. 'The Musical World'. *HW*, 29 July 1854, 561–7.

————. 'National Charter Association'. *RPI*, 23 March 1850, 152.

————. 'The Nelson Column'. *ILN*, 18 November 1843, 331.

————. 'The New English Opera-House, Strand'. *The Mirror of Literature, Amusement, and Instruction*, 2 August 1834, 1–2.

————. 'Notice to Advertisers'. *RWN*, 25 January 1852, 8.

————. 'Notices To Correspondents'. *RM*, 7 April 1849, 623.

————. 'Notices To Correspondents'. *RM*, 15 February 1851, 63.

————. 'Notices To Correspondents'. *RM*, 12 February 1853, 47.

————. 'Off to the Diggings!'. *HW*, 17 July 1852, 405–10.

————. 'The Open-Air Meeting in Trafalgar-square'. *The Times*, 7 March 1848, 8.

————. 'Our First Literary Arrivals'. *Empire*, 8 October 1852, 1490.

————. 'Our Name and Address'. *Puppet-Show*, 18 March 1848, 1–2.

————. 'Paul Advises'. *Paul Pry: The Reformer of the Age*, 5 March 1849, 3.

————. 'Political Meetings in the Country'. *RPI*, 23 March 1850, 160.

————. 'The Press and the Theatres'. *ILN Supplement*, 29 January 1853.

————. 'Prologue'. *Punch*, 5, 1843, 1.

————. 'Punch in Trouble'. *Empire*, 27 September 1855, 5.

————. 'The Puppet-Show'. *Puppet-Show*, 8 April 1848, 25–6.

————. 'The Real Murderer'. *All The Year Round*, 2 January 1864, 448.

————. 'Serious Riots in the Metropolis'. *Lloyd's Weekly London Newspaper*, 12 March 1848, 3.

————. 'The Story of the Strand'. *Strand Magazine*, January 1891, 4–13.

————. 'Street Musicians'. *RWN*, 9 June 1850, 4.

————. 'The Theatres'. *ILN*, 19 July 1845, 42.

————. 'The Theatres'. *ILN*, 27 December 1845, 413.

————. 'The Theatres'. *ILN*, 4 August 1849, 74.

————. 'To Editors and Others'. *MP*, I, 1856, 73.

————. 'To Our Reader'. *RM*, 7 November 1846, 16.

————. 'To Our Readers'. *RPI*, 11 May 1850, 1.

————. 'To the People of Great Britain and Northern Ireland'. *RPI*, 6 April 1850, 176.

————. 'To the Public'. *RPI*, 10 November 1849, 8.

————. 'Unworthy of Literary Notice'. *Puppet-Show*, 25 March 1848, 15.

————. 'Welcome to the Metropolis'. *Northern Star*, 23 November 1844, 1.

————. 'William and Robert Chambers'. *Dublin University Magazine*, February 1851, 177.

————. 'Young Australia Commercial Operations'. *MP*, I, 1856, 22.

Braddon, M.E. 'My First Novel'. *Idler*, July 1893, 19–30.

[Collins, Wilkie]. 'The Unknown Public'. *HW*, 21 August 1858, 217–22.

[Dickens, Charles]. 'A Detective Police Party'. *HW*, 27 July 1850, 409–14.

————. 'Down With the Tide'. *HW*, 5 February 1853, 481–5.

————. 'Preliminary Word'. *HW*, 30 March 1850, 1.

————. 'Where we stopped growing'. *HW*, 1 January 1853, 361–3.

[Forster, John]. 'Theatrical Examiner'. *Examiner*, 11 December 1836, 792.

GRACCHUS [probably Reynolds's younger brother Edward Reynolds]. 'National Prosperity: Opinions of Ledru-Rollin and Charles Dickens'. *RWN*, 16 June 1850, 3.

[Horne, R.H.]. 'Canvass Town'. *HW*, 18 June 1853, 361–7.

———. 'A Digger's Diary'. *HW*, 29 January 1853, 457–62.

———. 'A Digger's Diary'. *HW*, 19 February 1853, 545–51.

———. 'A Digger's Diary'. *HW*, 9 April 1853, 125–9.

———. 'A Digger's Diary'. *HW*, 3 September 1853, 6–11.

———. 'The Great Peace-Maker'. *HW*, 14 June 1851, 275–7.

———. 'The Pasha's New Boat'. *HW*, 22 November 1851, 209–13.

Hunt, Robert. 'Papier Mâché Manufacture'. *Art Journal*, November 1851, 277–8.

———. 'Visits to Art-Manufacturies'. *Art Journal*, September 1859, 273–4.

James, John Stanley ('the Vagabond'). 'A Night in the Model Lodging House'. *Argus*, 15 April 1876, 5.

[Jerrold, Douglas]. 'Preface'. *Douglas Jerrold's Shilling Magazine*, 1, 1845, iii–iv.

JUNIUS. 'A Few Words on the Newspaper Press'. *RPI*, 29 December 1849, 60.

Knight, Charles. *Knight's Cyclopaedia of London.* London: Charles Knight, 1851.

[Knight, Charles]. 'Preface'. *Penny Magazine*, 1, 1832, iii–iv.

———. 'Reading for All'. *Penny Magazine*, 1 March 1832.

[Lloyd, Edward], 'Preface'. *Lloyd's Weekly Miscellany*, 1, 1850, iii.

[Reynolds, Edward?] ('GRACCHUS'). 'National Prosperity: Opinions of Ledru-Rollin and Charles Dickens'. *RWN*, 16 June 1850, 3.

Reynolds, G.W.M. 'The Council of the National Parliamentary and Financial Reform Association: Scandalous Attempt to Betray the Chartist Cause'. *RPI*, 2 June 1850, 1.

[———] ('Max'). 'Reflections in a Horse-Pond'. *Bentley's Miscellany*, January 1837, 470–73.

———. 'The Swelling Tide of Emigration'. *RWN*, 17 October 1852, 1.

———. 'To Sir Joshua Walmsley, MP'. *RWN*, 23 June 1850, 1.

Rogerson, John Bolton. 'Walks In The Streets. – No. I'. *Bradshaw's Journal*, 19 March 1842, 312–15.

[Sala, G.A.]. 'The Key of the Street'. *HW*, 6 September 1851, 565–72.

Sinnett, Frederick. 'The Fiction Fields of Australia'. *Journal of Australasia*, 1, July–December 1856.

Stevenson, Robert Louis. 'Popular Authors'. *Scribners' Magazine*, July 1888, 122–8.

[Thackeray, W.M.]. 'Waiting at the Station'. *Punch*, 9 March 1850, 92–3.

VERECUNDIA. 'To The Editor Of The Times'. Times, 15 September 1849, 3.

Other Primary Materials

à Beckett, Arthur William. *The à Becketts of 'Punch': Memories of Fathers and Sons*. Westminster: Archibald Constable, 1903.

Anonymous. *Sinks of London Laid Open: A Pocket Companion for the Uninitiated. To which is added a Modern Flash Dictionary. Embellished with Humorous Illustrations by George Cruikshank.* London: J. Duncombe, 1848.

Bielefeld, Charles Frederick. *On the Use of Improved Papier Mâché in Furniture, in the Interior Decoration of Buildings, and in Works of Art.* 2nd edn. London: C.F. Bielefeld, 1850.

[————]. *Portable Buildings, designed and built by Charles F. Bielefeld, Patentee.* London: C.F. Bielefeld, 1853.

Braddon, M.E. *Rupert Godwin.* 2 vols. Leipzig: Bernhard Tauchnitz, 1867.

Brown, Henry. *Victoria, As I Found It.* London: T. Cautley Newby, 1862.

Browne, Edgar. *Phiz and Dickens as They Appeared to Edgar Browne.* London: J. Nisbet, 1913.

Burnand, F.C. *Records and Reminiscences, Personal and General.* 2 vols. London: Methuen, 1904.

Clacy, Mrs Charles. *A Lady's Visit to the Gold Diggings of Australia in 1852–53. Written on the Spot.* London: Hurst and Blackett, 1853.

Clark, Thomas. *A Letter Addressed to G.W.M. Reynolds, Reviewing his Conduct as a Professed Chartist, and also explaining Who He Is and What He Is, Together With Copious Extracts From His Most Indecent Writings. Also, A Few Words of Advice to his Brother Electors of Finsbury.* London: T. Clark, 1850.

Clarke, Marcus. *A Colonial City: High and Low Life. Selected Journalism of Marcus Clarke.* Edited by L.T. Hergenhan. St. Lucia, Queensland: University of Queensland Press, 1972.

Dickens, Charles. *Barnaby Rudge.* Edited by John Bowen. London: Penguin, 2003; first published 1841.

————. *Bleak House.* Edited by Stephen Gill. Oxford: Oxford University Press, 1996; reissued 2008; first published 1852–53.

————. *David Copperfield.* Edited by Nina Burgis. Oxford: Clarendon Press, 1981; first published 1849–50.

————. *Great Expectations.* Edited by Margaret Cardwell. Oxford: Clarendon Press, 1993; first published 1860–61.

————. *Little Dorrit.* Edited by Harvey Peter Sucksmith. Oxford: Clarendon Press, 1979; first published 1855–57.

————. *Martin Chuzzlewit.* Edited by Margaret Cardwell. Oxford: Clarendon Press, 1982; first published 1843–44.

————. *Nicholas Nickleby.* Edited by Paul Schlicke. Oxford: Oxford University Press, 1990; first published 1838–39.

————. *The Pilgrim Edition of the Letters of Charles Dickens.* Edited by Madeline House, Graham Storey, and Kathleen Tillotson (general editors). 12 vols. Oxford: Clarendon Press, 1965–2002.

————. *Sketches by Boz and Other Early Papers 1833–39.* Vol. 1 of *Dickens' Journalism.* Edited by Michael Slater. London: J.M. Dent, 1994.

————. *The Speeches of Charles Dickens.* Edited by K.J. Fielding. Oxford: Clarendon Press, 1960.

Dickens jnr., Charles, ed. *The Life of Charles James Mathews: Chiefly Autobiographical, with Selections from his Correspondents and Speeches.* 2 vols. London: Macmillan, 1879.

Dix, John. *Lions: Living and Dead; or, Personal Recollections of the 'Great and Gifted'.* 2nd edn. London: W. Tweedie, 1854.

Edwards, Henry Sutherland. *Personal Recollections.* London: Cassell & Company, 1900.

Edwards, P.D. *Dickens's 'Young Men': George Augustus Sala, Edmund Yates, and the World of Victorian Journalism.* Aldershot: Ashgate, 1997.

Engels, Friederich. *The Condition of the Working Class in England.* Edited by Victor Kiernan. London: Penguin, 1987.

Evans, Conway. *Reports Relating to the Sanitary Condition of the Strand District, London.* London: John Churchill, 1858. British Library MIC.A.6906. (17).

Fielding, K.J., ed. *The Speeches of Charles Dickens.* Oxford: Clarendon Press, 1960.

Fitzgerald, Percy. *The Garrick Club.* London: Elliot Stock, 1904.

———. *Memories of Charles Dickens: with an Account of 'Household Words' and 'All the Year Round' and of the Contributors Thereto.* Bristol: J.W. Arrowsmith; London: Simpkin, Marshall, Hamilton, Kent & Co., 1913.

———. 'Some Memories of Dickens and "Household Words"'. In *The Dickens Souvenir of 1912*, edited by Dion Clayton Calthorp and Max Pemberton, 22–28. London: Chapman & Hall, 1912.

Forster, John. *The Life of Charles Dickens.* With 500 portraits, facsimiles, and other illustrations, collected, arranged, and annotated by B.W. Matz. 2 vols. London: Chapman & Hall, 1911; first published 1872–74.

Haydon, G.H. *The Australian Emigrant, A Rambling Story, Containing As Much Fact As Fiction.* London: Arthur Hall, Virtue, and Co. and W. Roberts, Exeter, 1854.

Hemyng, Bracebridge. 'Prostitution in London'. In *London Labour and the London Poor*, Volume 4, 210–72. London: Griffin, Bohn, and Company, 1861–62.

Hergenhan, L.T., ed. *A Colonial City: High and Low Life. Selected Journalism of Marcus Clarke.* St. Lucia, Queensland: University of Queensland Press, 1972.

Hollingshead, John. *'Good old Gaiety': an Historiette and Remembrance.* London: Gaiety Theatre, 1903.

Holyoake, George Jacob. *The life and character of Richard Carlile.* London: James Watson, 1849.

Horne, R.H. *Australian Facts and Prospects: to which is prefixed The Author's Australian Autobiography.* London: Smith, Elder & Co, 1859.

———. *Orion: An Epic Poem, In Three Books.* London: J. Miller, 1843.

Howitt, William. *Land, Labour, and Gold or, Two Years in Victoria, with Visits to Sydney and Van Dieman's Land.* 2 vols. London: Longman, Brown, Green, and Longmans, 1855.

Jerrold, Douglas. *The History of St. Giles and St. James*. In *The Works of Douglas Jerrold*, edited by W. Blanchard Jerrold, 1: 5–397. London: Bradbury & Evans, 1863–64; first published 1847–49, first volume edition 1851.

Jerrold, Walter. *Douglas Jerrold: Dramatist and Wit*. 2 vols. London: Hodder & Stoughton, 1914.

Jerrold, W. Blanchard. 'Introductory Memoir'. In *The Works of Douglas Jerrold*, edited by W. Blanchard Jerrold, 1: v–xl. London: Bradbury & Evans, 1863–64.

Lamb, Charles and Mary. *The Works of Charles and Mary Lamb*. Edited by E.V. Lucas. 7 vols. London: Methuen, 1905.

Limner, Luke (pseudonym of John Leighton). *London Cries and Public Edifices: Sketches on the Spot*. London: Grant & Griffith, 1847.

Lindsey, G. 'Papier Mâché'. In *British Manufacturing Industries*, edited by G. Phillips Bevan, 165–80. London: Edward Stanford, 1876.

Masson, David. *Memories of London in the Forties*. Arranged for publication and annotated by his daughter Flora Masson. London: Blackwood, 1908.

Mayhew, Edward. *Stage Effect: or, the Principles which Command Dramatic Success in the Theatre*. London: C. Mitchell, 1840.

Mayhew, Henry. 'Dedication'. In *German Life and Manners as seen in Saxony at the Present Day: with an account of Village life – Town Life – Fashionable Life – Domestic Life – Married Life – School and University Life, &c., of Germany at the Present Time*, 1: iii–iv. London: Wm H. Allen & Co., 1864.

———. *London Labour and the London Poor*. 3 vols. London: Office of London Labour and the London Poor, 1851–52.

———. 'Preface'. In *The Upper Rhine: The Scenery of its Banks and the Manners of Its People. Illustrated by Birket Foster. Described by Henry Mayhew*, v–xii. London: George Routledge & Co., 1858.

McCrae, Hugh. 'My Father and My Father's Friends'. In *Story-Book Only*, 1–56. Sydney; London: Angus and Robertson, 1948; first published 1935.

McCulloch, J.R. *A Dictionary, Practical, Theoretical, and Historical, of Commerce and Commercial Navigation*. Edited by Hugh G. Reid, rev. edn. London: Longmans, Green & Co., 1875.

Moritz, C.P. With an introduction by P.E. Matheson. *Travels of Carl Philipp Moritz in England in 1782: A reprint of the English Translation of 1795*. London: Humphrey Milford, 1924.

Newton, H. Chance. *Crime and the Drama: or Dark Deeds Dramatized*. London: Stanley Paul, 1927.

Nicholson, Renton *Autobiography of a Fast Man*. London: [n.pub.], 1863.

Pugin, A. *Contrasts: or, A Parallel Between the Noble Edifices of the Middle Ages, and Corresponding Buildings of the Present Day; shewing The Present Decay of Taste. Accompanied by Appropriate Text*. 2nd edn. London: Charles Dolman, 1841.

Punch, The Writers of. *Punch's Pantomime: or, Harlequin King John and Magna Carta*. London: Punch Office, 13 Wellington Street, Strand, 1843.

Reach, Angus B. *London on the Thames: Or, Life Above and Below Bridge.* London: Vizetelly Brothers, 1848.

Rees, Thomas and John Britton. *Reminiscences of Literary London from 1779 to 1853; with Interesting Anecdotes of Publishers, Authors, and Book Auctioneers of that Period.* New York: Francis P. Harper, 1896; first published London, 1853.

Reynolds, G.W.M. *The Mysteries of London, Series I.* 2 vols. London: George Vickers, ? October 1844 – 26 September 1846.

———. *The Mysteries of London, Series II.* 2 vols. London: George Vickers, 3 October 1846–16 September 1848.

———. *The Necromancer.* Edited by Dick Collins. Kansas City: Valancourt Books, 2007; first published in *RM* December 1851–July 1852.

Reynolds, Susannah Frances. *Gretna Green: or, All For Love.* London: John Dicks, 1848.

Sala, George Augustus. *Echoes of the Year Eighteen Hundred and Eighty-Three.* London: Remington, 1884.

———. *The Life and Adventures of George Augustus Sala, Written by Himself.* 2nd edn. 2 vols. London: Cassell & Company, 1895.

———. *Twice Round the Clock; or The Hours of the Day and Night in London.* London: J. and R. Maxwell, 1859.

Schlesinger, Max. *Saunterings In and About London.* London: Nathaniel Cooke, 1853.

Smith, Albert. *The Drama Founded on the New Christmas Annual of Charles Dickens, Esq., Called The Battle of Life, Dramatised by Albert Smith, Esq. (Member of the Dramatic Author's Society), From early Proofs of the Work, By the Express Permission of the Author.* London: W.S. Johnson [1846].

[———]. *Novelty Fair; or, Hints for 1851.* London: T.H. Lacy, [n.d.].

Stirling, Edward. *Martin Chuzzlewit!: A Drama in Three Acts. Adapted From C. Dickens, Esq. Celebrated Work, by Edward Stirling, Esq.* Vol. 50 of *Duncombe's Edition [of British Theatre].* London: John Duncombe, [n.d.].

———. *Old Drury Lane: Fifty Years' Recollections of Author, Actor, and Manager.* 2 vols. London: Chatto and Windus, 1881.

Sutherland, Alexander. *Victoria and Its Metropolis, Past and Present.* 2 vols. Melbourne: McCarron & Bird, 1888.

Taithe, Bernard, ed. 'Part II: Answers to Correspondents'. In *The Essential Mayhew: Representing and Communicating the Poor*, edited by Bernard Taithe, 85–251. London: Rivers Oram Press, 1996.

Thackeray, William Makepeace. *The History of Pendennis.* Edited by John Sutherland. Oxford: Oxford University Press, 1994; first published 1850.

———. *Vanity Fair: A Novel without a Hero.* Edited by J.I.M. Stewart. London: Penguin, 1998; first published 1848.

Timbs, John. *The Year-Book of Facts in Science and Art.* London: David Bogue, 1854.

Tristan, Flora. *Flora Tristan's London Journal, 1840: A Survey of London Life in the 1830s*. Translated by Dennis Palmer and Giselle Pincett. London: Prior, 1980.

Vizetelly, Henry. *Glances back through Seventy Years: Autobiographical and Other Reminiscences*. 2 vols. London: Kegan Paul, 1893.

Yates, E.H. *Edmund Yates: His Recollections and Experiences*. 3rd edn. 2 vols. London: Richard Bentley, 1885.

Secondary Materials

Abler, Ronald, John S. Adams, and Peter Gould. *Spatial Organization: The Geographer's View of the World*. Englewood Cliffs, NJ: Prentice-Hall, 1971.

Ablow, Rachel, ed. *The Feeling of Reading: Affective Experience and Victorian Literature*. Ann Arbor: University of Michigan Press, 2010.

Ackroyd, Peter. *Dickens*. London: Minerva, 1991; first published Sinclair-Stevenson, 1990.

———. *London: The Biography*. London: Vintage, 2001.

Allen, Michael. *Charles Dickens and the Blacking Factory*. St. Leonards: Oxford-Stockley Publications, 2011.

Allen, Michelle. *Cleansing the City: Sanitary Geographies in Victorian London*. Athens, OH: Ohio University Press, 2008.

Allen, Rick, ed. 'Introduction'. In *The Moving Pageant: A Literary Sourcebook on London Street-Life, 1700–1914*, 1–25. London: Routledge, 1998.

———. 'Observing London Street-Life: G.A. Sala and A.J. Munby'. In *The Streets of London: From the Great Fire to the Great Stink*, edited by Tim Hitchcock and Heather Shore, foreword by Roy Porter, 198–214. London: Rivers Oram Press, 2003.

Allingham, Philip V. 'The Costuming and Set Design of Plays Adapted from Dickens's Christmas Books: Realisations of the Illustrations'. *Victorian Web*, accessed 1 November 2011. http://www.victorianweb.org/.

———. 'Dramatic Adaptations of Dickens's Novels'. *Victorian Web*, accessed 25 June 2010. http://www.victorianweb.org/.

Altick, Richard D. *The English Common Reader: A Social History of the Mass Reading Public 1800–1900*. Chicago: University of Chicago Press, 1957.

———. *The Shows of London*. Cambridge, MA: Belknap Press of Harvard University Press, 1978.

Anderson, Benedict. *Imagined Communities: Reflections on the Origin and Spread of Nationalism*. 3rd edn. London: Verso, 2006.

Andersson, Peter K. *Streetlife in Late Victorian London: The Constable and the Crowd*. Basingstoke: Palgrave Macmillan, 2013.

Appadurai, Arjun. 'The Production of Locality'. In *Modernity at Large: Cultural Dimensions of Globalization,* 178–99. Minneapolis: University of Minnesota Press, 1996.

Ashton, Rosemary. *142 Strand: A Radical Address in Victorian London.* London: Chatto & Windus, 2006.

Askew, M. and B. Hubber. 'The Colonial Reader Observed: Reading in Its Cultural Context'. In *The Book in Australia: Essays Towards a Cultural and Social History*, edited by D.H. Borchardt and Wallace Kirsop, 110–38. Clayton, Victoria: Australian Reference Publications in association with the Centre for Bibliographical and Textual Studies, Monash University, 1988.

Auerbach, Jeffrey A. *The Great Exhibition of 1851: A Nation on Display.* New Haven, CT: Yale University Press, 1999.

——— and Peter H. Hoffenberg, eds. *Britain, the Empire, and the World at the Great Exhibition of 1851.* Aldershot: Ashgate, 2008.

Ayres, Brenda. 'Temperance Magazines'. In *Dictionary of Nineteenth-Century Journalism in Great Britain and Ireland*, edited by Laurel Brake and Marysa Demoor, 618. Ghent; London: Academia Press and British Library, 2009.

Bagehot, Walter. 'Charles Dickens'. In *The Collected Works of Walter Bagehot*, edited by Norman St. John Stevas, 2: 77–107. London: The Economist, 1965–86.

Bailey, Craig Allen. 'The Irish Network: a Study of Ethnic Patronage in London, 1760–1840'. PhD diss., School of Advanced Study, University of London, 2004.

Bailey, Peter. 'Breaking the Sound Barrier'. In *Popular Culture and Performance in the Victorian City*, 194–211. Cambridge: Cambridge University Press, 1998.

———. 'Music Hall and the Knowingness of Popular Culture'. In *Popular Culture and Performance in the Victorian City*, 128–50. Cambridge: Cambridge University Press, 1998.

Baumgarten, Murray. 'Fictions of the City'. In *The Cambridge Companion to Charles Dickens*, edited by John O. Jordan, 106–19. Cambridge: Cambridge University Press, 2001.

Beetham, Margaret. 'Towards a Theory of the Periodical as a Publishing Genre'. In *Investigating Victorian Journalism*, edited by Laurel Brake, Aled Jones, and Lionel Madden, 19–32. Basingstoke: Macmillan, 1990.

———. 'Women and the Consumption of Print'. In *Women and Literature in Britain, 1800–1900*, edited by Joanne Shattock, 55–77. Cambridge: Cambridge University Press, 2001.

Benedict, Barbara M. 'Literary Miscellanies: the Cultural Mediation of Fragmented Feeling'. *English Literary History* 57, no. 2 (Summer 1990): 407–30.

Bennett, Scott. 'Revolutions in Thought: Serial Publication and the Mass Market for Reading'. In *The Victorian Periodical Press: Samplings and Soundings*, edited by Joanne Shattock and Michael Wolff, 225–53. Leicester: Leicester University Press, 1982; Toronto: Toronto University Press, 1982.

Bernstein, Carol L. *The Celebration of Scandal: Toward the Sublime in Victorian Urban Fiction.* University Park: Pennsylvania State University Press, 1991.

Bernstein, Susan David. *Roomscape: Women Writers in the British Museum from George Eliot to Virginia Woolf.* Edinburgh: Edinburgh University Press, 2013.

Berridge, V. 'Popular Sunday Newspapers and Mid-Victorian Society'. In *Newspaper History from the Seventeenth-Century to the Present Day*, edited by George Boyce, James Curran, and Pauline Wingate, 247–64. London: Constable, 1978.

Black, Barbara. *A Room of His Own: A Literary-Cultural Study of Victorian Clubland*. Ohio: Ohio University Press, 2012.

Blainey, Anne. *The Farthing Poet: A Biography of Richard Hengist Horne 1802–84, A Lesser Literary Lion*. London: Longmans Green & Co., 1968.

Blainey, Geoffrey. *The Tyranny of Distance: How Distance Shaped Australia's History*. 2nd edn. South Melbourne, Victoria: Sun Books, 1983; first published 1966.

Bloom, Harold. *The Anxiety of Influence: A Theory of Poetry*. 2nd edn. New York; Oxford: Oxford University Press, 1997.

Boase, G.C. 'Brooks, Charles William Shirley (1816–1874)'. Revised by H.C.G. Matthew. *Oxford Dictionary of National Biography* online edition. Accessed 11 August 2012. www.oxforddnb.com.

———. 'Nicholson, Renton (1809–1861)'. Revised by K.D. Reynolds. *Oxford Dictionary of National Biography* online edition. Accessed 11 August 2012. www.oxforddnb.com.

Boehm, Katharina and Josephine McDonagh. 'Introduction'. In 'New Agenda: Urban Mobility: New Maps of Victorian Britain', edited by Katharina Boehm and Josephine McDonagh, 194–200. Special issue, *Journal of Victorian Culture* 15, no. 2 (August 2010).

Bogle, Joanna. 'Chisholm, Caroline (1808–1877)'. *Oxford Dictionary of National Biography* online edition. Accessed 11 August 2012. www.oxforddnb.com.

Bolton, H. Philip. *Dickens Dramatized*. London: Mansell, 1987.

Booth, Michael R. *Theatre in the Victorian Age*. Cambridge: Cambridge University Press, 1991.

Borchardt, D.H. and Wallace Kirsop, eds. *The Book in Australia: Essays Towards a Cultural and Social History*. Clayton, Victoria: Australian Reference Publications in association with the Centre for Bibliographical and Textual Studies, Monash University, 1988.

———. 'Printing Comes to Australia'. In *The Book in Australia: Essays Towards a Cultural and Social History*, edited by D.H. Borchardt and Wallace Kirsop, 1–15. Clayton, Victoria: Australian Reference Publications in association with the Centre for Bibliographical and Textual Studies, Monash University, 1988.

Bowen, John. *Other Dickens*. Oxford: Oxford University Press, 2000.

Boyd, Kelly and Rohan McWilliam. 'Introduction: Rethinking the Victorians'. In *The Victorian Studies Reader*, edited by Kelly Boyd and Rohan McWilliam, 1–48. London; New York: Routledge, 2007.

Brantlinger, Patrick. *The Reading Lesson: The Threat of Mass Literacy in Nineteenth-Century British Fiction*. Bloomington: Indiana University Press, 1998.

Brake, Laurel. '*Examiner* [1808–1881]'. In *Dictionary of Nineteenth-Century Journalism in Great Britain and Ireland*, edited by Laurel Brake and Marysa Demoor, 211. Ghent; London: Academia Press and British Library, 2009.

―――. 'On Print Culture: The State We're In'. *Journal of Victorian Culture* 6, no.1 (Spring 2001): 125–36.

―――. *Print in Transition, 1850–1910: Studies in Media and Book History*. Basingstoke: Palgrave, 2001.

―――. '"Time's Turbulence": Mapping Journalism's Networks'. In 'Victorian Networks and the Periodical Press', edited by Alexis Easley, 115–27. Special issue, *Victorian Periodicals Review* 44, no. 2 (Summer 2011).

―――, Bill Bell, and David Finkelstein, eds. *Nineteenth-Century Media and the Construction of Identities*. Basingstoke: Palgrave, 2000.

――― and Marysa Demoor, eds. *Dictionary of Nineteenth-Century Journalism In Great Britain and Ireland*. Ghent; London: Academia Press and British Library, 2009.

―――, Aled Jones, and Lionel Madden, eds. *Investigating Victorian Journalism*. Basingstoke: Macmillan, 1990.

Bratton, Jacky. 'Anecdote and Mimicry as History'. In *New Readings in Theatre History*, 95–132. Cambridge: Cambridge University Press, 2003.

―――. *The Making of the West End Stage: Marriage, Management and the Mapping of Gender in London, 1830–1870*. Cambridge: Cambridge University Press, 2011.

Briggs, Asa. *Victorian Cities*. 2nd edn. Harmondsworth: Penguin, 1968.

Brooks, Peter. *The Melodramatic Imagination: Balzac, Henry James, Melodrama, and the Mode of Excess*. 2nd edn. New Haven, CT: Yale University Press, 1995.

Brown, Lucy. *Victorian News and Newspapers*. Oxford: Clarendon Press, 1985.

Brown-May, Andrew. 'In the Precincts of the Global City: The Transnational Network of Municipal Affairs in Melbourne, Australia, at the End of the Nineteenth-Century'. In *Another Global City: Historical Explorations into the Transnational Municipal Movement, 1850–2000*, edited by Pierre-Yves Saunier and Shane Ewen, 19–34. Basingstoke: Palgrave Macmillan, 2008.

―――. *Melbourne Street Life: The Itinerary of Our Days*. Kew, Victoria: Australian Scholarly Publishing, 1998.

Buckrich, Judith. 'Collins Street'. *eMelbourne: The City Past and Present (The Encyclopedia of Melbourne Online)*. Accessed 26 January 2012. http://www.emelbourne.net.au/.

Burford, E.J. *Wits, Wenchers and Wantons: London's Low Life: Covent Garden in the Eighteenth Century*. London: Hale, 1986.

Burke, Alan R. 'The Strategy and Theme of Urban Observation in *Bleak House*'. *Studies in English Literature 1500–1900* 9, no. 4, Nineteenth Century (Autumn 1969): 659–76.

Burke, Peter. 'Classifying Knowledge: Curricula, Libraries and Encyclopedias'. In *A Social History of Knowledge from Gutenberg to Diderot*, 81–115. Cambridge: Polity, 2000.

Burt, Daniel S. 'A Victorian Gothic: G.W.M. Reynolds's Mysteries of London'. *New York Literary Forum* 7 (1980): 141–58.

Buzard, James. *Disorienting Fiction: The Autoethnographic Work of Nineteenth-Century British Novels*. Princeton, NJ: Princeton University Press, 2005.

Campbell, Kate. 'Introduction: On Perceptions of Journalism'. In *Journalism, Literature and Modernity: From Hazlitt to Modernism*, edited by Kate Campbell, 1–14. Edinburgh: Edinburgh University Press, 2000.

Carver, Stephen James. 'The Wrongs and Crimes of the Poor: The Urban Underworld of *The Mysteries of London* in Context'. In *G.W.M. Reynolds: Nineteenth-Century Fiction, Politics and the Press*, edited by Anne Humpherys and Louis James, 149–62. Aldershot: Ashgate, 2008.

Castells, Manuel. *The Rise of the Network Society*. 2nd edn. Oxford: Blackwell, 2000.

Cathcart Borer, Mary. *The Story of Covent Garden*. London: Hale, 1984.

Chittick, Kathryn. *Dickens and the 1830s*. Cambridge: Cambridge University Press, 1990.

———. 'Dickens and Parliamentary Reporting in the 1830s'. *Victorian Periodicals Review* 21, no. 4 (Winter, 1988): 151–60.

Christ, Carol T. and John O. Jordan, eds. *Victorian Literature and the Victorian Visual Imagination*. Berkeley: University of California Press, 1995.

Clemm, Sabine. *Dickens, Journalism, and Nationhood: Mapping the World in Household Words*. London: Routledge, 2009.

Cockayne, Emily. *Hubbub: Filth, Noise and Stench in England 1600–1770*. New Haven, CT: Yale University Press, 2007.

Codell, Julie F. 'The Art Press and Its Parodies: Unravelling Networks in Swinburne's 1868 Academy Notes'. In 'Victorian Networks and the Periodical Press', edited by Alexis Easley, 165–83. Special issue, *Victorian Periodicals Review* 44, no. 2 (Summer 2011).

Collins, Dick. 'George William McArthur Reynolds: A Biographical Sketch'. In *The Necromancer*, edited by Dick Collins, vii–lvii. Kansas City: Valancourt Books, 2007; first published *RM* 1851–1.

Craig, Cairns. 'Benedict Anderson's Fictional Communities'. In *The Influence of Benedict Anderson*, edited by Alistair McCleery and Benjamin A. Brabon, 21–40. Edinburgh: Merchiston Publishing, 2007.

Crary, Jonathan. *Techniques of the Observer: On Vision and Modernity in the Nineteenth Century*. Cambridge, MA; London: MIT Press, 1990.

Dalziel, Margaret. 'The Most Popular Writer of Our Time'. In *Popular Fiction 100 Years Ago: An Unexplored Tract of Literary History*, 35–45. London: Cohen & West, 1957.

Dart, Gregory. '"Flash Style": Pierce Egan and Literary London, 1820–8'. *History Workshop Journal* 51 (Spring 2001): 181–205.

Davies, James A. *John Forster: A Literary Life*. Leicester: Leicester University Press, 1983.

Davis, Jim and Victor Emeljanow. *Reflecting the Audience: London Theatregoing, 1840–1880*. Hatfield: University of Hertfordshire Press; Iowa City: University of Iowa Press, 2001.

Davis, Lennard J. *Factual Fictions: The Origins of the English Novel*. New York: Columbia University Press, 1983.

Davis, Lloyd. 'Victorian Journalism and Victorian Fiction'. In *Victorian Journalism: Exotic and Domestic: Essays in Honour of P.D. Edwards*, edited by Barbara Garlick and Margaret Harris, 197–211. St. Lucia: University of Queensland Press, 1998.

Davis, Tracy C. 'Actresses and Prostitutes in Victorian London'. *Theatre Research International* 13 (1988): 221–34.

———. *Actresses as Working Women: Their Social Identity in Victorian Culture*. London: Routledge, 1991.

———. 'Amelia Chesson Enters the Fourth Estate: "She must, therefore, be considered a pioneer in lady journalism"'. Paper presented at the annual conference for the British Association for Victorian Studies, University of Birmingham, 1–3 September 2011.

Davison, Graeme. 'The European City in Australia'. *Journal of Urban History* 27 (2001): 779–93.

———. *The Rise and Fall of Marvellous Melbourne*. Melbourne: Melbourne University Press, 1978.

——— and David Dunstan. '"This Moral Pandemonium": Images of Low Life'. In *The Outcasts of Melbourne: Essays in Social History*, edited by Graeme Davison, David Dunstan, and Chris McConville, 29–57. Sydney: Allen & Unwin, 1985.

de Certeau, Michel. *The Practice of Everyday Life*. Translated by Steven Rendall. Berkeley, CA: University of California Press, 1984.

De Serville, Paul. 'Garrick Club'. *eMelbourne: The City Past and Present (The Encyclopedia of Melbourne Online)*. Accessed 20 January, 2012. http://www.emelbourne.net.au/.

Deane, Bradley. *The Making of the Victorian Novelist: Anxieties of Authorship in the Mass Market*. New York; London: Routledge, 2003.

Demoor, Marysa and Frederick Morel. 'Laurence Binyon and the Belgian Artistic Scene: Unearthing Unknown Brotherhoods'. In 'Victorian Networks and the Periodical Press', edited by Alexis Easley, 184–97. Special issue, *Victorian Periodicals Review* 44, no. 2 (Summer 2011).

Diamond, Michael. 'Charles Dickens as Villain and Hero in Reynolds's Newspaper'. *Dickensian* 98, no. 457 (Summer 2002): 127–38.

Dicks, Guy. *The John Dicks Press*. Published by the author, 2005.

Donald, James. *Imagining the Modern City*. London: Athlone Press, 1999.

Douglas-Fairhurst, Robert. *Becoming Dickens: The Invention of a Novelist*. Cambridge, MA; London: Belknap Press of Harvard University Press, 2011.

————. Introduction to *London Labour and the London Poor: a Selected Edition.* Edited by Robert Douglas-Fairhurst, xiii–xliii. Oxford: Oxford University Press, 2010.

Dowling, David. *The Business of Literary Circles in Nineteenth-Century America.* New York: Palgrave Macmillan, 2011.

Drew, John. 'Blanchard, [Samuel] Laman (1803–1845)'. In *Dictionary of Nineteenth-Century Journalism In Great Britain and Ireland*, edited by Laurel Brake and Marysa Demoor, 61. Ghent; London: Academia Press and British Library, 2009.

————. *Dickens the Journalist.* Basingstoke: Palgrave Macmillan, 2003.

Dyos, H.J. and Michael Wolff, eds. *The Victorian City: Images and Realities.* 2 vols. London: Routledge and Kegan Paul, 1973.

Earl, John and Michael Sel, eds. Foreword by Sir Donald Sinden. *The Theatres Trust Guide to British Theatres 1750–1950.* London: A. & C. Black, 2000.

Easley, Alexis, ed. 'Victorian Networks and the Periodical Press'. Special issue, *Victorian Periodicals Review* 44, no. 2 (Summer 2011).

Edwards, P.D. *Dickens's 'Young Men': George Augustus Sala, Edmund Yates, and the World of Victorian Journalism.* Aldershot: Ashgate, 1997.

Edwards, Percy J. *History of London Street Improvements 1855–1897.* London: London County Council, 1898.

Emmerson, George S. *John Scott Russell: A Great Victorian Engineer and Naval Architect.* London: John Murray, 1977.

Fawcett, F. Dubrez. *Dickens the Dramatist: On Stage, Screen, and Radio.* London: W.H. Allen, 1952.

Finn, Margot C. *After Chartism: Class and Nation in English Radical Politics, 1848–1874.* Cambridge: Cambridge University Press, 1993.

Flint, Kate. *The Victorians and the Visual Imagination.* Cambridge: Cambridge University Press, 2000.

Fox, Celina. 'Introduction: A Visitor's Guide to London World City, 1800–40'. In *London: World City, 1800–1840*, edited by Celina Fox, 11–20. New Haven, CT; London: Yale University Press, in association with the Museum of London, 1992.

Freedgood, Elaine. 'Groundless Optimism: regression in the service of the ego, England and Empire in Victorian ballooning memoirs'. In *Victorian Writing About Risk: Imagining a Safe England in a Dangerous World*, 74–98. Cambridge: Cambridge University Press, 2000.

Fryckstedt, Monica. 'Douglas Jerrold's Shilling Magazine'. *Victorian Periodicals Review* 19, no.1 (Spring, 1986): 2–27.

Gänzl, Kurt. 'Kenney, Charles Lamb (1821–1881)'. *Oxford Dictionary of National Biography* online edition. Accessed 11 August 2012. http://www.oxforddnb.com.

Garcha, Amanpal. *From Sketch to Novel: The Development of Victorian Fiction.* Cambridge: Cambridge University Press, 2009.

Gatrell, Vic. *City of Laughter: Sex and Satire in Eighteenth-Century London.* London: Atlantic Books, 2006.

———. *The First Bohemians: Life and Art in London's Golden Age.* London: Allen Lane, 2013.

Gibbon, Frank. 'R.H. Horne and Our Mutual Friend'. *Dickensian* 98, no. 2 (Summer 2002): 145–48.

Goodway, David. *London Chartism: 1838–1848.* Cambridge: Cambridge University Press, 1982.

Gordon, Charles (pseudonym of John Ashton). *Old Time Aldwych, Kingsway, and Neighbourhood.* London: T. Fisher Unwin, 1903.

Grande, James. 'Nineteenth-Century London in William Godwin's Diary'. In 'New Agenda: Urban Mobility: New Maps of Victorian Britain', edited by Katharina Boehm and Josephine McDonagh, 201–11. Special issue, *Journal of Victorian Culture* 15, no. 2 (August 2010).

Grenville, J.A.S. *Europe Reshaped: 1848–1878.* 2nd edn. Oxford: Blackwell, 2000.

Grossman, Jonathan H. *Dickens's Networks: Public Transport and the Novel.* Oxford: Oxford University Press, 2012.

Guivarc'h, Jean. 'Deux journalistes anglais de Paris en 1835 (G.W.M. Reynolds et W.M.T.)'. *Études Anglaises* 28, no. 2 (1975: avril/juin): 203–12.

Habermas, Jurgen, trans. by Thomas Berger with the assistance of Frederick Lawrence. *The Structural Transformation of the Public Sphere: An Inquiry into a Category of Bourgeois Society.* Cambridge: Polity Press, 1989; first published in German 1962.

Hall, Catherine and Sonya O. Rose. 'Introduction: being at home with the Empire'. In *At Home With the Empire: Metropolitan Culture and the Imperial World.* Edited by Catherine Hall and Sonya O. Rose, 1–31. Cambridge: Cambridge University Press, 2006.

Halliday, Stephen. *The Great Stink of London: Sir Joseph Bazalgette and the Cleansing of the Victorian Capital.* Stroud: Sutton Publishing, 1999.

Hamilton, Kristie. *America's Sketchbook: The Cultural Life of a Nineteenth-Century Literary Genre.* Athens, OH: Ohio State University Press, 1998.

Hamlin, Christopher. 'Simon, Sir John (1816–1904)'. *Oxford Dictionary of National Biography* online edition. Accessed 11 August 2012. http://www.oxforddnb.com.

Hansen, Adam. 'Exhibiting Vagrancy, 1851: Victorian London and the "Vagabond Savage"'. *Literary London: Interdisciplinary Studies in the Representation of London* 2, no. 2 (September 2004). Accessed 16 August 2012. http://www.literarylondon.org/london-journal/september2004/hansen.html.

Hansen, Peter H. 'Smith, Albert Richard (1816–1860)'. *Oxford Dictionary of National Biography* online edition. Accessed 11 August 2012. http://www.oxforddnb.com.

Harland-Lang, Antonia. 'Thackeray and Bohemia'. PhD diss., University of Cambridge, 2010.

Harris, Michael. 'The Book Trade in Public Spaces: London Street Booksellers, 1690–1850'. In *Fairs, Markets and the Itinerant Book Trade*, edited by Robin Myers, Michael Harris, and Giles Mandelbrote, 187–211. New Castle, DE: Oak Knoll Press; London: British Library, 2007.

Hartz, Louis, with contributions by Kenneth D. McRae and others. *The Founding of New Societies: Studies in the History of the United States, Latin America, South Africa, Canada, and Australia*. New York: Harcourt, Brace & World, 1964.

Hauser, Helen M. 'Miscellaneous Blood: GWM Reynolds, Dickens, and the Anatomical Moment'. PhD diss., University of California, Santa Cruz, 2008.

Haywood, Ian. 'George W.M. Reynolds and "The Trafalgar Square Revolution": radicalism, the carnivalesque and popular culture in mid-Victorian England'. *Journal of Victorian Culture* 7, no. 1 (2002): 23–59.

———. *The Revolution in Popular Literature: Politics, Print and the People 1790–1860*. Cambridge: Cambridge University Press, 2004.

Hearnshaw, F.J.C. *The Centenary History of King's College London: 1828–1928*. London: George G. Harrap, 1929.

Henderson, Ian. 'Trollope in Australia: Gentlemen, the Cringe'. Paper (supplied by the author) presented at the Second Commodities and Culture in the Colonial World Workshop: 'Commodities and Affect', Centre of Advanced Study in English, Jadavpur University, Kolkata, India, 12–14 January 2011. Also presented at an English/MCAS panel discussion, King's College London, 28 March 2011.

Henkin, David. *City Reading: Written Words and Public Spaces in Antebellum New York*. New York: Columbia University Press, 1998.

Hergenhan, Laurie, Ken Stewart, and Michael Wilding, eds. *Cyril Hopkins' Marcus Clarke*. North Melbourne, Victoria: Australian Scholarly Publishing, 2009.

Hergenhan, L.T. 'Introduction'. In *A Colonial City: High and Low Life. Selected Journalism of Marcus Clarke*, edited by L.T. Hergenhan, xv–xl. St. Lucia, Queensland: University of Queensland Press, 1972.

———. gen. ed. *The Penguin New Literary History of Australia*. Ringwood, Victoria; Harmondsworth: Penguin, 1988.

Hibbert, Christopher. *The Making of Charles Dickens*. Harmondsworth: Penguin, 1983; first published Longman, 1967.

Hirst, J.B. 'Keeping colonial history colonial: The Hartz thesis revisited'. *[Australian] Historical Studies* 21, no. 82 (April 1984): 85–104.

Hitchcock, Tim and Heather Shore, eds. 'Introduction'. In *The Streets of London: From the Great Fire to the Great Stink*, edited by Tim Hitchcock and Heather Shore, foreword by Roy Porter, 1–9. London: Rivers Oram Press, 2003.

Hobsbawm, E.J. *The Age of Capital: 1848–1875*. London: Sphere Books, 1985; first published Weidenfeld & Nicolson, 1975.

Hobson, G.D. 'Appendix A: Some of the Principal Sales held at Sotheby's'. In *Notes on the History of Sotheby's*, 21–34. London: Sotheby, Wilkinson & Hodge, 1917.

Hollington, Michael. 'Dickens, Sala, and the London Arcades'. *Dickens Quarterly* 28, no. 4 (December 2011): 273–84.

Holloway, Lewis and Phil Hubbard. *People and Place: The Extraordinary Geographies of Everyday Life*. Harlow: Prentice Hall, 2001.

Howsam, Leslie. *Old Books and New Histories: An Orientation to Studies in Book and Print Culture*. Toronto: University of Toronto Press, 2006.

Hughes, Linda K. and Michael Lund, eds. *The Victorian Serial*. Charlottesville; London: University Press of Virginia, 1991.

Humpherys, Anne. 'Generic Strands and Urban Twists: The Victorian Mysteries Novel'. *Victorian Studies* 34 (1991): 455–72.

———. 'The Geometry of the Modern City: G.W.M. Reynolds and The Mysteries of London'. *Browning Institute Studies* 11, no.13 (1983): 69–80.

———. 'An Introduction to G.W.M. Reynolds's "Encyclopedia of Tales"'. In *G.W.M. Reynolds: Nineteenth-Century Fiction, Politics and the Press*, edited by Anne Humpherys and Louis James, 123–33. Aldershot: Ashgate, 2008.

———. *Travels into the Poor Man's Country: The Work of Henry Mayhew*. Athens, GA: The University of Georgia Press, 1977.

———. 'Victorian Stage Adaptations and Appropriations'. In *Charles Dickens in Context*, edited by Sally Ledger and Holly Furneaux, 27–34. Cambridge: Cambridge University Press, 2011.

——— and Louis James, eds. *G.W.M. Reynolds: Nineteenth-Century Fiction, Politics and the Press*. Aldershot: Ashgate, 2008.

Hunt, Tristram. *Building Jerusalem: The Rise and Fall of the Victorian City*. London: Weidenfeld & Nicolson, 2004.

Jackson, Matthew O. *Social and Economic Networks*. Princeton, NJ; Woodstock: Princeton University Press, 2008.

Jaffe, Audrey. *Scenes of Sympathy: Identity and Representation in Victorian Fiction*. Ithaca, NY: Cornell University Press, 2000.

James, Louis. 'A Bibliography of Works by G.W.M. Reynolds'. In *G.W.M. Reynolds: Nineteenth-Century Fiction, Politics, and the Press*, edited by Anne Humpherys and Louis James, 273–78. Aldershot: Ashgate, 2008.

———. *Fiction for the Working Man 1830–1850: A Study of the Literature Produced for the Working Classes in Early Victorian Urban England*. London: Oxford University Press, 1963.

———. 'From Egan to Reynolds: The shaping of urban "Mysteries" in England and France, 1821–48'. *European Journal of English Studies* 14, no. 2 (August 2010): 95–106.

———. 'The Trouble With Betsy: periodicals and the common reader in mid-nineteenth-century England'. In *The Victorian Periodical Press: Samplings and Soundings*, edited by Joanne Shattock and Michael Wolff, 349–66. Leicester: Leicester University Press, 1982; Toronto: Toronto University Press, 1982.

———. 'The View from Brick Lane: Contrasting Perspectives in Working-Class and Middle-Class Fiction of the Early Victorian Period'. *Yearbook of English Studies* 11 (1981): 87–101.

John, Juliet. *Dickens's Villains: Melodrama, Character, Popular Culture*. Oxford: Oxford University Press, 2001.

———. 'Reynolds's Mysteries and Popular Culture'. In *G.W.M. Reynolds: Nineteenth-Century Fiction, Politics and the Press*, edited by Anne Humpherys and Louis James, 163–77. Aldershot: Ashgate, 2008.

Johns, Adrian. *The Nature of the Book: Print and Knowledge in the Making*. Chicago: University of Chicago Press, 1998.

———. *Piracy: the Intellectual Property Wars from Gutenberg to Gates*. Chicago: University of Chicago Press, 2009.

Jones, Aled. *Powers of the Press: Newspapers, Power and the Public in Nineteenth-Century England*. Aldershot: Scolar Press, 1996.

Jordan, John O. and Robert L. Patten, eds. *Literature in the Marketplace: Nineteenth-Century British Publishing and Reading Practices*. Cambridge: Cambridge University Press, 1995.

Joshi, Priya. *In Another Country: Colonialism, Culture, and the English Novel in India*. New York: Columbia University Press, 2002.

Kenyon-Jones, Christine. *King's College London: In the Service of Society*. London: King's College London, 2004.

King, Andrew. *The London Journal, 1845–83: Periodicals, Production and Gender*. Aldershot: Ashgate, 2004.

———. 'A Paradigm of Reading the Victorian Penny Weekly: Education of the Gaze and the *London Journal*'. In *Nineteenth-Century Media and the Construction of Identities*, edited by Laurel Brake, Bill Bell, and David Finkelstein, 77–92. Basingstoke: Palgrave, 2000.

———. '*Reynolds's Miscellany*, 1846–1849: Advertising Networks and Politics'. In *G.W.M. Reynolds: Nineteenth-Century Fiction, Politics, and the Press*, edited by Anne Humpherys and Louis James, 53–74. Aldershot: Ashgate, 2008.

——— and Fionnuala Dillane. 'Hunt, Thornton Leigh' (1810–1873)'. In *Dictionary of Nineteenth-Century Journalism in Great Britain and Ireland*, edited by Laurel Brake and Marysa Demoor, 297–98. Ghent; London: Academia Press and British Library, 2009.

Kirsop, Wallace. 'Bookselling and Publishing in the Nineteenth Century'. In *The Book in Australia: Essays Towards a Cultural and Social History*, edited by D.H. Borchardt and Wallace Kirsop, 16–42. Clayton, Victoria: Australian Reference Publications in association with the Centre for Bibliographical and Textual Studies, Monash University, 1988.

———. 'Cole's Book Arcade'. In *Worlds of Print: Diversity in the Book Trade*, edited by John Hinks and Catherine Armstrong, 31–40. New Castle, DE: Oak Knoll Press; London: British Library, 2006.

———. 'From Curry's to Collins Street, or How a Dubliner Became the "Melbourne Mudie"'. In *The Moving Market: Continuity and Change in the Book Trade*, edited by Peter Isaac and Barry McKay, 83–92. New Castle, DE: Oak Knoll Press, 2001.

Knight, Joseph. 'Keeley, Robert (1793–1869)'. Revised by Nilanjana Banerji. *Oxford Dictionary of National Biography* online edition. Accessed 11 August 2012. http://www.oxforddnb.com.

Knoke, David and James H. Kulinski. 'Network Analysis: Basic Concepts'. In *Markets, Hierarchies and Networks: The Coordination of Social Life*, edited by Graham Thompson and others, 173–82. London: SAGE in association with the Open University, 1991.

Koven, Seth. *Slumming: Sexual and Social Politics in Victorian London*. Princeton NJ; Woodstock: Princeton University Press, 2004.

Lacey, Candida Ann, ed. *Barbara Leigh Smith Bodichon and the Langham Place Group. Women's Source Library*. 2nd edn. New York and London: Routledge, 2001.

Landow, George P. 'The People's International League in "Hudson's Statue" (Annotation to Carlyle's "Hudson's Statue")'. *Victorian Web*. Accessed 2 June 2012. http://www.victorianweb.org/authors/carlyle/hudson/people.html.

Laquer, Thomas W. 'Bodies, Details, and the Humanitarian Narrative'. In *The New Cultural History*, edited by Lynn Hunt, 176–204. Berkeley, CA: University of California Press, 1989.

Large, David. 'London in the Year of Revolutions, 1848'. In *London in the Age of Reform*, edited by John Stevenson, 177–211. Oxford: Blackwell, 1977.

Latour, Bruno. *Reassembling the Social: An Introduction to Actor-Network-Theory*. Oxford: Oxford University Press, 2005.

Lauster, Martina. *Sketches of the Nineteenth Century: European Journalism and its Physiologies, 1830–1850*. Basingstoke: Palgrave Macmillan, 2007.

Law, Graham. 'Reynolds's "Memoirs" Series and "The Literature of the Kitchen"'. In *G.W.M. Reynolds: Nineteenth-Century Fiction, Politics and the Press*, edited by Anne Humpherys and Louis James, 201–12. Aldershot: Ashgate, 2008.

———. *Serializing Fiction in the Victorian Press*. Basingstoke: Palgrave, 2000.

Leary, Patrick. *The Punch Brotherhood: Table Talk and Print Culture in Mid-Victorian Britain*. London: British Library, 2010.

Ledger, Sally. *Dickens and the Popular Radical Imagination*. Cambridge: Cambridge University Press, 2007.

Lefebvre, Henri. *The Production of Space*. Translated by Donald Nicholson-Smith. Oxford: Blackwell, 1991.

Leighton, Mary Elizabeth and Lisa Surridge. 'The Plot Thickens: Toward a Narratological Analysis of Illustrated Serial Fiction in the 1860s'. *Victorian Studies* 51, no. 1 (Autumn 2008): 65–101.

Lewis, Miles. '11.02 Paper & Papier Mâché [2008 edition]'. In *Australian Building: A Cultural Investigation*. Accessed 30 April 2012. http://www.mileslewis.net/australian-building/.

Ley, J.W.T. *The Dickens Circle: A Narrative of the Novelist's Friendships*. London: Chapman & Hall, 1918.

Lindsay, Jack. *Charles Dickens: A Biographical and Critical Study*. London: Andrew Dakers, 1950.

Lohrli, Anne. *'Household Words' A Weekly Journal 1850–1859 Conducted by Charles Dickens, Table of Contents, List of Contributors and Their Contributions Based on the 'Household Words' Office Book.* Toronto: University of Toronto Press, 1973.

Mace, Rodney. *Trafalgar Square: Emblem of Empire.* London: Lawrence & Wishart, 2005; first published 1976.

Mack, Robert L. *The Wonderful and Surprising History of Sweeney Todd: The Life and Times of an Urban Legend.* London: Continuum, 2007.

Magee, Gary B. and Andrew S. Thompson. 'Networks and the British World'. In *Empire and Globalisation: Networks of People, Goods and Capital in the British World, c. 1850–1914*, 45–63. Cambridge: Cambridge University Press, 2010.

Magnet, Myron. *Dickens and the Social Order.* Philadelphia: University of Pennsylvania Press, 1985.

Mahood, Marguerite. *The Loaded Line: Australian Political Caricature 1788–1901.* Carlton, Victoria: Melbourne University Press, 1973.

———. 'Melbourne Punch and Its Early Artists'. *La Trobe Library Journal* 4 (October 1969): 65–81. Accessed 6 January 2014. http://www.slv.vic.gov.au/latrobejournal/issue/latrobe-04/t1-g-t1.html.

Maidment, B.E. 'The Mysteries of Reading: Text and Illustration in the Fiction of G.W.M. Reynolds'. In *G.W.M. Reynolds: Nineteenth-Century Fiction, Politics and the Press*, edited by Anne Humpherys and Louis James, 225–46. Aldershot: Ashgate, 2008.

———. *Reading Popular Prints 1790–1870.* Manchester and New York: Manchester University Press, 1996.

Mander, Raymond and Joe Mitchenson. *The Lost Theatres of London.* London: Rupert Hart-Davis, 1968.

Massey, Doreen. *For Space.* London: SAGE, 2005.

Mattelart, Armand. *Networking the World: 1794–2000.* Translated by Liz Carey-Libbrecht and James A. Cohen. Minneapolis; London: University of Minnesota Press, 2000.

Maxwell, Richard. 'G.M. Reynolds, Dickens, and the Mysteries of London'. *Nineteenth-Century Fiction* 32, no. 2 (1977): 188–213.

———. *The Mysteries of Paris and London.* Charlottesville, VA; London: University Press of Virginia, 1992.

Mayne, Alan. *The Imagined Slum: Newspaper Representation in Three Cities 1870–1914.* Leicester: Leicester University Press, 1993.

Mays, Kelly J. 'The Publishing World'. In *A Companion to the Victorian Novel*, edited by Patrick Brantlinger and William B. Thesing, 11–30. Malden, MA; Oxford: Blackwell, 2002.

McCalman, Iain. *Radical Underworld: Prophets, Revolutionaries, and Pornographers in London, 1795–1840.* 2nd edn. Oxford: Clarendon Press, 1993.

McCann, Andrew. *Marcus Clarke's Bohemia: Literature and Modernity in Colonial Melbourne*. Carlton, Victoria: Melbourne University Press, 2004.

McFadden, Margaret H. *Golden Cables of Sympathy: The Transatlantic Sources of Nineteenth-Century Feminism*. Lexington, KY: The University Press of Kentucky, 1999.

McWilliam, Rohan. 'The French Connection: G.W.M. Reynolds and the Outlaw Robert Macaire'. In *G.W.M. Reynolds: Nineteenth-Century Fiction, Politics and the Press*, edited by Anne Humpherys and Louis James, 33–49. Aldershot: Ashgate, 2008.

———. 'The Mysteries of GWM Reynolds: Radicalism and Melodrama in Victorian Britain'. In *Living and Learning: Essays in Honour of JFC Harrison*, edited by Malcolm Chase and Ian Dyck, 182–98. Aldershot: Scolar, 1996.

———. Talk of the Town: A History of the West End of London, 1800 to the Present (forthcoming).

Mee, Jon. *Conversable Worlds: Literature, Contention, and Community 1762 to 1830*. Oxford: Oxford University Press, 2011.

Meisel, Martin. *Realizations: Narrative, Pictorial and Theatrical Arts in Nineteenth-Century England*. Princeton, NJ: Princeton University Press, 1983.

Menke, Richard. *Telegraphic Realism: Victorian Fiction and Other Information Systems*. Stanford: Stanford University Press, 2008.

Miller, J. Hillis. 'The Fiction of Realism: Sketches by Boz, Oliver Twist, and Cruikshank's Illustrations'. In *Dickens Centennial Essays*, edited by Ada Nisbet and Blake Nevius, 85–153. Berkeley: University of California Press, 1971.

Mirmohamedi, Kylie and Susan K. Martin. *Colonial Dickens: What Australians Made of the World's Favourite Writer*. Melbourne: Australian Scholarly Publishing, 2012.

Morley, Malcolm. '*The Battle of Life* in the Theatre'. *Dickensian* 48, no. 302 (Spring 1952): 76–81.

———. 'The Cricket on the Stage'. *Dickensian* 48, no. 301 (Winter 1951–52): 17–23.

———. '*Martin Chuzzlewit* in the Theatre'. *Dickensian* 47, no. 298 (Spring 1951): 98–102.

———. 'Ring Up the Chimes'. *Dickensian* 47, no. 300 (Autumn 1951): 202–26.

Morretti, Franco. *Atlas of the European Novel: 1800–1900*. 2nd edn. London: Verso, 1999.

Morrison, Elizabeth. 'Serial Fiction in Australian Colonial Newspapers'. In *Literature in the Marketplace: Nineteenth-Century British Publishing and Reading Practices*, edited by John O. Jordan and Robert L. Patten, 306–23. Cambridge: Cambridge University Press, 1995.

Mullan, John. 'Sympathy and the Production of Society'. In *Sentiment and Sociability: The Language of Feeling in the Eighteenth Century*, 18–56. Oxford: Clarendon Press, 1988.

Nead, Lynda. *Victorian Babylon: People, Streets and Images in Nineteenth-Century London*. New Haven, CT: Yale University Press, 2000.

Newey, Katherine. *Women's Theatre Writing in Victorian Britain*. Basingstoke: Palgrave Macmillan, 2005.

Newman, Mark E.J. *Networks: An Introduction*. Oxford: Oxford University Press, 2010.

Nord, Deborah Epstein. 'The City as Theater: From Georgian to Early Victorian London'. *Victorian Studies* 31, no. 2 (Winter 1988): 159–88.

———. *Walking the Victorian Streets: Women, Representation and the City*. Ithaca, NY: Cornell University Press, 1995.

Ogborn, Miles and W.J. Withers. 'Introduction: Book Geographies, Book Histories'. In *Geographies of the Book*, edited by Miles Ogborn and W.J. Withers, 1–25. Farnham: Ashgate, 2010.

———, eds. *Geographies of the Book*. Farnham: Ashgate, 2010.

Ong, Walter J. *Orality and Literacy: The Technologizing of the Word*. London: Methuen, 1982.

Owens, Alastair, Nigel Jeffries, Karen Wehner, and Rupert Featherby. 'Fragments of the Modern City: Material Culture and the Rhythms of Everyday Life in Victorian London'. In 'New Agenda: Urban Mobility: New Maps of Victorian Britain', edited by Katharina Boehm and Josephine McDonagh, 212–25. Special issue, *Journal of Victorian Culture* 15, no. 2 (August 2010).

Paterson, Michael. *Voices from Dickens's London*. 2nd edn. Cincinnati, OH: David & Charles, 2007.

Patten, Robert L. 'Bogue, David (1807/8–1856)'. *Oxford Dictionary of National Biography* online edition. Accessed 24 May 2012. http://www.oxforddnb.com.

———. *Charles Dickens and 'Boz': The Birth of the Industrial-Age Author*. Cambridge: Cambridge University Press, 2012.

———. *Charles Dickens and His Publishers*. Oxford: Oxford University Press, 1978.

———. 'Dickens as Serial Author: A Case of Multiple Identities'. In *Nineteenth-Century Media and the Construction of Identities*, edited by Laurel Brake, Bill Bell, and David Finkelstein, 137–53. Basingstoke: Palgrave, 2000.

Pearl, Cyril. *Always Morning: The Life of Richard Henry 'Orion' Horne*. Melbourne: F.W. Cheshire, 1960.

———. 'Mr Dickens and Mr Reynolds'. In *Victorian Patchwork*, 67–94. London: Heinemann, 1972.

Peterson, Linda H. *Becoming a Woman of Letters: Myths of Authorship and Facts of the Victorian Market*. Princeton, NJ; Woodstock: Princeton University Press, 2009.

Pettitt, Clare. *Patent Inventions: Intellectual Property and the Victorian Novel*. Oxford: Oxford University Press, 2004.

Picard, Liza. *Victorian London: The Life of a City 1840–1870*. 2nd edn. London: Phoenix, 2006.

Pierce, Peter, ed. *The Cambridge History of Australian Literature*. Cambridge: Cambridge University Press, 2009.

Pike, David L. 'Afterimages of the Victorian City'. In 'New Agenda: Urban Mobility: New Maps of Victorian Britain', edited by Katharina Boehm and Josephine McDonagh, 254–67. Special issue, *Journal of Victorian Culture* 15, no. 2 (August 2010).

Piper, Andrew. *Dreaming in Books: The Making of the Bibliographic Imagination in the Romantic Age*. Chicago: University of Chicago Press, 2009.

Poovey, Mary. 'The Production of Abstract Space'. In *Making a Social Body: British Cultural Formation, 1830–1864*, 25–54. Chicago: University of Chicago Press, 1995.

Porter, Roy. *London: A Social History*. 3rd edn. London: Penguin, 2000.

Potts, Alex. 'Picturing the Modern Metropolis: Images of London in the Nineteenth Century'. *History Workshop Journal* 26, no. 1 (1988): 28–56.

Potts, E. Daniel and Annette Potts. *Young America and Australian Gold: Americans and the Gold Rush of the 1850s*. St. Lucia, Queensland: University of Queensland Press, 1974.

Powell, Kerry. *Women and Victorian Theatre*. Cambridge: Cambridge University Press, 1997.

———, ed. *The Cambridge Companion to Victorian and Edwardian Theatre*. Cambridge: Cambridge University Press, 2004.

Price, Leah. *The Anthology and the Rise of the Novel: From Richardson to George Eliot*. Cambridge: Cambridge University Press, 2000.

Purbrick, Louise, ed. *The Great Exhibition of 1851: New Interdisciplinary Essays*. Manchester: Manchester University Press, 2001.

Raven, James. *The Business of Books: Booksellers and the English Book Trade, 1450–1850*. New Haven, CT: Yale University Press, 2007.

———, Helen Small, and Naomi Tadmor, eds. *The Practice and Representation of Reading in England*. Cambridge: Cambridge University Press, 1996.

Richards, Jeffrey. *Sir Henry Irving: A Victorian Actor and His World*. London: Hambledon & London, 2005.

Richards, Thomas. *The Commodity Culture of Victorian England: Advertising and Spectacle, 1851–1914*. 2nd edn. London; New York: Verso, 1991; first published Stanford, CA: Stanford University Press, 1990.

Richardson, Ruth. *Dickens & the Workhouse: Oliver Twist & the London Poor*. Oxford: Oxford University Press, 2012.

Roe, Nicholas. 'Hunt, (James Henry) Leigh (1784–1859)'. *Oxford Dictionary of National Biography* online edition. Accessed 11 August 2012. http://www.oxforddnb.com.

Rose, Jonathan. *The Intellectual Life of the British Working Classes*. New Haven, CT; London: Yale University Press, 2001.

Rose, Joseph. 'Rereading the English Common Reader'. In *The Book History Reader*, edited by David Finkelstein and Alistair McCleery, 424–39. London: Routledge, 2002.

Rotunno, Laura. 'Blackfriars: The Post Office Magazine:A Nineteenth-Century Network of "The Happy Ignorant"'. In 'Victorian Networks and the Periodical Press', edited by Alexis Easley, 141–64. Special issue, *Victorian Periodicals Review* 44, no. 2 (Summer 2011).

Rowell, George. *The Victorian Theatre: A Survey*. London: Oxford University Press, 1956.

Royle, Edward. 'Holyoake, George Jacob (1817–1906)'. *Oxford Dictionary Of National Biography* online edition. Accessed 11 August, 2012. www. oxforddnb.com.

Rubery, Matthew. *The Novelty of Newspapers: Victorian Fiction after the Invention of the News*. Oxford: Oxford University Press, 2009.

———. 'Victorian Print Culture, Journalism and the Novel'. *Literature Compass* 7, no. 4 (2010): 290–300.

Russell, Gillian and Clara Tuite. 'Introducing Romantic Sociability'. In *Romantic Sociability: Social Networks and Literary Culture in Britain, 1770 – 1840*, edited by Gillian Russell and Clara Tuite, 1–23. Cambridge: Cambridge University Press, 2002.

Salmon, Richard. *Henry James and the Culture of Publicity*. Cambridge: Cambridge University Press, 1997.

Salzberg, Rosa. '"Per le Piaze & Sopra il Ponte": Reconstructing the Geography of Popular Print in Sixteenth-Century Venice'. In *Geographies of the Book*, edited by Miles Ogborn and Charles W. J. Withers, 111–31. Farnham: Ashgate, 2010.

Schlicke, Paul. 'Hazlitt, Horne, and the Spirit of the Age'. *Studies in English Literature* 45, no. 4 (Autumn 2005): 829–851.

Schlör, Joachim. *Nights in the Big City: Paris – Berlin – London 1840–1930*. Translated by Pierre Gottfried Imhof and Dafydd Rees Roberts. London: Reaktion Books, 1998; first published in German 1991.

Schumaker, Eri J. *A Concise Bibliography of The Complete Works of Richard H. Horne, 1802–1884*. Granville, OH: Granville Times Press, 1943.

Schwarzbach, F. S. *Dickens and the City*. London: Athlone Press, 1979.

Sedgwick, Eve Kosofsky. *Between Men: English Literature and Male Homosocial Desire*. New York: Columbia University Press, 1985.

Seed, David. 'Touring the Metropolis: The Shifting Subjects of Dickens's London Sketches'. *Yearbook of English Studies* 34, Nineteenth-Century Travel Writing (2004): 155–70.

Shattock, Joanne. 'Professional Networking, Masculine and Feminine'. In 'Victorian Networks and the Periodical Press', edited by Alexis Easley, 128–40. Special issue, *Victorian Periodicals Review* 44, no. 2 (Summer 2011).

——— and Michael Wolff, eds. *The Victorian Periodical Press: Samplings and Soundings*. Leicester: Leicester University Press; Toronto: Toronto University Press, 1982.

Shires, Linda M. 'The Author as Spectacle and Commodity: Elizabeth Barrett Browning and Thomas Hardy'. In *Victorian Literature and the Victorian Visual*

Imagination, edited by Carol T. Christ and John O. Jordan, 198–212. Berkeley: University of California Press, 1995.

Shirley, Michael H. 'G.W.M. Reynolds, *Reynolds's Newspaper* and Popular Politics'. In *G.W.M. Reynolds: Nineteenth-Century Fiction, Politics, and the Press*, edited by Anne Humpherys and Louis James, 75–89. Aldershot: Ashgate, 2008.

———. '"On the wings of everlasting power": GWM Reynolds and *Reynolds's Newspaper*, 1848–1876'. PhD diss., University of Illinois at Urbana Campaign, 1997.

Sicher, Efraim. *Rereading the City, Rereading Dickens: Representation, the Novel, and Urban Realism.* New York: AMS Press, 2003.

Sigel, Lisa Z. *Governing Pleasures: Pornography and Social Change in England, 1815–1914*. New Brunswick, NJ: Rutgers University Press, 2001.

Slater, Michael. *Charles Dickens*. New Haven, CT: Yale University Press, 2009.

———. *Douglas Jerrold: 1803–1857*. London: Duckworth, 2002.

———. 'Jerrold, William Douglas (1803–1857)'. In *Dictionary of Nineteenth-Century Journalism In Great Britain and Ireland*, edited by Laurel Brake and Marysa Demoor, 318. Ghent; London: Academia Press and British Library, 2009.

Sleight, Simon. 'Wavering between virtue and vice: constructions of youth in Australian cartoons of the late-Victorian era'. In *Drawing the Line: Using Cartoons as Historical Evidence*, edited by Richard Scully and Marian Quartly, 5.1–5.26. Melbourne: Monash University ePress, 2009.

———. *Young People and the Shaping of Public Space in Melbourne, 1870–1914*. Farnham: Ashgate, 2013.

Small, Helen. 'A Pulse of 124: Charles Dickens and a Pathology of the Mid-Victorian Reading Public'. In *The Practice and Representation of Reading in England*, edited by James Raven, Helen Small, and Naomi Tadmor, 263–90. Cambridge: Cambridge University Press, 1996.

Smith, Karl Ashley. *Dickens and the Unreal City: Searching for Spiritual Significance in Nineteenth-Century London*. Basingstoke: Palgrave Macmillan, 2008.

Sperber, Jonathan. *The European Revolutions, 1848–1851*. 2nd edn. Cambridge: Cambridge University Press, 2005.

St. Clair, William. *The Reading Nation in the Romantic Period*. Cambridge: Cambridge University Press, 2004.

Stephens, John Russell. 'Lacy, Thomas Hailes (1809–1873)'. *Oxford Dictionary Of National Biography* online edition. Accessed 11 August, 2012. http://www.oxforddnb.com.

———. *The Profession of the Playwright: British Theatre 1800–1900*. Cambridge: Cambridge University Press, 1992.

Sterne, Jonathan. *The Audible Past: Cultural Origins of Sound Reproduction*. Durham, NC; London: Duke University Press, 2003.

Stewart, Ken. 'Britain's Australia'. In *The Cambridge History of Australian Literature*, edited by Peter Pierce, 7–33. Cambridge: Cambridge University Press, 2009.

———. 'Journalism and the World of the Writer: The Production of Australian Literature, 1855–1915'. In *The Penguin New Literary History of Australia*, general editor Laurie Hergenhan, 174–93. Ringwood, Vic.; Harmondsworth: Penguin, 1988.

Stewart, Lurline, *Australian Periodicals With Literary Content 1821–1925: An Annotated Bibliography* (Melbourne: Australian Scholarly Publishing, 2003)

———. *James Smith: the Making of a Colonial Culture* (Sydney: Allen & Unwin, 1989)

Stokes, John. '"Encabsulation": Horse-Drawn Journeys in Late-Victorian Literature'. In *New Agenda: Urban Mobility: New Maps of Victorian Britain*, edited by Katharina Boehm and Josephine McDonagh, 239–53. Special issue, *Journal of Victorian Culture*, 15, no. 2 (August 2010).

Sutherland, John. *Victorian Fiction: Writers, Publishers, Readers*. Basingstoke: Macmillan, 1995.

Taithe, Bernard, ed. *The Essential Mayhew: Representing and Communicating the Poor*. London: Rivers Oram Press, 1996.

Tambling, Jeremy. *Going Astray: Dickens and London*. Harlow: Pearson Longman, 2009.

Thacker, Andrew. 'Theorising Space and Place in Modernism'. In *Moving Through Modernity: Space and Geography in Modernism*, 13–45. Manchester: Manchester University Press, 2003.

Thom, Colin. *Researching London's Houses*. London: Historical Publications, 2005.

Thomas, Trefor. 'G.W.M. Reynolds's *The Mysteries of London*: An Introduction'. In *The Mysteries of London, by G.W.M. Reynolds*, edited by Trefor Thomas, vii-xxvii. Keele: Keele University Press, 1996.

———. 'Rereading G. W. Reynolds's *The Mysteries of London*'. In *Rereading Victorian Fiction*, edited by Alice Jenkins and Juliet John, 59–80. Basingstoke: Macmillan, 2000.

Thornton, Sara. 'Reading the Dickens' Advertiser: Merging Paratext and Novel'. In *Advertising, Subjectivity, and the Nineteenth-Century Novel: Dickens, Balzac, and the Language of the Walls*, 63–118. Basingstoke: Palgrave Macmillan, 2009.

Tipping, Marjorie J. 'Sinnett, Frederick (1830–1866)'. *Australian Dictionary of Biography Online*. Accessed 25 January, 2012. http://adb.anu.edu.au/.

Tönnies, Ferdinand. *Community and Society: Gemeinschaft und Gesellschaft*. Edited and translated by Charles P. Loonis. Mineola, NY: Dover Publications, 2002; first published 1887; this edition originally published East Lansing: Michigan State University Press, 1957.

Topham, Jonathan R. 'The Mirror of Literature, Amusement and Instruction and cheap miscellanies in early nineteenth-century Britain'. In *Science in the*

Nineteenth-Century Periodical: Reading the Magazine of Nature, edited by Geoffrey Cantor, Gowan Dawson, Graeme Gooday, Richard Noakes, Sally Shuttleworth, and Jonathan R. Topham, 37–66. Cambridge: Cambridge University Press, 2004.

Turnbull, Clive. 'Whitehead, Charles (1804–1862)'. *Australian Dictionary of Biography Online*. Accessed 23 March, 2012. http://adb.anu.edu.au/.

Turner, Mark W. 'Companions, Supplements, and the Proliferation of Print in the 1830s'. *Victorian Periodicals Review* 43, no. 2 (Summer 2010): 119–32.

van der Merwe, Pieter. 'Stanfield, Clarkson (1793–1867)'. *Oxford Dictionary Of National Biography* online edition. Accessed 11 August, 2012. http://www.oxforddnb.com.

Vlock, Deborah. *Dickens, Novel Reading, and the Victorian Popular Theatre*. Cambridge: Cambridge University Press, 1998.

———. 'Mayhew, Horace (1816–1872)'. *Oxford Dictionary Of National Biography* online edition. Accessed 11 August, 2012. http://www.oxforddnb.com.

Walker, Shirley. 'Perceptions of Australia, 1855–1915'. In *The Penguin New Literary History of Australia*, general editor Laurie Hergenhan, 159–73. Ringwood, Vic.; Harmondsworth: Penguin, 1988.

Wall, Cynthia. '"At Shakespear's-Head, Over-Against Catherine-Street in the Strand": Forms of Address in the London Streets'. In *The Streets of London: From the Great Fire to the Great Stink*, edited by Tim Hitchcock and Heather Shore, foreword by Roy Porter, 10–26. London: Rivers Oram Press, 2003.

Waters, Catherine. *Commodity Culture in Dickens's Household Words: The Social Life of Goods*. Aldershot: Ashgate, 2008.

Watson, Nicola. *The Literary Tourist: Readers and Places in Romantic & Victorian Britain*. Basingstoke: Palgrave Macmillan, 2006.

Webber, Ronald. *Covent Garden: Mud-Salad Market*. London: J. M. Dent, 1969.

Webby, Elizabeth. 'The Beginnings of Literature in Colonial Australia'. In *The Cambridge History of Australian Literature*, edited by Peter Pierce, 34–51. Cambridge: Cambridge University Press, 2009.

———. 'Colonial Writers and Readers'. In *The Cambridge Companion to Australian Literature*, edited by Elizabeth Webby, 50–73. Cambridge: Cambridge University Press, 2000.

———. 'Journals in the Nineteenth Century'. *The Book in Australia: Essays Towards a Cultural and Social History*, edited by D.H. Borchardt and Wallace Kirsop, 110–38. Clayton, Victoria: Australian Reference Publications in association with the Centre for Bibliographical and Textual Studies, Monash University, 1988.

———. 'Writers, Printers, Readers: the Production of Australian Literature Before 1855'. In *The Penguin New Literary History of Australia*, general editor Laurie Hergenhan, 113–25. Ringwood, Vic.; Harmondsworth: Penguin, 1988.

Weiner, Joel H. *The War of the Unstamped: The Movement to Repeal the British Newspaper Tax, 1830 – 1836.* Ithaca, NY; London: Cornell University Press, 1969.

Wetherell, Charles. 'Historical Social Network Analysis'. *International Review of Social History* 43, supplement (1998): 125–44.

White, Jerry *London in the 19th Century: 'A Human Awful Wonder of God'.* London: Jonathan Cape, 2007.

Whitehead, Angus. 'The Will of Henry Banes, Landlord of Fountain Court, Strand, the Last Residence of William and Catherine Blake'. *Blake: An Illustrated Quarterly* 39, no. 2 (Fall 2005): 78–99.

Wilde, William H., Joy Hooton and Barry Andrews, eds. *The Oxford Companion to Australian Literature.* 2nd edn. Melbourne; Oxford: Oxford University Press, 1994.

Wilding, Michael. *Marcus Clarke.* Melbourne; Oxford: Oxford University Press, 1977.

Williams, Raymond. *The Country and The City.* 2nd edn. London: Hogarth Press, 1985; first published Chatto & Windus 1973.

Williams, Tony. *The Representation of London in Regency and Victorian Drama (1821–1881).* Lewiston, NY; Lampeter: Edwin Mellen Press, 2000.

Wilson, A.E. *The Lyceum: Illustrated from the Raymond Mander and Joe Mitchenson Theatre Collection.* London: Dennis Yates, 1952.

Wolfreys, Julian. *Writing London: The Trace of the Urban Text from Blake to Dickens.* Basingstoke: Macmillan, 1998.

Woloch, Alex. *The One vs. the Many: Minor Characters and the Space of the Protagonist in the Realist Novel.* Princeton, NJ: Princeton University Press, 2003.

Wright, Thomas. *The Life of Charles Dickens.* London: Henry Jenkins, 1935.

Wynne, Deborah. 'Responses to the 1851 Great Exhibition in *Household Words*'. *Dickensian* 97, no. 3 (Winter 2001): 228–34.

———. *The Sensation Novel and the Victorian Family Magazine.* Basingstoke: Palgrave, 2001.

Yeo, Eileen. 'Mayhew as Social Investigator'. In *The Unknown Mayhew: Selections from the Morning Chronicle 1849–1850*, edited by E.P. Thompson and Eileen Yeo, 56–104. 2nd edn. Harmondsworth: Penguin, 1984.

Web Resources

Ancestry.co.uk: UK Census Records
   http://www.ancestry.co.uk/
Austlit: The Australian Literature Resource
   http://www.austlit.edu.au/
Australian Building: A Cultural Investigation, 2008
   http://www.mileslewis.net/australian-building/

Australian Dictionary of Biography Online
   http://adb.anu.edu.au/
British Periodicals Online
   http://britishperiodicals.chadwyck.co.uk
eMelbourne: The City Past and Present (The Encyclopedia of Melbourne Online)
   http://www.emelbourne.net.au/
Hansard Online
   http://hansard.millbanksystems.com
The John Johnson Collection of Printed Ephemera Online
   http://johnjohnson.chadwyck.co.uk/
London Low Life: Street Culture, Social Reform, and the Victorian Underworld
   http://www.amdigital.co.uk/Collections/London-Low-Life.aspx
London Topographical Society
   http://www.topsoc.org/home
MOTCO: UK Directory and Image Database – Antique Maps, Prints and Books
   http://www.motco.com/
Nineteenth-Century British Library Newspapers
   http://newspapers.bl.uk/blcs/
Old Bailey Proceedings Online
   http://www.oldbaileyonline.org
The Oxford Dictionary of National Biography
   http://www.oxforddnb.com/
The Oxford English Dictionary
   http://oed.com
State Library of Victoria Digitised Collections
   http://www.slv.vic.gov.au/
Survey of London: volume 36: Covent Garden. Edited by F.H.W. Sheppard (1970)
   http://www.british-history.ac.uk/source.aspx?pubid=362
The Times Digital Archive, 1785–1985
   http://archive.timesonline.co.uk/tol/archive/
Trove
   http://trove.nla.gov.au/
The Victorian Plays Project
   http://victorian.worc.ac.uk/modx/
The Victorian Web
   http://www.victorianweb.org/
Walter Thornbury's Old and New London, III (1878)
   http://www.british-history.ac.uk/source.aspx?pubid=341
The Wellesley Index of Victorian Periodicals, 1824–1900
   http://wellesley.chadwyck.com/

Index

For Product Safety Concerns and Information please contact our EU
representative GPSR@taylorandfrancis.com
Taylor & Francis Verlag GmbH, Kaufingerstraße 24, 80331 München, Germany

www.ingramcontent.com/pod-product-compliance
Ingram Content Group UK Ltd.
Pitfield, Milton Keynes, MK11 3LW, UK
UKHW021009180425
457613UK00019B/876